Unemployment and Activation Policies in Europe and the US

THE FUTURE OF WORK AND EMPLOYMENT

The future of work and employment has rarely been as opaque as it is now and never as speculated upon. This important series will explore the biggest issues facing the modern workforce, policy-makers and businesses today. Its books will include topics as diverse as the rise of the gig economy to the role of platform companies and an ageing workforce. Book proposals on topics such as employment (in)security, inclusivity, equity, remote teams, wellbeing, AI, digitalization and voice will be welcomed. Books will be theoretically rigorous and empirically grounded but also will light the way for future research and debate in the field of employment relations.

For a full list of Edward Elgar published titles, including the titles in this series, visit our website at www.e-elgar.com.

Unemployment and Activation Policies in Europe and the US

Edited by

Henning Jørgensen

Professor and Research Manager, University College Northern Jutland, Denmark

Michaela Schulze

Professor of Political Science, University of Applied Labour Studies, Germany

THE FUTURE OF WORK AND EMPLOYMENT

EE Edward **Elgar**
PUBLISHING

Cheltenham, UK • Northampton, MA, USA

Published by
Edward Elgar Publishing Limited
The Lypiatts
15 Lansdown Road
Cheltenham
Glos GL50 2JA
UK

Edward Elgar Publishing, Inc.
William Pratt House
9 Dewey Court
Northampton
Massachusetts 01060
USA

A catalogue record for this book
is available from the British Library

Library of Congress Control Number: 2024944488

This book is available electronically in the **Elgar**online
Sociology, Social Policy and Education subject collection
https://doi.org/10.4337/9781035325610

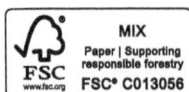

MIX
Paper | Supporting
responsible forestry
FSC
www.fsc.org   FSC® C013056

ISBN 978 1 0353 2560 3 (cased)
ISBN 978 1 0353 2561 0 (eBook)

Printed and bound in Great Britain by
TJ Books Limited, Padstow, Cornwall

Contents

Tables

Contributors

Giuliano Bonoli is Professor of Social Policy at the Swiss Graduate School for Public Administration at the University of Lausanne. He has been involved in several national and international research projects on social policies. His work has focused on pension reform, labour market and family policies. He has published some fifty articles in journals such as *Policy & Politics*, *Journal of European Social Policy*, *European Sociological Review*.

Daniel Clegg is Professor of Comparative Social Policy and Head of Social Policy, School of Social and Political Science, University of Edinburgh. He has a PhD from the European University Institute and worked previously at the universities of Stirling and Oxford and at Sciences Po Paris. His research interests are in the causes and consequences of cross-national variations in labour market policies and social security for people of working age. He is co-editor (with Niccolò Durazzi) of the *Handbook of Labour Market Policy in Advanced Democracies* (Edward Elgar, 2023).

Begoña Cueto is Professor of Applied Economics at the University of Oviedo. Her research area focuses on labour economics, labour market policy evaluation and self-employment, on which she has published several peer-reviewed journal articles and book chapters. She regularly collaborates with public administrations and social partners to carry out public policy evaluation and labour market analysis.

Werner Eichhorst studied sociology, political science, psychology, and public policy and administration at the universities of Tuebingen and Konstanz, where he graduated as Diplom-Verwaltungswissenschaftler in 1995. From 1996 to 1999 he was doctoral and post-doctoral fellow at the Max Planck Institute for the Study of Societies in Cologne. In fall 1998 he received his doctoral degree from the University of Konstanz. He joined the IZA Institute of Labor Economics in 2005 and is Coordinator of Labor Market and Social Policy in Europe there. Since November 2017 he has been an honorary professor at Bremen University, affiliated with the Research Center on Inequality and Social Policy SOCIUM.

Ian Greer is Research Professor and Director of the Ithaca Co-Lab at Cornell University's School of Industrial and Labor Relations. He has published numerous peer-reviewed journal articles on industrial relations and welfare states and is co-author of *Marketization: How Capitalist Exchange Disciplines Workers and Subverts Democracy* (Bloomsbury, 2022).

Ivan Harsløf is Associate Professor at the Department of Social Work, Child Welfare and Social Policy, Oslo Metropolitan University, Norway. He has a Master's in social studies and a PhD in sociology. Before OsloMet, he worked at the Danish National Institute of Social Research, and Norwegian Social Research. His research interests span the areas of activation and vocational rehabilitation, inequalities in health, new social risks, and professionals in the social services.

Aleksander Heikkinen is a doctoral researcher in social and public policy at the University of Helsinki. In his PhD dissertation, he is examining the digitalization and automation of social security administration, focusing on the intersection of technology and welfare provision. Before starting his doctoral studies, he worked at the Finnish Prime Minister's office and as an external consultant for the OECD.

Silvia Hofbauer is a lawyer. She is a labour market expert and Head of the Labour Market and Integration Department of the Vienna Chamber of Labour. She has been a member of the advisory boards of the Labour Market Service in Austria since its inception on regional and national level. She was a long-standing board member of the Vienna Employee Promotion Fund. Her main areas of expertise are qualification and labour market policy for young people as well as European labour market policy.

Henning Jørgensen has been Professor in Political Science at Aalborg University since the late 1980s and is now Research Manager at University College Northern Jutland in Denmark. He has also been Director of ETUI in Brussels and director of CARMA at Aalborg University. He has published more than sixty books and many articles on collective regulations, labour market and social policies, welfare state developments, education and vocational training, leadership and competence developments, changes in values and interests of wage earners, and trade union renewal. He has been engaged in both international and national policy discussions, think tanks and evaluations. He has also been a widely consulted expert and commentator.

Mads Peter Klindt is Associate Professor in the Department of Politics and Society, Aalborg University. Mads Peter's research focuses on flexicurity and the dynamics of labour market regulation, unemployment insurance, active labour market policy and training. He has also contributed to the evaluation of organizational reform and partnership, working across public services, and, more recently, on unions and the green transition. His work has been published in various outlets, including *Journal of Common Market Studies*, *International Journal of Lifelong Education*, *Transfer* and *Public Management Review*.

Ferry Koster is Professor of Work and Institutions – Technological and Social Innovation at the department of Public Administration and Sociology of Erasmus University, Rotterdam, the Netherlands. His research focuses on labour market developments in relation to labour market institutions. He is specifically interested in the role of employers in these developments and has published extensively on this topic.

Ivar Lødemel is Professor of Comparative Social Policy and Founding Research Director of the Research Group for Inclusive Social Welfare Policies (GIV) at Oslo Metropolitan University. He trained and worked as a social worker before completing a PhD at the London School of Economics in 1989. He was research director at Fafo Institute for Applied Social Science (Oslo), before joining Oslo Metropolitan University in 2001. His main current areas of research are cross-Atlantic comparative studies of activation programmes and global studies about the relationship between poverty and shame.

Laureano Martinez is Assistant Professor at the Complutense University of Madrid. His research interests focus on social and employment policies, active labour market policies, and the link between employment and social protection. In addition to his research activities, he has collaborated with different local and regional governments in the design and evaluation of social inclusion policies.

Michaela Schulze is Professor of Political Science at the University of Applied Labour Studies (HdBA) at the Campus Schwerin. Before joining the HdBA in 2019 she was Interim Professor at the University of Trier and Post-Doc researcher at the University of Kassel and Siegen. Her research focuses on the developments of active labour market policies in a comparative perspective and on the changes within public employment services. In addition, she has recently done more research on the implications of the different crisis scenarios for the welfare state and especially for the public employment services and the labour market policy in general.

Simon Theurl is a researcher and expert in labour market economics and policies at the Arbeiterkammer (Chamber of Labour) in Austria. He is a member of the Directorate of the Public Employment Service Vienna and teaches economics at the University of Graz. Previously, he served as a lecturer at the University of Applied Sciences (BFI) in the Department of Monetary Theory and Policy and in the Department of European Integration. He also held a lecturing position at the Business University Vienna. His research primarily focuses on labour market policies and labour market segmentation, with a recent emphasis on Job Guarantee Schemes.

Romke van der Veen is Professor of Sociology of Work and Organization at the Department of Public Administration and Sociology of Erasmus University, Rotterdam, the Netherlands. His research focuses on the development and implementation of social policy, in particular social security and labour market policies, health care policies and pension policies, and on the governance and administration of social policies.

Minna van Gerven is Professor of Social Policy at University of Helsinki. Before returning to Finland, she had an extensive academic career in the Netherlands, at the universities of Tilburg, Amsterdam and Twente. Her work and career to date are strongly interdisciplinary with a core focus on social policy. Most of her publications are on topics of politics and policies of activation, in addition to labour market and EU social policy. She currently runs a project relating to digital welfare states, and the digitalization and automation of social security systems.

1. Introduction: unemployment and activation policies in Europe and the US

Henning Jørgensen and Michaela Schulze

CURRENT STATE OF RESEARCH

Unemployment hurts. It is harmful. It is negative for the individual person, the family, the local community, and for the whole society and economy. It has psychological effects, it can be a driver for poverty, and it presents a fiscal and social threat to the welfare state. Unemployment has consequences persisting over a life span and it produces higher chances of new unemployment periods (Fervers 2021). No wonder that the public sector has been trying to cope with unemployment as an economic, social, and political issue.

In times of crises, unemployment is an emotionally charged topic. The welfare state functions here as a stabilizer providing protection and frictional benefits (e.g. short-time allowance). Our economies and welfare states are dependent upon skilled workers. Taxes and contributions enable us to bridge the time of unemployment. However, paid work has a high significance for modern societies. Unemployment is accepted as a temporary incident in which people are covered by benefits. Protection against unemployment is also part of the UN Declaration of Human Rights. Article 23 stipulates the right to work and the free choice of employment this way: "Everyone has the right to work, to free choice of employment, to just and favourable condition of work and to protection against unemployment." Human dignity and equal pay are also stressed in the declaration.

Unemployment became the key organizing concept for state interventions in the labour market in the second half of the 20th century. This is also a result of continuously rising unemployment rates and persistent long-term unemployment. Many countries had to admit that unemployment will remain. Passive policy approaches of compensation had been questioned increasingly. Discussions about more active measures emerged. The OECD Jobs Study in 1994 (OECD 1994) and the European Employment Strategy in 1997 (CEC

1999) paved the way for a changed mindset. Welfare states have to address effectiveness and reform their instruments to integrate people into the labour market. Still, the picture of the unemployed changed, too. Market orientation and self-responsibility became major debates. Politicians and scientists inspired the debate likewise.

During a longer period of time, labour market policies have been developed to address problems stemming from unemployment developments. Active labour market policies (ALMPs) were first developed in the Nordic countries to reduce structural unemployment and to ensure a counter-cyclical policy avoiding inflationary bottlenecks in the labour market and being a guarantee for income support (Clegg and Durazzi 2023). Sweden had already started this process in the 1950s, based on a Rehn–Meidner model or theory, and Denmark took the lead during the 1990s with a policy mix of general and selective measures. Among which was "activation", but in a special form, with vocational training and formal education at the centre. Activation reduced unemployment rapidly. This triggered an international discussion on activation.

Soon, other countries also developed and implemented activation, mostly in demanding versions. An "activation paradigm" (Weishaupt 2011) made its way in many Anglo-Saxon and European countries. Bonoli characterizes this development as an activation turn (Bonoli 2010). Activation has become the single most important approach to tackling the unemployment problem. The OECD and the EU have played important roles in providing argumentation and some empirical evidence for member countries to implement activation policies. But not all European countries have made activation policies central in national policy-making – even if they pay lip service to the concept and EU proposals in political declarations. Most countries conduct activation, but policies are different in magnitude, logics, instruments, institutional arrangements, and results. This reflects the fact that each country adapts activation to its own histories, institution, and actor systems.

Activation aims at *bringing unemployed people quickly back into the open labour market by restoring a balance between rights and duties,* stressing the importance of the latter. People should not rely on the public sector for economic support without being prepared to recognize and actively work on giving something back to society. A new "moral economy" should be operational and change the concept of unemployment, putting the attitudes and behaviour of the unemployed person to a test. This means actively seeking jobs and participating in activities as obligation. Otherwise, sanctions should be used to discipline them. The duty to work received prominence in public debates and initiatives, and "threat effects" were included in policies from the late 1990s.

Soon, activation was also an *object of research*. Scientific investigations of activation have been strong during the last 25 years. Activation has become a research topic in its own right (Clasen and Mascarò 2022, 2023). Discussions as to the rationale, instruments, results, and consequences of activation have been intense. However, most studies have been national historical and empirical investigations, also with a bias towards a certain Western Eurocentrism in empirical analysis. Especially during the last 20 years, an increased research effort in the policy field of activation is in evidence. It is difficult to point to examples of studies as "classics" among the comprehensive literature, but let us just consider a few examples now.

One of the first coherent studies was the book *Workfare States* by Jamie Peck, published in 2001 (Peck 2001). He shows the workfare pioneer position of the United States by analysing activation (workfare) reforms. Making work a condition for the receipt of benefits was highlighted as a major element of the workfare ideology. He saw the first tendencies of a policy spillover of workfare ideology to Europe. In the same year, Lødemel and Trickey (2001) published a collection on workfare with the expressive title, *An offer you can't refuse*, built on US examples of "hard" activation, stressing obligations and threat of sanctions in the event that unemployed people did not comply with the wishes of the authorities. The starting point for the discussions was the tension between, on the one hand, the profile of traditional labour market and social policy, cushioning social risks, and responding to the demands for social protection, and on the other hand the new demanding activation. After the first decade or more of activation experiments, Joel F. Handler published a comparative study on *Social citizenship and workfare in the United States and Western Europe* (Handler 2004). Here a strong social policy angle supplements the labour market perspectives, and paradoxes of inclusion policy were highlighted. Handler shows the fundamental change in the meaning of citizenship and the administration of social policy in European countries. Conditionality, obligation, and contracts speak for a changed welfare state rationale.

It was clear from the literature that pressure on welfare states was rising and that the "Golden Age" of welfare security and expansion had come to an end. Activation targeted more and more groups, and the aim was to activate the whole employment system. A European perspective was represented by Clasen and Clegg (2011) in *Regulating the risk of unemployment: National adaptations to post-industrial labour markets in Europe*. At this stage more comparative aspects were developed, bringing into focus the different ways of performing activation and using public money on activities. *Activation or workfare? Governance in the neo-liberal convergence* was a new book by Lødemel and Moreira, published in 2014. Further aspects and dimensions of activation were uncovered, but a positive attitude towards engaging public authorities and private providers in activation was dominant (Lødemel and Moreira 2023).

Typologies of activation policies have been proposed, and one of the most advanced and used was developed by Giuliano Bonoli (2010, 2013). Workfare policy forms a contrast with investment-oriented policy (see next chapter). Quite a number of contributions have also tried to analyse and assess different instruments and results of activation. Focus has been both on inputs (how policies are targeted) and on outputs (integration results or the lack of these). Evaluations by economists have weakened optimism as to results in a number of ways. Political science studies have highlighted the connection to partisan politics and the importance of implementation processes. Sociological studies often concentrate on experiences of unemployment and ways of coping with problems – including the interplay with street-level bureaucrats. The literature has become enormous, and more multi-disciplinary in character.

Governance reforms with New Public Management (NPM) at the centre have been studied carefully, together with analyses of street-level bureaucrats and their interplay with citizens. *Frontline delivery of welfare-to-work policies in Europe: Activating the unemployed*, edited by Rik van Berkel et al. (2017), shows how different administrative reforms have impacts on local behaviour, on the results produced, and on the content of policies as well. Frontline workers are having a crucial role in determining what kind of activation or welfare-to-work arrangements to establish, and how these affect the situation and lives of the people they target. Governance of activation has both vertical and horizontal aspects. Brodkin and Marston (2013) have made a collection of important contributions in *Work and the welfare state: Street-level organiza- tions and workfare politics*, and their findings are supplemented by Bernardo Zacka's *When the state meets the street* (2017), which stresses that public service is also moral agency. It is obvious here that there is continuous research focus on the role of street-level bureaucrats as the producers and deliverer of social services. They are, however, complaining of lack of time and resources, high caseload, and burdens from manuals and reporting systems. Success of reforms is also contingent on subnational governance capabilities, including coordination and collaboration between actors and agencies.

Among the latest comprehensive publications on activation, we find *Work and the social safety net*, edited by Besharov and Call (2023), with a dominant US focus but also addressing European developments, and *Handbook of labour market policy in advanced democracies*, edited by Clegg and Durazzi (2023). This last anthology has again a broader outlook, advocating ALMP to cope with a lot of new social risks, including demographic changes, digital- ization, and structural change. Governments change their way of addressing labour market risks, but they do not retreat from conducting ALMP. This is an important finding. However, activation needs closer analytical and empirical investigations than those produced to date, to build on comparative political economy and comparative social policy. Again: it is a research topic of its own, still in development.

HISTORICAL ROOTS OF ACTIVATION

For a better understanding of current activation research, it is important to look at the common historical roots of LMP and activation (Weishaupt 2019: 672ff.). In the first period from the middle of the 19th century to the end of World War II, many countries had established local and national unemployment protection systems with differences in timing and focus. Some over-simplification cannot be avoided when trying today to reconstruct more than fifty years of policy developments. Research on these developments is mostly part of country studies on activation to attest continuity and/or change in institutions or mindsets. Often the question of paradigmatic changes (Hall 1993) is addressed.

Some states are forerunners, in a *first period*, as they implemented a national unemployment insurance comparatively early. Prominent examples are France (1905), Norway (1906), Denmark (1907), the Netherlands (1916), and Finland (1921). It has to be highlighted here, that Great Britain had its first national unemployment insurance and labour administration in 1911. Moreover, some countries followed the idea of the Ghent system. Here the main responsibility for unemployment insurance is held by the trade unions rather than by the government. In this first period, the main foundations of the unemployment benefit systems had been established.

In the *second period*, a first milestone for the later activation policy was introduced, in the 1960s and in many countries (Weishaupt 2019: 673). All Western welfare states focused more on placement, qualification and counselling. On the basis of the recommendations of the OECD in 1964, the term "active labour market policy" – with its Swedish heritage – became a framework for debates on labour market policy. The Rehn–Meidner model was targeting full employment, mobility, wage equality, and structural change at the same time. More countries developed clearer aims of active labour market policy, structures of modernized labour administrations, and a set of labour market policy instruments. One result is that many countries increased their budgets for this policy field and modernized their labour market policy institutions (e.g. Germany and Denmark in 1969).

The *third period* (from the 1970s to the 1990s) was characterized by new challenges in the labour market and different responses by the countries (Weishaupt 2019: 673f.). Countries were facing inflation and rising unemployment as economic crises were putting policies to a severe test. Again, the OCED suggested several policy options to address the challenges. These were not limited to early retirement, the implementation of a subsidized labour market, or long-term training for the unemployed. Some countries seemed to be more successful, mostly those (such as the Nordic countries) that focused on extended employment (e.g. employment in childcare facilities or elderly care facilities). Other countries were faced with low employment, high taxes, and fees. In this context, Germany had been labelled as the sick man of Europe (Eichhorst et al. 2008).

The *fourth period* started in the 1990s and is characterized as the beginning of creation and implementation of activation (Weishaupt 2019, Bonoli 2010). The "old" system of helping the needy unemployed people through so-called "passive" benefits was politically assessed as not only ineffective and inefficient, but also lacking a social dimension as benefit recipients were allegedly incentivized to remain dependent on the welfare state (Weishaupt 2011, Wright 2016). The Clinton welfare reform in the US in 1996 had some impacts on the debate about activation, while some countries also started on a reform path. The impetus was to expand activation measures to wider groups of welfare recipients of working age, especially sole parents with children. The UK had already embarked on welfare reforms in the late 1980s. Both the OECD Jobs Study (1994) and the European Employment Strategy (CEC 1999) had a broader impact for the implementation of activation. Some countries had introduced activation early on (e.g. Denmark in 1993/1994). It became popular to use an "active"/"passive" distinction in policies, but this is a bit misleading insofar as it gives different values to different policies. More functions are in fact attached to both kind of measures. Activation did not involve simply an increase on spending with regard to "active" measures relative to "passive" ones (unemployment insurance (UI) and unemployment assistance (UA)). You cannot understand activation from the side of public expenditures. It is about the working and effectiveness of arrangements and measures as to employment results, and norms build into these. And there is also a need to take account of the interactions between measures and institutions, as potential complementarities between policy instruments and institutions exist too.

According to this logic, somehow passive grants have a negative stigma, as people are not earning any reward, whereas active measures are seen as positive, as people give something in exchange for the benefits. In Germany, for example, there was a huge debate on the fact that the welfare state is enshrined in the German constitution. Activation reforms change not only the general principles but also the concept of the citizen as a market-compliant worker ("marktkonformer Arbeitsbürger", Segbers 2016). Some common trends are obvious in this period: e.g. a stronger linkage between benefits and rewards and between rights and duties, aggravated access to benefits, reduction of benefit level or length, reform of the administrations, and the inclusion of New Public Management (NPM) principles and high priority for efficiency and professionalism. The activation turn was followed by manuals and management by results. Full employment had now been substituted by increasing the supply of labour and putting pressure on unemployed persons as first priorities in LMP. Both macro and micro levels are involved. Different versions and *waves of demanding activation*, with economic incentives and sanctions included, have been seen from the beginning of the 2000s. American "workfare" inspired some European systems enough to copy this model, while others developed alternative "welfare-to-work" or "work-first" approaches. Australia even privatized the employment system and dissolved the public employment system (PES) in the mid-1990s. Pressure on the unemployed was growing stronger. "Someone has to do the dirty work", a private caseworker said (Maron 2011: 9). "Workfare", conditionality, and austerity were mushrooming. "We have ended welfare as we know it", President Bill Clinton could proudly announce. Now "learnfare" – policies inspired by human capital concepts – had become much less popular. And the EU placed its social dimension on the back seat until the second half of the 2010s.

It can be argued that at the time of writing, in 2024, we have entered a *fifth period*. And we have more arguments for this change in activation. Some of the most important ones are the following. Lessons had been learned during multiple crises with unemployment rising despite "hard" activation, and activation systems have already been changed as a response to the pandemic experiences. Since the mid-2010s, the EU institutions and the OECD have reformed their earlier neo-liberal views as to labour market policies, and in a number of member states you could again see intensified use of training and education. And activation is becoming less coercive in more places. Finally, New Public Governance (NPG), with user involvement and network governance, challenges NPM and top-down steering.

The activation arrangements are now characterized by early and more individualized activation – including co-production and co-creation practices (Brandsen et al. 2018). This is also a result of the Covid-19 experiences, during which "normal" activation was impossible. New ways of conducting interviews and discussing activities were introduced. Recently, the OECD has highlighted three main developments (OECD 2022): understanding job-seekers' needs and targeting support; digitalization of services and measures; and matching of labour supply and demand. Traditional and newer activation measures go hand in hand. Virtual meetings have become prominent in more places. Positive attitudes on the part of unemployed people have paved the way for more IT-based interactions and negotiations. Activation might become less demanding and aggressive, relying less on sanctions and more on positive motivation of unemployed individuals. Nudging has been a new practice as well as a renewed economic philosophy within the public institutions (building on behavioural economics). And at the same time, the authorities are experimenting with using AI in their work, including predictive AI.

New encounters between unemployed persons and public authorities are being installed, but these are presenting problems in the employment system with regard to handling hybridity to reach new goals of activation, as NPG brings yet another logic into the system besides bureaucracy and NPM (Nielsen and Andersen 2024). Austerity failed to support working people, especially in Southern Europe, Ireland, and some other countries. Austerity was stifling domestic demand and was responsible for skyrocketing youth unemployment in Mediterranean countries. The PES systems were having very difficult times from 2008 to 2013/2014. At that stage, times were changing again. The European Pillar of Social Rights (2017) proclaims a right to "active support for employment". Once more, the EU has been strengthening its social dimension.

And perhaps even more importantly, human capital approaches seem to be regaining popularity in an increasing number of systems. This seems partly inspired by more political interest in investment-oriented strategies (Garritzmann et al. 2022, Scalise and Hemerijck 2024), but it is also a result of policy lessons over time within the activation paradigm. Investments in capabilities are different from focusing on more existing capacities. Linkages from the micro level to the meso and macro levels are desirable, and the state is trying to strengthen its interventions. The role of the state has been increased again – governance experiments with social investments have resulted in new and popular ways of activating people, while trying to coordinate between levels with the help of more collective actors. The EU Commission is also trying to promote policies that will support human capital building and the creation of high-quality jobs (EU 2020). But it is still member states that decide on policies and priorities.

As we are entering a fifth period of activation, we also need a new scientific recording of developments and changes. This is exactly what we are trying to provide with this anthology, building on national analysis and comparative considerations as to new balances of instruments in activation, new measures and governance practices, and partly new philosophies. The historical roots to activation and the Covid-19 experiences with their lessons learned, now in a period with both unemployment and lack of manpower in more sectors, are a way of stressing the need for giving an up-to-date account of what is happening in activation in the US and Europe and in trying to draw some conclusions as to the state of the art and the future of activation. This might also involve re-marking the boundaries of what is covered by "activation". We will have more to say in the next chapter on new insights and transformations.

From this short overview of developments, it is obvious that activation has become both a central part of the policies of the welfare states and a challenge, as it has been developed as part of a "new active welfare state" (Bonoli and Natali 2012). The political efforts to "activate" include not only unemployed persons, but also caseworkers, the administrative system, and the whole social system. But new ideas and reconfiguration of content of activation arrangements, tools, and approaches, together with new governance experiments, are present, which calls for new considerations as to concepts, theories, and methodologies, as well as established lessons regarding activation and labour market policies. With this collection of new contributions, we will try to enlighten, document, and critically discuss the activation policies and programmes implemented and look for renewals.

We can conclude that there are lots of differences in approaches to activation, such as its configuration, producing a complexity of policy interventions, and that policies give rise to tensions and conflicts that often provide results contradictory to the intentions of the policy-makers. The traditional distinction between policy-making and administration needs to be challenged. Activation research has clearly produced both empirical and conceptual advances during recent years. We know a lot more now than a decade or more ago. But still, comprehensive and international comparative analysis is missing – also because of the fact that concepts, hypotheses, and methodologies have not been developed consistently until now with consensus in the scientific community (Clasen et al. 2016). Generative mechanisms of activation and actor systems involved in systems are to be sought now.

ARGUMENTS AS TO THE COMPLEXITY OF RESEARCH ON ACTIVATION

Research on activation is in no way easy. Clasen and Mascarò have argued in their recent articles, "Activation: A thematic and conceptual review" (2022) and "Activation: a research topic in its own right?" (2023), that even though there is a bulk of research, there is also a lack of conceptual clarity. This is obvious from the research discussed above and stressed earlier in parts of the literature (Martin 2016, Clasen et al. 2016). The terms used range from activation in "hard" and "soft" editions, via active labour market policy, to workfare, and sometimes with very different meanings and conceptualizations.

More *concepts* were proposed in the early stages of activation research. During the first 10–15 years of investigations, concepts had a rather general character, using over-simplified descriptions and then evolving into more sophisticated forms. But on occasion concepts were still "bent" to fit the available empirical material. Concepts had to comply better with empirical experiences. Progress was to be seen. Now, it is no go with convenience samples. We need sampling based on consistent criteria. And we, still, need more comparative research, strong longitudinal data about developments, and big sampling exercises from which we can understand the main components and their interplay better and build solid theoretical constructions.

The comprehensive activation literature is also a test bed for analysing the role and place of concept formation in theory building – outside daily familiarity criteria. In-depth criteria for concept formation relates to dimensions included under the concept (Gerring 1999). No doubt, there is room for improvement in this respect. Coherence and differentiation are key. We have discussions ranging from the independent status of activation (Clasen and Mascarò 2023), to the political objectives and elements of activation policies (Weishaupt 2011, Bonoli 2013), to the philosophy or rationale of activation (Hansen 2019, Nielsen and Larsen 2024) – if a single one were ever supplied. But we are still without a strong and accepted theory of activation, building on the formation of empirical generalizations as to forces, forms, processes, and consequences. This is contrary to the situation with ALMP. Here you do not stop with a framework for organizing analysis, but put things together in a theory of public interventions in the labour market. The Rehn–Meidner model was a theoretical construction and a way of conquering unemployment and ensuring counter-cyclical interventions without producing inflation and bottlenecks in the labour market, specifying elements in interventions and the backing up of collaboration between collective actors.

There is – we think – a *difference between ALMP and activation* that needs to be stressed. In their recent book *Handbook of labour market policy in advanced democracies* (2023), Clegg and Durazzi define LMP as "policy interventions that explicitly aim to shape the labour market risks confronting workers" (ibid.: 5). This is a broad definition, reflecting the traditional interest in unemployment insurance, benefits, pensions, and activities of the PES, all services, measures, and supports for workers and ways of matching supply and demand. This also includes employers. It is a set of multi-purpose tools. Activation is more focused on influencing the attitudes and behaviour of unemployed people in order to help them quickly back into the labour market. Some call it "coercion against unemployed individuals" (Raffass 2017: 349), while others see activation as "demands on standby-ability" (Bengtsson 2014) and many see activation as a productive way of assisting the unemployed to get off benefits and into the working community (Martin 2016). But activation is a supply-sided policy only. Interventions are not addressing the employers and the macro-balances of the labour market directly. Activation might not be seen as the crucial arena in mediating the relationship between democracy and capitalism in affluent societies, as is being said about LMP (ibid.). ALMP is covering more kinds of functions and sub-policies: allocation, qualification, employment provision and assistance, occupational health and safety, besides economic support (Schulze and Jørgensen 2023). Activation might be seen as most closely connected to the second and third functions here.

The activation reforms have had different policy profiles and concrete arrangements. Thus, we cannot use one single activation umbrella to give an appropriate description – even if some have tried to figure out a common moral economy of activation (Hansen 2019). Policies developed at the central level are not the exact way of experiencing a policy, because policy programmes are reinterpretations and local implementations that might differ to some extent from the intentions of the policy-makers. Programmes are confronted with a lot of tensions and difficulties during the implementation processes. And central to this are the local street-level bureaucrats (Lipsky 2010) and their organized interplay with "clients" (Brodkin and Marston 2013). This allows the realization and implementation of policy. A lot of implementation studies during other decades have witnessed this crucial difference between formulations of public policies and the results of implementation and adoption.

The reference groups of activation have become broad. It is not only people on unemployment benefits and in receipt of social assistance that are addressed now, but also people on sickness allowance, people with disabilities, homeless people, immigrants and refugees, and other groups as well. You can no longer talk of a core interactive group of people "having" activation, as in principle all unemployed persons in the adult population are included. All should, potentially, be "conducting" some kind of activation.

We need to start with differentiation, making it clear what qualifies as activation and what does not. If activation shares all concepts with ALMP or social policy, there will be no distinctive contribution to our common knowledge base. The *social policy* narrative of "helping others" is not very helpful in defining activation, because mandatory activation is intimately connected to influencing unemployed persons' extrinsic motivation and linked to sanctions as well. Social policy is traditionally seen as the provision of human need for subsistence and care and levelling out opportunities. Social policy and ALMP operate at the collective level. Activation is incentive based and demanding, and is without such levelling out mechanisms. It operates on the individual level. However, more people in the target group do not respond very well to economic incentives because they have other kinds of problems and have little space for economic calculation – thus partly undermining the fundamental instrument of activation. Often, more "soft" ways of talking to people bring better behavioural results, we have learned. It is not traditional analysis of social rights, welfare expenditures, and poverty questions that brings us much needed information regarding the determinants of activation. We are rewarded when focusing on dispositional elements in activation, from the environmental aspects. Activation programmes function differently, according to variations in instruments and target groups, and diverse economic situations. Activation is also different from pensions and other cash transfers that are entitlement programmes. It entails discretionary spending on activities with another rationale and much insecure results.

All this means that activation is different from a traditional social right policy of the "old" welfare state. It is a new policy of the "active" welfare state. Intersection of these policies is most central to the welfare state (Heidenreich and Rice 2016). The locus of activation is discussed in Clasen and Mascarò (2023), and we return to this in the next chapter. Activation is not a government service activity only – activation is mandatory – and it is often broader than public-sector activity. Private providers and non-profit organizations also engage in activation, complementing and sometimes substituting public service and intervention. However, the complementary relationships are defined mostly by public decision-making and framing.

Accompanying the conceptual and theoretical problems, are methodological problems. Both quantitative and qualitative methods, and also mixed methods, have been used. Often quantitative analysis uses official data on expenditures, numbers of participants, and immediate employment results. But aggregate expenditure data need to be disaggregated as to separate programmes. And here there are problems using quantitative data for analysing activation. Available statistics – especially the OECD database (started in 1985) and the EU statistics (see OECD 2018) – do not correspond directly with activation concepts. The OECD defines the aim of ALMP as to bring more people into the labour force and into jobs. From this perspective, several requirements need to be fulfilled in particular. The state has to ensure that there is motivation and incentives to seek employment. Moreover, employability has to be increased, and support to find a suitable employment is part of the OECD understanding. Furthermore, it is necessary to expand employment opportunities for jobseekers outside the labour force. Finally, a balanced implementation of ALMP is only necessary when it is implemented by efficient labour market institutions (Greve 2018: 112). The data available from the OECD are comprehensive and – as they go beyond the European perspective – more suitable in terms of comparability with the results of our book. However, we see some flaws. It is, for example, not possible to find an equivalent to Bonoli's concept of "incentive reinforcement", strongly represented in research. We also know that decentralization of policies results in under-reporting. Municipalities use money for more kinds of purposes and complement state money in activities. There are a lot of diverse local and regional activities, and this makes the OECD data less reliable (Clasen et al. 2016). Furthermore, marketization bring insecurity as to reporting of activities and expenditures. And quasi-markets have been part of activation from the start in almost all systems. Moreover, the OECD category "direct job creation" does not differentiate between public employment schemes (for core workers) and activation arrangements for people difficult to place in a job. But the OECD database is important insofar as it provides some comparative figures and references, and we have encouraged the use of these.

To the above quantitative research problems, could be added the partial lack of generalizations from case studies based on individual interviews and local implementation process descriptions. And the majority of case studies seldom use a common operationalization of the activation concept. This is to say that public expenditure data will not present a fully reliable and valid picture of activation. Spending data are a commonly used comparative indication, but also an incomplete one, being composed on a programme level and not on a policy level. Methodological problems are clearly visible, and add to the analytical ones in studying activation policies and results.

BASIC ELEMENTS IN ACTIVATION PROGRAMMES

The countries examined are mostly Continental European and Anglo-Saxon ones, including the US. Over time, more exceptions from the activation "industry" of these countries have been recorded. Special editions of activation in Southern European countries, for example, are visible (Moreira et al. 2015, Valadas 2022). One result of the studies is that policies, steering instruments, and political ideas simply differ across countries, localities, and time. Tracing activation policy change and identifying forces and mechanisms remains the central aim of social science here (Clasen and Mascarò 2022). Shifting focus from the central policy level to programmes and implementation will uncover new dimensions and ways of operating.

Despite national differences in policy objectives, a variety of existing elements of programmes can be identified – always in mixed combination. The most common and shared elements on the input side can be recorded as:

- The *individualization and contractualization of staff–client relations* – producing a tension between disciplining and facilitating elements with more target groups included. There is also compulsory participation in job training and other activities (van Berkel and Valkenburg 2007, Sol and Westerveld 2005, Sol 2010, Weishaupt et al. 2023).
- *Use of economic incentives* – negative and positive – in order to realize wanted behaviour or preventing other kinds of unwanted behaviour. At the same time, the *threat of sanctions* is expected to best influence the behaviour of the unemployed people (Dinan 2019, Knotz 2019, Brussig 2019).
- Tightened and frequently time-limited *benefit eligibility* (Immervoll 2010, Langenbucher 2015, Wright 2016, Raffass 2017).
- *Time limits* on benefit receipt (Besharov and Call 2023). Generous benefits and longer periods of support are supposed to create disincentives to actively seeking jobs in the open labour market.

- A "performance revolution" in the introduction of *new performance man-agement systems* through management-by-objectives (MBO) and other control functions (Nunn 2013, van Berkel, Larsen, and Casswell 2017).
- Measurement and evaluation of the effects of employment policy by the help of micro data and *"evidence-based" methodologies* (including RCT), using individual data and having self-employment as the central criteria of success (Andersen 2020, Besharov and Call 2023).
- The *decentralization of administrative tasks* (and at times in the context of re-centralization of authority, including municipalization of employment policy in more countries) (van Berkel and Borghi 2007, Knuth and Larsen 2010, van Berkel et al. 2017, van Berkel, Larsen, and Casswell 2017, Weishaupt et al. 2023).
- Increased inter-agency cooperation and the creation of so-called *"one-stop shops"*, whereby various services ranging from job placement to benefit receipt are being integrated, often in the context of harmonizing different types of benefits and a re-categorization of risk (Clasen and Clegg 2011, 2022, Weishaupt 2014, Finn and Peromingo 2019, Klindt et al. 2020).
- *Privatization and/or marketization*, including both competitive tenders when it comes to the delivery of services and the (partial) outsourcing of PES tasks to private providers (Finn 2010, Whitworth 2016, Maron 2022, Murphy and McGann 2023).

The last five elements sum up administrative and operational changes in imple-menting activation policies, trying to consolidate the administration of polices and to place efficiency at the centre. Institutional context counts (Fuertes et al. 2021). All nine elements are combined in different ways in individual systems. And they are topics in most investigations. To this could be added the impli-cations of multiple crises on activation now investigated: Covid as catalyst for digitalization, new formats of guidance, and counselling. Analysis has also shown that registering a diversity of activation policies and implementation arrangements is most important. Fragmentation of administrative systems is to be seen almost everywhere. While governments in Europe shared almost the same vision and faced almost the same challenges, their reform trajecto-ries differed as noted due to varying institutional "starting points", political ideologies, and the number and strength of the actors involved in designing the reform steps. Moreover, the reforms are a continuous process, leading to frequent adaptions and more radical reform steps after new governments have taken office and new lessons learned. In addition, local and regional imple-mentation processes count for different results.

This way of formulating activation elements also entails some demarcations of what are not to be counted as central elements of activation. These consist of pensions, transfers, and welfare arrangements not directly attached to the labour market. Benefit retrenchment is only indirectly part of activation. The way of operating in activation is limited in a number of ways, and a definition and a research agenda must take stock of this (see next chapter).

The elements that are included operate both separately and in tandem. Privatization and marketization did have a strong attraction during the first decade of the 21st century, and both elements were expanded until disappointing results again decreased their popularity in more systems. Often they were too expensive and provided fewer results than expected according to many national assessments of best activation strategy (Roche and Griffin 2023). Bureaucracy, however, was expanding strongly because of tendering processes, monitoring systems, negotiations, and contract disputes. The most radical use of privatization has been seen in Australia. Unemployed people simply became profit units in operations. But today, this country too is reorienting its activation policy towards more public foundation and organization as it has proven difficult to "buy and sell the poor" (O'Sullivan et al. 2021). Still, private providers are part of the activation "industry".

Seen from the output side, analysis and evaluations differ as to methodologies and results. Traditional economic models for individuals' decisions as to work and jobseeking operate with levels for benefits as the most important factor behind wishes not to take up work. Inactivity should be conquered. No one had "the right to be lazy", opined German chancellor Gerhard Schröder. To sum up the economic philosophy behind these neo-liberalizations (Cahill et al. 2018), the reservation wage should be as low as possible – with the help of people accepting "bad" job offers. Then a de facto wage floor is established, we are told. But this position misses the fact that there are big differences in national levels for benefits, unemployment support periods, etc., and these are often more decisive in the quality of offers jobseekers will be given and the way they are treated in meetings and interactions. Mainstream economists pay special attention to obstacles to efforts and negative results. These include windfall profits (or in German, "Mitnahmeeffekte") – as new employment would have been the result without a wage subsidy – as well as swing-door effects (due to the absence of firm integration into the labour market), and substitutions and displacement effects. Neo-classical-oriented researchers might prefer market solutions to public interventions, and among the last one "hard" activation measures are advocated. This is based on new behavioural economics with nudging at the centre. In a German formulation, you have to both "fordern und fördern" (demand and enable) in activation. It is also of importance that fiscal issues are framed differently in systems, affecting policies and reforms and thus contextualizing struggles between actors and organizations at all levels.

Policy learning is needed. According to the OECD in 2015, the countries that had implemented the "hardest" activation approaches were Australia,

Austria, Denmark, New Zealand, Switzerland, and the United Kingdom. Recent assessments will include more countries, including Germany and the Netherlands. The Hartz reforms in Germany from 2005 were indicative for the direction of many activation policies in a second wave of reforms. During the Great Recession of 2008 to 2013, activation measures were not suspended but actually strengthened in a number of systems with "work-first" arrangements. Activation strategies were part of neo-liberal developments taking place, as also witnessed by the EU "austerity policies" (Rubery 2011, Crespy 2020). The aims included work motivation to be kept high, job search encouraged, labour supply improved, and overall ensuring that "work pays". Public cuts were part of these efforts. Strict budgets and strict activation were to follow each other. But new experiences have brought new insights and reconfigurations. And the Covid-19 period brought new directions. Social investment thoughts and initiatives are slowly gaining ground. However, a dualization between the "haves" and the "have-nots" is still a big problem. Those who have no or low education, manual skills only, or a migrant background, will often face problems finding a decent and lasting job.

Some countries – such as Ireland and Finland – have had big problems implementing activation measures. Southern European countries have had weak administrative set-up for developing activation programmes. These countries often lack both institutional settings and collective actors responsible for implementing activation policies. Anglo-American systems have been lacking last-resort safety nets and well-funded institutions. Vertical coordination problems have been huge in most systems (Mering 2021). This has also been a problem for the European Employment Strategy during the last two decades. Activation cannot avoid barriers, tensions, conflicts, and contradictions.

However, the Covid-19 pandemic with its lockdowns, closed borders, limitations to social contact, and mandatory closures of firms together with new policies did bring activation measures to break with the past. Other results were produced by new procedures and arrangements. Job requirements, monitoring practices, and sanctions were abolished in shorter periods of time or were radically changed during lockdowns. Now policies for securing existing jobs, employment, and income support were being implemented, recasting neo-Keynesian recipes to a broken economic and social order. Job retention schemes were used strongly (Ebbinghaus and Lehner 2022). Jobseekers had new and more positive experiences with job centres and other public services. E-services were mushrooming at many places. But short-time reactions are to be distinguished from more long-term effects.

A post-Covid-19 period has started, and future policies to be developed might look different from the well-known activation policies. Yet many think it is too early to estimate the future direction of activation and employment protection overall (Natali 2022: 25ff.). We think a new phase has been started, also because recent challenges (e.g. skill shortage) will remain central tasks for activation and LMP. A broadened perspective, to keep one eye on people inside and outside the labour market, is necessary for successful activation policy. New ways and instruments need to be tested. The openness for that varies tremendously. There are massive differences in timing, frequency, and arrangement of activation programmes between different countries and within the countries themselves. Again: the result is an activation complexity. This needs to be investigated and compared systematically, and that is an aim of this book, building on comprehensive and strong activation research.

QUESTIONS THAT ARE ADDRESSED BY THIS BOOK

We have tried to take up a broad activation perspective, so far. We discussed the current state of research and made clear that there is still room for more and more advanced research in this field. There are further questions to be addressed. One rather radical question can be raised. Is the activation paradigm soon coming to an end – and with it the scientific research practices now steering many activation programmes around Europe and the US after the Covid-19 crisis? This could be argued not only because of internal contradictions in the paradigm, but also because of the shortcomings of activation to help activate, reorganize, and modernize labour market policy in times of structural change and new challenges from the corona crisis, climate change, demographic developments, new economic business models, inequality, insecurity, and instability in a number of arrangements (Martin 2016, Brussig 2019). Alternatively, is activation here to stay as a new way of making political interventions into the labour market and developing new capabilities and transformations?

Innovation in policy-making and implementation might run into big troubles with activation as a dominant paradigm because of internal deficits and external lack of results. Research carried out within an activation frame is also seen by more researchers as unable to direct discussions and decisions about these questions (Serrano Pascual and Magnusson 2007, Brussig 2019). Will activation – as we know it – perhaps fail, and the evaluation practices and micro-based research programmes fail as well? Or will everything be back to a new "normal" soon? Assessments must be based not only on a number of facts and experiences from the last decades but also on the new situation brought about by the coronavirus crisis and the economic situation following this, and how it is going to be handled by those in power positions. Political will and distribution of power in each political system seem to be most important. It is one thing to understand future challenges, but another to cope with these in a responsible, fair, innovative, and effective way.

Our research agenda becomes broad. We will have to engage in discussions as to the definition and classification of activation. Clarification of central concepts matters. The effects of activation are only recently being investigated from more angles, and more research in this respect is urgently needed (Ahmad et al. 2019). It seems obvious that both a longer-term perspective as well as analysis with a short-term perspective are called for, with regard to both national developments and comparative accounts. Focus on the subnational level will reveal more pressing problems – as to youth unemployment, unequal opportunities, cultural diversity, etc. Focus on the international can reveal new regulations and policy renewals. Activation needs help and learning from many actors and places: other policies, the employers, the social partners, and the persons involved.

Several possible topics, themes, and areas can be identified to give new projects a clearer structure and to overcome some of the concrete and method-ological questions touched upon here. We are particularly interested in a *balanced theoretical perspective*, linking activation and ALMP to other concepts (e.g. social investment); a *methodological perspective*, involving concepts to measure and evaluate activation (policies) in a comparative manner; qualita-tive, quantitative, and mixed methods and their challenges besides *empirical perspectives*; country profiles and clusters, common developments, and chal-lenges (including polarization of the labour market, the role of the business cycle, crises, and digitalization). Some of these topics will form a basis for considerations as to the *future perspectives on activation* (sustainable models).

To address some of these research questions, we have decided to focus on country-specific profiles of the activation policy at this stage. We assume that the detailed understanding of the country experts might contribute to a deeper understanding of the policy field. Experimenters and researchers may find current information on the activation arrangements in the countries included in this volume. However, the book also aims to encourage younger researchers and students to recognize that it is worth studying activation reforms and arrangements from a comparative perspective on the way forwards to stronger theory building.

ORGANIZATION OF THE ANTHOLOGY

This book is a history of collaboration among researchers from many coun-tries. The selection and participation of authors and the guidelines given to them have been part of the overall efforts to treat activation from a distinct historical–empirical, analytical-informed, and forward-mapping perspective. National developments and especially the learning potential of the Covid-19 period, its aftermath, and the way of transforming activation arrangements, have been given special focus. We look at the issues from political, policy, and polity angles without forgetting economic and cultural ones. And we see the implementation of policies, the actors involved, and the consequences of policies as having huge importance besides formal political decisions made at top level. However, as, for example, the UK and Austrian experiences are telling us, partisan politics and central steering are still having a big say. Contextualization is always needed. But implementation has logics of its own, which have to be investigated. The activation of a national system bears all the elements of political and administrative institutions (Ladner and Sager 2022), including actors and organizations in conflict and collaboration, processes of programming, reorganization, and delivering services and interventions – all on behalf of society in order to secure human well-being. The interests and ways of conducting public policies on the side of public employees are to be included in investigations.

Many empirical, analytical, and normative issues are raised in the book. Struggles as to understandings and explanations are part of endeavours to analyse and transform activation. This is witnessed by new experiences and a possible new phase of activation.

The book is organized as follows. Next, in Chapter 2, we will discuss the analytical and normative foundation of the book. We present the current debates and our understandings of activation from a retrospective and current perspective. Moreover, national accounts are given, in alphabetical order of countries.

In "Crisis and political power relations: the development of activation policies in Austria before and after COVID", Simon Theurl and Silvia Hofbauer examine the activation path in this country since the 1980s. The authors start here because it became clear that the macroeconomic policies aiming at full employment by fiscal and monetary policies were no longer effective to address unemployment and structural changes. Subsequently, Theurl and Hofbauer discuss the origins of activation in the 1990s and the main principles of activation. The authors further show that the right-wing government (2000 to 2007) had a crucial impact in tightening sanctions and activation measures. Additionally, they point out that the government broke with a tradition of incorporation of unions. The position of social partners has shifted towards the capital side. In subsequent years, several activation reforms had been passed for special vulnerable groups (e.g. for older unemployed or long-term unemployed). The time between 2017 and 2019 is described as activation with a xenophobic slant. Migration as a labour market and welfare state threat became a strong discourse. At the same time, activation measures were tightened. Finally, the impact of Covid-19 is discussed. As in Germany, there were short-term work allowances and other measures to stabilize the labour market. Some unique programmes are also presented. The most prominent example is – for sure – the job guarantee experiment in Gramatneusiedl, which offers a job for all inhabitants of the community.

Henning Jørgensen and Mads Peter Klindt discuss in "The Danish case: activation in flux and fraught with tensions" the recent trends in Denmark. This country was long seen as a model for successful activation policy, which is discussed by the authors first. The model comprised a dynamic labour market, high employment, low unemployment, and protection against unemployment that was generous and always targeted towards human capital (activation). But the authors also show the way in which this beautiful swan transformed to an ugly duckling. Changes in activation were closely connected to a paradigm shift from the demand to the supply side. Economic incentives were placed as instruments in a pivotal position vis-à-vis the individual – as had happened before in most other European countries. Moreover, Jørgensen and Klindt discuss activation principles and instruments used, and the change from human-capital reorientation to work-first approaches in Danish activation policy. A special aspect of the Danish case has long been the strong incorporation of social partners in the field of social policy. The authors show that the social partners have been pushed out of the political arena, to be lobbyists only. Recent developments include both some human capital elements and a government wish to substitute the job centres with new organizations.

Minna van Gerven and Aleksander Hekkinen analyse the developments in Finland. Their chapter, "Activation in the universal welfare state: the case of Finland", underscores the tension between universalism and activation policies, emphasizing individual responsibilities over collective rights, potentially exacerbating existing inequalities and inclusive activation. The special configuration of the Finnish welfare state and the unemployment system are discussed. This also includes activation measures, which comprise sanctions, obligations, and monetary incentives in order to force integration into the labour market. As in other countries, Finland also expanded the group of people affected by activation. However, the country has gone a way that is the opposite to most European countries. The largest reform of the 2010s was the re-centralization of the social assistance benefit, which shifted administration of the last-resort benefit from the municipalities to the central social security institution (Kela). The authors discuss the recent emphasis of activation policy too. Finland is, again, somehow outstanding. Starting in 2020 (until 2027), a parliamentary committee has been working on a general overhaul of the passive social security system. The goal of this reform is to create a simpler and more functional system that enables people to combine work and social security in ever-changing life situations. This also affects the activation debate substantially.

Werner Eichhorst and Michaela Schulze present the activation path in Germany. In their chapter, "An activation U-turn? From pro-market employment orientation to investment in human capital", the authors show a substantial shift from welfare without work to a model of employment-oriented active labour market and activating labour market policies, combined with a renewed set-up of governance in this policy area. The activation path in Germany started with the much-debated Hartz reforms in the early 2000s. Until the 2010s, the activation path was characterized by instruments that stressed integration into the labour market rather than investments in human capital. Combined with a strong economy and a partly deregulated labour market, this has helped overcome mass unemployment and stimulate significant job growth, not least in the service economy. However, this was associated with rising inequality within the labour market and considerable political uneasiness regarding the downsides of labour market divides and demanding aspects of activation. More recently, the authors see an activation U-turn. Form the late 2010s on, Germany has taken an activation path that is more oriented towards human capital investment. Newer reforms aim at integrating vulnerable groups (long-term unemployed) and investing in employees (further training).

Romke van der Veen and Ferry Koster discuss in their chapter, "Activation policies in the Netherlands: the vicissitudes of general social policy and activating labour market policies since the 1990s", the developments in social policies in the Netherlands. They focus on social security and labour market policies in general and activation policies in particular, and the relation between the policy fields. Here the authors contrast the earlier and the latest reforms. Finally, they also try to examine the future prospects of activation specifically and of labour market policy more generally. Van der Veen and Koster observe a development towards increasing control of costs and take-up in social security, towards flexibilization in labour market policies, and towards an increasing specificity, targeting, and (some) retrenchment in activation policies. These policies have resulted in an increasing labour market participation, in control of the take-up of social security, but also in a highly dualized labour market and a still-fragile position of vulnerable groups with a weak labour market position.

Ivan Harsløf and Ivar Lødemel have contributed a chapter, "Norway: activation in the labouring society", which critically assesses the evolution and configuration of activation in Norway. Through a historical review of developments in employment and activation policies, the authors show the historical development and general traits of activation in their country. They also examine the activation programmes and measures for the unemployed, for recipients of health-related benefits and of the minimum income scheme. This analysis is followed by a discussion of the important role played by the social partners in decisions on employment policies and their implementation. In addition, they provide an account of the special employment measures that were adopted to tackle the challenges and implications according to activation imposed by the Covid-19 pandemic. Finally, the future direction of activation is discussed. Compared with other countries, it is obvious that Norway has strict availability requirements and criteria for what is considered a suitable job. However, such rules have often not been implemented or followed up very enthusiastically by the national authorities' representatives at the local level. They also see signs of increasing human capital investments.

Laureano Martinez and Begoña Cueto have provided the chapter, "Institutional fragmentation and low effectiveness in the Spanish activation turn", which deals with the main developments and implementations of activation in Spain. It does this by analysing the institutional setting of employment policy and activation, and the outcomes of activation in terms of spending for activation. Evidence has shown that the activation policies effort is relatively low, and it misallocated expenditure and limited effectiveness of the measures due to a low capacity to implement social programmes from an underfunded and poorly coordinated administrative system. The crisis triggered by the Covid-19 pandemic has highlighted the limitations of activation policies and has led to some changes that, in addition to addressing the deficits in system coordination, seem to be oriented towards a reinforcement of the enabling instruments of activation. As a distinctive feature, given the insufficient funding that has been characteristic for active policies in Spain, the role of the European Recovery Fund can provide a boost to activation measures by closing this shortfall.

Giuliano Bonoli discusses in his contribution, "Switzerland: activation in a fragmented welfare state", the activation configurations and developments in Switzerland. Activation in this country is described as being fragmented and decentralized, as there are significant differences across programmes and cantons. Besides a general activation turn, there is no uniform activation strategy in the country. This is especially the case with social assistance, a scheme that is entirely governed by the cantons and the municipalities. To show these differences, Bonoli sketches the development of activation across the various schemes that make up the Swiss social security system. Moreover, given the fragmented structure of the Swiss welfare state, the three main social security schemes, i.e. unemployment insurance, disability insurance, and social assistance, are discussed separately with regard to activation. In addition, the chapter addresses the normative question coordination in highly fragmented systems and also asks for possible future developments of activation policy in Switzerland.

Daniel Clegg discusses in his chapter, "Between extension and emasculation: the UK activation regime in the 21st century", the activation perspective on the United Kingdom. It starts with a brief sketch of the way to activation. Afterwards, Clegg outlines a number of core features that differentiate the UK's activation regime most markedly from those found in other advanced democracies, especially elsewhere in Europe. Some of the relevant features are comparatively modest benefits, limited public expenditures for activation, and a highly centralized governance. Next, he describes the evolution of the UK activation regime in the two decades between the turn of the new millennium and the onset of the Covid-19 pandemic. In the first period, the gradual extension of active welfare principles to an even larger population of working-age benefit claimants and a substantial expansion of in-work benefits is recognizable. In the second, structural reform of the benefit system built on some of these developments, but at the same time sharp cuts to expenditure on both benefits and services time further weakened the modest enabling features of the UK activation regime. Finally, the prospects for the future of activation in the UK in the light of debates around policies to respond to the aftershocks of the pandemic and the UK's current political and economic direction are discussed briefly.

Ian Greer opens up a new activation perspective in his chapter, "Activation in the United States: low effort, fragmented administration, and poor performance", which describes the character and spending of activation in the US. Greer presents some details on the historical development of activation (workfare) and relevant social policy programmes (e.g. AFDC/TANF). Afterwards, the author discusses three main points that contribute to a market-driven social policy and labour market policy. First, the reasons for low spending (compared with European measures) for benefits related to activation/workfare and training or employment services are analysed. Second, fragmented administration as an obstacle for an extensive activation is considered. The lack of institutionalized structures is discussed as an aspect of the American way of workfare. And lastly, the author notes the poor performance of the American system.

Finally, in Chapter 13, we try to extract central statements as to the development of and investigations into activation, and we attempt to point to ways ahead in analysis. This includes a proposal for a new typology of activation strategies.

Tracing national policy developments is – still – the preferred way of analysing activation. This is also witnessed in the current anthology. Comparative studies of activation will normally have a macro-level focus in trying to find forms and determinants of cross-national variations in the design and implementation of activation and outcomes. But national studies have the advantage of bringing more kinds of actors and administrative systems to the forefront in analysing activation reforms.

It is not primarily "what works" that is highlighted in this volume, but why and how activation is developed in different ways in national systems. Change mechanisms behind policy choices are sought now. The countries represented are not selected on the basis of size, importance, or distinctiveness, but mostly because of author representation and coverage of different families of welfare systems (Anglo-American, Nordic, Continental, and Southern-European ones). Distinguished and internationally well-known scholars are contributing.

This edited volume has its limitations too, in respect of basing chapters on national developments and a number of comparative figures and considerations. Secondly, there is a strong limitation in the lack of contributions from Eastern European countries. We have not succeeded in including authors from these countries in our collaborative research. But these countries have special political, institutional, and social conditions for practising activation. There is a particular geographical and institutional "problematique" attached to Eastern European activation. Many kinds of findings and clarifications are, fortunately, to be found in the rich activation literature on Western European and US developments. Activation research can proceed.

REFERENCES

Ahmad, N., Svarer, M. and Naveed, A. (2019) 'The effect of active labour market programmes and benefit sanctions on reducing unemployment duration', *Journal of Labour Research*, 40(2), pp. 202–229.

Andersen, N. A. (2020) 'Fra opkvaliferingseffekt til motivationseffekt: Effektevalueringers rammesætning af den aktive arbejdsmarkedspolitik', in Klindt, M. P., Rasmussen, S. and Jørgensen, H. (eds.) *Aktiv arbejdsmarkedspolitik – Etablering, udvikling og fremtid*. Copenhagen: DJØF-Forlag, pp. 171–194.

Bengtsson, M. (2014) 'Towards standby-ability: Swedish and Danish activation policies in flux', *International Journal of Social Welfare*, 23(S1), pp. 54–70. https://doi .org/10.1111/ijsw.12075.

Besharov, D. and Call, D. (eds.) (2023) *Work and the social safety net: Labor activation in Europe and the United States*. New York: Oxford University Press.

Bonoli, G. (2010) 'The political economy of active labor-market policy', *Politics & Society*, 38(4), pp. 435–457. Doi: 10.1177/0032329210381235.

Bonoli, G. (2013) *The origins of active social policy: Labour market and childcare policies in a comparative perspective*. Oxford: Oxford University Press.

Bonoli, G. and Natali, D. (eds.) (2012) *The politics of the new welfare state*. Oxford: Oxford University Press.

Brandsen, T., Bram, V. and Stehen, T. (eds.) (2018) *Co-production and co-creation: Engaging citizens in public services*. New York: Routledge.

Brodkin, E. Z. and Marston, G. (eds.) (2013) *Work and the welfare state: Street-level organizations and workfare politics*. Georgetown, Washington DC: Georgetown University Press.

Brussig, M. (2019) 'Was kommt nach der Aktivierung? Neue Leitbilder der Arbeitsmarktpolitik', *Arbeit*, 28(2), pp. 101–123. https:// doi .org/ 10 .1515/ arbeit -2019–0008.

Cahill, D., Cooper, M., Konings, M. and Primrose, D. (eds.) (2018) *The SAGE handbook of neoliberalism*. London: Sage.

CEC (Commission of the European Communities) (1999) *The European employment strategy: Investing in people; investing in more and better jobs*. Luxembourg: Office for Official Publications of the European Communities.

Clasen, J. and Clegg, D. (eds.) (2011) *Regulating the risk of unemployment: National adaptation to post-industrial labour markets in Europe*. Oxford: Oxford University Press.

Clasen, J. and Clegg, D. (2022) 'European labour markets and social policy: Recent search and future direction', in Nelsen, K., Nieuwenhuis, R. and Yerkes, M. A. (eds.) *Social policy in changing European societies: Research agenda for the 21st century*. Cheltenham, UK and Northampton, MA, USA: Edward Elgar Publishing, pp. 187–201.

Clasen, J. and Mascarò, C. (2022) 'Activation: A thematic and conceptual review', *Journal of European Social Policy*, 32(4), pp. 484–494. https://doi.org/10.1177/09589287221089477.

Clasen, J. and Mascarò, C. (2023) 'Activation: A research topic in its own right?', in Clegg, D. and Durazzi, N. (eds.) *Handbook of active labour market policy in advanced democracies*. Cheltenham, UK and Northampton, MA, USA: Edward Elgar Publishing, pp. 44–53.

Clasen, J., Clegg, D. and Goerne, A. (2016) 'Comparative social policy analysis and active labour market policy: Putting quality before quantity', *Journal of Social Policy*, 45(1), pp. 21–38. https://doi.org/10.1017/S0047279415000434.

Clegg, D. and Durazzi, N. (eds.) (2023) *Handbook of labour market policy in advanced democracies*. Cheltenham, UK and Northampton, MA, USA: Edward Elgar Publishing.

Crespy, A. (2020) 'The EU's socioeconomic governance 10 years after the crisis: Muddling through and the revolt against austerity', *Journal of Common Market Studies*, 58(1), pp. 133–146. https://doi.org/10.1111/jcms.13083.

Dinan, S. (2019) 'A typology of activation incentives', *Social Policy and Administration*, 53(1), pp. 1–15. https://doi.org/10.1111/spol.12456.

Ebbinghaus, B. and Lehner, L. (2022) 'Cui bono – business or labour? Job retention policies during the COVID-19 pandemic in Europe', *Transfer: European Review of Labour and Research,* 28(1), pp. 47–64. https://doi.org/10.1177/10242589221079151.

Eichhorst, W., Kaufmann, O. and Konle-Seidl, R. (eds.) (2008) *Bringing the jobless into work? Experiences with activation schemes in Europe and the US*. Berlin/Heidelberg: Springer.

EU (2020) *European Commission: A strong social europe for just transitions*, Communication, Brussels.

Fervers, L. (2021) 'Healing or deepening the scars of unemployment? The impact of activation policies on unemployed people', *Work, Employment & Society*, 35(1), pp. 3–20. https://doi.org/10.1177/0950017019882904.

Finn, D. (2010) 'Outsourcing employment programmes: Contract design and differential prices', *European Journal of Social Security*, 12(9), pp. 189–302. https://doi.org/10.1177/138826271001200403.

Finn, D. and Peromingo, M. (2019) *Key developments, role and organization of Public Employment Services in Great Britain, Belgium-Flanders and Germany*. Geneva: ILO.

Fuertes, V., McQuaid, R. W. and Heidenreich, M. (2021) 'Institutional logics of service provision: The national and urban governance of activation policies in three European countries', *Journal of European Social Policy*, 31(1), pp. 92–107. https://doi.org/10.1177/0958928720974178.

Garritzmann, J. L, Häusermann, S. and Palier, B. (eds.) (2022) *The world politics of social investment*, vols. I–II. Oxford: Oxford University Press.

Gerring J. (1999) 'What makes a concept good? A criterial framework for understanding concept formation in the social sciences', *Polity*, 31(3), pp. 357–393. https://doi.org/10.2307/3235246.

Greve, B. (2018) *Social and labour market policy: The basics*. New York: Routledge.

Hall, P. (1993) 'Policy paradigms, social learning, and the State: The case of economic policymaking in Britain', *Comparative Politics*, 25(3), pp. 275–296. https://doi.org/10.2307/422246.

Handler, J. F. (2004) *Social citizenship and workfare in the United States and Western Europe: The paradox of inclusion*. New York: Cambridge University Press.

Hansen, M. P. (2019) *The moral economy of activation: Ideas, politics and policies*. Bristol: Policy Press.

Heidenreich, M. and Rice, D. (2016) *Integrating soocial and employment policies in Europe: Active inclusion and challenges for local welfare governance*. Cheltenham, UK and Northampton, MA, USA: Edward Elgar Publishing.

Immervoll, H. (2010) *Minimum-income benefits in OECD countries: Policy design, effectiveness and challenges*. Paris: OECD.

Klindt, M. P., Rasmussen, S. and Jørgensen, H. (eds.) (2020) *Aktiv arbejdsmarkedspolitik – etablering, udvikling og fremtid*. DJØF, Copenhagen.

Knotz, C. (2019) 'Why countries "get tough on the work-shy": The role of adverse economic conditions', *Journal of Social Policy*, 48(3), pp. 615–634. https://doi.org/10.1017/S0047279418000740.

Knuth, M. and Larsen, F. (2010) 'Increasing roles for municipalities in delivering public employment services: The cases of Germany and Denmark', *European Journal of Social Security*, 12(3), pp. 174–200. https://doi.org/10.1177/138826271001200301.

Ladner, A. and Sager, F. (eds.) (2022) *Handbook on the Politics of Public Administration*. Cheltenham, UK and Northampton, MA, USA: Edward Elgar Publishing.

Langenbucher, K. (2015) *How demanding is eligibility criteria for unemployment benefits for OECD and EU countries*. Paris: OECD.

Lipsky, M. (2010 (1989)) *Street-level bureaucracy: Dilemmas of the individual in public services*. New York: Russell Sage Foundation.

Lødemel, I. and Moreira, A. (eds.) (2014) *Activation or workfare? Governance and the neo-liberal convergenc*e. Oxford: Oxford University Press.

Lødemel, I. and Moreira, A. (2023) 'Activation in eight european social assistance programs', in Besharov, D. J. and Call, D. M. (eds.) *Work and the social safety net: Labor activation in Europe and the United States*. Oxford: Oxford University Press, pp. 91–121.

Lødemel, I. and Trickey, H. (eds.) (2001) *"An offer you can't refuse": Workfare in international perspective*. Bristol: Policy Press.

Maron, A. (2011) Competing state projects in the heterarchic state: Governance as a neo-liberal political strategy. Manuscript, University of Negev, Israel.

Maron, A. (2022) 'Public sector, private delivery: Service workers and the negotiation of blurred boundaries in a neoliberal state', *Work, Employment and Society*, 36(6), pp. 1060–1077. https://doi.org/10.1177/09500170211001272.

Martin, J. P. (2016) *Whither activation policies? Reflections for the future*. IZA Policy Paper No. 114. Bonn: Institue of Labor Economics (IZA).

Mering, T. (2021) 'Activation and new governance of labour market policies in Central and Eastern European countries', *Problemy Polityki Społecznej*, 54, pp. 31–47. https://doi.org/10.31971/pps/145155.

Moreira, A., Domínguez, A. A., Antunes, C., Karamessini, M., Raitano, M. and Glatzer, M. (2015) 'Austerity-driven labour market reforms in Southern Europe:

Eroding the security of labour market insiders', *European Journal of Social Security*, 17(2), pp. 202–225. https://doi.org/10.1177/138826271501700204.

Murphy, M. P. and McGann, M. (2023) 'A period of contention? The politics of post-crisis activation reform and the creeping marketisation of public employment services', *Irish Political Studies*, 38(1), pp. 120–144. https://doi.org/10.1080/07907184.2022.2044313.

Natali, D. (2022) 'Covid-19 and the opportunity to change the neoliberal agenda: Evidence from socio-employment policy responses across Europe', *Transfer: European Review of Labour and Research*, 28(1), pp. 15–30. https://doi.org/10.1177/10242589221097231.

Nielsen, M. H. and Andersen, N. A. (2024) 'Ignoring by complying: How public officials handle hybrifity to pursue the goals of new public management', *Public Administration*, 104(1), https://doi.org/10.1111/padm.12979.

Nielsen, N. A. and Larsen, F. (2024) 'Activation Policy: bruised and battered but still standing', *Policy and Society*, 43(2), pp. 127–140.

Nunn, A. (2013) *Review of performance management in Public Employment Services*. Brussels: The European Commission.

O'Sullivan, S., McGann, M. and Considine, M. (2021) *Buying and selling the poor: Inside Australia's privatised welfare-to-work market*. Sydney: Sydney University Press.

OECD (1994) *The OECD Jobs Study: Facts, analysis, strategies*. Paris: OECD.

OECD (2015) *OECD economic outlook 2015*. Paris: OECD.

OECD (2018) *Statistical profiling in Public Employment Services: An international comparison*. Paris: OECD Social, Employment and Migration Working Papers.

OECD (2022) *Harnessing digitalisation in Public Employment Services to connect people with jobs*. Paris: OECD Policy Brief on Active Labor Market Policies.

Peck, J. (2001) *Workfare states*. New York: Guildford.

Raffass, T. (2017) 'Demanding activation', *Journal of Social Policy*, 46(2), pp. 349–365. https://doi.org/10.1017/S004727941600057X.

Roche, Z. and Griffin, R. (2023) 'Activation through marketisation as a process of ignorancing', *Social Policy and Administration*, 57(5), pp. 565–579. https://doi.org/10.1111/spol.12871.

Rubery, J. (2011) 'Reconstruction amid deconstruction: Or why we need more social in European social models', *Work, Employment and Society*, 25(4), pp. 658–674. https://doi.org/10.1177/0950017011419718.

Scalise, G. and Hemerijck, A. (2024) 'Subnational social investment in three European cities: An exploratory comparison', in *Journal of Social Policy*, 53(2), pp. 530–550.

Schulze, M. and Jørgensen, H. (2023) 'Active labour market policy', in van Gerven, M., Rothmayr Allison, C. and Schubert, K. (eds.) *Encyclopedia of public policy*. Cham: Springer International Publishing, pp. 1–6.

Segbers, F. (2016) 'Das Menschenbild von Hartz IV: Die Pädagogisierung von Armut, die Zentralität von Erwerbsarbeit und autoritärer Sozialstaat', in Anhorn, R. and Balzereit, M. (eds.) *Handbuch Therapeutisierung und Soziale Arbeit: Perspektiven kritischer Sozialer Arbeit*. Berlin: Springer, pp. 687–708.

Serrano Pascual, A. and Magnusson, L. (eds.) (2007) *Reshaping welfare states and activation regimes in Europe*. Brussels: Peter Lang.

Sol, E. (2010) 'Vouchers, NPM and the provision of Public Employment Services', *European Journal of Social Security*, 12(4), pp. 343–357. https://doi.org/10.1177/138826271001200406.

Sol, E. and Westerveld, M. (eds.) (2005) *Contractualism in employment services: A new form of welfare state governance*. The Hague: Kluwer.

Valadas, C. (2022) 'The activation of employment policy in Southern Europe: The case of Portugal and the translation of external pressures into policies and processes', in Brown, M. and Briguglio, M. (eds.) *Social welfare issues in Southern Europe*. New York: Routledge, pp. 59–77.

Van Berkel, R. and Borghi, V. (2007) 'New modes of governance in activation policies', *International Journal of Sociology and Social Policy*, 27(9–10), pp. 412–424. https://doi.org/10.1108/01443330710773854.

Van Berkel, R. and Valkenburg, B. (2007) *Making it personal: Individualizing activation services in the EU*. Bristol: Policy Press.

Van Berkel, R., Larsen, F. and Casswell, D. (2017) 'Introduction: Frontline delivery of welfare-to-work in different European contexts', *International Social Security Review*, 71(4), pp. 3–11. https://doi.org/10.1111/issr.12186.

Van Berkel, R., Caswell, D., Kupka, P. and Larsen, F. (eds.) (2017) *Frontline delivery of welfare-to-work policies in Europe: Activating the unemployed*. London: Routledge.

Weishaupt, T. J. (2011) *From the manpower revolution to the activation paradigm: Explaining institutional continuity and change in an integrating Europe*. Amsterdam: Amsterdam University Press.

Weishaupt, T. J. (2014) *Central steering and local autonomy in Public Employment Services*. Brussels: The European Commission.

Weishaupt, T. J. (2019) 'Arbeitsmarktpolitik', in Obinger, H. and Schmidt, M. G. (eds.) *Handbuch Sozialpolitik*. Wiesbaden: Springer, pp. 669–696.

Weishaupt, T. J., Jørgensen, H. and Nunn, A. (2023) 'Activation in Public Employment Services in Europe', in Besharov, D. and Call, D. (eds.) *Work and the Social Safety Net - Labor Activation in Europe and the United States*. New York: Oxford University Press, pp. 204–241.

Whitworth, A. (2016) 'Neoliberal paternalism and paradoxical subjects: Confusion and contradiction in UK activation policy', *Critical Social Policy*, 36(3), pp 412–431. https://doi.org/10.1177/0261018315624442.

Wright, S. (2016) 'Conceptualizing the active welfare subject: Welfare reform in discourse, policy and lived experience', in *Policy and Politics*, 44(2), pp. 235–252. https://doi.org/10.1332/030557314X13904856745154.

Zacka, B. (2017) *When the state meets the street: Public service and moral agency*. Cambridge: The Belknap Press of Harvard University Press.

2. Understandings of activation

Henning Jørgensen and Michaela Schulze

In the literature concerning activation, there are many positions as to description and conceptualization. Much ambiguity and a lot of inconsistencies are present as well. This stems from a rationale behind activation as policy, programme, institution, actors, implementation, and result. Thus, classification is difficult. Activation can be characterized as both discursive frames of politics, policies, implementation arrangements, evaluation practices, and scientific support, and public debates. Approaches and understandings differ. In Germany we might call this difference "Leitbilder", diverse ways of sharing understanding of goals, means, processes, and mechanisms. More readings and ways of scanning the landscape of activation are possible (Klammer and Leiber 2004, Brussig 2019, Clasen and Mascarò 2022, 2023). The authors argue that there is a noticeable lack of conceptual clarity within research on activation. This makes it difficult to specify mechanisms and to analyse more than incremental changes. We agree.

As a heuristic tool, the paradigm concept of Peter Hall (1993) could also be used. Hall works out three types or levels of policy change, while each has a higher amount of change. According to Hall, there will only be a shift of paradigm where both instruments, steering principles and narratives and rationales, are changed at the same time. New instruments will only be a first-order change. More waves of activation can be identified and the use of a paradigm shift is also represented in the literature (Weishaupt 2011, Schulze and Jørgensen 2018). But this is only one kind of exercise.

Still, there is no shared or common understanding of activation, but many ways of interpreting the DNA of activation or the basic elements and mechanisms as well as drivers for activation. The chapter is structured as follows. First, conceptual challenges towards theory and understandings are discussed. Second, themes in activation research are scrutinized. Third, questions of analysing implementation and accountability are touched upon before the future of activation is addressed.

DIFFERENT CONCEPTUALIZATIONS AND TYPOLOGIES

Understanding activation in the OECD countries has changed over time, but now a number of statements provide context to their way of reasoning (Bonoli 2022, Greve 2023). The objective of an effective activation policy for jobseekers and other disadvantaged groups is to bring more people into the labour force and into jobs, as quickly as possible. In particular, this requires ensuring that people have the motivation and incentives to seek employment, so as to increase their employability; helping them to find suitable employment; expanding employment opportunities for jobseekers and people outside the labour force; and managing the implementation of activation policy through efficient labour market institutions and processes.

Clasen and Mascarò (2022) find that a common understanding involves a shift in the balance between rights and obligations, and a stronger need for participation in activation programmes aimed at labour market entry; this includes job search activities, training, and subsidized employment, i.e. strong linkage between benefit entitlement and behavioural requirements of job search conditionality. Besharov and Call (2023a) have summarized the most common programmatic and administrative changes that are distinguishable. The authors note tighter eligibility criteria and job search requirements, and the requirement to accept suitable jobs, time limits, benefit step-downs, earning disregards, job readiness assistance, job training, and enhanced case monitoring under programmatic changes. According to the authors, governance changes are the consolidation of administration of services, decentralization of administration or programme authority, synchronization of benefits across safety net programmes, and outsourcing services (Besharov and Call 2023b: 7). However, these criteria are only applicable to a European perspective. Nevertheless, they provide important insights concerning the policy changes. But besides these programmatic changes, we still miss a fully developed and accepted theoretical understanding of activation. More connections between empirical findings and analytical insights and theory building are still to be discovered and formulated. Here typologies are of help.

Giuliano Bonoli (2010) has assisted us a lot with such an effort that transcends simple one-factor differentiation (welfare–workfare, human-capital building–incentives-based activation). He has put two parallel dimensions together: human capital investment (none, weak, strong) and promarket orientation (weak or strong). Four ideal-types of activation are identified (see ibid., Table 1, p. 441): employment assistance, occupation, upskilling, and incentive reinforcement. *Incentive reinforcement* is strong promarket employment orientation and no investment in human capital: tax credits, in-work benefits, time limits on benefit receipt, benefits reductions, benefit conditionality. *Employment assistance* covers strong promarket employment orientation and weak human-capital investment: placement service, job subsidies, counselling, job-search programmes. *Occupation* stands for weak promarket employment orientation and weak investment in human capital: job-creation schemes in the public sector, non-employment-related training programmes. And *upskilling* equals strong promarket employment orientation and strong human-capital investment: job-related vocational training.

The typology summarizes many of the concepts and elements used in analysis and evaluations during the last decade or more. It has been of more than heuristic value for scholars, as it has been used a lot. Still, it is focusing on orientations in *programmes* predominantly. Only indirectly are activation strategies identified too.

However, there might be more as to the classification of activation *strategies* and/or *types of policies* than these ideal-type elements. (We also need to remember that an ideal-type is not an ideal but a heuristic tool.) Here a first and simple *three-fold differentiation* is proposed based on the special way conceptualizations are formulated in relation to the existing welfare state policies: (A) as a new and special type of policy, (B) as part of neo-liberal employment policy or a Third Way edition of employment policy, and (C) as being strongly related to and forming a special part of ALMP. These policy understandings can be specified.

A: Special Kind of Policy

Activation can be seen as *a separate and new type of policy* developed during the last decades in most Western countries. This was early on a clear position. A new paradigm was being established. According to this understanding, activation must be analysed as a special and innovative way of modernizing part of the national social protection system. Unemployed people are mostly given a "Sicilian offer" – "An offer you can't refuse" (Lødemel and Trickey 2001, Lødemel and Moreira 2014) – to help them back into the open labour market in a paternalistic way. Obligations and demands are the important claims of recipients of public support (Peck 2001). New work tests, conditioning cash benefits on participation in different kinds of work activities, including welfare-to-work programmes, are central to an understanding. The welfare state is no longer to be a "static" protection system but a "dynamic" system to help people to manage their own life by finding a job and thus leaving the public support system (financial self-sufficiency/autonomy). Activation should help individuals to enter economic competition and the public sector will remove barriers to the open labour market (such as a division between "insiders" and "outsiders"). If the requests of the PES are not followed, sanctions are implemented immediately.

This position finds activation to be the core of *workfare* – putting welfare recipients to work, having discipline produced and secured by making benefits conditional. Workfare in a US version has been transformed to European ways of activating people. This workfarist pressure on unemployed people can also be supported by reactivating the frontline workers and the system of social protection. Country-by-country analysis has shown this as part of welfare state change (Barbier and Ludwig-Mayerhofer 2004, Clasen and Clegg 2011). But occupying centre stage are the efforts to discipline and push unemployed people back to work, especially using economic incentives and sanctions (Knotz 2019). In addition, individual responsibility is stressed again and again. Differences in national strategies and organizational arrangements have been analysed within this interpretation of policy renewal (Kluve et al. 2007). Activation is the corner concept. ALMP is to be seen as a minor element of activation only (Barbier 2004, Lødemel and Moreira 2014), or totally absent. Activation is equal to *a workfare strategy* in many understandings (Lødemel and Trickey 2001, Lind and Møller 2006), and this also implies extensive individualization (Eversberg 2016).

B: Part of Neo-liberal Employment Policy

Another way of seeing and defining activation is to *place it within the concept of neo-liberal employment policies*, as efforts to increase supply of labour at the macro level and to strengthen discipline and work ethics within the labour force at the micro level. Often activation is seen as a strategy to give the welfare state a new rationale and ethos, including new ways of handling people (Whitworth 2016). "The activation paradigm in social policy is part and parcel of the austerity regime" (Raffass 2015: 357). It can be seen as a neo-liberal policy stating that unemployment is functional to the benefit of the employers and the economy. Social protection is closely connected to neo-liberal politics and morals, according to a lot of analysis (Rubery 2011, Bengtsson et al. 2017). In Europe, it is not traditional conservative or traditional values being promoted – as in the US with religious and family values in front – but neo-liberal ones, stressing individual responsibility, duties, and morale combined with the expression of freedom through competition (van Berkel and Møller 2002). Reducing spending on passive benefits and increasing employment and productivity also form part of the intentions. Moreover, it is argued that there is a need to reduce the risk of moral hazard inherent in public support. But policies have more kinds of functionalities than the many understandings of a new paradigm.

The "old" welfare state simply distributed benefits according to status – unemployed, sick, retired, invalid, etc. But the objective of the new welfare state is to give each individual the means necessary to change this status (van Berkel and Møller 2002, van Berkel et al. 2018). Activation in human capital as well as activation in health have been amongst the most important ways of doing this in the hope of improving employability. Often the new activation paradigm is seen as a neo-liberal and paternalistic policy development (Whitworth 2016). This might threaten "individual autonomy" in the eye of more researchers (Betzelt and Bothfeld 2011, Betzler 2013, Bothfeld 2017). But activation is also seen as a special element in a broader "active social policy" renewal (Bonoli 2013, 2022, Clasen et al. 2016). The change of paradigm can be realized in incremental ways, we are told (Bothfeld and Rosenthal 2014). We have a lot of social policy research now on activation stressing the threats to citizens and the welfare state (Williams 2021, Nelson et al. 2022). As to activation, we can talk of *a work-first strategy*.

Some of these thoughts – including morale – have been adopted by the "New Left" in the expression of a "Third Way" social democracy movement (Giddens 2009). The individual responsibility vis-à-vis society is a starting point for understanding activation and the aim is to be able to find means of self-help and not to be "helped" by society any longer. "No one has the right to be lazy," as former chancellor Gerhard Schröder formulated the basic thought. Any kind of "assistance" will imply control and new sanctions in case an individual cannot find a job themselves. It is not that "you are on your own", but a society's request for efforts to find a job or first to improve your "capital", your qualifications, and your willingness to meet a job offer require self-motivation (Morel et al. 2012, Brodkin and Marston 2013). Investments are central, but monitoring, claims, and eventually sanctions are also to be used in relation to benefit recipients. The individual should internalize constraints in the form of an ethic of reciprocity between the individual and the state. The Third Way formulation would be "between the individual and the community." Self-discipline, self-improvement, and self-reliance are, according to former UK prime minister Gordon Brown (2009), the most important ingredients in finding valuable employment. A new way of looking at citizenship arises. Citizenship is an achievement – not a status. This is what Franz Segbers calls the "marktkonforme Arbeitsbürger" (market-compliant working citizen) (Segbers 2016). Paid work is the one and only decent integration mechanism. Different forms of "welfare-to-work" or "work-first" arrangements are central here. Activation is seen as the diamond of employment policy. It has become status as a paradigm (Bonoli 2010, Bothfeld and Rosenthal 2014, Schulze and Jørgensen 2018).

C: Special Edition of ALMP

Finally, activation can be seen as *just one of other possible versions of active labour market policy* (ALMP), originally developed during the 1950s and 1960s in Sweden, following a Rehn–Meidner model of general economic policy and active selective interventions within the labour market in order to secure or restore full employment. The example of Danish developments is instructive here. During the 1990s, Denmark renewed the concept of a Rehn–Meidner policy mix and made interventions with the help of individual action plans, including extensive use of training and education. An expansive fiscal policy was implemented at the same time. The policy mix was a success, reducing unemployment quickly and improving employment. Denmark became the darling of the European "activation" designs of the early 2000s and the Danish "flexicurity" labour market model was a benchmark when included in the European Employment Strategy in 2007. However, from 2003 a new liberal-conservative government in Denmark took office and slowly abolished this first "learnfare" version of activation, substituting it with welfare-to-work arrangements much more in accordance with neo-liberal thoughts and models. Labour market policy was transformed into employment policy (Jørgensen 2009, 2020). Ideally, a high road to full employment with human capital building, upskilling, and creation of quality jobs should be followed. Increasingly, *a social investment strategy* lies behind many policy proposals. Social investment (Hemerijck 2017) stresses the investment in human capital to compensate inequalities. We find this strategy in many social policy fields. As we have mentioned above, Bonoli also addressed this point in his classification of active labour market policy (2010, 2022).

In this conceptualization, activation is seen and analysed along well-known LMP ideas and models, giving way to different political and ideological editions of activation (Strandh 2001, Danforth 2014). And with solidaristic elements – among these investments in training and education of unemployed people – it has been interpreted as part of labour market reforms of the 2000s (Thelen 2014). Activation is one of the "multi-purpose tools" of ALMP (Brussig 2019, Cronert 2022). And wage earners are to have both rights and obligations in modern welfare states even if activation stresses obligations relative to rights by making claims on participants in labour market programmes. These will include job search activities, training, education, resource clarification measures, or subsidized employment. Here ALMP is seen as the paradigmatic type of policy.

These three ways of classifying activation related to established welfare policies – or deviating from these – might not be the only possible ones. But the positions are developed from already-established ways of analysing and theorizing post-war welfare arrangements and provide another ordering of contributions. It should also be remembered that ALMP comprised efforts to bring mobility and "the security of the wings" for established workers, while activation mostly addresses the access of more vulnerable and inactive groups to the open labour market. However, we can see that some countries have changed their activation strategy. In Germany, one can see a clear shift from activation for unemployed persons to investment in human capital for all citizens ("activation for all") (see Eichhorst and Schulze in this volume). The same is true with other countries, as documented in the chapters that follow.

At the same time, there are arguments against a clear separation of activation strategies and policies. A working line has been part of Scandinavian LMP for more than sixty years and here it is nothing new to stress duties, but on a foundation of more basic rights as citizens and as wage earners. In other systems without such a path dependency, new duties and threat of sanctions might seem a break with basic social rights in the welfare state. Then it could be appealing to talk of a quite new type of policy. The relationship between activation and neo-liberalizations of the welfare state – especially in the form of marketization and management steering – seems obvious, but it could also be argued that the disciplinary elements in activation represent nothing else other than a new way of stressing the (Protestant) working ethic. They correspond perfectly well to old employer wishes and demands too. The connections between activation and neo-liberalizations are perhaps more complex than supposed in a large part of the literature. And finally, the way of conceptualizing activation as one version of ALMP is challenged in other parts of the literature. Some see activation as broader than ALMP because of the reformulation of aims and policies of the welfare state (Bengtsson 2014). Then we are closer to position (B) in our differentiation of activation policies.

One central experience is that it will be necessary to talk more about the activation policies implemented. More than one activation strategy and one coherent philosophy and policy rationale has been recorded.

Activation programmes have been specified as having more ways of conducting welfare-to-work and workfare, as documented in Bonoli's typology. But there have been few efforts – if any – to analytically challenge or develop the notion of *human capital* in activation research. To be a contrasting picture to coercive approaches only is unambitious, and even misleading. It is a wrong track, we think, to accept the underlying neoclassical human capital theory (HCT), advocated by the Chicago School of Economics (Becker 1976) and having a huge impact on a broad range of disciplines and research activities. The theory is about maximizing own economic interests and is strongly connected to methodological individualism and rational choice. Activation thus should be a product of sequences of rational actions to maximize individual rewards (Udehn 2001). This is, however, not the basis for activation programmes of, for example, the Danish system during the 1990s or the present Norwegian and German ones.

For decades, HCT has been a cornerstone in analysis of investment and economic development. Human capital is defined by the OECD as productive wealth embodied in labour, skills and knowledge (OECD 2001). It refers to the different stocks of knowledge that persons have acquired to increase productivity. Education is seen as an *investment* because it is supposed to increase productivity and earnings. It is key to economic growth in the theory. A micro-economic version of HCT has won hegemony from the 1990s in many systems. And the concept is rather undisputedly used in activation research.

However, there is not much of the human in human capital. It is mostly about economic purposes of education. This is also the subject of most criticisms (Tan 2014), addressing methodological, practical, empirical, and moral aspects of the theory. Knowledge and skills are not only for competitiveness; they are also about enhanced ways of living and democratic competences. HCT is at best rather incomplete as an economic theory and it is disturbingly used in activation research without questioning the functionalist and reductionist basis of the conceptualization. Skills are not only rational monetary rewards via productivity in the market, but also to be seen as politically and socially constructed (Read 2009). Non-pecuniary rewards are part of activation and HCT ignores more aspects of skill production, organizing, occupational fields, and the institutional production of public goods. The social and political organization of life has causal impacts on individuals and collectivities. Collective elements, connectedness, and holistic views of labour and activation ought to be a starting point.

A broader concept of "human capital" could include investments in health, motivation, skills, and abilities that can develop *capabilities* (Sen 1999). This was exactly what was done in Denmark in the 1990s, when starting up activation. Individual action plans were created in tandem between workless people and frontline workers. More than skills for productive use were considered in the approach. Elements in human capital (England and Folbre 2023) could better be seen as capabilities:

1. *physical functioning* (to be healthy, having education and skills, and emotions in balance),
2. *cognitive functioning* (using language, reason, skills, and being "mentally healthy"),
3. *self-control* (using self-discipline to be a responsible person and having work ethics), and
4. *caring* (in terms of services and attitudes, and displaying altruism too).

These capabilities reflect basic human needs in order to participate in collective contributions to the well-being of others. And they supplement each other. Frontline workers also need to care about clients and show it in activities. And it is political and social choices made – not rational ones (Brown et al. 2020) – that gives activation different appearances and directions. Activation is not without disagreements between political and professional actors either, we know, but there has been no place for this in HCT.

At the micro level, human capital theory ignores types of rationality other than instrumental ones (motivation and individuals as utility maximisers). At the macro level, HCT ignores the functioning of institutions and complementarities between these and the labour market, including the governance thereof. Future activation research could analytically benefit from using capabilities and ways of developing and organizing these as the basis for understanding programmes, and then differentiate between these with respect to strategies and programming of "human capital" formation. We think a reconceptualization from human capital investments to developing capabilities will pay off.

TOPICS IN ACTIVATION RESEARCH

In a recent review article, Clasen and Mascarò (2022) include a welcome overview of themes and aims within the activation literature. They indicate eight different themes in old and new literature on activation:

1. *National developments as to policy changes.* Here individual countries are the normal research topic, but a few comparative analyses are also recorded. Questions of policy changes with a shift of balance between rights and obligations and a stronger linkage between benefit entitlements and behavioural requirements of job search conditionality are addressed.
2. *Classifications of models of activation.* Here policies are again the main theme. However, there are few contributions overall, especially if dichotomous classifications are left aside.
3. *Causes of activation policies.* Here we find contributions that try to figure out political, administrative, and other forces behind policy changes.
4. *Activation as part of welfare state reform*, with stronger need for participating in programmes aimed at labour market entry, but also redefining citizenship and individualizing problems.
5. *Effect studies of activation.* This kind of evaluation study has become a whole industry, covering both general effects of activation measures and special effects as to particular target groups. Besides traditional mainstream economic studies, there are policy studies in which more than immediate employment goals are addressed.

6. *Labour market integration and activation.* Broader welfare questions as to special vulnerable and precarious groups are raised and analysed.
7. *Research on implementation.* Here the governance of activation and coordination of efforts are discussed, including what happens when "the state meets the street" (Zacka 2017).
8. *Activation as a question of "deservingness" and marketization practices.* Questions of legitimacy and functionality are raised in connection with popular and political understandings of activation.

This classification of Clasen and Mascarò is a helpful way of introducing the growing literature on activation policies and arrangements. An administrative polity dimension is perhaps the most difficult to cope with in such an overview. But such kinds of decentralized studies are essential in dealing with activation arrangements and policy developments (van Berkel et al. 2017). Debates on deservingness (Laenen 2021) are still ongoing, but it is perhaps difficult to see how this relates directly to questions of marketization. And the relationships among deservingness, the role of street-level bureaucrats, and principles of new public management (e.g. efficiency) have to be brought into focus too (Jilke and Tummers 2018, Senghaas 2021).

Some other problems with this classification could perhaps be raised, especially regarding the position and importance of implementation studies, as street-level bureaucracy studies seem difficult to place. Most likely, this topic can be located at the interface between themes 6, 7, and 8. The encounter between the public sector and citizens is of crucial importance and needs more elaboration, we think; and the next section is dedicated to this special research and policy issue. How is the interplay between street-level bureaucrats and involved citizens with individual and structural barriers to employment arranged and processed, and what results are to be expected? More aspects of activation are attached to this encounter – including accountability and the increasing use of algorithms in activation practice. The way of conceptualizing the involved citizens – as consumers, service receivers, or fellow citizens – should also be addressed.

The public sector activates policies through its administration and the interplay with citizens, organizations, and firms. But the territorial organization of the national state and allocation of tasks to different levels and actors also have an impact on the functioning of the administration. Implementation is in no way a pure technical matter. Nothing can fully escape politics and political accountability. Neither can activation (Jantz and Jann 2013). This also goes with *performance management systems and evaluations*. They demand a huge data production and collection and measurable activities of the institutions involved. Naming, blaming, and shaming often follows evaluations. And some kinds of hard activation measures are normally advocated this way – mostly by economists. It could also be said that accountability becomes reformulated administratively. Performance management systems make classifications and exclusions. They also try to take over political decisions.

The same goes with *evidence-based evaluations*. Some objectives and legitimizations are given dominance this way and such evaluations are also used for agenda-setting purposes. They are not neutral, objective, and reflexive in character. But they have been heavily used to support activation. Evaluations of activation – and especially effect studies – focus on individual programmes and how individuals quickly find a job in the first labour market after participation in arrangements. Micro data are used to document individual employment results. Short-time effects are measured most often, even if longer time periods can bring more positive replacement results (Martin 2015, Pinto 2019). Most activation policies give priority to the speed and quantity of re-employment, with the disadvantage of long-lasting job placements and quality of jobs. Matthew effects have been one of the results, activation risks producing more precarious work for some groups. There has been a rich scholarly debate over the effectiveness and possible bias against special groups of workless people. Privatization and outsourcing of incentive reinforcement are often reported as having creaming and parking as side effects (Maron 2022). Here private instead of public law is dominant and this is a blurred boundary between the state and the market.

Economic studies might – as indicated – also try to calculate deadweight, selection, and substitution effects besides individual job outcomes. However, one might see this as a limitation and in three respects. First, there will be no data and assessment of *the interplay* between different measures and different policy areas and the way this influences the functioning of the labour market. Other consequences such as displacement and distribution effects are easily neglected, too. Packages of programmes and policy area interplay need to be studied much more. Equity-efficiency trade-offs should not be ignored either. Second, evaluations of supply-side effects are also *forgetting the demand side* and the dynamic interplay with employer decisions and behaviour. Their view of programmes seems strongly to influence their behaviour, according to a comparative analysis of Sweden and Switzerland (Fossati et al. 2021). Comparative analysis of 25 countries seems to confirm this finding (Haapanala 2022). Activation is dependent on employers having strong results. They are the gatekeepers of employment. They decide who fills jobs and how jobs are developed. They are in a pivotal position as to success or failure of activation (Ingold and McGurk 2023). The labour market has demand-side barriers in hiring and retaining workers, and the public supply of childcare facilities and other services are also of high importance. So are the actions of the PES. Third, the important *processes* creating the content of activation measures and new job opportunities are not always considered. There are limitations as to valid results in a number of effect studies using individual data for assessing employment results of individual programmes. It is difficult to measure how employment effects can improve the life of people in vulnerable positions. Processes are producing different results – also some not foreseen in policy formulations.

A special problem has been that jobseekers are often placed in low-wage jobs with limited duration. They return to the PES system very frequently. Activation seldom offers strong career prospects. But activation can – seen from a macro perspective – lower unemployment rates by shortening spells and by improving work motivation, and it increases the supply of labour (Martin 2015, 2016, Pinto 2019). But it is no high road to full employment and sustainability. Empirically, it is indicated (Haapanala 2022) that coercive activation trying to place clients in jobs quickly and discipline jobseekers by giving sanctions for non-compliance can be related to an expansion of precarious employment – even if it was not the intended consequence. Then punitive policies might also put a downward pressure on wages and give job holders and trade unions problems. Punitive workfare programmes are among the most contested ones. Too strong emphasis on coercive measures relative to capability building ("human capital"-oriented activation) also risks having short-time gains only. Upskilling policies are more productive when viewed from a 2- to 5-year perspective (Card et al. 2018). Quality jobs and more lasting sustainable jobs are in demand in case activation proves more successful in the future. But it is too simple and misleading to speak of "good" human capital investments and "bad" coercive policies. They perform very differently seen in a short- or a long-time perspective (ibid.). And coercive elements are often combined with service and help for improvement of abilities in programmes. This also makes assessments more difficult.

New understandings in *evidence-informed* evaluations might be holding ground now, substituting evidence-based ones. This is also a step away from technocratic policy-making. Actors at all levels have a right to participate in lesson-learning and improvement of activities.

Then we come back to the old distinction between politics and administration. It needs reformulation (Ladner and Sager 2022). The interrelationship of politics, policy, and polity is instructive and productive – also in the dealing with the many empirical, analytical, and normative issues of activation. Here, future activation studies might find help in part of recent political science advances.

FROM POLICY TO PRACTICE: ANALYSING POLITICS, POLICY, AND POLITY

Activation policies are complex entities made up of many actors, ideas, processes, and implementation structures. Policy processes are situated within an environment of multiple actors and organizations at all levels in a system. Researchers need to make a distinction between activation *policy* (with goals and principal aspirations of activation and renewal of social assistance, including a set of rules and sanctions) and activation *programmes and instruments* used (activation rules and sanctions in use) when studying activation.

A political science perspective might help to clarify some of the different aspects of activation policies and activation that are in use. You can fruitfully utilize the concepts of politics, policy, and polity (see Bekkers et al. 2017, Bell and Hindmore 2009, Capato et al. 2020, Berg-Schlosser et al. 2020, St. Denny and Zittoun 2024). A most useful distinction is between *policy* and *politics*. It is much more than a linguistic problem. These two wordings exist in English only, while other languages use just one word for the political phenomenon that also addresses historical legacies in the individual countries. A social construction is seen as part of this understanding of what political affairs are all about. To complement understandings, you need to add *polity*, referring to the institutional structures and administrative programming of policies.

First, the politics–policy dyad is to be reflected upon. We have two words covering the same semantic field – thanks to the historical developments of the UK. Politics is about the emergence of public policy vis-à-vis certain collective problems in society and how changes occur over time – in our case, unemployment. According to mainstream political science, politics is always struggles for power and exercise of this in separate fields or society at large. Political parties and parliaments are most central. But lobbyism and copycat behaviour can easily disturb policy-making processes, giving slow reaction times, and unequal access and power distributions. This we know. Politics is showing a willingness to act and policy is ways of finding "solutions" to common collective problems in specific political areas.

David Easton (1953, 1965) talked of politics as "the authoritative allocation of values for a society." Values can be both material and symbolic. Harald D. Lasswell (1951) adopted a definition of politics as "who gets what, when and how" (p. 3). That means a study of *policy-making processes and valued outcomes*. Lasswell called for a focus upon "the fundamental problems of man in society, rather than the topical issues of the moment." Thus, we also need to reflect upon the question, is activation to be termed activities dealing with more than the topical issues of the moment? And is activation to be described as a paradigm of its own or is it part of other policy paradigms? Analytically, a clear distinction on power/influence on the one hand and public problems and solutions on the other was made. Contexts are most important too, as Lasswell stated again and again.

A policy-centred approach focuses on the policy-making processes, implementation, and complexities in these processes and the context. Policy is politics in action. This problem-centred approach also includes a horizontal perspective on processes. Thus, a dual dimension of the political emerges. Many kinds of actors and ideas are involved, including collective values and goals, and many kinds of results are to be analysed. Policies are on-going processes of interactions and problem-solving activities. Collective problems are at the centre of focus and how well these problems are conquered. This is a genuine activation problematic.

Policy-oriented studies are, thus, occupied with the problem-centred activities of the public sector in interactions with the surrounding society. Here, a more processual definition is grounded. It is not a question of power "over" others, but "power of" something or "power to" do something related to the social order of society. Governments not only power but also puzzle in a collective way on behalf of all of us. Social learning is part of these processes dealing with collective uncertainty. In mainstream (American) political science, a *power-centred approach* is still dominant. But a policy-oriented approach is becoming more and more influential. In a traditional political science approach, politics is seen as a battle for power rather than activities linked to the solution of collective problems. Vertical power relationships are made central, disregarding many problems in society including unemployment and troublesome work in PES and educational institutions.

In a way, we can say that "policy determines politics". Policies also create specific areas of power resources to be used by actors in dealing with the problems. Processes of institutionalization and institutional arrangements have also stressed the importance of *polity* – the third dimension. Polity defines strategic opportunities and constraints that both public and private actors face during the processes. This is not reflected directly in Bonoli's ideal-types of activation. While policy is having the content of policies at centre stage, polity refers to the administrative and institutional structures of a political system and the way they influence processes and results. Governance reforms count. Special capacities and limitations are brought into the picture with the polity dimension.

This implies that politics is not only the exercise of power to design activation programs, but also the positioning of a question mark against that power. The policy dimension – the "what, when, and how" questions – is also about drivers of public policy, complexity of interactions and dynamic implementation, and outcomes and impacts of public action. A lot of puzzles of policy-making have already been discovered, including the use of third-party mechanisms and private actors. Public policies also have unintended results that must form part of studies. Public employees and other actors interact at the local level; they negotiate and experience conflict while trying to address collective problems. Sometimes they also counteract central initiatives.

In many policy studies, a policy cycle model (Howlett et al. 2009, Howlett 2011, Schulze 2012) has been used, specifying different stages. But it can only be of heuristic value as no clear real separation of the different "stages" is to be found (problem definition, agenda-setting, policy formulation, decision-making, implementation, and policy evaluation). The policy stage model can, however, remind us of the need to have a dynamic analytical understanding of the activation phenomenon. Policy-oriented studies will use the complexities of relationships between politics, policy, and polity as both a starting point and a point of reference for explanations of activation.

IMPLEMENTATION AND ACCOUNTABILITY

What happens when citizens meet the public authority in activation spaces and arrangements, is both a question of empirical investigation and an analytical problem of using such findings in relation to what was expected to happen, according to central decisions and administrative programming. Official objectives and formulations seldom fit with reality. This is also a way of saying that the political expectations are filtered and dashed by a number of administrative reformulations and by the designing of implementation frames, as well as – most importantly – by the interactions between citizens and representatives of the authorities (Zacka 2017, Nielsen and Andersen 2024). Here, at the street level, policies and polity are reframed and changed by the interactions themselves and the resulting behaviour on both sides. Questions of autonomy, practising accountability, and policy delivery are at stake.

The frontline workers ("street-level bureaucrats") are acting not simply as bureaucrats but also as partners in public encounters that can bring results not foreseen at all in formal policy-making. Substantive findings in a lot of implementation studies witness a big difference between formal political science perspectives and a realist perspective of actual behaviour and importance of local interactions, especially since the Third Wave of implementation research (Sætren 2020). This calls for further clarification of the dichotomy between politics and implementation and a realist perspective in activation research on how discretion and accountability are practised at the decental level. One could also say that bureaucracy is politics (Frederickson et al. 2016).

As to the first question, we need to have empirical accounts of what actually happens at the street level of government and relate this to the expectation and reality level (Hupe 2019, 2022, Hawkins 2022). Discrepancies are not to be operational or acceptable, according to a formalist conception. But the reality is that the official objectives formulated and decided upon in policies are reinterpreted in programmes and implemented in accordance with local needs and processes that can deviate strongly from central expectations.

The dichotomy of politics versus administration reduces implementation to a technical question while in reality it is a number of interpretations, ways of using discretion on the side of employees, and concrete interactions, processes with, and various feedback from unemployed people and people on social assistance that produces results often not foreseen. It is not simply rule application but a craft-based and creative use of competences on the side of public employees when they decide to act for reasons not recognized by official policy. More than legal aspects are at stake (Ladner and Sager 2022). Also, normative, ethical, moral, and organizational reasons are involved in professional practice (Freidson 2001, Zacka 2017). Rule application is, in practice, to be seen more as an art and craft by itself – and not a technocratic exercise only.

The use of a dominant top-down perspective thus seems to need supplementary approaches. But the question of accountability is also giving this top-down perspective relevance. It is a question of acting on behalf of a number of accountability issues and forums, including citizens as participants and co-producers of policies. Street-level bureaucrats also have more kinds of feedback. And they are part of local organizations protecting interests of their own (Brodkin and Marsden 2013).

Professionalism is actually demonstrated in balancing different accountabilities when they use their discretion in the processes (Svensson and Evetts 2010, Noordegraaf 2020). Discretion is both a question of space for action and a way of behaving. Formally granted space is needed to act, and is used in different ways, adapted to the special encounter. Formal rules are generally less important than other demands and considerations. Policy programmes and local and individual circumstances are being considered and connected in actions, starting with screening of unemployed people, information, communication, interactions, and decisions as to activation forms, benefits, and sanctions. Encounters are communicative and relational situations. These processes cannot avoid tensions, ambivalence, and dilemmas. There is a complexity of joint action, recognized from the beginning in implementation research (Pressman and Wildavsky 1984) and analysed also today (Olsen 2022). You have ambivalence in translations, relationships, and in organization. Handling of such ambivalences are difficult. Trade-offs in power-based decisions are to be made justifiable. This also calls for an empirical-based bottom-up perspective in implementation research – and multiple methods of investigation.

However, it is not individual street-level bureaucrats and decentral leaders only who influence the result of processes. Also of relevance are *collective policy adjustments* from below. Local authorities, municipalities, and cities make their own implementation design and actions in processes using more institutional logics and relying on professional accountability (Fuertes et al. 2021). Private providers look to their own interests too. All those decisions made at the local level and the way citizens involved react to the ways of being treated and the services or arrangements provided will change policy. Even within a work-first system, decentralized actors might start developing capabilities with physical training, care, psychological help, language courses, and vocational training. The expected policy and the one realized seldom correspond to each other. Ways of changing policy are recorded as different ways of "policy drift" (Mahoney and Thelen 2010).

The lack of correspondence between official expectations and final implementation results in activation have had new central initiatives produced. One of them was stronger NPM steering through manuals, standards, monitoring, performance management, and evaluation. These efforts have tried to narrow the room for discretion. This steering strategy is full of conflicts between levels within the state system and the decentralized level in trying to defend a political and administrative autonomy, now with more success. Professionalism is to be increasingly stressed again. Another strategy is more digitalization. The use of algorithms is a new way of trying to eliminate errors in human treatment of citizens, to decide eligibility and fines and other administrative choices. Technological solutions to implementation problems are, however, less effective in the case of caring professions where analogous interactions with people are required in order to have individual treatment, to engage in dialogues, and to build trust. It is a central part of the service delivery and it is a test of professionalism on the side of the semi-professionals. Thus, you have more kinds of tensions and conflicts embedded in implementation of activation policies, including multi-level conflicts within the state system.

Accountability then becomes a central question – a question of fair treatment, impartiality, correctness, justice, and effectiveness. As a public employee or leader, you cannot avoid being held accountable (Jantz and Jann 2013, Zacka 2017). Efforts to do so will create unjust and perverse results. It is necessary to act in accordance with law and formal instructions, but also to be responsible and flexible as to the wishes, hopes, and situations of the citizens involved. Job Centre employees often deal with complex cases. Decisions can be full of dilemmas. But a case cannot be ignored. Decisions have to be made and justified. The daily, "dirty" work means tensions. A behavioural response is to seek coherence. But a well-known coping strategy is also to create stereotypes and classify clients and treat them differently (Ingram and Schneider 2015). This is a defensive and unjust way of using discretion. Jobseekers with disadvantaged backgrounds have been the losers of the economic prosperity also because of priorities and coping strategies in the PES systems. A broader debate on vulnerable groups in activation has developed, in which the question addressed is how the hard-to-place unemployed can be integrated into the open labour market. Often new formats are claimed (Andersen et al. 2017).

From the street level via organizations and interorganizational networks to the macro-level of the state, accountability is a collective effort to help in securing human well-being. All public actors want to behave in a professional way – not as a bureaucrat. And citizens have more roles in actions and encounters with the public sector. They are rule followers in having rights and duties to observe; they are increasingly co-producers of public service provisions, voters, and now and then activists. They experience, assess, challenge, accept, or oppose policies and treatments. The relationship between local authority representatives and citizens decides much of the fate of individual activation arrangements and policy initiatives, but also the output legitimization of the public sector (Rothstein 2021). Activation also rests on a social contract between citizens and the public institutions – even more important than input legitimization.

ACTIVATION AND THE FUTURE

This short overview is in no way exhaustive. Activation can be viewed and approached via other channels and ways of definition; it can be analysed differently as well. In the case of our joint work, we tried to clarify different forms of understandings, analytical statements, and ways of analysing activation. More stepping stones towards the building of a more comprehensive theory are to be found. Ideas, models, and steering principles travel across borders, but policy-making at the central level is not the same as policies implemented. How path-dependent, path-shaping, or path-breaking are developments then? It would be important to have comparative analysis clarifying whether activation arrangements have been part of processes of "policy diffusion" or "policy transfer" (Marsh and Sharman 2009) or perhaps "policy circulation" (de Oliveira 2021). This calls for both historical and systematic comparative analysis (and proper funding of such international cooperation with many countries included). The place and importance of the EU level and the OECD in this respect also need more clarification, as do the imponderables and the transformation of the post-industrial welfare states (Nielsen and Hammerslev 2024).

Even more important, however, is to figure out what kind of future activation we are going to experience. Is the activation paradigm soon coming to an end? This was a provocative central question. Termination of activation could be argued not only because of limits to the paradigm that have been revealed in coping with crisis and growing unemployment and inequalities. But here, there must again be place for differentiation. Countries with well-funded and accepted public institutions and coordination mechanisms might have better chances of success with activation than liberal systems. Upskilling and reskilling in order to meet the demands of a more technologically advanced and digitalized labour market and tailored support and help to vulnerable groups – such as low-skilled, young, female, non-standard, and immigrant workers – seem needed. And this is in progress in more places, even though activation will still have many national variations. Does activation need help from other policies, organizations, and/or collective actors to be successful? These are important questions to answer.

We argue that activation is here to stay. A fifth phase has started with new response mechanisms built into activation practices and a partial revival of "social investment" initiatives at policy level. There is a growing awareness of the importance of capability-building measures. But activation, vocational training, and the education systems should be much stronger connected to produce better reintegration. This implies that the formal educational system should be supplemented by upskilling and reskilling initiatives for the whole working populations.

The Covid-19 pandemic and its aftermath changed the cards on the table. It was a focus event and it worked – in the short run – as an accelerator for new Keynesian and "human capital" policies (Madsen 2023). Education and training, upskilling and reskilling on more equal and non-discriminatory terms, are again given priority in a number of systems according to the following contributions. Some social scientists even think that we are at the beginning of a new Great Transformation 2.0 with disruption of old regulations and policies (Ferrera et al. 2024). This might be too premature a conclusion because one will also find economic and political pressure to rebalance national budgets and renew ALMP along well-known economic models. More kinds of struggles are taking place. But people pushed out of employment during the pandemic must be reintegrated and new inequalities have to be conquered. Now labour shortages from 2022 also indicate that proper policy responses have not been found yet. Activation is in flux. The "human capital" concept needs a new and broader interpretation outside orthodox economic thinking as indicated above. It is more about developing capabilities.

Activation can be studied at macro-, meso-, and micro levels. The research agenda must be broad. We will have to engage in discussions as to *definition and classification* of activation. Clarification of central concepts matters, and we will also have to engage in constructive exchange as to the analytical strength of basic concepts. We will look forward to more and new analysis of the use of activation in different national system and – hopefully – also some comparative investigations. The effects of activation are only recently being investigated from more angles, and more research in this respect is urgently needed (Ahmad et al. 2019). It seems obvious that both a *longer* time perspective and analysis with a *short* time perspective are called for. The experiences during the Covid-19 period are most important to investigate and assess, also because of the fact that the future – or the end – of the activation paradigm must be addressed and new policies need to be formulated.

REFERENCES

Ahmad, N., Svarer, M. and Naveed, A. (2019) 'The effect of active labour market programmes and benefit sanctions on reducing unemployment duration', *Journal of Labour Research*, 40(2), pp. 202–229.

Andersen, N. A., Caswell, D. and Larsen, F. (2017) 'A new approach to helping the hard-to-place unemployed', *European Journal of Social Security*, 19(4), pp. 335–352. https://doi.org/10.1177/1388262717745193.

Barbier, J.-C. (2004) 'Systems of Social Protection in Europe: Two Contrasted Paths to Activation, and Maybe a Third', in Lind, J., Knudsen, H. and Jørgensen, H. (eds.) *Labour and Employment Regulation in Europe*. Brussels: Peter Lang, pp. 233–253.

Barbier, J.-C. and Ludwig-Mayerhofter, W. (2004) 'Introduction: the many worlds of activation', *European Societies*, 6(4), pp. 423–436. https:// doi .org/ 10 .1080/ 1461669042000275845.

Becker, G. S. (1976) *The Economic Approach to Human Behavior*. Chicago: University of Chicago Press.

Bekkers, V., Fenger, M. and Scholten, P. (2017) *Public Policy in Action*. Cheltenham, UK and Northampton, MA, USA: Edward Elgar Publishing.

Bell, S. and Hindmore, A. (2009) *Rethinking Governance: The Centrality of the State in Modern Society*. Cambridge: Cambridge University Press.

Bengtsson, M. (2014) 'Towards standby-ability: Swedish and Danish activation policies in flux', *International Journal of Social Welfare*, 23(S1), pp. 54–70.

Bengtsson, M., de la Porte, C. and Jacobsson, K. (2017) 'Labour Market Policy under conditions of permanent austerity: Any signs of social investment?', *Social Policy and Administration*, 51(2), pp. 367–388. https://doi.org/10.1111/spol.12292.

Berg-Schlosser, D., Badie, B. and Morlino, L. (eds.) (2020) *The SAGE Handbook of Political Science. Vol. 1–3*. London: Sage.

Besharov, D. and Call, D. (eds.) (2023a) *Work and the Social Safety Net: Labor Activation in Europe and the United States*. New York: Oxford University Press.

Besharov, D. and Call, D. (2023b) 'Introduction: European and US Experiences with Labor Activation', in Besharov, D. and Call, D. (eds.) *Work and the Social Safety Net: Labor Activation in Europe and the United States*. New York: Oxford University Press, pp. 1–24.

Betzelt, S. and Bothfeld, S. (eds.) (2011) *Activation and Labour Market Reforms in Europe: Challenges to Social Citizenship*. Basingstoke: Palgrave Macmillan.

Betzler, M. (ed.) (2013) *Autonomie der Person*. Münster: Mentis.

Bonoli, G. (2010) 'The political economy of active labor-market policy', *Politics & Society*, 38(4), pp. 435–457. Doi: 10.1177/0032329210381235.

Bonoli, G. (2013) *The Origins of Active Social Policy: MCPCP*. Oxford: Oxford University Press.

Bonoli, G. (2022) 'Research on Active Social Policy', in Nelson, K., Nieuwenhuis, R. and Yerkes, M. (eds.) *Social Policy in Changing European Societies: Research Agendas for the 21st Century*. Cheltenham, UK and Northampton, MA, USA: Edward Elgar Publishing, pp. 120–134.

Bothfeld, S. (2017) 'Autonomie: Ein Kernbegriff moderner Sozialstaatlichkeit', *Zeitschrift für Sozialreform*, 63(3), pp. 355–387. https://doi.org/10.1515/zsr-2017-0017.

Bothfeld, S. and Rosenthal, P. (2014) 'Paradigmenwechsel durch inkrementellen Wandel', *WSI-Mitteilungen*, 67(3), pp. 199–206. https://doi.org/10.57 1/0342–300X-2014–3-199.

Brodkin, E. Z. and Marston, G. (eds.) (2013) *Work and the Welfare State: Street-level Organizations and Workfare Politics*. Georgetown, Washington DC: Georgetown University Press.

Brown, G. (2009) *Address to the Labour Congress*. Brighton, September 29, 2009.

Brown, P., Lauder, H. and Cheung, S. Y. (2020) *The Death of Human Capital? Its Failed Promise and How to Renew It in an Age of Disruption*. Oxford: Oxford University Press.

Brussig, M. (2019) 'Was kommt nach der Aktivierung? Neue Leitbilder der Arbeitsmarktpolitik', *Arbeit*, 28(2), pp. 101–123. https://doi.org/10.1515/arbeit-2019–0008.

Capato, G., Howlett, M. and Fraser, S. (eds.) (2020) *A Modern Guide to Public Policy*. Cheltenham, UK and Northampton, MA, USA: Edward Edgar Publishing.

Card, D., Kluve, J. and Weber, A. (2018) 'What works? A meta analysis of recent active labor market program evaluations', *Journal of European Economic Association*, 16(3), pp. 894–931. https://doi.org/10.1093/jeea/jvx028.

Clasen, J. and Clegg, D. (eds.) (2011) *Regulating the Risk of Unemployment: National Adaptation to Post-industrial Labour Markets in Europe*. Oxford: Oxford University Press.

Clasen, J., Clegg, D. and Goerne, A. (2016) 'Comparative social policy analysis and active labour market policy: Putting quality before quantity', *Journal of Social Policy*, 45(1), pp. 21–38. https://doi.org/10.1017/S0047279415000434.

Clasen, J. and Mascarò, C. (2022) 'Activation: a thematic and conceptual review', *Journal of European Social Policy*, 32(4), pp. 484–494. Doi: 10.1177/095892872 21089477.

Clasen, J. and Mascarò, C. (2023) 'Activation: a research topic in its own right?', in Clegg, D. and Durazzi, N. (eds.) *Handbook of Active Labour Market Policy in Advanced Democracies*. Cheltenham, UK and Northampton, MA, USA: Edward Elgar Publishing, pp. 44–53.

Cronert, A. (2022) 'The multi-tool nature of active labour market policy and its implications for partisan politics in advanced democracies', *Social Policy & Society*, 21(2), pp. 210–226. https://doi.org/10.1017/S1474746420000597.

Danforth, B. (2014) 'Worlds of welfare in time: A historical reassessment of the three-world typology', *Journal of European Social Policy*, 24(2), pp. 164–182. https://doi.org/10.1177/0958928713517919.

de Oliveira, O. P. (ed.) (2021) *Handbook of Policy Transfer, Diffusion and Circulation*. Cheltenham, UK and Northampton, MA, USA: Edward Elgar Publishing.

Easton, D. (1953) *The Political System: An Inquiry into the State of Political Science*. New York: Alfred A. Knopf.

Easton, D. (1965) *A Systems Analysis of Political Life*. New York: John Wiley & Sons.

England, P. and Folbre, N. (2023) 'Reconceptualizing Human Capital', in Tåhlin, M. (ed.) *A Research Agenda for Skills and Inequality*. Cheltenham, UK and Northampton, MA, USA: Edward Elgar Publishing, pp. 177–195.

Eversberg, D. (2016) 'Beyond individualization: The German "activation toolbox"', *Critical Social Policy*, 36(2), pp. 167–186. https:// doi .org/ 10 .1177/ 0261018315620868.

Ferrera, M., Miró, J. and Ronchi, S. (2024) *Social Reformism 2.0: Work, Welfare and Progressive Politics in the 21st Century*. Cheltenham, UK and Northampton, MA, USA: Edward Elgar Publishing.

Fossati, F., Liechti, F. and Wilson, A. (2021) 'Participation in labour market programmes: A positive or negative signal of employability?', *Acta Sociologica*, 64(1), pp. 70–85. https://doi.org/10.1177/0001699320902837.

Frederickson, H. G., Smith, K. B., Larimer, C. and Licari, M. J. (2016) *The Public Administration Theory Primer*. New York: Routledge.

Freidson, E. (2001) *Professionalism, the Third Logic: On the Practice of Knowledge*. Chicago: Chicago University Press.

Fuertes, V., McQuaid, R. W. and Heidenreich, M. (2021) 'Institutional logics of service provision: The national and urban governance of activation policies in three European countries', *Journal of European Social Policy*, 31(1), pp. 92–107. https:// doi.org/10.1177/0958928720974178.

Giddens, A. (2009) *The Third Way: The Renewal of Social Democracy*. Cambridge: Polity Press.

Greve, B. (ed.) (2023) *Welfare States in a Turbulent Era*. Cheltenham, UK and Northampton, MA, USA: Edward Elgar Publishing.

Haapanala, H. (2022) 'Carrots or sticks? A multilevel analysis of active labour market policies and non-standard employment in Europe', *Social Policy and Administration*, 56(3), pp. 360–377. https://doi.org/10.1111/spol.12770.

Hall, P. (1993) 'Policy paradigms, social learning and the state: The case of economic policymaking in Britain', *Comparative Politics* 25(3), pp. 275–296. https://doi.org/ 10.2307/422246.

Hawkins, K. (2022) 'Discretion and Accountability: Notes on Perspectives and Avoidance', in Hupe, P. (ed.) *The Politics of the Public Encounter: What Happens When Citizens Meet the State*. Cheltenham, UK and Northampton, MA, USA: Edward Elgar Publishing, pp. 78–105.

Hemerijck, A. (ed.) (2017) *The Uses of Social Investment*. Oxford: Oxford University Press.

Howlett, M. (2011) *Designing Public Policies: Principles and Instruments*. London: Routledge.

Howlett, M., Ramesh, M. and Perl, A. (2009) *Studying Public Policy: Policy Cycles and Policy Subsystems*. Toronto, ON: Oxford University Press.

Hupe, P. (ed.) (2019) *Research Handbook of Street-level Bureaucracy: The Ground Floor of Government in Context*. Cheltenham, UK and Northampton, MA, USA: Edward Elgar Publishing.

Hupe, P. (2022) 'The Politics of the Public Encounter', in *The Politics of the Public Encounter: What Happens When Citizens Meet the State*. Cheltenham, UK and Northampton, MA, USA: Edward Elgar Publishing, pp. 19–38.

Ingold, J. and McGurk, P. (eds.) (2023) *Employer Engagement: Making Active Market Policies Work*. Bristol: Bristol University Press.

Ingram, H. and Schneider, A. L. (2015) 'Making Distinctions: The Social Construction of Target Groups', in Fischer, F., Torgerson, D., Durnová, A. and Orsini, M. (eds.) *Handbook of Critical Policy Studies*. Cheltenham, UK and Northampton, MA, USA: Edward Elgar Publishing, pp. 259–273.

Jantz, B. and Jann, W. (2013) 'Mapping accountability changes in labour market administrations: From concentrated to shared accountability?' *International Review of Administrative Sciences*, 79(2), pp. 227–248. https:// doi .org/ 10 .1177/ 0020852313477764.

Jilke, S. and Tummers, L. (2018) 'Which clients are deserving of help? A theoretical model and experimental test', *Journal of Public Administration Research and Theory*, 28(2), pp. 226–238. https://doi.org/10.1093/jopart/muy002.

Jørgensen, H. (2009) 'From a beautiful swan to an ugly duckling: The renewal of Danish activation policy since 2003', *European Journal of Social Security*, 11(4), pp. 337–367. https://doi.org/10.1177/138826270901100401.

Jørgensen, H. (2020) 'Arven fra Rehn-Meidner-modellen: Idégrundlag og erfaringslære for aktiv arbejdsmarkedspolitik', in Klindt, M. P., Rasmussen, S. and Jørgensen, H. (eds.) *Aktiv arbejdsmarkedspolitik: Etablering, udvikling og fremtid*. Copenhagen: DJØF-Forlag, pp. 51–88.

Klammer, U. and Leiber, S. (2004) 'Aktivierung und Eigenverantwortung in europäisch-vergleichende Perspektive', *WSI Mitteilungen*, 57(9), pp. 514–521.

Kluve, J., Card, D., Fertig, M., Góra, M., Jacobi, L., Jensen, P., Leetmaa, R., Nima, L., Patacchini, E., Schaffner, S., Schmidt, C. M., Klaauw, B. and Weber, A. (2007) *Active Labour Market Policies in Europe: Performance and Perspectives*. Berlin: Springer Verlag.

Knotz, C. (2019) 'Why countries "get tough on the work-shy": The role of adverse economic conditions', *Journal of Social Policy*, 48(3), pp. 615–634. https://doi.org/ 10.1017/S0047279418000740.

Ladner, A. and Sager, F. (eds.) (2022) *Handbook on the Politics of Public Administration*. Cheltenham, UK and Northampton, MA, USA: Edward Elgar Publishing.

Laenen, T. (2021) *Welfare Deservingness and Welfare Policy: Popular Deservingness Opinions and Their Interaction with Welfare State Policies*. Cheltenham, UK and Northampton, MA, USA: Edward Elgar Publishing.

Lasswell, H. D. (1951) 'The Policy Orientation', in Lernerand, D. and Lasswell, H. D. (eds.) *The Policy Sciences: Recent Developments in Scope and Method*. Stanford, CA: Stanford University Press, pp. 3–15.

Lind, J. and Møller, I. H. (2006) 'Activation for what purpose? Lessons from Denmark', *International Journal of Sociology and Social Policy*, 26(1–2), pp. 5–19. https://doi .org/10.1108/01443330610644399.

Lødemel, I. and Moreira, A. (eds.) (2014) *Activation or Workfare? Governance and the Neo-liberal Convergence*. Oxford: Oxford University Press.

Lødemel, I. and Trickey, H. (eds.) (2001) *'An Offer You Can't Refuse': Workfare in International Perspective*. Bristol: Policy Press.

Madsen, M. O. (2023) 'Keynesian Economics Steering is Back: End of Liberal Economic Policy?', in Greve, B. (ed.) *Welfare States in a Turbulent Era*. Cheltenham, UK and Northampton, MA, USA: Edward Elgar Publishing, pp. 98–111.

Mahoney, J. and Thelen, K. (2010) *Explaining Institutional Change: Ambiguity, Agency, and Power*. Cambridge: Cambridge University Press.

Maron, A. (2022) 'Public sector, private delivery: Service workers and the negotiation of blurred boundaries in a neoliberal state', *Work, Employment and Society*, 36(6), pp. 1060–1077. https://doi.org/10.1177/09500170211001272.

Marsh, D. and Sharman, J. C. (2009) 'Policy diffusion and policy transfer', *Policy Studies*, 33(6), pp. 269–288. https://doi.org/10.1080/01442870902863851.

Martin, J. P. (2015) 'Activation and active labour market policies in OECD countries: Stylised facts and evidence on their effectiveness', *IZA Journal of Labour Policy*, 4(4), pp. 1–29. https://doi.org/10.1186/s40173–015–0032-y.

Martin, J. P. (2016) *Whither Activation Policies? Reflections for the Future*. IZA Policy Paper No. 114. Bonn: Institute of Labor Economics (IZA).

Morel, N., Palier, B. and Palme, J. (eds.) (2012) *Towards a Social Investment Welfare State? Ideas, Polices and Challenges*. Bristol: Policy Press.

Nelson, K., Niewenhuis, R. and Yerkes, M. (eds.) (2022) *Social Policy in Changing European Societies: Research Agendas for the 21st Century*. Cheltenham, UK and Northampton, MA, USA: Edward Elgar Publishing.

Nielsen, M. H. and Andersen, N. A. (2024) 'Ignoring by complying: How public officials handle hybridity to pursue the goals of new public management', *Public Administration* 102(1) (in publication). https://doi.org/10.1111/padm.12979.

Nielsen, S. P. P. and Hammerslev, O. (eds.) (2024) *Transformations of European Welfare States and Social Rights: Regulation, Professionals, and Citizens*. Cham: Palgrave Macmillan.

Noordegraaf, M. (2020) 'Protective or connective professionalism? How connected professionals can (still) act as autonomous and authoritative experts', *Journal of Professions and Organization*, 7(2), pp. 205–223. https:// doi .org/ 10 .1093/ jpo/ joaa011.

OECD (2001) *OECD Economic Outlook 2015*. Paris: OECD.

Olsen, G. (2022) 'Ambivalence in activation encounters', *European Journal of Social Work*, 25(4), pp. 564–576. https://doi.org/10.1080/13691457.2021.1995705.

Peck, J. (2001) *Workfare States*. New York: Guilford.

Pinto, M. (2019) 'Exploring activation: A cross-country analysis of active labour market policies in Europe', *Social Science Research*, 81, pp. 91–105. https://doi.org/10.1016/j.ssresearch.2019.03.001.

Pressman, J. L. and Wildavsky, A. (1984) *Implementation: How Great Expectations in Washington are Dashed in Oakland or, Why It's Amazing the Federal Programs Work At All, This Being a Saga of the Economic Development Administration as Told by Two Sympathetic Observers who Seek to Build Morals on a Foundation of Ruined Hopes*. 3rd Edition. Berkeley, CA: University of California Press.

Raffass, T. (2015) 'Demanding activation', *Journal of Social Policy*, 46(2), pp. 349–365. https://doi.org/10.1017/S004727941600057X.

Read, J. (2009) 'A genealogy of homo economicus: Neoliberalism and the production of subjectivity', *Foucault Studies*, 6, pp. 25–36. https:// doi .org/ 10 .22439/ fs .v0i0 .2465.

Rothstein, B. (2021) *Controlling Corruption: The Social Contract Approach*. Oxford: Oxford University Press.

Rubery, J. (2011) 'Reconstruction amid deconstruction: Or why we need more social in European social models', *Work, Employment and Society*, 25(4), pp. 658–674. https://doi.org/10.1177/0950017011419718.

Sætren, H. (2020) 'Implementation', in Berg-Schlosser, D., Badie, B. and Morlino, L. (eds.) *The SAGE Handbook of Political Science: Vol. 3*. London: Sage, pp. 1001–1022.

Schulze, M. (2012) *Gewerkschaften im Umbau des Sozialstaats: Der Einfluss der Dachverbände im Welfare-to-Work-Reformprozess in Dänemark, Deutschland und den USA*. Wiesbaden: VS-Verlag für Sozialwissenschaften.

Schulze, M. and Jørgensen, H. (2018) 'Das Aktivierungsparadima als dominantes Prinzip der Arbeitsmarktpolitk in Deutschland und Dänemark', *Sozialer Fortschritt*, 67(8–9), pp. 627–643. https://doi.org/10.3790/sfo.67.8–9.627.

Segbers, F. (2016) 'Das Menschenbild von Hartz IV: Die Pädagogisierung von Armut, die Zentralität von Erwerbsarbeit und autoritärer Sozialstaat', in Anhorn, R. and Balzereit, M. (eds.) *Handbuch Therapeutisierung und Soziale Arbeit: Perspektiven kritischer Sozialer Arbeit*. Berlin: Springer, pp. 687–708.

Sen, A. (1999) *Development as Freedom*. New York: Knopf.

Senghaas, M. (2021) 'Street-level judgements about welfare deservingness: How Jobcentre advisors decide about the individual mix of "support" and "demand" in the delivery of activation policies', *Social Policy and Society*, 20(3), pp. 385–399. https://doi.org/10.1017/S1474746420000408.

St. Denny, E. and Zittoun, P. (eds.) (2024) *Handbook of Teaching Public Policy*. Cheltenham, UK and Northampton, MA, USA: Edward Elgar Publishing.

Strandh, M. (2001) 'State intervention and mental well-being among the unemployed', *Journal of Social Policy*, 30(1), pp. 57–80. https:// doi .org/ 10 .1017/ S0047279400006176.

Svensson, L. G. and Evetts, J. (eds.) (2010) *Sociology of Profession: Continental and Anglo-Saxon Traditions*. Borås: Daidalos.

Tan, E. (2014) 'Human capital theory: a holistic criticism', *Review of Educational Research*, 84(3), pp. 411–445. https://doi.org/10.3102/0034654314532696.

Thelen, K. (2014) *Varieties of Capitalism and the New Politics of Social Solidarity*. New York: Cambridge University Press.

Udehn, L. (2001) *Methodological Individualism*. London: Routledge.

Van Berkel, R., Caswell, D., Kupka, P. and Larsen, F. (eds.) (2017) *Frontline Delivery of Welfare-to-Work Policies in Europe: Activating the Unemployed*. London: Routledge.

Van Berkel, R., Larsen, F. and Casswell, D. (2018) 'Introduction: Frontline delivery of welfare-to-work in different European contexts', *International Social Security Review*, 71(4), pp. 3–11. https://doi.org/10.1111/issr.12186.

Van Berkel, R. and Møller, I. H. (eds.) (2002) *Active Social Policies in the EU: Inclusion through participation?* Bristol: Policy Press.

Weishaupt, T. J. (2011) *From the Manpower Revolution to the Activation Paradigm: Explaining Institutional Continuity and Change in an Integrating Europe*. Amsterdam: Amsterdam University Press.

Whitworth, A. (2016) 'Neoliberal paternalism and paradoxical subjects: Confusion and contradiction in UK activation policy', *Critical Social Policy*, 36(3), pp 412–431. https://doi.org/10.1177/0261018315624442.

Williams, F. (2021) *Social Policy: A Critical and Intersectional Analysis*. Cambridge: Polity.

Zacka, B. (2017) *When the State Meets the Street: Public Service and Moral Agency*. Cambridge, MA: The Belknap Press of Harvard University Press.

3. Crisis and political power relations: the development of activation policies in Austria before and after COVID

Simon Theurl and Silvia Hofbauer

INTRODUCTION

The economic impact of the COVID-19 pandemic has led to a number of departures from the economic policies of recent decades and pushed labour market activation policies to their limits. In 2020, the European Commission suspended the deficit rules of the EU Stability Pact, allowing for generous government interventions to stabilise the economy and mitigate social distortions. While the activation approach in labour market policy (LMP) was temporarily abandoned, easing of fiscal policy allowed for an expansion of LMP measures. As the economy has recovered since 2021, a return to a policy of labour market activation can also be observed. However, the current inflation crisis, high inflation expectations, demographic change and the climate crisis also pose extraordinary challenges for LMP in the immediate and near future. In this chapter, we examine the development of the activation approach in Austria, and outline continuities and changes in the context of economic crises and political power relations.

Crises on the labour market reveal the limits of LMP and can lead to temporary or lasting departures from common perceptions of problems and the solutions that are developed on the basis of those perceptions. The economic growth regime of the post-war period came up against its limits, leading to a paradigm shift in Austrian LMPs from the 1980s onwards. Most significantly, macroeconomic policies that aimed for full employment through expansionary fiscal and monetary policies were abandoned. Instead, policy makers relied on LMPs, which are naturally interwoven with the logic of unemployment insurance, especially the requirement of "willingness to work".

After the expansion of active LMP, the concept of "activating" jobseekers was incorporated into a range of labour market and welfare systems in various forms and to varying degrees on a trans-national, European scale (Weishaupt,

2011). In the mid-1980s, Austria also gave way to international economic and political pressure and abandoned the Austro-Keynesian policy. Thereby, social partnership, which had played a crucial role during Austro-Keynesian demand management, remained influential. A crucial element of activating LMP was the shift in the perception of the underlying causes of unemployment. They are no longer located in a lack of economic demand, which could be managed through macroeconomic policies by the government, but on the supply side among the unemployed themselves. Since then, putting pressure on jobseekers has become an elementary strategy of LMP.

Since establishment of the activation approach, various crises have rocked the Austrian labour market, manifesting themselves in rising unemployment. Given that unemployment has a range of causes (Rothschild, 1994) and is not solely a question of (un)willingness to work, the effectiveness of labour market activation policies is limited. It comes as no surprise, that policy makers relied more strongly on active LMPs to deal with different crises on the Austrian labour market. The failure of activation measures to cope with crisis, therefore partly explains policy shifts during times of crisis such as COVID. To understand whether such a shift is temporary or permanent, ideological views of political players, the institutional setting – in Austria the strength of social partners, who manage the Public Employment Service together with the government – as well as power relations between labour and capital in general, must be considered.

In the literature, the term "activation" remains ambiguous. A broad definition, which understands activation as efforts to promote employability and labour market participation for both uninsured and insured unemployed people, allows us to maintain country-specific terms. Following Bonoli's typology (Bonoli in this book), we analyse activation policies along the following dimensions: "the scope of activation in general", "focus groups of activation", "labour market performance", "activation benefits", "strictness clusters" and "the governance of activation". Additionally, we distinguish between a "decommodifying" work first ideology and the inclusion perspective, to link the development of activation policies to political power relations.

Some studies use the term "workfare" to describe the change from the post-war Keynesian welfare state to a "Schumpeterian workfare state" (Atzmüller, 2009; Peck, 2001, 2003). Activation policies are seen as a key element, as social welfare benefits are increasingly conditioned towards the acceptance of any job offer, while monitoring and sanctions of the welfare beneficiaries increase. The welfare state gets reoriented, away from its decommodifying character towards commodification. The primary aim of LMP is the fastest possible re-employment of unemployed persons.

This can be contrasted with the inclusion perspective. Advocates of this approach place social participation in the foreground (Kronauer, 2002). Work is understood as a social relationship that creates a sense of purpose (Jahoda, 1995). Based on shared experiences in the work process, this can even provide the basis for joint protests and contribute to an improvement in working conditions (Kronauer, 2019). Importantly, from an inclusion perspective, the positive aspects of work crucially depend on the quality of work and its social recognition. Employment is understood as an important social relation, but the aim of LMP is empowerment of people through education or public job offers, rather than unconditional employment.

In Austria, the various political power relations can be roughly divided between the opposing poles of inclusion and decommodification on the side of labour and commodification on the side of capital.

An overview of research on the development of activation policies from the perspective of inclusion is provided by Marcel Fink et al. (2018). Peter Streckeisen, Karin Scherschel and Manfred Krenn examine labour market activation policies in the context of new forms of precarious employment relationships (Streckeisen et al., 2012). Roland Atzmüller (2009) and Markus Griesser (2019) examine the development of the workfare state in Austria. Marcel Fink et al. (2018) and Emerich Talos, Theurl Simon, Christine Stelzer-Orthofer and Dennis Tamesberger describe the development of LMP under the two right-wing conservative coalition governments of the Austrian People's Party (ÖVP) and the Freedom Party of Austria (FPÖ) (Stelzer-Orthofer & Tamesberger, 2018; Tálos, 2006a, 2019; Theurl, 2019). We will build on this research and outline changes and developments in Austrian LMP since the 1980s in the context of political power relations and crises on the labour market.

First, we will describe the emergence of the activation approach in Austria and outline the major historical developments. We will then describe the key elements of activation policy in Austria today. After that, we will look at the development of LMP since 2000 against the backdrop of political power relations and crises or problems on the labour market. We will highlight departures from the activation paradigm and discuss to what extent these form a suitable basis for a new LMP approach and whether such a change is emerging in Austria.

ORIGINS OF ACTIVATION POLICIES IN AUSTRIA

Active LMP has played an important role in Austria's political system for decades and has its origins in the trade union movement. The first Labour Market Promotion Act (AMFG) was passed in 1968/1969, when power relations shifted towards capital, during the first and only government with the Austrian People's Party (ÖVP) solely in power. That Act deviated radically from the original bill (Lechner et al., 1993), all non-market measures were cut back and the instruments were geared almost exclusively to the supply of labour (Lechner et al., 1993), hence on activation.

In the 1980s, Austria abandoned Austro-Keynesian demand management. In the search for new solutions for raising unemployment, Alfred Dallinger (SPÖ), then minister of social affairs, initiated a series of LMP projects that were later referred to as "experimental LMP" (Lechner et al., 2017). Those included a broad set of active LMPs, as well as initial activation and training measures, which form the core of today's LMP. Even though the idea of activation was part of the "experimental LMP", other measurements remained dominant. Parallel to the evolution of LMP, the development of the Unemployment Insurance Act (ALVG) up to the 1990s shows both reductions in benefits and expansions in eligibility (Tálos, 2006b), mirroring first developments of an internationally uprising activation paradigm. Moreover, in 1994, the Labour Market Promotion Act (AMFG) was passed, defining the responsibilities of the newly created and spun-off Public Employment Service Austria (AMS). That Act sets out the task of "efficient job placement" and thus legally establishes the basis for the introduction of a policy of labour market activation.

Atzmüller (2009) identifies the first signs of a workfare-oriented shift in LMP in Austria as starting in the 1990s. In contrast to other countries, however, no clear switch to a policy of labour market activation can be identified in Austria (Streckeisen, 2012).

MAIN PRINCIPLES OF ACTIVATION POLICIES

The tools and objectives of LMP have not changed significantly since the 1980s. Most marked was the shift in the perception of the problem of unemployment to a purely supply-side view and the associated reduction of full employment policy to the limited scope of LMP. According to the current way of thinking, LMP is intended to increase the functioning of the labour market through targeted measures (BMA, 2021).

The Public Employment Service Act (AMSG) defines the task of the Public Employment Service Austria (AMS). In addition to efficient job placement, it has been stipulated since 1994 that the AMS's task is to prevent and eliminate unemployment within the framework of the federal government's policy of full employment. In the interest of an active LMP, the supply and demand for labour is to be harmonised as completely, economically sensibly and sustainably as possible, while maintaining social and economic principles. The Public Employment Service Act places the task of the AMS in the context of the federal government's policy of full employment, yet no such policy exists. Instead of an explicit strategy of full employment, on its website the Federal Ministry of Labour and Economy (BMAW) refers back to the LMP of the

AMS, namely to the targets set annually by the Ministry of Labour. These tie a portion of the LMP budget to certain groups of people and measures and are not a replacement for an economic employment or development strategy.

The numerous LMP instruments are divided into three areas: employment, training and support. Table 3.1 illustrates the funding categories and their uptake in 2022, thereby reflecting the LMP measures to address the COVID-19 crisis.

Table 3.1   Funding cases 2022

Funding cases 2022	Number of funding cases[*]	%
All subsidies	**629,597**	**100**
Employment	**290,356**	**46**
Company integration subsidies	86,649	14
Short-time work subsidies	171,930	27
Socio-economic enterprises	28,033	4
Training	**262,498**	**42**
Work foundations	11,808	2
Educational measures	171,442	27
Course costs	20,591	3
Apprenticeship funding	17,764	3
Training for employees	14,685	2
Subsidies to cover the cost of living	176,736	28
Support	**231,994**	**37**
Counselling and guidance facilities	214,472	34
Business start-up subsidies	9,061	1

Note: [*] For the calculation of funding cases, a person is counted in all categories in which he/she appears, but only once in total.
Source: Own calculation (dnet.at).

Participation in LMP measures is mandatory for the unemployed, and non-compliance is subject to sanctions. As a result, active LMP – with a few exceptions – can also be understood as a welfare-to-work approach. Naturally, active LMP reaches its limits if it is not accompanied by a corresponding economic policy geared to creating or securing good jobs that provide a living wage.

Austria has moderate mobility requirements compared with other countries. However, Austria is among the top countries in terms of "job search" requirements and "monitoring" of the unemployed (Immervoll & Knotz, 2018). When considering sanctions for "refusal and repeated refusal of job offers" and for "refusal and repeated refusal to participate in ALMPs" separately (OECD, 2023), Austria posts the second-highest figures after Sweden in comparison with Germany, Sweden, and the United Kingdom. While no entitlement to training or guidance services applies, counselling appointments, participation in training courses, and applications to companies are mandatory. Failure or refusal to attend is sanctioned by the suspension of unemployment benefits for a period of four to six weeks (§ 10 ALVG). After the third suspension, unemployment benefits are completely withdrawn on the grounds of unwillingness to work (§ 9 ALVG). The rules on "reasonableness" stipulate that job offers for which relocation is necessary must be accepted if the jobseeker has no care obligations and the employer provides accommodation at the place of work (§ 9 ALVG).

In Austria, it is possible to receive unemployment benefits until retirement. The level of unemployment benefits is relatively low in international comparison and is in the lower third (OECD, 2019). As a rule, unemployment benefits amount to 55% of the net income received one year prior to unemployment (§ 21 ALG). Unemployment benefits are not a living wage and recipients of unemployment benefits are at increased risk of poverty, which has a negative impact on their chances of re-employment (Schönherr et al., 2014). In addition, unemployment benefits are not index linked, and the transition to emergency assistance means that in many cases, depending on age and years of contributions, the benefits (§ 36 ALVG) are capped below the poverty line after a short period of time.

The establishment of the AMS resulted in substantial change to the structures for shaping LMP. As before, the responsible federal minister exerts a decisive influence through LMP targets, which must also be implemented by the AMS. Priorities to be addressed by the AMS are set out in those targets. The Board of Directors has a decisive role as the supreme body of the AMS. This committee is made up of equal numbers of representatives of the federal government, employees and employers. The Board of Directors decides on the specific objectives to be pursued by the AMS and on funding conditions, and also appoints the management of the AMS at the federal and provincial levels. The decision on which measures and strategies will actually be implemented is decided at the provincial level, likewise on a tripartite basis. This structure also makes it possible to take regional differences into account and to use a variety of methods and projects. Another particular feature is the structural involvement of the social partners. Their competencies go beyond a supervisory board function. They help decide how the budget of the AMS is used (Tálos, 2017), but not the amount that is used. As a result, LMP through the AMS also depends largely on the respective government and the budget it allocates to LMP. In fact, most decisions in the bodies of the AMS are made unanimously.

Nevertheless, political conditions are also reflected in the AMS, as the respective federal government also has a say through the government curia.

TRENDS ON THE LABOUR MARKET AND LABOUR MARKET POLICY

In Austria, unemployment has seen an upward trend since the 1990s (Figure 3.1). The number of unemployed people registered with the AMS[1] increased from 255,560 in 1997 to 402,078 in 2021. The financial crisis of 2007/2008 and the prolonged recession led to a sharp rise in unemployment in the following decade. Owing to demographic change and the strong economy, the labour market has been recovering since 2016. That was interrupted by the COVID-19 pandemic, but the trend resumed in 2020. In 2022, the number of unemployed people reached the 332,645 mark again for the first time, a lower level than in 2013 (360,723). Current developments – in particular the increasing demand for labour – are largely shaped by demographic trends and pose a particular challenge for LMP.

The number of people in training increased from 20,930 in 1997 to 73,190 in 2010 and has remained around that level since then (Figure 3.1). However, due to the steady rise in unemployment, the training rate fell from around 23% in 2010 to 17% in 2021 and rose in 2022, due to the sharp decline of unemployment, to 21%. From the cohorts of 1968 onwards, an expansion in education can be observed in Austria (Horvath et al., 2021). While the proportion of the labour force with higher formal qualifications is rising, opportunities on the labour market for people with at most a basic school leaving certificate have declined. Against this backdrop, training measures are an important component of LMP. The stagnation in training nevertheless seems to reflect disillusionment with the potential of established training measures. At the same time, this coincides with the EU sovereign debt crisis and the accompanying austerity policies. During periods of austerity, governments often tighten rules relating to the unemployed, while cutting LMP measures (Knotz, 2019).

Support and guidance for jobseekers plays a key role in LMP, because the quality of job search assistance depends on it, as does the choice of training measures and, not least, sanctions for misconduct. There was a significant increase in expenditure on AMS staff between 1985 and 1996, indicating an expansion of its workforce (Figure 3.2). Since then, spending has remained largely stable despite the rising number of unemployed people. Recent years from 2018 onwards have seen staffing cuts, with the exception of the COVID crisis years from 2020 to 2022 (Achleitner et al., 2022; Feigl, Marterbauer, & Schultheiss, 2020; Feigl, Marterbauer, Schultheiß, & Schweitzer, 2020, 2021).

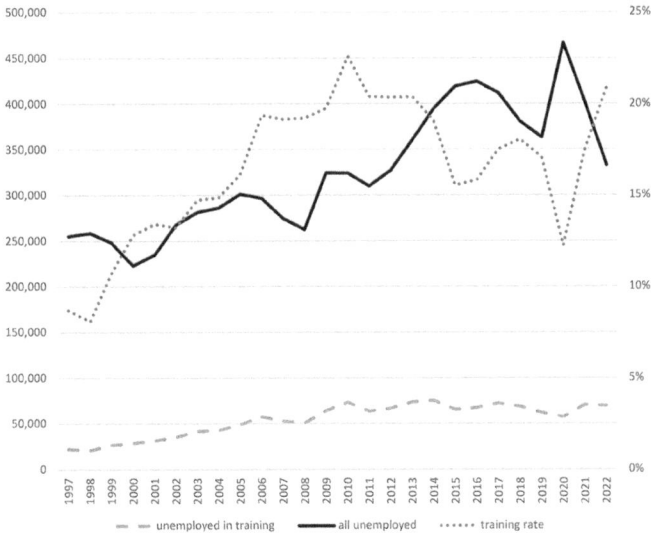

Note: Own calculations; the "training rate" is the number of all unemployed in training divided by all unemployed (including those in training).
Source: AMDB (n.d.).

Figure 3.1   *Decreasing training rate after 2010*

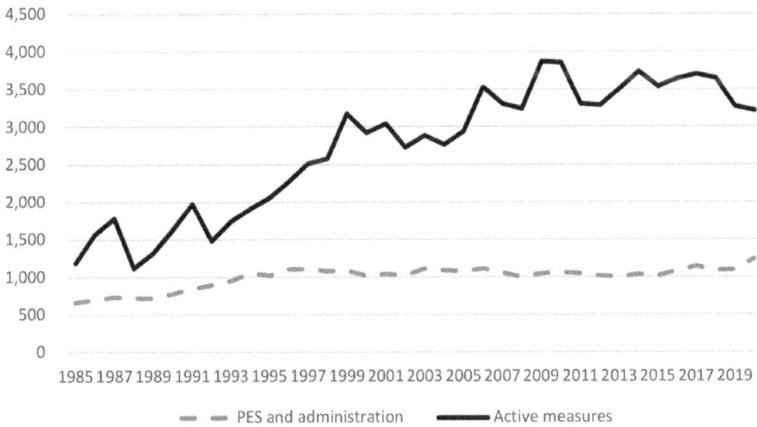

Note: Own calculation; inflation-adjusted spending.
Source: OECD.

Figure 3.2   *Case management and active measures*

The Change of Government, 2000–2007: Tightening of Activation Measures

In 2000, for the first time in the Second Republic, a right-wing conservative government coalition was formed between the Austrian People's Party (ÖVP) and the Freedom Party of Austria (FPÖ)/Alliance for the Future of Austria (BZÖ). The Schüssel I government from 2000 to 2003 and the Schüssel II government from 2004 to 2007 stepped up the workfareist reorientation of Austria's LMP (Theurl, 2018). During those legislative terms, the governing parties made cuts in benefits, tightened the rules on sanctions and cut the funds for active LMP (Fink, 2006). The government broke with the democratic tradition in Austria and weakened the position of the social partners, amounting to a shift of power towards the side of capital (Tálos, 2006a).

In 2000, the eligibility for unemployment insurance was tightened by increasing the length of employment required in order to qualify for unemployment benefits. That worsened the situation of those in unsteady (discontinuous) employment in particular. The elimination of the appreciation and index-linking of unemployment benefits was of particular significance (Nagl, 2022). It meant that the ÖVP and the FPÖ introduced an inflation-related depression in unemployment benefits.

In 2004, the Labour Market Reform Act (BGBl. I No. 77/2004) implemented a social partnership agreement with respect to reasonable commuting times, occupational and remuneration protection, as well as an adjustment of the rules on sanctions. The reasonable commuting time was increased to two hours for full-time employment and to one-and-a-half hours for part-time employment, although longer commuting times may be considered reasonable in exceptional cases. The applicable occupational protection was limited to 100 days. In return, the workers' representatives succeeded in extending wage protection to 80% of the last income for 120 days and to 75% for the remaining period of receiving benefits. Since then, sanctions can be increased by an additional two weeks in the case of untrue statements about part-time employment. The ongoing tightening of unemployment benefits is also reflected in the sanctions imposed. Suspensions of unemployment benefits increased five-fold between 1990 and 2005 (Atzmüller, 2009).

Overall, the restructuring of the labour market regime was less pronounced than announced in the government's manifesto. During its legislative term, the federal government was too preoccupied with reform of the pension system (Tálos, 2006a). Moreover, strong social partnership played a role in preventing a more radical paradigm shift in Austria (Soentken & Weishaupt, 2015).

The Financial and Economic Crisis of 2007 and the Following Years

The coalition of SPÖ and the ÖVP took office in 2007. The government merged the Ministry of Labour, which had traditionally been occupied by the SPÖ before 2000, and the Ministry of Economics under ÖVP leadership. That led to criticism that this would favour the interests of business over those of workers and give the ÖVP greater influence over LMP. In the short legislative period before 2008, the provisions of the Unemployment Insurance Act were tightened still further, but the scope of people covered by it was also expanded.

The increasingly restrictive provisions of the Unemployment Insurance Act had led to an increase in litigation in the second half of the 1990s (Atzmüller et al., 2012). Points of contention concerned, among other things, the allocation to a socio-economic enterprise (SÖB)[2] (Atzmüller et al., 2012). In 2007, an amendment to Section 9 of the Unemployment Insurance Act was enacted, in which the definition of willingness to work was adjusted and formed the basis for sanctions imposed by the AMS. The amendment provided a legal basis for many of the aforementioned controversial measures by the AMS. At the same time, enforcement of the law was extended to private organisations commissioned by the AMS. Since then, refusal of an assignment by a "socio-economic labour leasing enterprise"[3] (SÖBÜ) to a transitional job can be sanctioned. This led to criticism that this amendment amounted to creeping privatisation of the labour market administration (Atzmüller et al., 2012).

The proportion of atypical employment[4] relationships had also increased in Austria (dnet.at, own calculations). By 2003, the number of self-employed forms of employment increased sharply, reaching 108,772 in 2008. While the 2007 amendment included further tightening of the provisions of the Unemployment Insurance Act, the governing coalition facilitated access for young people to unemployment insurance. Against the background of increasing atypical employment relationships, the federal government also expanded the group of insured persons to include "freelancers" and put them on an equal footing with "genuine" employees (Nagl, 2022). In 2009, the possibility of self-insurance for self-employed persons on an elective basis was extended by the next government (Nagl, 2022).

The government was dissolved by the ÖVP's coalition partner in 2008. After new elections, 2008 saw another coalition between the SPÖ and the ÖVP, again with a Social Democratic labour minister. Following new elections, the legislative term was extended. After the ÖVP once again disbanded the coalition in 2017, this period – which was marked by the effects of the banking and financial crisis and the expansion of the labour force due to the new Member States that joined the EU in 2004 – came to an end. There was a clear focus on expanding training measures.

Stagnation in the wake of the global economic and financial crisis posed particular challenges in terms of LMP. The crisis management measures strongly target people who are in employment or who lose their jobs due to external economic circumstances. These people do not fit the explanatory model behind the debate about "disincentives", "moral hazard" and the like. Moreover, employed people do not fall into unemployment benefit legislation. Accordingly, activation measures take a back seat.

In addition, against the background of a shortage of skilled workers, measures to promote training for the unemployed were launched. It was recognised that earning a living wage during an apprenticeship is a key factor when it comes to completing the apprenticeship. Accordingly, a training bonus was introduced in 2008, which participants received. However, this was abolished in 2011, as the importance of training declined again (Löffler and Schmid 2011). The varying importance accorded to training has been reflected in the history of LMP since 2000, alternating between fulfilling a need for skilled workers through training and more restrictive placement measures.

Against the backdrop of rising youth unemployment, the federal government took a series of steps. In 2008, the training guarantee for people aged up to 18 years was introduced. In the course of that, the number and quality of supra-company apprenticeship workshops was expanded, and apprenticeship support was improved – both of which come under the scope of the AMS. The Compulsory Training Act also introduced a training obligation. That provided for compulsory training even after the end of compulsory schooling until the age of 18 and came into force in July 2017. The core of the training obligation is to accompany young people until they complete their education or a vocational training programme. The training guarantee was extended to the age of 25 years. Since 2013, the AMS has been promoting intensive training courses for skilled workers (Nagl & Jandl-Gartner, 2022). This programme is designed for adults who want to earn an apprenticeship certificate in a shorter time. With the federal law (Nagl, 2022), the federal government clarified at the same time that the refusal to participate in training measures prescribed by the AMS is to be considered as unwillingness to work and can be sanctioned.

In addition to the economic slump caused by the financial and economic crisis, this can be explained by an expansion of the labour supply. This is due to the entry of workers from eight out of ten of the countries that joined the European Union in 2004 and, to a lesser extent, to the increasing participation of women in the labour force (Fink et al., 2018). The pension reforms of the first decade of the 21st century are another factor behind the increase in labour supply. This explains the longer duration of unemployment episodes and, in part, the high proportion of unemployed people aged 50 and over (Fink et al., 2018). The increase in the proportion of long-term unemployed persons, which rose from 14% in 2009 to 35% in 2017, is particularly striking and since then became increasingly recognised by LMP authorities as a problem.

Against the backdrop of rising unemployment among older people, the federal government introduced a number of measures. In 2014, these included the retraining programmes that were introduced and the promotion of part-time work for people with a certified incapacity to work or disability (Nagl & Jandl-Gartner, 2022).

A special feature is the education allowance introduced in 1999, which – together with the solidarity premium introduced in 2013 and the partial retirement scheme – promotes the reduction of working hours by compensating for income losses from unemployment insurance funds (Figerl et al., 2021). The solidarity bonus, as well as the "block version" scheme of partial retirement, are tied to the condition that a previously unemployed person is hired. Likewise, in 2013, caregiver leave was introduced in connection with relaxation of the conditions for recipients of unemployment benefits who are caregivers (Nagl, 2022). That subsidises private care services from unemployment insurance funds.

The sharp rise in long-term unemployment also pushed the policy of labour market activation to its limits, because the causes of long-term unemployment range from the material, physical and psychological deprivation of those concerned to discrimination when hiring. From 2010 to 2017, the number of long-term unemployed[5] as a proportion of all unemployed people (AMS, 2023) ranges from 14% to 29%.

The federal government responded to rising long-term unemployment with the "Aktion 20,000" (20,000 Campaign) (Hausegger et al., 2019; Sozialministerium, 2019; Walch & Dorofeenko, 2020). These were publicly subsidised jobs with the federal government, municipalities and socio-economic enterprises, with the aim of integrating the long-term unemployed over the age of 50 into the labour market. The federal government of that time thereby picked up where the "8,000 Campaign" had left off in the 1980s and 1990s. Job guarantee-like measures can be categorised under labour market activation policy (Brown & Koettl, 2015), because the goal of reintegration into the labour market is paramount. However, due to non-market employment in the public sector, these measures are in line with the principle of decommodification and regard the political sphere as responsible for guaranteeing full employment (Tamesberger & Theurl, 2019). Furthermore, the "20,000 Campaign" was voluntary, hence opposing the activation paradigm.

The Years 2017–2019, Return of the Policy of Labour Market Activation with a Xenophobic Slant

In Austria, there were signs of an economic recovery from 2015 onwards and the situation on the labour market also began to improve in 2016 (Figure 3.2). Against the backdrop of the short-term surge in migration in 2015, the ÖVP focused heavily on illegal migration and presented it as a security and social policy problem. After new elections, from which the ÖVP emerged as the party with the most votes, a right-wing conservative coalition of the ÖVP and the FPÖ took power in December 2017. The government's labour market policies followed on seamlessly from those of the 2000–2007 ÖVP/FPÖ coalition government and again included stepping up negative incentives (Theurl, 2018, 2019). The government's LMP once again focused on reforming unemployment benefits. However, it was presented as if it primarily involved a worsening of welfare benefits, especially for migrants, who were implicitly accused of systematic benefits fraud. Again, the right-wing coalition deviated from the democratic traditions in Austria, weakened social partnership and threatened to seriously decline their source of income.

As one of its first labour market policies, the right-wing conservative federal government ended the "20,000 Campaign" in February 2018. That step was taken despite the promising results of the evaluation of the pilot project published by the previous government (Sozialministerium, 2017). Further cuts in LMP particularly affected benefits for people granted asylum and subsidiary protection, as well as people with a migrant background. The federal government cut funding for the integration year from 100 to 50 million euros and support measures for people granted asylum and subsidiary protection by 80 million euros. Overall, the budget of the AMS for language courses and validation (nostrification) of foreign titles and degrees was cut by 120 million euros. At the same time, the system of means-tested minimum benefits was undermined and given the stigmatising name of "social assistance". The level of the benefits was reduced, with the amount linked to German language skills and the number of children in the joint household. In the public debate, it was argued that this would particularly affect families with a migrant background. Regulations in the field of social assistance have a direct impact on unemployment benefits. Many people receive very low unemployment benefits and receive a top-up to reach the level of social assistance. Accordingly, this measure also led to a reduction in benefits for people with low incomes and low unemployment benefits.

The federal government's line on LMP is also reflected in sanctions imposed by the AMS. These jumped from 6,376 unemployment benefits sanctions in 2017 to 10,750 sanctions in 2018 (Figure 3.3).

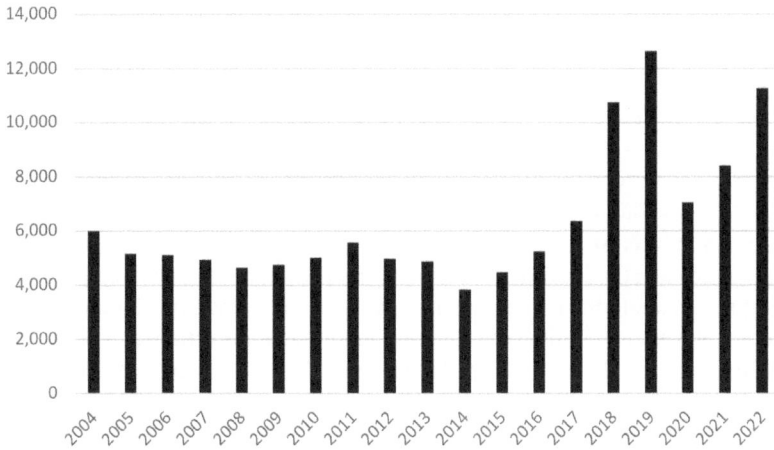

Source: Data cube: alv/wvl823 on 24.01.2023.

Figure 3.3   Sanctions

In 2019, the coalition between the ÖVP and the FPÖ was dissolved, following a vote of no confidence in Parliament. A transitional caretaker government followed between June 2019 and January 2020. That was succeeded in 2020 by a coalition between the ÖVP and the Greens. In 2021, the ministries of Labour and Economics were merged, as in 2007, again under the leadership of the ÖVP.

In terms of LMP, the ÖVP, in coalition with the Greens, also attempted to reform the unemployment benefits system, with a focus on higher incentives to work. At the same time, the draft budget for 2020 (Feigl, Marterbauer, & Schultheiss, 2020) provided for severe cuts in the LMP budget, as well as the staff of the AMS. In the scope of the "free play of forces" (i.e. the formation of spontaneous parliamentary majorities) ahead of the last general election (National Council election), a pact between several parliamentary parties abolished the system of taking into consideration the level of income of the recipient's partner when deciding on emergency assistance. Previously, a means test was used to determine eligibility for "emergency assistance", and the total household income was considered. That significantly improved the level of unemployment benefits for some recipients of emergency assistance.

COVID-19: LABOUR MARKET POLICY IN CRISIS MODE

The COVID-19 pandemic shaped LMP in 2020–2022. The legislative terms in which the ÖVP, as the party with the most votes, formed a coalition with the FPÖ and later with the Greens, illustrate their tough welfare-to-work programme. Nevertheless, efforts to expand the policy of labour market activation were temporarily set aside. The reason for this was the impact of the lockdowns on the labour market and on the administrative activities of the AMS. As before, to tackle the financial and economic crisis in 2007 and the following years, the federal government relied on short-time work and training measures. In addition, temporary financial subsidies were granted to recipients of unemployment benefits in order to mitigate social distortions.

The measures taken to contain the pandemic had an immense impact on the labour market. Some of those effects were felt until the end of 2022. At the time of the first lockdown, Austria experienced the sharpest drop in employment ever recorded in the Second Republic. Unemployment rose to 466,746 in 2020. It fell back in 2022 with the easing of COVID measures and strong economic conditions.

To mitigate the economic impact of the COVID-19 crisis, the federal government awarded a number of business grants (Badelt, 2021), and a short-time work model that was easy to access, and that provided wage replacement benefits graded progressively according to earnings (Tamesberger & Theurl, 2021). The administration of short-time work and the increase in unemployment abruptly increased the AMS's staffing needs, temporarily pushing the service to its limits. In order to cope with the high volume of short-time work applications and settlements, the number of staff was temporarily increased in place of implementing the reduction planned for 2020 (Feigl, Marterbauer, & Schultheiss, 2020; Feigl, Marterbauer, Schultheiß, & Schweitzer, 2020, 2021). At the same time, the AMS temporarily stopped personal contact with jobseekers during the lockdown and largely refrained from monitoring and sanctions. Compared with Germany, where the sanctions were suspended on an experimental basis and by means of a moratorium for one year beyond the COVID crisis, in Austria an ad-hoc, temporary decision was taken by the AMS. Once healthcare policy was relaxed and the economy picked up, sanctions were quickly reimposed (Figure 3.3).

With regard to the LMP budget, the federal government likewise reversed its planned cuts (Feigl, Marterbauer, & Schultheiss, 2020; Feigl, Marterbauer, Schultheiß, & Schweitzer, 2020, 2021) and made additional funds available to deal with the crisis. Those were provided for employment promotion and training instruments.

Under the title of "restart bonus" between 15 June 2020 and 31 December 2021, the restrictions on the group of persons eligible for income supplementation benefits were removed (Nagl & Jandl-Gartner, 2022). This is an income subsidy that is granted for a maximum of 28 weeks and is intended to make it more attractive to return to a relatively low-paid job.

The "Springboard" programme (Nagl & Jandl-Gartner, 2022) comprises a set of common LMP measures: wage subsidies for employers and employees, subsidised jobs in socio-economic enterprises, and supporting measures for companies. The target group was people who have been unemployed for more than two years, people aged 50+ and people with health impairments. The programme provided for a preceding counselling and matching process, followed by work training of up to 13 weeks, and then – for up to 12 months – supported employment in a socio-economic labour leasing or commercial enterprise.

Under the title "Job Drive", apprenticeships were funded from 31 December 2022 to the end of December 2022. With the education bonus, benefits supplementary to unemployment benefits – which are granted in some cases in the case of participation in training – were increased from €2 to €6 per day. That represents an additional €180 per month; as unemployment benefit payments decrease, it is a growing incentive to participate in training. Accordingly, this instrument is one of the few LMP measures that provides positive incentives. The education bonus stands out from the other LMP measures because it is a purely positive incentive to participate in training.

In the field of unemployment benefits, there were temporary increases and one-time payments (Nagl & Jandl-Gartner, 2022). From March to September 2021, emergency assistance was raised to the level of unemployment benefits. People who received unemployment benefits in the months of May to August 2020 also received one-time payments of €450 euros. One-time payments of between €300 and €450 were again paid for the months September to November 2020. One-time payments of €150 were granted for the months of November to December 2021 and in January and February 2022.

In October 2020, Sven Hergovic (SPÖ), then head of the regional Public Employment Service Austria in Lower Austria, initiated a job-guarantee experiment for all long-term unemployed in Gramatneusiedl. Extending the idea of the "Aktion 8,000" and "Aktion 20,000" the programme guaranteed jobs for all long-term unemployed. First evaluations show strong positive impacts of programme participation on participants' economic (employment, income, security) and non-economic (social recognition, time-structure, time-preference) wellbeing (Kasy & Lehner, 2022).

CONCLUSION/FUTURE DEBATES/ FUTURE DIRECTION OF ACTIVATION POLICIES?

Changes and developments in Austrian LMP were shaped by the political balance of power and party-political ideas on reducing unemployment. As the last decades have made clear, the ÖVP and FPÖ pursue the implementation of a stringent welfare-to-work approach (Peck, 2003) and rely on disincentives and sanctions. However, wage subsidies are also understood by representatives of capital as a suitable LMP instrument. Both are consistent with a supply-side perception of unemployment that is also typical of workfareist LMP. The SPÖ's approach to LMP includes social policy ambitions that are based on the concept of participation (Kronauer, 2002, 2019) and decommodification. However, in some respects that can also be categorised as a soft welfare-to-work approach (Peck, 2003), active LMP is an integral part of unemployment insurance and its logics.

Economic crises might trigger LMP experiments, which can promote the inclusion of other approaches in the scope of LMP. For example, short-time work has become established as an LMP instrument in Austria since the financial crisis of 2007 and the following years. At the same time, the SPÖ is trying to implement variations of the concept of a state job guarantee on the basis of the steadily increasing number of long-term unemployed, particularly among older people. However, no clear alternative to the activation paradigm is yet discernible. Also, so far there are no attempts to counter the slowly but rising amount of atypical employment that can be linked to the rise of the activation paradigm.

Moreover, recent decades also show that activation policies are insufficient to resolve crises. The exceptional situation at the height of the COVID-19 pandemic led to a temporary departure from the LMP reforms outlined in the government manifesto. But, as the labour market recovered, the issue of LMP reform came back to the fore. COVID crisis programme funding expires in 2023 (Achleitner et al., 2022) and the 2023–2026 budget plan calls for a return to pre-crisis budget austerity. In December 2022, Labour Minister Kocher (ÖVP) announced failure of the negotiations on the reform of unemployment insurance, but also noted that he can implement central points directly through targets issued to the AMS. That includes the sanctions imposed by the AMS offices, which are already on the rise again.

The inflation and inflationary crisis has a particularly marked impact on recipients of unemployment benefits and is likely to shape economic developments over the next few years. In response to inflation, the federal government decided to index-link social benefits, but explicitly excluded unemployment benefits. Unemployment benefits are not adjusted for inflation, so inflation results in a depression in real benefits. The resulting decline of real UE (unemployment) Benefits is completely in line with activation policies. As the labour minister in office is a trained economist and in favour of degressive UE Benefits, it can be inferred that the decision to exclude UE Benefits from inflation adjustments was on purpose.

Overall, the situation on the labour market is marked by increasing demand for labour, which is likely to be maintained in the coming years due to demographic change. We can only speculate at times about the extent to which economic stagnation could counteract that. Against the background of the increasing demand for labour, employee representatives argue that productivity and health can be increased by reducing working hours, thus enabling people to work longer into old age. At the same time, they emphasise the importance of training measures. Combined with the urgent need for a socio-ecological transformation to mitigate the climate crisis, it seems sensible to pursue an LMP that relocates workers to socially and environmentally sustainable enterprises and that takes advantage of the natural decline in labour force participation caused by demographic change. Employers' representatives, in line with the ÖVP, however, are focusing more on activating the labour force and extending working hours, especially through measures to raise the de-facto retirement age.

With reference to overcoming the climate crisis, the expansion of renewable technologies and ecological production techniques is increasingly being financed globally. Rising industrial policy spending in the US and China is also increasing pressure in Europe to move away from the market-centric policies of recent decades and expand support for the environmental transformation. A European socio-ecological industrial policy would be most successful if it were supported by a corresponding LMP. Experiences gained from the LMP response to the COVID crisis, as well as from the LMP pilot projects, could be harnessed to address the climate crisis and establish a new transformation model.

NOTES

1. We define unemployed people as all people registered as unemployed with the AMS, plus people in training.
2. Socio-economic enterprises are companies that specialise in the reintegration of the unemployed and provide transitional jobs subsidised by the AMS.
3. They act as temporary employment agencies.
4. "Marginally employed", "freelancers", "marginally employed freelancers" and the "new self-employed" are grouped together as atypical employees.
5. For the calculation of the number of people in long-term unemployment, status interruptions of <= 62 days are not included.

REFERENCES

Achleitner, S., Feigl, G., Marterbauer, M., Muckenhuber, M., Premrov, T., Mader, K., Raith, A., Schnell, P., Soder, M., & Theurl, S. (2022). *Budgetanalyse 2023–2026: Soziale Handschrift gefragt. Materialien zu Wirtschaft und Gesellschaft: Nr. 237.* Kammer für Arbeiter und Angestellte für Wien. https://resolver.obvsg.at/urn:nbn: at:at-akw:g-5750881

AMDB. (n.d.). *Arbeitsmarktdatenbank.* https://arbeitsmarktdatenbank.at/

AMS. (2023). *Fachbegriffe.* AMS. https://www.ams.at/arbeitsmarktdaten-und-medien/ arbeitsmarkt-daten-und-arbeitsmarkt-forschung/fachbegriffe#langzeitbeschftigungs lose

Atzmüller, R. (2009). Die Entwicklung der Arbeitsmarktpolitik in Österreich. Dimensionen von Workfare in der österreichischen Sozialpolitik. *Kurswechsel, 2009*(4), 24–34.

Atzmüller, R., Krenn, M., & Papouschek, U. (2012). Innere Aushöhlung und Fragmentierung des österreichischen Modells: Zur Entwicklung von Erwerbslosigkeit, prekärer Beschäftigung und Arbeitsmarktpolitik. In P. Streckeisen, K. Scherschel, & M. Krenn (Eds.), *International labour studies: Bd. 2. Neue Prekarität: Die Folgen aktivierender Arbeitsmarktpolitik - europäische Länder im Vergleich* (pp. 75–110). Campus-Verl.

Badelt, C. (2021). *Österreichs Wirtschaftspolitik in COVID-19 -Zeiten und danach: Eine Einschätzung zur Jahreswende 2020/21* (WIFO Monatsberichte No. 1). Wien. https://www.wifo.ac.at/jart/prj3/wifo/resources/person_dokument/person _dokument.jart?publikationsid=66829&mime_type=application/pdf

BMA (2021). Arbeitsmarktpolitik Österreich – ein Überblick: Berichtsjahr 2020. https://www.google.com/url?sa=t&rct=j&q=&esrc=s&source=web&cd=&ved = 2ahUKEwjq7 rq9oK78AhW NRPEDHb4vC -UQFnoECA8QAQ & url = https %3A%2F%2Fwww.bmaw.gv.at%2Fdam%2Fjcr%3A1c0bfc61-abad-484c-a8ce -a4b18d9fc055 %2 FArbeitsma rktpolitik %2520 %25C3 %2596sterreich %2520 - %2520ein %2520 %25C3 %259Cberblick _Berichtsjahr %25202020 .pdf & usg = AOvVaw3ArRdTAefMQK97jD2mbHj3

Brown, A. J. G., & Koettl, J. (2015). Active labor market programs – employment gain or fiscal drain? *IZA Journal of Labor Economics, 4*(1). https://doi.org/10.1186/ s40172–015–0025–5

dnet.at. *Arbeitsmarktdaten online: atypische Beschäftigte.* https://www.dnet.at/bali/ Tabellen/taArbeitsmarkt.aspx

Feigl, G., Marterbauer, M., & Schultheiss, J. (2020). *Budget 2020: Schritte zur Überwindung der Corona Krise: AK-Budgetanalyse zum Entwurf des Bundesvoranschlags 2020 und darüber hinaus. Materialien zu Wirtschaft und Gesellschaft.* https://resolver.obvsg.at/urn:nbn:at:at-akw:g-3461950

Feigl, G., Marterbauer, M., Schultheiß, J., & Schweitzer, T. (2020). *Zu spät, zu wenig, nicht ausreichend fokussiert. Budgetpolitik in der Corona-Krise: Analyse des Bundesvoranschlags 2021 und darüber hinaus. Materialien zu Wirtschaft und Gesellschaft: Vol. 205.* Kammer für Arbeiter und Angestellte für Wien.

Feigl, G., Marterbauer, M., Schultheiß, J., & Schweitzer, T. (2021). *Budget 2022: Unausgewogene Steuerreform, erkennbarer Klimaschwerpunkt, Mittel für Armutsbekämpfung, Pflege und Bildung fehlen. Materialien zu Wirtschaft und Gesellschaft: Vol. 229.* Kammer für Arbeiter und Angestellte für Wien.

Figerl, J., Tamesberger, D., & Theurl, S. (2021). Umverteilung von Arbeit(-szeit): Eine (Netto)Kostenschätzung für ein staatlich gefördertes Arbeitszeitverkürzungsmodell. *Momentum Quarterly – Zeitschrift für Sozialen Fortschritt, 10*(1), 3. https://doi.org/ 10.15203/momentumquarterly.vol10.no1.p3–19

Fink, M. (2006). Zwischen „Beschäftigungsrekord" und „Rekordarbeitslosigkeit": Arbeitsmarkt und Arbeitsmarktpolitik unter Schwarz-Blau/Orange. In E. Tálos (Ed.), *Schwarz-blau: Eine Bilanz des „Neu-Regierens"* (pp. 170–187). Lit.

Fink, M., Titelbach, G., & Mürzl, E. (2018). Arbeitslosigkeit – Die sozialen Folgen für Betroffene und Angehörige. https://emedien.arbeiterkammer.at/viewer/resolver?urn =urn:nbn:at:at-akw:g-3392460

Griesser, M. (2019). Deutungsrahmen der aktiven Arbeitsmarktpolitik: ein deutsch-österreichischer Vergleich von diskursiven Frames aus Anlass von 50 Jahren Arbeits(markt)förderungsgesetz. *Momentum Quarterly – Zeitschrift für Sozialen Fortschritt, 8*(3), 166. https://doi.org/10.15203/momentumquarterly.vol8 .no3.p166–182

Hausegger, T., Krüse, T., & Hager, I. (2019). Evaluation der Aktion 20.000: Endbericht. *Prospect, Reserch & Solution* (Studie im Auftrag des Bundesministeriums für Arbeit, Soziales, Gesundheit und Konsumentenschutz).

Horvath, T., Huemer, U., Hyll, W., & Mahringer, H. (2021). *Erwerbs- und Einkommensverläufe in Österreich.: Ein Vergleich der Entwicklung von vier Geburtsjahrgängen seit den 1970er-Jahren.* Wien. WIFO.

Immervoll, H., & Knotz, C. M. (2018). How demanding are activation requirements for jobseekers? *IZA Discussion Paper Series* (11704). https://repec.iza.org/dp11704.pdf

Jahoda, M. (1995). *Wieviel Arbeit braucht der Mensch? Arbeit und Arbeitslosigkeit im 20. Jahrhundert* (Repr. der 3. Aufl. von 1986). Psychologie-Verl.-Union. https:// permalink.obvsg.at/AC01266675

Kasy, M., & Lehner, L. (2022). Employing the unemployed of Marienthal: Evaluation of a guaranteed job program. *INET Oxford Working Paper* (29).

Knotz, C. (2019). Why countries 'get tough on the work-shy': The role of adverse economic conditions. *Journal of Social Policy, 48*(03), 615–634. https://doi.org/10 .1017/S0047279418000740

Kronauer, M. (2002). *Exklusion: Die Gefährdung des Sozialen im hoch entwickelten Kapitalismus.* Campus.

Kronauer, M. (2019). Konzepte der Teilhabe: Bedingungsloses Grundeinkommen oder Recht auf Arbeit? *PROKLA. Zeitschrift für Kritische Sozialwissenschaft, 49*(197), 617–630. https://doi.org/10.32387/prokla.v49i197.1847

Lechner, F., Reiter, W., Wetzel, P., & Willsberger, B. (2017). *Die experimentelle Arbeitsmarktpolitik der 1980er- und 1990er-Jahre in Österreich: Rückschlüsse und Perspektiven für Gegenwart und Zukunft der aktiven Arbeitsmarktpolitik; herausgegeben vom Arbeitsmarktservice Österreich.* Arbeitsmarktservice Österreich; Lechner, Reiter & Riesenfelder Sozialforschung OG. AMS report. http://www .ams-forschungsnetzwerk.at/deutsch/publikationen/BibShow.asp?id=12232&sid= 749004852&look=2&jahr=2017

Lechner, F., Reiter, W., & Marius, W. (1993). Arbeitsmarktverwaltung und Sozialpartnerschaft. In *Emmerich, Tálos (1993): Sozialpartnerschaft: Kontinuität und Wandel eines Modells* (pp. 207–227). Verlag für Gesellschaftskritik.

Nagl, I. (2022). *Legistische Änderungen in der österreichischen Arbeitsmarktpolitik 1998–2022: Dokumentations – Stand November 2022.* Bundesministerium für Arbeit und Wirtschaft. https:// www .bmdw .gv .at/ dam/ bmdwgvat/ Fotos -und

-Anlagen/Services/Publikationen/Arbeitsmarkt/Legistische-%C3%84nderungen-in
-der-%C3%B6sterr.-AMP-1998–2020_Stand-1.10.2020.pdf

Nagl, I., & Jandl-Gartner, T. (2022). *Aktive Arbeitsmarktpolitik in Österreich
2014 bis 2022: Dokumentation.* Bundesministerium für Arbeit und Wirtschaft.
https:// www .bmdw .gv .at/ dam/ bmdwgvat/ Fotos -und -Anlagen/ Services/
Publikationen/ Arbeitsmarkt/ FINAL _Aktive -AMP -in - %C3 %96sterreich -2014 - -
-2021_Dokumentation.pdf

OECD. (2019). *Benefits and wages.* https://doi.org/10.1787/0cc0d0e5-en

OECD. (2023). *How demanding are activation requirements for jobseekers?* https://
www.oecd.org/social/strictness-benefit-eligibility.htm

Peck, J. (2001). *Workfare states.* Guilford Press.

Peck, J. (2003). The rise of the workfare state. *Kurswechsel* (3), 76–87.

Rothschild, K. W. (1994). *Theorien der Arbeitslosigkeit: Einführung* (2. Aufl.).
Oldenbourg.

Schmid, K., & Löffler, R. (2011). Qualifizierungsbonus: Zentrale Ergebnisse einer
aktuellen Evvaluation im Auftrag des AMS Österreich. AMS Info, No. s170.
Arbeitsmarktservice Österreich.

Schönherr, D., Hacker, E., Hofinger, C., & Michenthaler, G. (2014). Existenzsicherung
bei Arbeitslosigkeit: Individuelle Strategien zur Existenzsicherung bei
Arbeitslosigkeit in Wien. SORA, IFES (Studie im Auftrag der Arbeiterkammer
Wien). https:// www .arbeiterkammer .at/ infopool/ wien/ Existenzsicherung _bei
_Arbeitslosigkeit_2014.pdf

Soentken, M., & Weishaupt, J. T. (2015). When social partners unite – Explaining continuity and change in Austrian and Dutch Labour market governance. *Social Policy
& Administration, 49*(5), 593–611. https://doi.org/10.1111/spol.12100

Sozialministerium (2017). Zwischenbericht zur Aktion 20.000: Bilanz zum Ende des
der Pilotphase, November 24. https:// images .derstandard .at/ 2018/ 01/ 02/ zwisch
enberichtzuraktion20.000.pdf

Sozialministerium (2019). Zwischenbericht zur Aktion 20.000: Bilanz zum Ende der
Pilotphase. https://www.sozialministerium.at/cms/site/attachments/0/0/1/CH3582/
CMS1511508633739/zwischenbericht_zur_aktion_20.000.pdf

Stelzer-Orthofer, C., & Tamesberger, D. (2018). Die Arbeitsmarktpolitische Agenda
der schwarz-blauen Regierung: Symbolische Politik oder radikaler Umbau? *WISO,
2018*(3), 15–43.

Streckeisen, P. (2012). Wege zur neuen Prekarität: Die aktivierungspolitische
Wende zwischen internationalem Trend und länderspezifischer Geschichte. In P.
Streckeisen, K. Scherschel, & M. Krenn (Eds.), *International labour studies: Bd.
2. Neue Prekarität: Die Folgen aktivierender Arbeitsmarktpolitik – europäische
Länder im Vergleich* (pp. 177–196). Campus-Verl.

Streckeisen, P., Scherschel, K., & Krenn, M. (Eds.). (2012). *International labour
studies: Bd. 2. Neue Prekarität: Die Folgen aktivierender Arbeitsmarktpolitik -
europäische Länder im Vergleich.* Campus-Verl.

Tálos, E. (Ed.). (2006a). *Schwarz-blau: Eine Bilanz des „Neu-Regierens".* Lit.

Tálos, E. (2006b). Sozialpolitik: Zwischen Expanson und Restriktion. In H. Dachs
(Ed.), *Politik in Österreich: Das Handbuch* (pp. 624–636). Manz.

Tálos, E. (2017). Sozialpartnerschaft: Ein zentraler Gestaltungsfaktor im Österreich der
Zweiten Republik. In M. Krempl & J. Thaler (Eds.), *100 Jahre Arbeitsmarktverwaltung*
(pp. 159–182). V&R unipress. https://doi.org/10.14220/9783737007443.159

Tálos, E. (Ed.). (2019). *Politik und Zeitgeschichte. Die Schwarz-Blaue Wende in
Österreich: Eine Bilanz.* Verlag.

Tamesberger, D., & Theurl, S. (2019). Vorschlag für eine Jobgarantie für Langzeitarbeitslose in Österreich. *Wirtschaft und Gesellschaft, 45*(4), 471–495.

Tamesberger, D., & Theurl, S. (2021). Design and Take Up of Austria's Coronavirus Short Time Work Model. *ICAE Working paper series, 2021*(127). https://www.jku.at/fileadmin/gruppen/108/ICAE_Working_Papers/wp127.pdf

Theurl, S. (2018). Arbeitsmarktpolitik Reloaded: Hartz IV für Österreich. *KuWe, 3,* 75–82.

Theurl, S. (2019). Arbeitsmarktpolitik der Schwarz-Blauen Bundesregierung. In M. Haselwanter, E. Hussl, & H. Schreiber (Eds.), *Gaismair-Jahrbuch: 20 (2020). Im Labyrinth der Zuversicht* (pp. 33–43). Studien Verlag.

Walch, D., & Dorofeenko, V. (2020). Untersuchung der fiskalischen Effekte der Beschäftigungsaktion 20.000. *IHS Projektbericht.* https:// irihs .ihs .ac .at/ id/ eprint/ 5435/ 1/ ihs -report -2020 -walch -dorofeenko -fiskalische -effekte -b eschaeftig ungsaktion-20000.pdf

Weishaupt, J. T. (2011). *From the Manpower Revolution to the Activation Paradigm: Explaining Institutional Continuity and Change in an Integrating Europe. Changing Welfare States.* Amsterdam University Press.

4. The Danish case: activation in flux and fraught with tensions

Henning Jørgensen and Mads Peter Klindt

INTRODUCTION: ACTIVATION IN FLUX

All kinds of analysis of activation seem to have reference to the Danish case. In increasing and different ways, Denmark has provided a "model country" in the scholarly debate about activation and welfare reform. But the Danish case is also misunderstood as to changing content of activation, from human capital investments to work-first approaches and evidence-based initiatives. What happened during the 1990s and what is happening now represent diverse ways of practicing activation. Policy developments have been non-linear, featuring shifting policy priorities, different narratives and principles, and new implementation arrangements. Experiences of change are many. In this chapter, we will try to document this and explain some of the change mechanisms and the collective actors responsible for the developments.

Among traits and in portraits of Denmark, a dynamic labor market, high employment, and low unemployment are always mentioned. Denmark "punch[es] above its weight in meeting the challenges of our time", according to former US president Barack Obama (2016, speech, National Archives). The country's success in organizing and governing society – including activation – in models of cooperation has received widespread attention. Expenditures for labor market policy (LMP) have consistently been among the highest seen comparatively. In 2005, almost 4.5% of GNP was used on passive as well as active measures (OECD statistics). Active measures have been dominant. Denmark was also the first country to officially use the word "activation" in an LMP context in the 1990s.

The first elements of LMP were introduced before World War 2, but mostly as instruments of income replacement. Post-war developments included the implementation of new policies, addressing labor market risks. The state defined rules concerning employment relations, protected workers, and rebalanced the asymmetrical power relationship between employers and employees, but employers also received help as to the supply of manpower with labor exchange and some qualification of wage earners.

A new center-left government implemented an ALMP in 1994, abolishing former requalifying rules, and introduced new "activation" as part of ALMP. The activation policy of the 1990s had training and education as the most important instruments, trying to remove barriers to job placement. Individual action plans were starting points for activities – replacing job offers – and the plans sought to balance the situation and wishes of each unemployed person with the prospects of the local and regional labor market. People on social assistance were not included in activation at that time.

Ten years later, however, cash transfers and interventions were transformed and partly limited to job search conditionality. Individual action plans were replaced by narrow job plans. And the unemployment benefit period has been reduced from 7 to 2 years only. Activation has been transformed into a variety of the welfare-to-work policy, already introduced in many western countries. Unemployed persons' rights to benefits became contingent on participation in work-related or other activities. Now people on social assistance and other "problem groups" were included too.

However, in contrast to "workfare" programs in the US and elsewhere in Europe that were primarily job focused, training and education made up the bulk of the Danish activation activities at first (Rosdahl and Weise, 2001). Moreover, implementation was strongly influenced by the social partners. The philosophy behind Danish activation was to turn the social safety net into a "trampoline' with the help of investments in human capital (Jørgensen, 2002, 2009; Kvist, 2003).

The positive employment developments in the 1990s subsequently spurred massive interest in Danish "flexicurity" (OECD, 2004; Wilthagen and Tros, 2004; Jørgensen and Madsen, 2007). A flexible labor market combined with generous unemployment benefits and training-based ALMP exemplified a "golden triangle" and a third way beyond liberal and coordinated market economies delivering both competitiveness and social cohesion.

Thinktanks, research institutions, and policymakers were discussing how to imitate the model, while Danish government officials were touring European capitals explaining the "hidden formula". Interest peaked in 2007 when the European Commission adopted flexicurity and integrated the concept in the European Employment Strategy (EES). New policy recommendations were clearly inspired by the Danish model, particularly regarding how countries should implement ALMP (Klindt, 2011). The EU looked to Denmark for new inspiration and activation targets were included in the EES (Casey, 2004).

The global financial crisis changed the cards on the table, and interest in flexicurity faded. However, activation was now mushrooming all around Europe, with Denmark still seen as a model country (Lødemel and Moreira,

2014, 2022). But the Danish experiences during the last 20 years do not provide many arguments for Denmark's having role-model status. A shift of narrative and philosophy to work-first principles started in 2003. It has proven difficult, though, to "make work pay" according to neo-liberal theories and protagonists in a Danish context. Incentive reinforcement has been lacking long-term job gains (Card et al., 2018), and some collective actors and decentralized organizations have often been counteracting central steering efforts during the two decades. Tensions, dilemmas, and trade-offs are visible.

This chapter analyses changes to activation and ALMP in Denmark since the turn of the millennium. We focus the analysis on particularly interrelated developments: (1) the gradual shift from a "train-first" or human capital approach to more work-first approaches to activation from unemployment benefit recipients; (2) the diffusion of the activation regime to other target groups in and outside the labor market; (3) more governance reforms and the fall of Danish regional corporatism; and (4) the COVID-19 experiences and latest developments, questioning the activation arrangements. Finally, discussion as to the future of activation brings us to a conclusion.

HISTORICAL CHANGE: FROM THE SECURITY OF THE WINGS TO CONDITIONALITY AND PUNISHMENT

Introduction of "activation" in Denmark in the 1990s was a shift from redistribution to intervention as dominant philosophy and a way of improving "the security of the wings" for wage earners. They should acquire the ability to move on a shifting labor market with the help of better qualifications. At the same time, employers should be given services enabling them to participate in activation. The goal was a balanced labor market development – quantitatively, qualitatively, and geographically.

Formerly, LMP efforts were concentrated on economic compensation and matching of open jobs and people seeking jobs. In 1969, Denmark established a public employment system (PES) for matching and guidance of both wage earners and employers. The economic crisis in the 1970s and 1980s called for some new offers to unemployed people to re-enter employment, and some new measures. However, the unemployment figures were still high and growing. A shift of government in 1993, finally, paved the way for reform and stronger interventions.

The ALMP of the 1990s had a focus on insured people (and partly the employees). This has since changed, with all benefit recipients now target groups. The distinction between insured and non-insured people has been broken down. During the last 20 years, *the job perspective* has become totally dominating in the employment system – and for social policy as well, with large parts of this policy absorbed in employment policy.

Comparatively, it is unique that activation was coordinated with other labor market initiatives and economic policy in the 1990s. Denmark pursued a new kind of *progressive policy mix* of expansive fiscal policy and ALMP, including activation of the unemployed, leave schemes for employed persons (which would create job openings), and a revitalized public employment service (PES) mandated and better equipped to tackle structural challenges in the regional labor market (Larsen, 2013). The results were remarkable and noticed internationally. Some researchers even called it a "Danish miracle" (Torfing, 1999). Unemployment dropped from 12.4% in 1993 to less than 5% five years later, with no negative inflationary side effects. In the same period, more than 300,000 new jobs were created.

We will document how the Danish realities have changed since 2000 – incrementally though radically. Firstly, *the activation policy of the 1990s*, which as noted was based on a "train-first" model, *was gradually transformed to a more rigid work-first version of activation, even though the toolkits of activation were broadened*. Denmark thereby conformed to the European workfare mainstream for more researchers (Kvist and Haarsløf, 2014). The process has even been described as a backward-mapping Hans Christian Andersen fairytale: "From a Beautiful Swan to an Ugly Duckling"[1] (Jørgensen, 2009). Changes in activation were closely connected to a broader shift of paradigm in economic theory, from the demand to the supply side. Economic incentives were placed as instruments in a pivotal position vis-à-vis the individual, as had happened before in most other European countries. No policy mix was any longer to be seen. Diffusion or circulation of ideas and ideologies is, however, also a way of creating different policy and polity results. And there is more to the Danish developments that occurred during the last 20 years.

Secondly, *ALMP was replaced by a so-called evidence-based employment policy* focusing almost exclusively on rapid and job-oriented activation. The leave schemes for employed persons, established in 1994, were terminated while the activation regime was expanded to include more and more groups. This was accompanied by a discourse framing that all persons, even the hardest to place, were "ready for activity" (Hansen, 2019). Sticks and carrots in the form of lower benefits and tax cuts for low-income groups also became part of Danish reform practice in the new millennium.

Thirdly, these policy changes took place next to – and were underpinned by – *a range of governance reforms*. New Public Management (NPM) reforms have been many. Most significantly, the state-run PES – that was anchored in regional labor market committees responsible for activation of insured persons with corporatism as a guiding principle – was abolished over a two-year process from 2007 to 2009. Today, the implementation of all activation resides with 94 job centers run by the municipalities on which the social partners have minimal leverage.

The Danish activation regime has been decentralized and stripped of its main corporatist traits, yet the state maintains strong steering from a distance. By use of NPM, including performance management, contracting, and reimbursement rules, the state provides clear economic incentives as to how the municipalities should prioritize among different activation instruments. Consequently, work-oriented activation has become the "golden standard" across the municipalities, albeit a few still focus on training.

Historically, this amounted to *the Danish "learn-fare" strategy's being deactivated and a new work-first strategy being the replacement.* This started with an "employment" reform in 2003. Unemployed people had to find a job as soon as possible and be self-supporting. This could also be called a movement away from capabilities towards strengthening the motivation and activation of unemployed people, also using threats of punishment.

Following this has been a partial shift in arrangements and instruments, downplaying the role of education and training to the benefit of private-sector activation and wage subsidies. The social partners have been sidelined. Finally, a new form of research and evaluation has been implemented, using mainstream economists as policy advisers and their recommendations of incentives and sanctions, search activities, and handing over of responsibility to the individual. A shift of status at the individual level is key – regardless of groups, situations, and contexts. No macro perspective is left. An evidence-based literature – with RCT as a central reference to an ideal evaluation model – has supported this shift towards a punitive approach. "Hard" activation is still popular with many economists and politicians. But the work-first strategy did also show its limits from the financial crisis on. The municipalities were given full responsibility in 2009 to design and implement "employment policy", but within a central steering and monitoring system. Since then, the municipalities have been complaining about the state's way of steering. And during the last 7–8 years, more local autonomy has actually been given to the municipalities.

It was only from 2015–2016 that a partial shift of strategy was to be seen at the central level. It had become clear that activation was not very useful where jobs are not there to place people in. Threats do not by themselves create job opportunities. More talks with unemployed people were to be a replacement for harder activation measures. The rights and duties to have activation offers changed a bit. A more flexible way of re-entering the unemployment support system was introduced. And the municipalities were rewarded with more freedom as to priorities. However, a new form of benchmarking from the evidence-based steering system was a central way of having a bureaucratic hold in the municipalities. And a new state reimbursement system was installed in 2009, putting more financial pressure on municipalities to find jobs for jobseekers. From 2019 the reimbursement system was changed again and transformed into (reduced) economic grants.

Still, it is supply-sided efforts only that are at stake and an object for evaluations. The demand side is partly a blind spot in policy, narratives, and interventions. But a special arrangement is the active integration of unemployment insurance funds (of a "Ghent" type) in start-up talks during an unemployment period. Common talks with job center representatives and members are also a way of controlling and advising people. Stronger coordination between the public sector and the private system is clearly required. From 2024, the unemployment insurance funds will have responsibility for contact and talks with members during the first three months of unemployment. This is also a kind of partial privatization.

There are some indications that the "train-first" or human capital model was on the way back to a revival during recent years, not everywhere but in some municipalities and sometimes not directly linked to activation. Since 2015, government rhetoric has also become more nuanced and education for unemployed persons is no longer articulated as a waste of money.

The OECD figures for Danish unemployment developments 2000–2021 are to be found in the Finnish chapter (by Minna van Gerven and Aleksander Heikkinen) in this volume.

PRINCIPLES AND INSTRUMENTS USED

The ALMP rationale was to have a balanced labor market development by having full employment as the top priority, and job matching and qualification arrangements as the next priority. This was to the advantage of both wage earners and employers, it was said.

However, during the 2000s these priorities in policy were abandoned, paving the way for neo-liberalizations aiming at improving labor supply and putting pressure on the individual wage earner. Activation ideas were copied from the Netherlands and the Anglo-Saxon world by a right-wing government and the new principles of "employment policy" were to be supported by administrative reforms and new steering arrangements. Work-first principles were soon visible in governmental policy with a dominant ethics of self-responsibility. Duties were celebrated over social rights in policy narratives. But the public sector still had a responsibility for enabling people to manage risks and to find employment.

The actor system operating was then put under pressure, leaving fewer places for the labor market organizations – in continental places and in the EU called "the social partners" – to influence policy developments. A regionalized ALMP was soon being replaced by municipality-run employment policies. A logic of commodification was underpinning policy reforms and administrative tracks of reforms from 2003 to 2015.

The instruments used were also given new priorities. The Danish activation toolbox officially includes the following four instruments:[2] wage subsidy job, company internship, job training schemes and utility job (the last one introduced in 2014), and guidance and skill formation (training and ordinary education).

Using Peck and Theodore's (2000) raw distinction between different forms of welfare-to-work programming, these instruments can be categorized as either work-first or human capital approaches to workfare/activation. Additional differentiations are used (see for instance Bonoli, 2010, 2013). And more types of instruments go into the decentralized programming and implementation.

Wage subsidy jobs and company internships (or "subsidized employment") are instruments in which the unemployed person works on a full-time basis in a private company or a public service provider for a longer or shorter period while receiving benefits and maybe a small additional allowance. Obviously, they both represent work-first, albeit not the harshest version of the model.

Work-intensive activation has been criticized for promoting precarious employment and fueling working poverty, but research has also uncovered that it can provide a stepping-stone for persons between education and work or between jobs (Rosholm and Svarer, 2020).

Job training and utility jobs are in the work-first category. A utility job is an activation job in the public sector where the unemployed person makes a "useful contribution to society" in return for social assistance. Unofficially, the goal is to enhance the "threat effect" of activation and thus to prevent people from applying for benefits in the first place (Rosholm and Svarer, 2004). An evaluation supports that this is in fact the main effect of the instrument (DAMVAD, 2015). But the evaluation literature is far from conclusive.

Guidance and skill formation is a more ambiguous instrument consisting of two subcategories: (1) training and ordinary education, and (2) other types of guidance and skill formation. The former clearly represents the human capital model. The latter subcategory covers various courses arranged for persons recently unemployed. Insured persons are categorized as "ready for work" per definition, hence courses for this group would often be about CV writing and job seeking.

The Danish employment policy includes a fifth instrument: *adult apprentice*. This is an adult taking ordinary vocational training while receiving a higher salary than under normal conditions. The company employing the apprentice is reimbursed accordingly by the municipality. The scheme provides an opportunity for skill formation such as the ordinary education instrument, but in a strict sense it does not count as activation. It is a decentralized measure to keep human capital formation going. At the end of the day, it is still a supply-side intervention using training to bring people back into employment. No demand-side interventions are present.

FROM HUMAN CAPITAL TO WORK-FIRST APPROACHES

Using the rough distinction between human capital and work-first, Figure 4.1 depicts the trajectory of Danish activation policy vis-à-vis insured persons during the last 20 years. The impression is the gradual but persistent fall of the Danish train-first approach. The work-first model has become prevalent, while human capital activation constitutes only a fraction of the level it had in the 1990s and early 2000s. The development did not happen overnight but over some 10 years.

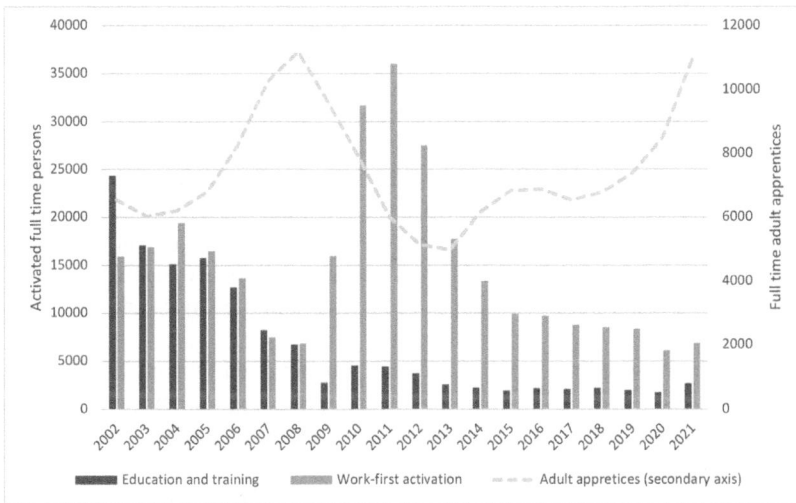

Figure 4.1   Human capital and work-first activation of insured persons 2002–21

Institutional changes often come about in small piecemeal steps rather than abrupt wholesale transformation (Streeck and Thelen, 2005). Gradual change modes include *displacement, layering, conversion and exhaustion*. Conversion occurs when formal rules largely stay the same but are interpreted in a new way and redeployed for new purposes (Mahoney and Thelen, 2010). From an empirical viewpoint, this description is not far from what happened in Denmark a few years after 2001 when a new Liberal–Conservative coalition government took office. The activation rule basically looked the same, unemployed persons still had the "right and duty" to participate in activation, and most of the instruments in the activation toolbox were continued. However, discourse, goals, guiding principles, and rule enforcement changed soon.

ALMP was transformed and renamed active employment policy (AEP) with new priorities and a recalibration of instruments and implementation structures, not forgetting huge reductions in funding for activation. The new goal was to increase effective labor supply if not just to get people off the dole as quickly as possible thereby saving taxpayers' money. Structural unemployment was seen as due to lack of motivation on the side of the unemployed (according to mainstream economist and political actors), not to lack of qualifications as had been the analysis in the early 1990s.

From 2003, a new activation approach had taken shape. The Liberal Minister of Employment, Claus Hjort Frederiksen, stated the following about his mission: "It's about making life more difficult for people in the unemployment system (...) if we had a country, where people would obviously benefit from having a job, we could save ourselves a great deal of the inconvenience" (interview with Claus Hjort Frederiksen, 28 August 2013, our translation).

The implications of the institutional conversion were manifold. First, with fewer funds for ordinary education, the PES and the municipalities' use of the instrument started to fade, while inexpensive activation offers gained prominence. Next, instead of individual action plans, caseworkers were now instructed to devise narrow *job plans* only. Furthermore, conditionality in the activation system was strengthened and its disciplinary elements, which had always existed but had seldom been used, came up front (Larsen, 2013; Hansen, 2019).

When the new regime reached its peak, unemployed persons had to document that they applied for four jobs every week, even when they were in mandatory activation. This was a direct order from the liberal minister himself. Reasonable arguments for refusing a job offer, for instance low skill match or long transportation time, were minimized. Under the new AEP, most people were fit for most jobs according to official assessment.

A tougher stance was adopted vis-à-vis young people and specially arranged courses were continuously put in place to ensure that all were activated immediately. The content was less important, and sometimes courses seemed like a waste of time, not to say totally ridiculous. Even mainstream economists deeply involved in advocating and designing strong work-first activation in Denmark now admit that many of the activation measures, including the use of economic incentives, did not work the way supposed. People at the edge of the labor market seldom respond to both the incentives and the threats of sanctions (Svarer and Naveed, 2019).

When introduced in 1994, activation was mainly targeted towards persons with unemployment insurance. The rules also applied to a proportion of the uninsured, but many social assistance recipients were deemed unfit for work and hence exempted from activation duty. The same applied for persons on sickness benefits. In 1994, the ratio between insured and uninsured persons in activation was 2 to 1. In 2003 it was 1:1 (Danmarks Statistik, 2004, p. 55). Since then, uninsured groups have constituted most of the clients enrolled in the system. Developments since 2007 are documented in Figure 4.2.

More and more groups have been included in activation, and measures with a disciplining threat attached have been implemented, most strongly in the period between 2005 and 2015. In 2013, sanctions were given in such a number that this even exceeded the number of people on social assistance. Some persons had sanctions given more times during the year. Public debates on the functioning of the municipal job centers began. Political action was again required.

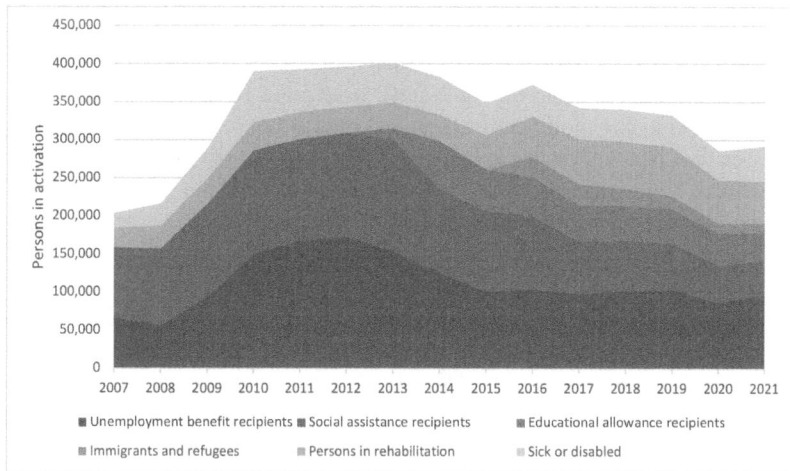

Figure 4.2   Activation of different target groups 2007–21

When considering the political climate surrounding the state-run PES in the early 2000s, there was a window for conversion: the Social Democratic party and the trade unions were historically weak, and the economic upturn encouraged PES staff to focus more on work-oriented activation than lengthy training measures. Within the public social services (PSS) responsible for implementing social policy, the situation was different. No powerful trade union or interest group defended the uninsured, let alone the sick or immigrants and refugees. However, the social and health workers in the municipalities gave these groups a voice and they turned out to be the strongest opposition to government's next mission, which was to extend the activation regime to the social policy domain.

The most important step in this process was the introduction of a set of methods to assess and categorize the work capability of social assistance and sickness benefit recipients. Effectively a kind of layering, these methods included: the workability assessment method, the resource profile, the visitation toolbox, the dialogue guide, and the profiling system.

Most noticeable is the profiling system introduced in 2004, in which social assistance claimants were to be placed in one of five categories, according to the degree of match between their resources and competences on the one side, and the demands of the labor market on the other. Claimants in categories 1 to 3 were deemed to have a high or some degree of match and therefore subject to activation duty. Claimants in the last categories were deemed to have little or no match and were exempted. Later, the five categories were reduced to three, and then two. Now, everyone is confronted with activation requirement (Andersen and Jørgensen, 2020). Officially, the authorities no longer use the word "unemployed". These people have been transformed to "jobseekers". They are cast in commodity terms, and this should motivate people to sell their labor on the open market, try to incentivize frontline people and case managers to be "hard" on putting pressure on claimants, and try to have the employment system increase the supply of labor.

The introduction and revisions of the described tools were essentially levers instigated to gradually expand the scope of the work-first policy. Yet they were also instruments for intervening with the work ethos of social workers and undermining their traditional occupational professionalism (Baadsgaard et al., 2014). According to Claus Hjort Frederiksen, many social workers were overprotecting their clients. Consequently, use of the tools was compulsory to the caseworkers in the PSS. Their implementation standardized the meeting between citizens and the municipality. They described in detail how to assess, categorize, and treat the unemployed, including how to (re)write job plans. Difficulties were to be handled in accordance with centrally made manuals. In the new methodology for casework in the PSS, job placement and earning an income was considered the solution to individual problems. The same philosophy by and large characterized the government's approach to persons on sickness benefits. Among the people in activation after 2007 were people on sick allowances, people with functional disabilities, alcoholics, mentally ill persons, and even cancer patients (Hansen, 2019; Nørup, 2020).

Alongside the institutional changes in the PSS and the transformation of social and labor market policy into an all-encompassing AEP, the government consolidated its achievements by using *evidence-based policy*. On behalf of the government, the Ministry of Employment constructed a database consisting of evidence of effects of welfare-to-work programs, all based on peer-reviewed (often Anglo-Saxon) economic research results. Research later documented, however, that the government's concept of "evidence" was inherently biased. It was constructed in a way that clearly undermined the human capital model and favored work-first including welfare reductions (Andersen and Jørgensen, 2020). In fact, the strategy of punishing unemployed persons economically has generally proven ineffective when assessed for its employment results (Hussain et al., 2021).

Nevertheless, by referring to the central authorities' own "evidence", the government legitimized several cutbacks to social assistance and unemployment benefits. Rates were reduced and the continuation of social assistance after two years was tied to a minimum work requirement of ordinary employment (the so-called 450-hour rule). Furthermore, from 2013 the unemployment benefit period was shortened from four years to two only, now compromising the balance between flexibility and security in the flexicurity system (Jørgensen and Klindt, 2018). Two years for activation measures compromises some of the possibilities for longer-lasting skill formations.

However, it was towards immigrants and refugees the government adopted the most rigorous policy. They were no longer treated on an equal basis in the Danish system. Researchers have pointed out that the policies represent a kind of graduated citizenship (Betzeld and Bothfeld, 2011; Nørup, 2020). The outright intention was to prevent refugees from seeking asylum in Denmark or encourage them to leave once they had arrived. With a changing economic situation and a beginning of lack of manpower, Danish employers started, however, to integrate some of these people.

This also illustrates the fact that labor market institutions are deeply political; they have distributional consequences and are fraught with tension (Thelen, 2014, p. 54).[3] The practical is political.

GOVERNANCE REFORMS AND THE FALL OF CORPORATISM

A restructuring of the public sector with the help of NPM was generally executed in Denmark in this period. Private-sector logics and management practices were used at all levels. This also changed the conditions for street-level bureaucrats to implement policies. The unemployed people had to learn to be "active" to receive public support. Labor market institutions were "neo-liberalized".

The Liberal–Conservative coalition government 2001–2011 practiced layering and displacement,[4] initially via marketization and later through a comprehensive governance reform. Starting in 2003, the government took steps towards contracting out the implementation of employment services for selected target groups. Outsourcing promised more efficient and cost-effective solutions, along with a reduction in bureaucracy. A new market and control functions within the PES were created and activation firms mushroomed in the 2000s. Denmark was actually one of the early adopters of quasi-markets and no slow modernizer.

However, results were not in line with expectations. Reports of "creaming" and "parking" of unemployed persons, and growing transaction costs, discredited the marketization experiment (Bredgaard and Larsen, 2007; Larsen, 2013). Moreover, some frontline people were engaging in selection practices and developing own coping strategies when facing limited time and resources, high caseloads, and pressures to meet organizational targets. Re-regulation followed, activation became a shrinking market, and after a few booming years in the 2000s the level of contracting out declined.

In terms of displacement, the abolition of the state-run PES and handover of full responsibility for AEP to the municipalities in 2009 was more effective and lasting. Embedded in a larger polity reform, the number of municipalities was reduced from 271 to 98 in 2007 (Weishaupt, 2011; Jørgensen and Schulze, 2018). In the same connection, 14 PES regions were consolidated into four larger employment regions. An important reform element was the creation of job centers integrating the services of the PES (insured) and PSS (uninsured) in the same organizational frame from 2007.

This was also an idea copied from the Netherlands (Marsh and Sharman, 2009). A total of 91 (now 94) new local labor market boards were formed including private interest representation, but without the former PES regions' decision-making competences and stripped of economic muscles. *The social partners were sidelined* and managers and employees in the job centers would no longer really take notice of their input and reactions. The employer organizations and trade unions jointly protested in 2008, albeit without success (Jørgensen, 2009).

The next step was taken in 2009, when 77 joint job centers were reorganized as 14 experimental job centers and transferred to the municipalities. *The state-run PES was thus finally dissolved and full municipalization completed.* This implied that local politicians and job center leaders became the new important decision-makers.

While responsibility for implementation was decentralized, *control and monitoring were centralized* and contractualism introduced at all levels as in most continental employment systems (van Berkel and Borghi, 2008; van Berkel et al., 2017). Contracts with the Central Labour Market Agency oblige the municipalities to arrange conveniently-timed job interviews and submit activation offers to unemployed persons. Failure to comply may result in intensified supervision. Later direct interventions from above was a possibility and a threat. Outcome-based pay-for-performance schemes had been implemented too. Private providers should have a chance. This kind of optimism soon eroded.

Moreover, a new economic steering system was introduced in 2009. According to this system, the municipalities now had to the pay the bill for benefits including activation. Collectively, the municipalities are reimbursed by the state, but for the individual municipality a so-called staircase model applies now. Reimbursements are reduced the longer benefit recipients are out of work or activation. The reimbursement rule produces incentives for rapid and cheap activation and disincentives for training, as training naturally is more expensive than work-first measures and may increase the locking-in effect (Klindt et al., 2020).

Control measures for staff and clients were strengthened too. With the introduction of NPM in relation to governance reform, activities and operational codes changed again. The professional autonomy of job center staff was reduced as in other European countries (Noordegraaf and Steijn, 2014; van Berkel et al., 2017). The front-line workers, of which only some 40% had a relevant social worker education (Baadsgaard et al., 2014), received new instructions regarding how they should carry out the work, including more frequent job meetings with benefit claimants. With standardization, new tasks, performance measurement, and an increasing number of clients, they had less autonomy in case handling. But the unemployed persons still have some rights. It was not a workfare system established but a system in which it was no longer important to support "jobseekers" gaining the qualifications and work experience required to be in demand in the open labor market. In reality, it was to treat unemployment as if it is a standardized, constant, and measurable phenomenon (Dall and Danneris, 2019).

Finally, threats and use of sanctions vis-à-vis benefit recipients were institutionalized. Incentives for "good" behavior and penalties for non-compliance were advocated and used. The risk of being sanctioned for non-compliance is a central part of the AEP's discourse accomplishing the new (Protestant) work ethic. Job center caseworkers, caught between a rock and a hard place, are obliged to enforce the policy, and have done, though mostly regarding people on social assistance.

The work-first model was consolidated, the economic steering system probably being one of the most influential elements. Most municipalities have "learned" how to behave to maximize financial gains or reduce losses and this is evident from activation statistics. Figure 4.1 depicts how work-first activation skyrocketed after 2009, education and training nosediving even further.

However, differences in local activation strategies do exist despite all the central control efforts. Among the municipalities, a number are investment oriented and still use training to a great extent or have rediscovered the instrument (Klindt and Ravn, 2019). Most municipalities, though, give priority to work-first activation, in particular supported employment.

THE IMPACT OF COVID-19 AND NEW TENSIONS

Efforts to control the municipalities directly from above have created new tensions in the employment system. Centralization versus decentralization has become one of the new significant conflict dynamics.

During the last 7–8 years, the municipalities – in particular, the largest ones – have been advocating for more freedom to create their own individual service delivery strategies (Andersen and Larsen, 2018; Andersen and Jørgensen, 2020). And they have partly succeeded. Some slack has been provided even though the steering system is still operational. Increased freedom from the side of the municipalities as to activities is counteracted from 2016 by a new ladder of decreasing state funding of benefits the longer people stay unemployed. From 2019 new ways of allocating money from the state to the municipalities were introduced.

The basic schism between work-first and human capital, and bourgeois aversion of the latter, is also less pronounced in Denmark. A reform in 2015 reduced a couple of work-first elements and tried to reintroduce education and real job brokering as a central task in the job centers next to activation. The reform introduced economic incentives for taking up short-time jobs, thereby supporting more flexible rules for regaining the right for unemployment benefits. Nudging now also became part of the repertoire of the authorities. The demands on the street-level bureaucrats to find new jobs and training opportunities grew once more – but again with different local strategies as a frame. A classification of unemployed people as ready for job or ready for activation as the central criteria was implemented. But no strong "train-first" strategy has been reintroduced.

The *COVID-19 pandemic* showed an unprecedented political response as labor market interventions and new income support systems intertwined. The pandemic called for comprehensive economic support from the state to firms and wage earners during 2020, 2021, and 2022. Wage subsidies up to 75% of people's income have been implemented, and firms were given additional help from the state, during several rounds. Borrowing money for these arrangements was no problem for the Danish state. Budgets were almost in balance again by the end of 2022. A big surplus was produced in 2023.

COVID-19, naturally, closed down a lot of activities. Activation was suspended during many months, e-based contacts established for most unemployed people, and new experiences were made. This was successfully done. Digital solutions to many problems have from 2021 been a new strategy of the authorities, even though face-to-face meetings have been reintroduced from

2022. But digitalization is now seen as a common solution to many of the bureaucratic problems within the system. At the same time, you might easily forget that not all citizens are capable of handling this new technology without big problems. A new normal has not been established yet, giving us no secure knowledge as to the future direction of activation in Denmark. More local projects trying to use AI have been started – and closed again. The authorities have difficulties in dealing with the new (hidden) technology.

It was also important that *crisis corporatism re-emerged* in Denmark: 17 corporatist agreements with the social partners were made in 2020 and seven new during 2021. It is still to be assessed whether this is a more permanent change back to traditional corporatist arrangements or if it is a COVID-19 phenomenon only. The political and parliamentary situation clearly influences the use of tripartite rounds of negotiations in Denmark. It seems to be a general lesson learned in Denmark that more coordinated efforts and common understandings are more easily created in case interested organizations are included in political processes.

The municipalities have shown that they consider economic incentives most important when making decisions as to how to cope with labor market problems. Economic gains – up to 100% reimbursement from the state – when using the special measure adult apprentice have resulted in increased placement of unemployed people in this arrangement. In a way, the municipalities reintroduce a kind of human capital approach by this priority. But the measure is placed outside the list of activation offers that have a much lower reimbursement base. New weight has also been given to guidance and information activities by the municipalities.

From 2024, immigrants and refugees must do 37 hours of weekly work in activation in order to receive support. This is a way of putting even more pressure on foreign people, following "ethnicing" of activation in Denmark, Norway, and Sweden (Parsland, 2023). But it will be difficult for the municipalities to find more than the 20,000 new utility jobs required.

Even if economic developments since 2022 have brought a shortage of labor and other problems back on the political agenda, basic labor exchange has not been strengthened by the municipalities. Very few percentages of the common shift of jobs in Denmark – around 1 million per year, equal to one third of the whole labor force – go via the job centers. This again raises questions as to the role of the municipalities in a decentralized and less coordinated policy and activation system – and to the role of employers as well. These questions address cost, flexibility, and quality. They are not taking part in implementation of activation as was the case in the 1990s.

The formation of a centre-left, center-right coalition and majority government in December 2022 again seems to signal a change of arrangements and instruments. The government simply wants to dissolve the job centers, cut expenditures by 3 billion Danish kroner, equal to more than a quarter of the total budget, and create a new system also based on outsourcing and marketization. That is the plan. Strong criticism of job center behavior – including on TV programs – have paved the way for political "action" to renew the activation system and to get rid of inhumane treatment. A small group of economists and advisors has been given responsibility to come up with proposals and a blueprint for a new system in June 2024. The cuts in budgets have already been decided on by parliament and the job centers have started dismissing employees. Quiet quitting has also started because of the unknown future. This is a difficult moment for employment policy. It is partly paralyzed at the time of writing in early 2024. However, institutional rearrangements might not be equal to totally new principles, but clearly new priorities of instruments.

DISCUSSION AND CONCLUSION

The international status as a role model in ALMPs and activation for Denmark has been slowly undermined. And this was done deliberately, according to partisan politics and neo-liberal forces in society and because of a weakening of the labor movement. More waves of reforms have partly reduced "the security of the wings" for wage earners with more pressure placed on the unemployed and on trade unions. De-corporatization has been an element in policy and polity renewals.

Promotion of labor market participation as a way of fighting marginalization and exclusion has been a political issue and a policy priority since the late 1990s in most European countries – alongside retrenchment discussions. Activation became popular generally. But the Danish (and Nordic) tradition of active LMP was started decades before and had a "working" line that was strengthened by the Danish LMP reforms of the 1990s. Here a progressive policy mix of fiscal and ALMP elements paved the way for improvements of balances within the labor market. Denmark broke away from the European unemployment developments this way. And when "flexicurity" received its formulation for the labor market system, a new interest and wish to learn about the Danish "miracle" started. But political developments in Denmark soon put an end to this miracle.

The change in activation principles recorded is from an interventionist policy trying to have "the security of the wings" for wage earners established by upskilling and reskilling to work-first principles for increasing the labor supply and individualize responsibilities. Economic incentives and sanctions are to help this change of mind and behavior. At the same time, a new decentralized municipal system has implied almost 94 different activation policies, but with the state in a central monitoring and steering position. Especially during the last 7–8 years, the municipalities have had more degrees of freedom, but still within work-first principles and policy recommendations. At the moment, a replacement of the existing job center system is in the pipeline.

The activation policy of the 1990s empowered the unemployed people with strong influence on their individual action plan and its implementation. This ended in 2003. Especially from 2007, more "work-first" elements and a new actor system with municipalities at the center did transform the policy, but operational reforms also contributed to the results. Now job plans and activation was made by the authorities. Activation has a defining ambiguity of support and punishment being embedded in stronger logics of policies and politics that are in no way one dimensional or clear. Some rights are preserved, while duties have been strengthened alongside central monitoring and steering of the municipalities who make different strategic choices. More collective logics are now at work.[5] Social policy was made part of employment policy, but a clash of rationales, principles, and understandings has also been the result.

Activation policies are politically debatable. Assessments and evaluations do not tell us of negative results only (Kluve, 2010; Card et al., 2018, Rosholm and Svarer, 2020). Positive outcomes can be delivered. The building up of capabilities and productive ways of (re)entering the labor market for people on unemployment benefits and social assistance have been a Danish way of com-bining ALMP with work-first approaches. This is witnessed in the still-growing employment and decreasing unemployment figures. Unemployment is down to 3% at the time of writing. However, the downsizing of education and training as central activation instruments, especially since 2010, does place a serious challenge to both the employment and the "flexicurity" system.

The shift of responsibility to the municipalities in 2009 and the dissolving of the state-run PES were not supportive of the security elements in Danish flex-icurity. Different local strategies, fragmentation, and tensions between levels have been the result. But the political will to re-install a state-run PES has not existed until now (Klindt and Jørgensen, 2018).

The content of activation policies has changed radically from those of the 1990s. Endogenous change has portrayed the Danish developments. Displacement, conversion, layering, and exhaustion require active cultivation by collective actors whose interests are fostered by the new arrangements and processes. The highly praised Danish "flexicurity" system or the "Golden Triangle" (Hansen and Leschke, 2022) was in fact jeopardized in two of the three corners of the triangle – e.g. cuts in social security in the form of eco-nomic compensation for unemployment and in ALMP converted into more kinds of a work-first system. Activation might be running into severe troubles after years of conflict-ridden developments and after the experiences under COVID-19.

A number of political and institutional changes in the Danish system sums up to a paradigmatic shift during the first decade of the new century, according to the conceptualization of Peter Hall (1993). It is not only a shift in instruments and operational procedures that have taken place, but also a shift in activation philosophy, guiding principles, and rationale. From a logic of human capital investment to a logic of commodification is a big change. But basic instruments used persist.

Table 4.1   Institutional changes in the Danish activation system 2003–2022

	Displacement	**Layering**	**Conversion**	**Exhaustion**
Content	"Work first" initiatives (incentives and sanctions) From individual action plans to job plans Profiling	Outsourcing of activation Marketization Stricter eligibility Unemployment benefit period 2 years	From need orientation to "quickest possible way into job" Municipalization Education downsized	The state-run PES system exhausted during the period 2003–2009 Regional ALMP dissolved
Process	Centralized decentralization, reform creates 94 job centers "Nudging" introduced Job centers to be abolished/ changed in 2025	Municipalization changes actor system One-step job centers Performance management systems	The social partners in advisory roles New evaluation practices. Municipalities look to own finances	From corporative actors to local politicians as decision-makers

In Table 4.1, we have summarized the types of institutional changes of Danish activation after 2003.

Different interests exist in the system. Local decision-makers do not share central problem definitions and do not always follow implementation instructions, also because of a problem exacerbated by the financial squeeze on the municipalities. This highlights the structural and inbuilt tensions between the local and the central level. It also implies problems and ethical dilemmas for the implementation agents. But criticism also pointed to the fact that municipalization reduces societal problems to local ones of bad administration rather than bad policy.

However, the local municipalities and their delivery strategies are not totally controllable from the center (Klindt and Ravn, 2020). Different local strategies have been the result and the encounter processes between the representatives of the municipalities and the citizens are of special importance (Hupe, 2022).

Changes in street-level practice can be caused by substantive policy changes at the central level or by using local and regional instruments and arrangements in a special way – or both. Co-production and co-creation strategies are now mushrooming in municipalities. Municipalities have more options included in their operation, but they still will have to comply with measurement goals and data set-up within the central employment system.

The administrative reforms are also influencing the content of policy (Larsen, 2013). The way you plan and install certain ways of handling problems and ways of meeting the people involved, you also change the way unemployed people and the system meet each other. It has been difficult to find a balance between welfare, conditionality, and co-creation (Caswell and Larsen, 2020).

However, the COVID-19 period reconfirmed the importance of the state and public-sector interventions in providing public goods and security to people and firms. A shift of interest from solely supply-sided policy towards demand-side might follow. The socioeconomic environment is undergoing change too due to the dual transition to a green and digital future. Thus, activation has to be seen in relation to questions of employment, labor market balance, structural change, and economic growth as well. This is not offered today with the existing supply-sided activation, perhaps also neglecting institutions helping with coordination and cooperation.

The future is unknown, and also to the municipalities, as the new center-right government has the intention to dissolve the job centers, introduce more contracting out, and has already decided on big cuts in budgets. Debates on the future of activation have also shown that activation needs more than a brush-up to be able to have the Danish labor market system "punch above its weight" once again.

NOTES

1. The original fairytale is called *The Ugly Duckling*. It tells the story of a male cygnet who is born in a duck yard. The other ducks, except for his mother, call him the ugly duckling because of his size and grey color. Ultimately, the ugly duckling wishes to die but then sees his reflection in a lake. He has transformed into a beautiful adult swan and is happily united with other swans, who bow to his honor (see: https://andersen.sdu.dk/vaerk/hersholt/ TheUglyDuckling.html).
2. A detailed overview can be accessed on the webpage of STAR (the Danish Government's Agency for Labour Market and Recruitment): https://star.dk/ indsatser-og-ordninger/
3. Agents that are disadvantaged by the institutional design push for change, while institutional winners will resist change and try to maintain the status quo. Conversion is the preferred mode when the targeted institution exhibits

a high level of discretion in rule interpretation and when institutional defenders' veto possibilities are relatively weak (Mahoney and Thelen, 2010). If defenders are somehow more entrenched and have the capacity of resisting conversion, change agents can switch to *layering*, which implies that new rules are attached to the existing institutional setup, thereby "changing the ways in which the original rules structure behaviour" (ibid., 16–17). Administrative reforms contributed to this.

4.   When the strategies of conversion and layering encounter difficulty, change agents may opt for a third mode of change: *Displacement*. This entails breakdown of institutions and replacement with new ones, yet displacement can be a gradual process as well. It occurs when the new institutions are introduced stepwise and during a period compete with the old institutional set-up (Mahoney and Thelen, 2010).

5.   Dichotomous classifications in the literature (Torfing, 1999; Barbier, 2004; Taylor-Gooby, 2004) have big difficulties dealing with the Danish case. They are oversimplifications. Categorization as to more axes of promotion of labor market participation and elements of "learnfare" is called for. Both demanding and enabling elements are to be found in activation programs. Even within a single program, more forms of these elements might be present.

REFERENCES

Andersen, N.A. and Jørgensen, H. (2020): "Udviklingslinjer og sporskifte i dansk arbejdsmarkeds- og beskæftigelsespolitik", pp. 80–118 in M.P. Klindt, S. Rasmussen and H. Jørgensen (eds.): *Aktiv arbejdsmarkedspolitik – Etablering, udvikling og fremtid*, DJØF-Forlaget, Copenhagen.

Andersen, N.A. and Larsen, F. (2018): *Beskæftigelse for alle? Den kommunale beskæftigelsespolitik på kontanthjælpsområdet siden 2000*, Frydenlund, Copenhagen.

Baadsgaard, K., Jørgensen, H., Nørup, I. and Olesen, S.P. (2014): *Jobcentre og klemte kvalifikationer*, Aalborg Universitetsforlag, Aalborg.

Barbier, J.-C. (2004): "Systems of social protection in Europe: Two contrasted paths to activation, and maybe a third", pp. 233–154 in J. Lind, H. Knudsen, and J. Jørgensen (eds.): *Labour and Employment Regulation in Europe*, Peter Lang, Brussels.

Betzeld, S. and Bothfeld, S. (eds.) (2011): *Activation and Labour Market Reforms in Europe: Challenges to Social Citizenship*, Palgrave Macmillan, Basingstoke.

Bonoli, G. (2010): "The political economy of active labour market policies", pp. 435–457 in *Politics and Society*, vol. 38, no 4.

Bonoli, G. (2013): *The Origins of Active Social Policy: Labour Market and Childcare Policies in a Comparative Perspective*, Oxford University Press, Oxford.

Bredgaard, T. and Larsen, F. (2007): "Implementing public employment policy: What happens when non-public agencies take over?", pp. 287–300 in *International Journal of Sociology and Social Policy*, vol. 27, no. 7–8.

Card, D., Kluve, J. and Weber, A. (2018): "What works? A meta analysis of recent active labour market program evaluations", pp. 494–931 in *Journal of European Economic Association*, vol. 16, no. 3.

Casey, B.H. (2004): "The OECD Jobs Study and the European Employment Strategy: Two views of the labour market and the welfare state", pp. 329–352 in *European Journal of Industrial Relations*, vol. 10, no. 3.

Caswell, D. and Larsen, F. (2020): "Co-creation in an era of welfare conditionality: Lessons from Denmark", in *Journal of Social Policy*, doi.101017/S004727941000065.

Dall, T. and Danneris, S. (2019): "Reconsidering 'what works' in welfare-to-work with the vulnerable unemployed: The potential of relational causality as an alternative approach", pp. 582–596 in *Social Policy and Society*, vol. 18, no. 4.

DAMVAD (2015): *Kvalitativ evaluering af nytte-indsats*, STAR, Copenhagen.

Danmarks Statistik (2004): Statistikbank, København (http://www.dst.dk).

Hall, P.A. (1993): "Policy paradigms, social learning and the state: The case of economic policymaking in Britain", pp. 275–296 in *Comparative Politics*, vol. 25, no. 3.

Hansen, M.P. (2019): *The Moral Economy of Activation: Ideas, Politics and Policies*, Policy Press, Bristol.

Hansen, M.P. and Leschke, J. (2022): "Reforming the ideal(ised) model(s) of danish labour market policies", pp. 39–56 in A.H. Krogh, A. Agger and P. Triantafillou (eds.): *Public Governance in Denmark: Meeting the Global Mega-Challenges of the 21st Century?*, Emerald Publishing, Bingley.

Hupe, P. (2022): "The politics of the public encounter", pp. 19–38 in P. Hupe: *The Politics of the Public Encounter: What Happens When Citizens Meet the State*, Edward Elgar Publishing, Cheltenham, UK and Northampton, MA, USA.

Hussain, M.A., Ejrnæs, M. and Larsen, J.E. (2021): "Are benefit reductions an effective activation strategy? The case of the lowest benefit recipients in Denmark", pp. 569–587 in *Journal of Social Policy*, vol. 50, no. 3.

Jørgensen, H. (2002): *Consensus, Coordination and Conflict. The Policy-Making Process in Denmark*, Edward Elgar Publishing, Cheltenham, UK.

Jørgensen, H. (2009): "From a beautiful swan to an ugly duckling: The renewal of Danish activation policy since 2003", pp. 337–367 in *European Journal of Social Security*, vol. 11, no. 4.

Jørgensen, H. and Klindt, M.P. (2018): "Revisiting Danish flexicurity after a decade of reform: Does the labour market still work for everyone?", pp. 134–151 in M. Fabian and R. Breunig (eds.): *Hybrid Public Policy Innovations: Contemporary Policy Beyond Ideology*, Routledge, New York.

Jørgensen, H. and Madsen, P.K. (eds.) (2007): *Flexicurity and Beyond*, DJØF Publishing, Copenhagen.

Jørgensen, H. and Schulze, M. (2018): "Das Aktivierungsparadigma als dominantes Prinzip der Arbeitsmarktpolitik in Deutschland und Dänemark", pp. 627–643 in *Sozialer Fortschritt*, vol. 67, no. 8–9.

Klindt, M.P. (2011): "From rhetorical action to policy learning: Understanding the European Commission's elaboration of the flexicurity concept", pp. 971–994 in *Journal of Common Market Studies*, vol. 49, no. 5.

Klindt, M.P. and Jørgensen, H. (2018): "Revisiting Danish Flexicurity after a decade of reform", pp. 134–151 in M. Fabian and R. Breuning (eds.): *Hybrid Public Policy Innovations*, Routledge, New York, NY.

Klindt, M.P. and Ravn, R. (2019): "Den 'rådne banan' er human kapital – en analyse af kommunernes brug af uddannelse i beskæftigelsesindsatsen", pp. 48–71 in *Tidsskrift for Arbejdsliv*, vol. 21, no. 1.

Klindt, M.P. and Ravn, R. (2020): "Kommunernes redskabsanvendelse i beskæftigelsesindsatsen", pp. 221–146 in M.P. Klindt, S. Rasmussen and H. Jørgensen (eds.):

Aktiv Arbejdsmarkedspolitik – Etablering, udvikling og fremtid, DJØF-Forlag, Copenhagen.

Klindt, M.P., Rasmussen, S. and Jørgensen, H. (2020): *Aktiv arbejdsmarkedspolitik – Etablering, udvikling og fremtid*, DFØF-Forlaget, Copenhagen.

Kluve, J. (2010): "The effectiveness of European labour market programs", pp. 904–918 in *Labour Economics*, vol. 17, no. 6.

Kvist, J. (2003): "Scandinavian activation strategies in the 1990s: Recasting social citizenship and the Scandinavian Welfare Model", pp. 223–248 in *Revue Francoise des Affaires Sociales*, vol. 4.

Kvist, J. and Harsløf, I. (2014): "Workfare with welfare revisited: Investigating dual tracks for insiders and outsiders", pp. 48–68 in I. Lødemel and A. Moreira (eds.): *Activation or Welfare? Governance and the Neo-liberal Convergence*, Oxford University Press, Oxford.

Larsen, F. (2013): "Active labour market reform in Denmark: The role of governance in policy change", pp. 103–123 in E. Brodkin and G. Mardsdon (eds.): *Work and the Welfare State: Street-level Organizations and Workfare Policies*, Georgetown University Press, Georgetown.

Lødemel, I. and Moreira, A. (eds.) (2014): *Activation or Workfare? Governance and the Neo-liberal Convergence*, Oxford University Press, Oxford.

Lødemel, I. and Morieira, A. (2022): "Activation in eight European countries", pp. 92–123 in Besharov, D. and Call, D. (eds.): *Work and the Social Safety Net: Labor Activation in Europe and the United States*, Oxford University Press, New York.

Mahoney, J. and Thelen, K. (2010): *Explaining Institutional Change: Ambiguity, Agency, and Power*, Cambridge University Press, New York, NY.

Marsh, D. and Sharman, J.C. (2009): "Policy diffusion and policy transfer", pp. 169–288 in *Policy Studies*, vol. 30, no. 3.

Noordegraaf, M. and Steijn, B. (eds.) (2014): *Professionals under Pressure*, Amsterdam University Press, Amsterdam.

Nørup, I. (2020): "Sammensmeltning af social- og beskæftigelsespolitik: reformer af indsatsen for borgere på kanten af og uden for arbejdsmarkedet", pp. 247–272 in M.P. Klindt, S. Rasmussen and H. Jørgensen (eds.): *Aktiv arbejdsmarkedspolitik – Etablering, udvikling og fremtid*, DJØF-Forlag, Copenhagen.

OECD (2004): *Employment Outlook*, OECD, Paris.

Parsland, E. (2023): "'Ethnicing' activation as a standard story in a Swedish municipal labour market programme", in *Nordic Social Work Research*, doi .org/ 10 .1080/ 2156857x.2023.2188484.

Peck, J. and Theodore, N. (2000): "Searching for best practice in welfare-to-work: The means, the method and the message", pp. 81–94 in *Policy and Politics*, vol. 29, no. 1.

Rosdahl, A. and Weise, H. (2001): "When all must be active: Workfare in Denmark", pp. 159–180 in I. Lødemel and H. Trickey (eds.): *"An Offer You Can't Refuse": Workfare in International Perspective*, The Polity Press, Bristol, UK.

Rosholm, M. and Svarer, M. (2004): *Estimating the Threat Effect of Active Labour Market Programmes*, IZA Discussion Paper No. 1300.

Rosholm, M. and Svarer, M. (2020): *Evaluering af offentlige løntilskud til ledige*, Metrica, London.

Streeck, W. and Thelen, K. (2005): *Beyond Continuity: Institutional Change in Advanced Political Economies*, Oxford University Press, Oxford.

Svarer, M. and Naveed, A. (2019): "The effect of active labour market programs and benefit sanction on reducing unemployment", pp. 202–229 in *Journal of Labor Research*, vol. 40, no. 2.

Taylor-Gooby, P. (2004): "New risks and social change", pp. 1–27 in P. Taylor-Gooby (ed.): *New Risks, New Welfare?*, Oxford University Press, Oxford.

Thelen, K. (2014): *Varieties of Capitalism and the New Politics of Social Solidarity*, Cambridge University Press, New York, NY.

Torfing, J. (1999): "Workfare with welfare: Recent reforms of the Danish welfare state", pp. 5–28 in *Journal of European Social Policy*, vol. 9, no. 5.

van Bergel, R. and Borghi, V. (2008): "Review article: The governance of activation", pp. 393–402 in *Social Policy and Society*, vol. 7, no. 3.

van Bergel, R., Caswell, D., Kupka, P. and Larsen, F. (eds.) (2017): *Frontline Delivery of Welfare-to-Work Policies in Europe*, Routledge, London.

Weishaupt, T.J. (2011): *From the Manpower Revolution to the Activation Paradigm: Explaining Institutional Continuity and Change in an Integrating Europe*, Amsterdam University Press, Amsterdam.

Wilthagen, T. and Tros, F. (2004): "The concept of 'flexicurity': A new approach to regulating employment and labour markets", pp. 166–186 in *Transfer: European Review of Labour and Research*, no. 2.

5.   Activation in the universal welfare state: the case of Finland

Minna van Gerven and Aleksander Heikkinen

1.   INTRODUCTION TO THE ACTIVATION IN THE "NORDIC WAY"

As the chapters of this book convey, activation regimes are not the same in all countries (see also Bonoli, 2022). Numerous studies suggest the distinctive activation regime in the Nordic countries, focusing on investment in human capital (Bonoli, 2022; Johansson & Hvinden, 2007) instead of stringent measures to push people into the labour market (such as severe benefit conditionality and sanctions; see, e.g., Bonoli, 2022). This article re-evaluates the modern-day discussion of universalist activation by analysing the developments and present-day activation practices in the Finnish welfare state. The chapter seeks to answer the question, how has the Finnish activation policy been developed in recent decades and to what extent does it still adhere to the Nordic values of universalism?

Universalism may constitute an uneasy match with activation. Generally speaking, universalism upholds the political ideal that "people in the same situation should be treated the same" (Saikkonen & Ylikännö, 2020, p. 146; see also Anttonen et al., 2012; Kildal & Kuhnle, 2005), whereas activation is generally targeted at individuals to a differing extent to facilitate their (re)entry into the labour market. The inclusive membership embedded in universalism ties it into a strong normative understanding of social justice and equality in a society that "should be structured so that the greatest possible amount of liberty is given to its members" (Rawls, 1971, p. 202). The active turn in the 1990s has changed much of the political environment in which universal welfare states exist. The commitment to activation reforms has been seen to erode individual liberties and social rights and replace these with individual responsibilities and conditionality. In this way, the targeted logic of activation trumps the ideas of inclusiveness and generosity of social protection (Bonoli, 2010, 2022). The scope of activation, and the conditional requirements surrounding these policies have been targeted to an ever-larger group of inactive people (e.g., those with disabilities or care responsibilities).

Although the universalist regime of activation emphasizes social justice and fairness, the Finnish interpretation of it does not imply that everybody must receive the same benefits and services (Anttonen et al., 2012, pp. 3–4). Rather, targeting has been an element in universal welfare states for decades (Anttonen et al., 2012; Kuhnle, 2011; Saikkonen & Ylikännö, 2020). The child benefit is the exemplar of the targeted nature of universal systems (Jacques & Noël, 2018), being exclusively available to some of the population only (families with children). Wrapped around the virtue of equality and social justice, universalism can thus be seen as compatible with targeting, *if it results in protecting the least well off* (Andersen, 2012, p. 166). In this way, if following the Rawlsian ideals of accepting inequalities, activation can be just only if "the worst off will be better off than they might be under an equal distribution" (Rawls, 1971, p. 266). In this chapter, we *critically assess the extent to which and how the activation policies in Finland support or undermine the "Nordic principles" of universalism*. The analysis is based on an extensive review of the literature, policy documents and descriptive statistics as well as tracing the process of activation policies between 1990 and 2023 in Finland.

The structure of the chapter is as follows. First, a short outline is given of the historic developments in activation in Finland. Next, the current activation regime is discussed in relation to the economic and social disparities of activation. The chapter ends with a prognosis of the future and the conclusion.

2. THE TURBULENT ROAD TO A NORDIC WELFARE STATE

The route of the Finnish welfare state to a Nordic welfare state has been long and difficult. Up to the 1950s, Finland was one of the poorest countries in Europe. After World War II, the country made staggering progress by transforming from an agricultural society into a post-industrial leader in just a few decades. As for welfare state development, however, Finland has been portrayed as the "light version" of the Nordic welfare state (see, e.g. Kangas, 2019). The country only achieved the same level of social protection as other Nordic countries in the 1980s; it has never attained the same levels of employment and public service provision of its Nordic peers (Lehtonen et al., 2001, pp. 110, 112). Referring to the birth of the universal schemes in Finland, Kangas and Saloniemi (2013) have shown that universalism emerged from compromises demanded by the agrarian parties, rather than being initiated by social democratic party ideals in the other Nordic countries. The cornerstones of universalism became the pension (implemented 1939), the sickness benefit (1963), and the child benefit (1948) schemes, but the employment-related schemes, such as the work accident (1894) and unemployment schemes (1917) were designed around principles of workers' insurance schemes (Kangas & Saloniemi, 2013). As for services, the responsibilities of municipalities to provide universal health care and subjective rights to childcare and education have been essential in the development of Finnish universalism, but this does not extend to employment services, with the exception of the social work.

The splendid welfare state expansion in Finland, however, came to an abrupt halt in the early 1990s. The fall of the Soviet Union, among other things, pushed the Finnish economy into a deep economic recession (1991–1995). The long period of economic growth and almost full employment of the previous decade was suddenly transformed into corporate bankruptcies, a decreased standard of living for households, a large-scale banking crisis that eventually led to significant public finance problems (Kalela et al., 2001, p. 3), and austerity that scarred the public sector for decades. The Finnish activation policy originated from this unprecedented economic recession (see, e.g., Saikku, 2018a; Julkunen, 2013; Karjalainen, 2013). The main focus was to establish a statutory basis for activation and target mostly the long-term unemployed and especially the young (Karjalainen, 2013, p. 220) by cutting their rights and increasing the responsibility to undertake training, employment, or other offers. Despite the reasonably quick economic recovery, the new activation regime was introduced to address "benefit dependency" and "incentive traps" (Lehtonen et al., 2001, p. 110; also: Karjalainen, 2013, p. 221; Saikku, 2018b, p. 23), matters that have remained the key concerns in the political debate ever since. The recessions left a long shadow that still frames political decisions. As will be elaborated more in the fourth section, the political ideals of activation have shifted from "universalism to selectivism", where activation responsibilities are stressed at the expense of social rights (Kuivalainen & Niemelä, 2010).

3.   THE FINNISH UNEMPLOYMENT SYSTEMS: A MIX OF EVERYTHING

As discussed in the previous section, the Finnish activation regime grew out of an exceptionally deep "great recession" in the 1990s. At its peak, unemployment rose from the pre-recession level of 3% in 1990 to 18% in 1993 (Simpura et al., 2001, p. 129). Although the recession was short and the recovery had already started by 1994, it cast a long shadow: high unemployment persisted and remained at over 10% for the rest of the century (Simpura et al., 2001, p. 129) and long-term unemployment persisted at over 29% from 1992 to 2000 (OECD, 2023b).

From this background, high levels of (long-term) unemployment combined with the scarcity of public resources, and the Finnish labour market policy was reinvented in the 1990s. Prior to this, Finland was committed to achieving full employment. As articulated in the 1987 employment law, the government was responsible for arranging at least temporary employment for all citizens (after a certain period of unemployment). This "job guarantee" was abolished in 1993. The obligation of the state was refined in the 1995 constitutional rights reform into "a pursuit" of securing everyone "the right to work" (Lehtonen et al., 2001, pp. 110, 112). At the same time, to deal with the fiscal pressures and rapid growth in unemployment, social security systems were exposed to "cheese slicer" cuts and greater emphasis was put on means-testing (Julkunen, 2001, 2013, p. 34). Eventually, about a hundred important cuts were conducted in social policy and social benefits (Lehtonen et al., 2001, p. 113), impacting upon both the level and coverage of benefits and services (Kautto, 2004; van Gerven, 2008) for the decades to come.

In 1994, a new unemployment benefit, "the labour market subsidy", scheme was introduced alongside *the basic and earnings-related social insurance systems and means-tested (last resort) social assistance*. The combination of these four schemes guarantees adequate livelihood for unemployed residents regardless of their work history. In this respect, Finland still adheres to a de-commodifying regime, as Esping-Andersen (1990) suggested for the social democratic regime. The four unemployment protection schemes, however, produce very different levels of protection. The unemployed with a work record and insured by unemployment insurance funds can access higher benefits from the trade union governed fund, namely *the earnings-related unemployment insurance benefit (työttömyysvakuutus)*. The unemployed with a work record, but not a member of the fund, can receive *a basic unemployment insurance benefit (peruspäiväraha)*. In the 1990s, *the labour market subsidy (työmarkkinatuki)* scheme that provides basic security for those without a work record, mostly young people entering the labour market for the first time (Ylikännö, 2011, p. 206) and the long-term unemployed who have received the maximum length of the unemployment insurance benefits, was created (Lehtonen et al., 2001, p. 110).[1] The labour market subsidy is a means-tested benefit paid at a flat rate and its level is low, but it can be paid in exceptional circumstances for an unlimited duration. Finally, there is *social assistance (toimeentulotuki)*, with inherent needs- and means-testing requirements, targeted at people unable to work. The people who can still work (at least partially) must apply for the labour market subsidy instead. Social assistance in Finland, however, has the peculiarity that it is commonly paid to top up other social security benefits (such as the labour market subsidy, and sick pay). Social assistance is paid if one's income from benefits or work remains below the minimum threshold. Given the low level of labour market subsidy benefits, recipients must also often apply for social assistance. Social assistance is the last-resort benefit, paid without a maximum duration (as long as the person satisfies the requirements) and in the Nordic tradition it is closely linked to public services (social work and health services). The extensive coverage of unemployment protection in Finland may echo the ideals of universalism from the past but, as Table 5.1 shows, the rights of recipients vary greatly.

Table 5.1   *Main characteristics of Finnish unemployment benefit schemes*

	Earnings related	Basic insurance	Labour market subsidy	Social assistance
General obligation	To be registered as unemployed, job-seekers must be between 18 and 64 years of age, resident in Finland and meet the following requirements: (1) fit for work, (2) available for employment, and (3) looking for a full-time job			Need and means test, registered at public employment services (PES)
Target	Job-seekers (18–64) with work record and membership of a fund	Job-seekers (18–64) with work record	Job-seekers without work record or whose eligibility has exceeded insurance benefit	No work record or ability *or* whose income is under the minimum threshold
Duration	400 days	400 days	Unlimited	Unlimited (need/means-test)
Level	Earnings related (€37.21/day plus earnings-related part)	Flat rate (€37.21/day – €744.20 month)	Flat-rate (€37.21/day – €744.20 month)	Basic assistance, depends on household (€555.11 per month basic amount for single)
Relation to activation	Via PES, focus on re-entry to work or education	Via PES, focus on re-entry to work or education	Via PES, focus on rehabilitation, employment experiences and social integration	Via PES/ social services, focus on social integration, rehabilitation (and work experiences)

Note: The basic unemployment allowance is payable for a maximum period of 300 days (with work history shorter than 3 years), 400 days (in normal cases) and for 500 days (if older than 58 years).
Source: Missoc (2022); van Gerven et al. (2022); Kela (2023).

To receive any of the unemployment benefits, claimants must be registered as a job-seeker and must comply with the public employment services (PES) requirements (such as making an employment plan, reporting regularly, and accepting work or training if provided). In the case of social assistance, claimants are often freed from these obligations, but if a claimant has not registered for PES the basic amount of their social assistance benefit may be reduced. The basic requirement for able-bodied job-seekers is to apply for four jobs per month. This can be adjusted according to job availability and the job-seeker's functional capacity. Sanctions apply if a claimant does not adhere to rules or work with authorities on a work search plan. In this, activation services have become an important element in managing and assessing entry into the labour market. The PES provision in Finland has predominantly been developed among the municipal and regional services (TE-toimisto), that aim at intensifying cooperation and coordination between service providers and improving the implementation of activation policies (Karjalainen, 2013, p. 220; Saikku, 2018b, p. 23, 2018a, p. 107). After the turn of the millennium, the scope of activation has been broadened to cover all working-age people. For example, most early-exit schemes were removed by 2000 (Gould & Saurama, 2004) and an intermediate labour market and services were created to support hard-to-employ claimants' working capacity and rehabilitation (Karjalainen, 2013). At the same time, more activating (workfare) principles were imported into the PES and municipal social assistance system (Kuivalainen & Niemelä, 2010) by adding sanctions for non-compliance.[2] Job-seekers' obligations (e.g., job search plans, regular reporting) and monetary incentives have been a common strategy to diminish benefit dependency and to make the regular labour market more attractive (Saikku, 2018b, p. 23). Although the rights within the unemployment protection schemes are clearly established, the obligations related to benefit claims have increased considerably under the label of activation (van Gerven, 2008; van Gerven et al., 2022).

4.   CURRENT ACTIVATION FOCUS

As already suggested, the current activation regime in Finland has its roots in the great recession of the 1990s. The route to recovery has been slow, and the crises in recent decades have each put the unemployment protection systems to a continuing test. Here, Finland has fared reasonably well. As Figure 5.1 portrays, the unemployment rates in Finland have been decreasing with the exceptions of economic downturns around the financial crisis and COVID-19. The levels are higher than in Denmark, but close to those of Sweden and lower than the EU average.

As Figure 5.1 also shows, the financial crisis in the 2010s proved to be a déjà-vu from the previous recession. However, although there was a sudden

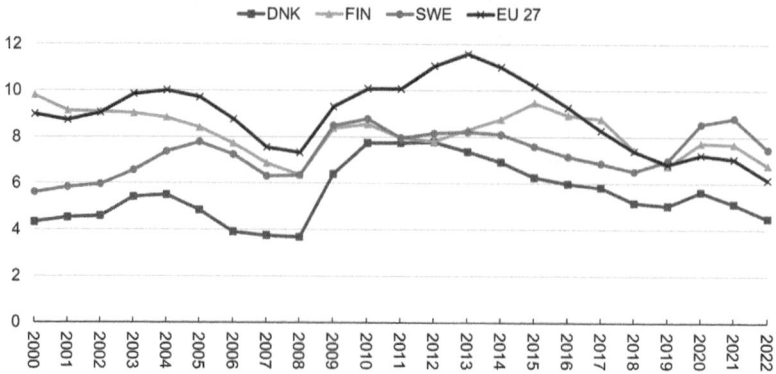

Figure 5.1   *Unemployment rates (total, % of labour force) in Denmark,*
                     Finland, Sweden and EU 27, 2000–2022

rise in unemployment, the impact of the financial crisis was different. Being
a global crisis, this led to decreased exports and a larger fall in GDP than in
the 1990s recession (Kangas, 2019). Employment developed more favourably
than in the earlier recession and, consequently, the gravity of social policy
reforms remained less severe than that of the 1990s (Kangas, 2019). However,
the financial crisis gave rise to yet another wave of structural unemployment.
In 2015, the number of job-seekers was still above 350,000, of which over 31%
was long-term (Saikku, 2018a, p. 107).

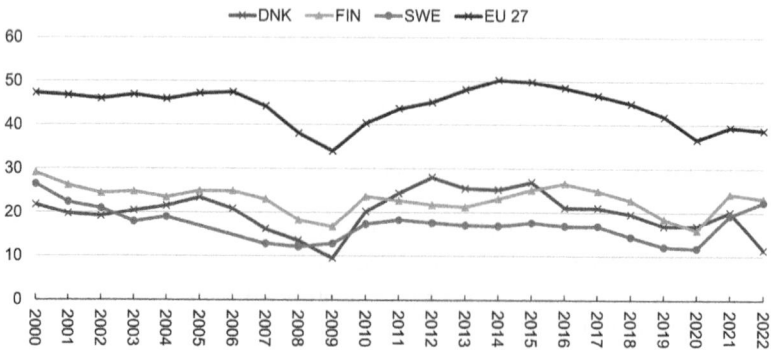

Figure 5.2   *Long-term unemployment rates (total, % of unemployed) in*
                     Denmark, Finland, Sweden and EU 27, 2000–2022

After peaking in the great recession (23.6%), the long-term unemployment trend decreased slowly until 2013. Thereafter, it fluctuated upwards, reaching 26.6% in 2016. Thereafter, the rate began to decline over the next few years, reaching 11.7% in 2020. However, this came to a stop in 2021 (due to the COVID-19 pandemic) when the long-term unemployment increased to 24.2%. As of 2022, Finland's long-term unemployment rate stands at 23.1%. While this rate is lower than the EU average (38.8%), it remains higher than the neighbouring countries, Sweden (22.4%) and Denmark (11.4%).

The activation regime in Finland has aimed to strengthen the incentives for work and inclusion of more extensive groups of inactive people into the labour market. For example, by extending the privileged earned income in unemployment benefits, reducing the length of benefits, the obligation to accept work has been the favourite political solution for activating the inactive and making part-time work more attractive. The largest reform of the 2010s was the re-centralization of the social assistance benefit, which shifted the administration of the last-resort benefit from the municipalities to the central social security institution, Kela. In this, Finland went in the opposite direction to other European countries aiming at decentralization of such benefits. Although not introduced as an activation reform, it affected the financial support and social welfare services of the unemployed greatly (Saikku, 2018b, p. 26) and led to exclusion of some of the most vulnerable in society because of their inability to process the digital claim system (see van Gerven and Ruckenstein, forthcoming).

The dominant trends in the current Finnish activation policy have been *the intensification of employment services* (Saikku, 2018b, p. 25; Karjalainen, 2013, pp. 220–221) and *integration of social security benefits and services* (van Gerven et al., 2022, 2023). As for these goals, activating services are more strongly geared towards long-term unemployment, and hard-to-employ people with often accumulated issues related to skills, health and ability to work. To improve the professional rehabilitation of psychologically deficient clients, a co-service pilot for labour and welfare administration was started in 2002. These *labour force service centres* (TYPs) brought together labour administration, municipalities and the Social Insurance Institution of Finland (Kela), responsible for implementing social insurance benefit (Saikku, 2018b, pp. 24–25). At the same time, access to welfare benefits (labour market subsidy and social assistance) was tightened for these hard-to-employ people. In a 2006 reform of the labour market subsidy (HE 164/2005), the conditionality of this benefit was increased and municipalities were given financial incentives for efficient unemployment reduction. In legislation that came into force in 2010, the age limit for mandatory participation in rehabilitative services was removed (HE 194/2009), broadening its target group to over 25-year-old people as well (van Gerven, 2008).

Another focus activation group has been young people. The focus of activating youth has a similar sound to the European ambitions of getting young people into the labour market. In 2005, the Finnish government launched a "youth guarantee" scheme to reduce youth unemployment and marginalization. Before the reform, the young were in the same service system as the other unemployed: after becoming unemployed an activation plan (on which all activation is based) was drafted for all job-seekers within five months of unemployment, which did not necessarily include any activation measures. After the reform, young job-seekers (aged 17–24) had preparatory counselling within their first month of unemployment; their individualized job search plan had to be drafted within the first three months of their unemployment; and the plan had to include agreed-upon activation measures. This plan was mutually binding; the employment offices had to offer the activation measures, and the young job-seeker had to participate (as non-compliance could result in sanctions) (Hämäläinen, Hämäläinen & Tuomola, 2014, p. 3). The activation of the young has remained strongly on the agenda. In 2013, the government launched a youth guarantee program for people under 25 years old and recently extended it to cover those under 30 as well. They are provided with either a job, an internship, training, a workshop or a rehabilitation place within three months of becoming unemployed. It changed little from the previous (1997) social guarantee for young people program, except in combining the previous programs available for the young and increasing obligations for the public employment offices (te-toimisto) regarding activation of unemployed job-seekers aged under 30 (Lähteenmaa, 2021). A further boost was the "Youth guarantee towards community guarantee", as a part of the Sipilä cabinet's spearhead project. The resources for the guarantee were cut (Lähteenmaa, 2021), but a one-stop service, "Ohjaamo advisory service", was created as low-threshold multidisciplinary service points for people under the age of 30, offering outreach youth work and workshops.

The main element of the activation services remains with the Labour force service centres (TYPs), cemented in legislation in 2015 (Act 1369/2014), which have intensified the activation services at the local level. The TYP law retained the previous division of labour between the municipalities, social security benefit administration (Kela) and labour administration but also strengthened the cooperation between central and local actors in addressing the active inclusion of hard-to-employ people (Saikku, 2018b, p. 25). Supporting unemployed people's *ability to work* became the central theme of the policy and remains so in 2023. The changes were accompanied by tighter integration of benefits and services by adding stricter activation conditions and sanctions and the increasing role of incentives and municipalities' responsibilities towards hard-to-employ people (Karjalainen, 2013, pp. 220–221). An important rationale underlining the TYP law was to provide municipalities with better capabilities in influencing the content of the services provided for long-term unemployed people and to incentivize municipalities in providing services for this target group (Saikku, 2018a, p. 113).

At the same time, the responsibilities of job-seekers have been intensified. Facing the pertinent structural unemployment in the aftermath of the financial crisis, the newly elected centre-right Sipilä cabinet (2015–2017 with the Centre party, the National Coalition party, and the Finns Party/later with Blue Reform) set out a reform process to find a new activation model for the future. To date, consecutive governments have joined the search and have initiated various "activation policy models". Although suggested activation models are seen to be different, they have generally tightened unemployment security conditions, increased activation requirements and introduced sanctions. In retrospect, the Sipilä cabinet's initial and "notorious" Activation Model (HE 124/2017) increased the conditionality of both the basic unemployment benefits and income-related schemes. It institutionalized stringent obligations to accept (any) work or activity, and reductions if activation requirements were not met. The "benefit cutter" – central to the policy – encountered fierce criticism and was valid only between 1.1.2018 and 31.12.2019.[3] In June 2018, the Sipilä Government presented a new version of the policy: the so-called "activation model 2", which stipulated that the unemployed must apply for at least four jobs per month to avoid sanctions. Again, faced with intense criticism, "Model 2" was not even presented to parliament. It did, however, make a (silent) comeback with the Marin cabinet (2019–2023 with Social Democrats, Centre Party, Green League, Left Alliance and Swedish People's party), when they introduced the "Nordic employment service model" (Pohjoismainen työpalvelumalli) (HE 167/2021). With a more fashionable framing, the Nordic activation model greatly resembled the previous activation Model 2 by the Sipilä government: job-seekers had to apply for at least four jobs within a month; the first meeting with PES takes place sooner, and the guidance was intensified. However, there was one significant deviation from the previous "Model 2": sanctions under the Nordic model were considerably smoothened.[4] At the same time, the Marin cabinet blended honey with vinegar as they made a historic and painful removal of the unemployment pension scheme, previously providing an early retirement path by allowing the extension of the days of unemployment allowance for older job-seekers.

To make the Nordic employment service model work, however, requires considerable investment in public (employment) services. The Nordic peculiarity has been the important role of public spending in kind (van Gerven, 2022). This refers to public investments in (universal) public services, including free education and heavily subsidized health care and childcare. In 2022, Finland allocated 29.0% of its GDP to social spending, a significantly higher proportion than in other Nordic countries (Denmark 26.2%, Iceland 20.8,

Norway 20.7% and Sweden 23.7%) and well above the OECD average of 21.1% (OECD, 2023c).

In terms of labour market policy expenditure, however, the tables are turning. In the area of employment, the Finnish social policy invests highly on passive spending, much more than in other Nordic countries. In 2021, for instance, Finland's spending on active labour market policies only accounted for 0.83% of GDP, whereas passive measures were almost twice that, up to 1.54% (OECD, 2023a). The same figures for Denmark are 1.65% and 1.41% and for Sweden 1.05% and 0.74%, respectively (OECD, 2023a).

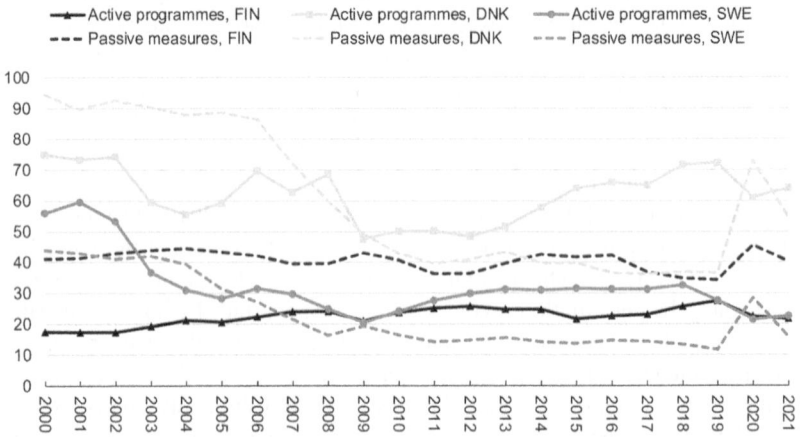

Figure 5.3   *Spending on passive and active labour market policies per unemployed (as a % of GDP per capita) in Denmark, Finland and Sweden, 2000–2021*

Source: LMP spending data (in NC) retrieved from OECD's (2023a) Labour Market Programmes database and deflated to constant (2015) prices using indexes from OECD's (2024) Annual GDP and Components - Expenditure Approach database. Unemployment data retrieved from OECD's (2023d) Annual Labour Force Statistics database, and GDP per capita (at constant 2015 prices) calculated based on OECD's (2023e) Social Expenditure - Reference series.

Figure 5.3 clearly illustrates this point by presenting the public expenditure on active and passive labour market policies per unemployed people (as a percentage of GDP/capita) in Finland, Sweden, and Denmark. Finland is spending less on ALMP's per unemployed than Denmark and Sweden. In contrast, Finland's public spending is primarily geared towards passive measures (unemployment benefits) and the level of spending on active measures has remained reasonably stable over a long period of time, despite the policies on intensifying the employment services as discussed above. The data show a slowly growing trend in spending in active policies, but the difference from Denmark remains considerable, and also from Sweden, where spending on passive measures has been generally declining since 2004 (excluding the recent increase in 2020).

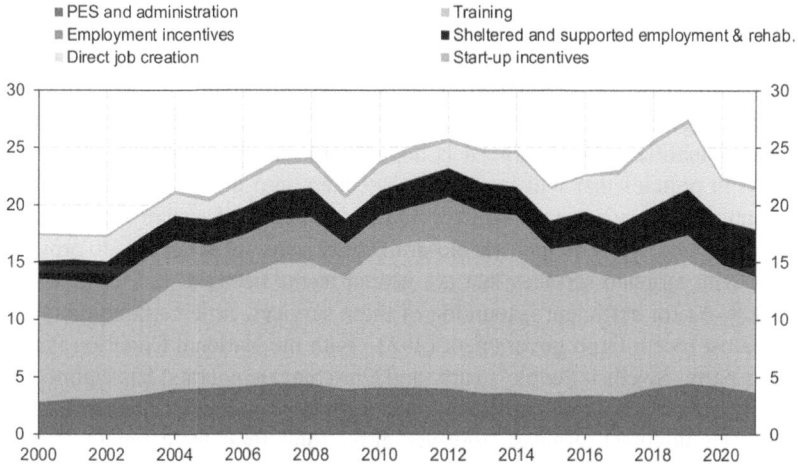

Figure 5.4   *Spending on ALMP programmes per unemployed (as a % of GDP per capita) in Finland, 2000–2021*

Source: LMP spending data (in NC) retrieved from OECD's (2023a) Labour Market Programmes database and deflated to constant (2015) prices using indexes from OECD's (2024) Annual GDP and Components - Expenditure Approach database. Unemployment data retrieved from OECD's (2023d) Annual Labour Force Statistics database, and GDP per capita (at constant 2015 prices) calculated based on OECD's (2023e) Social Expenditure - Reference series.

Figure 5.4 displays ALMP expenditure per unemployed person (as a percentage of GDP/capita) disaggregated by ALMP measures in Finland. The figure shows that most activation investments are made in training services. This increased significantly between 2000 and 2011, but has remained reasonably stable since. As for other types of ALMP measures, spending has not varied much over the period analysed, with the exception of the slight increases in direct job creation and sheltered employment between 2016 and 2019. Overall, the disparity between active and passive spending seems more pronounced in Finland than among its Nordic neighbours, which will make it challenging to achieve the "Nordic model" any time soon.

Much, however, has been changing during the writing of this chapter. As for activation services, important parts of the Finnish activation regime are currently under construction. After a series of local government pilots,[5] from 1.1.2025 onwards, PES services will be permanently transferred from regional PES offices to municipalities (HE 207/2022). In line with the conventional decentralization thesis (Jans et al., 2016), the transfer of PES services to municipalities is expected to bring services closer to customers. With the transfer, employment services, municipal education services and economic services will be the responsibility of the same (local) organizer (TEM, 2023). By restructuring the funding incentive structure for municipalities (shifting the funding and payment responsibility of basic unemployment allowance to municipalities), the reform, it is hoped, will incentivize municipalities to invest in policies that will integrate job-seekers into the labour market. The decentralized services are also expected to support the faster re-employment of job-seekers, as municipalities closer to the citizens are better able to provide them with targeted services that are geared to the needs of the local labour market. As for sufficient resourcing of these services, little certainty obtains. The most recent Orpo government (2023– with the National Coalition Party, Finns party, Swedish People's party and Christian Democrats) has claimed in its "work first" coalition agreement, that sufficient funding will be targeted at public employment services. However, at the same time, the cabinet wants to impose considerable cost containment on the municipalities, shift considerably more responsibility onto the citizens for their own livelihood, and cut the benefit levels directly and indirectly (through freezing of indexation) to make work more attractive than being on welfare. The Orpo cabinet also wants to remove most of the financial incentives to take up part-time work and thus encourage people to find full-time employment (VN, 2023).

5.   THE FUTURE OF THE FINNISH WELFARE STATE

Universalist welfare states are often seen to generate high-quality outcomes, frequently with very high levels of public spending. Finland, wishing to belong to this "AAA"-rated Nordic family of nations, has embraced the Nordic commitment to alleviating social harm by extensive state regulation, yet the country has been lagging behind its Nordic neighbours when compared with macro indicators such as employment rates, productiveness and competitiveness. As extensively discussed above, the Finnish social security and activation services have been undergoing considerable reform during the writing of this chapter. The passiveness of unemployment benefit system and complexity of the various benefit systems have provoked a thorough-going political project in Finland. Since 2020, a parliamentary committee has been working on an overhaul of the passive social security system in Finland. The goal of this reform is to initiate "a more simple and functional system – from a person's point of view – that enables people to combine work and social security in ever[-]changing life situations" (VN, 2020; STM, 2023; Sosiaaliturvakomitea, 2022, p. 7). The current systems demonstrate the main challenges: the complexity of the systems, reconciliation of work and benefits, and integration of benefits and services (VN, 2020).

The process began in 2020 and will continue until 2027, extending (at least) over two cabinet periods. The parliamentary committee, including all political parties, cadres of civil servants and other relevant stakeholders, has recently outlined that the basic benefit system (including the basic unemployment benefit and labour market subsidy) should be unified under one benefit scheme, and better integration of benefits and services must follow. This is hoped to close incentive traps and increase the motivation to seek employment.

As it seems now, the future of Finnish activation policies will follow its set course. It will most likely combine income security (both earnings-related and a broader scope of basic provision) with targeted employment services. As for activation measures, the main focus has been on human capital investments, with strong pro-labour market orientation incorporating more (targeted) responsibilities to seek employment and enhance an individual's own employability. The famous experiment on universal basic income between 2017 and 2018 was an interesting time in the history of Finnish social security that attracted great attention worldwide because of its nationwide, controlled, randomized trial set-up (Kangas et al., 2021). The results, showing increased well-being but only a modest increase in employment, however, did not convince the political decision-makers of the desirability of a non-conditional benefit scheme (Kangas, 2021). Other experiments (such as negative income tax trials, participation income) have been under discussion, but no political mandate has been given yet. What is certain, however, is that the new Finnish social policy paradigm will centre on conditional benefit provision, where establishing a right to social protection and services requires a personal meeting or some level of politically accepted social risk (unemployment, illness, etc.). In this sense, political ideals of universalism are not fully compatible with these aspirations. But we will conclude on this in the final section.

The Finnish labour market policy has fared reasonably well at times of crisis, including the financial crisis as well as the COVID-19 pandemic in the 2020s. Massive investments in the economy, with a combination of flexibility for employers and security for workers, led to successful buffering against restriction measures and their negative outcomes during the pandemic (Greve at al., 2021). The unemployment rates naturally peaked during the pandemic, and were particularly high among the young and migrant populations. Unemployment after COVID-19 decreased rapidly and the employment rate in

2022 was at an all-time high (74.5% in October) (Statistics Finland, 2023), as was the number of job vacancies (TEM, 2022). The increase in employment rates has been explained by the integration of people outside of employment, whereas the pertinent unemployment rates indicate signs of structural unemployment and a mismatch between labour market demand and supply from the pool of job-seekers (Pylkkänen, 2022; Mähönen, Alatalo & Ylikännö, 2022). In the extension of exceptionally high inflation (see, e.g., Greve et al., 2023), however, employment has been decreasing in 2023 and the prospects of an economic downturn in a rapidly ageing society have daunting connotations. The activation regime will be put to the test again.

6.   CONCLUSION

This chapter has explored the interplay between activation policies and Nordic universalism, focusing on Finland. It set out to investigate *how the Finnish activation policy has been developed in recent decades and how far it still adheres to the Nordic values of universalism.*

The chapter delves into the historical evolution of activation policies in Finland between 1990 and 2023, outlining the current structure of unemployment benefit schemes and their consequences. Derived from the findings from the process of tracing of activation policies and statistical information, it appears that Finland retains elements of universalism by offering various unemployment schemes for different circumstances, emphasizing inclusiveness. However, this inclusivity coexists with targeting, raising questions about equality and uniformity. Unemployment schemes for different situations (from basic security to earnings-related and minimum assistance) still suggest a strong reliance on inclusiveness inherent in universalism. The plans to simplify the benefit system also follow the intention to secure basic protection in addition to earnings-related and means-tested benefit schemes. At the same time, the systems cater to various groups of the unemployed and come with very different entitlements and benefits geared to these systems. We see strong targeting traits within universalism (see also Saikkonen & Ylikännö, 2020) and the plurality of income protection system structures (also Johansson & Hvinden, 2007), which question the actualization of equality and uniformity, integral elements of universalism.

In this sense, then, Finland's unemployment benefit system reflects the welfare state's path-dependent trajectory, aiming to include diverse societal groups. The Finnish activation may adhere to the Rawlsian approach by recognizing the stratification in society and aiming to cover the most vulnerable via broad basic coverage. However, it provides stronger protection to those with earnings-related schemes and weaker support to those reliant on basic benefits. The analysis underscores the fundamental tension between universalism and activation policies, emphasizing individual responsibilities over collective rights, potentially exacerbating existing inequalities. Activation services in Finland emphasize equality in principle but often not in practice, as benefit systems shape services available for the unemployed. Abundant research has shown that the benefit systems in Finland strongly direct the repertoire of services available to the unemployed (van Gerven et al., 2022). The indicators above show how social spending on active policies per unemployed has not fluctuated much, not even during the worst economic period. This suggests that activation services have little ability to respond to increasing demands for multifaceted activation. Neither is the heavier investment in training, as the disaggregation of ALMP spending shows, likely to benefit those closer to the labour market rather than meet the needs of people at its margins, particularly those at greater distance from the labour market who particularly need more holistic services addressing skills to manage their everyday lives. The reality of street-level delivery of activation is that it faces ever more complex problems, and this is not reflected in the investments in active measures geared to them. A recent OECD (2020) report has shown that the majority of the long-term unemployed in Finland have multiple barriers to unemployment, making the need for more tailored activation programs high. This would suggest that the need for "universal" or inclusive activation is only growing, but macro-indicators suggest that the institutional grounds for this do not appear to be very solid.

The analysis shows that universalism is a social policy principle that is not always easily reconciled within activation policy. The weakest point might be the attention of activation measures to individual responsibilities instead of social (collective) rights. Targeting within universalism would require the protection of the most vulnerable. At least based on the evidence presented above, it seems likely that targeting active measures to those better off strengthens the "Matthew effect" (Bonoli, 2022), rather protecting the vulnerable.

NOTES

1. People of 18–24 years of age must have applied for study.
2. From 1998, individual job-search plans were introduced as a part of a public employment administration reform (Act 1353/1997). The essence of this reform was to increase activation efforts on job search in the private sector by granting the unemployed rights and obligations to fixed-term interviews and job-search plans (Lehtonen, 2001, p. 110; Saikku 2018b, p. 23; Kautto, 2004, p. 20).
3. Aiming to encourage activation of the unemployed, it decreased the unemployment duration periods and increased the employment rate. The model furthermore stipulated that the unemployed must meet an "activity

condition" to avoid the curtailment of benefits. This condition could be met by spending 18 hours in paid employment, earning at least €24 as a self-employed person or participating in employment-promoting services, training or education at the employment office for five days within three months after becoming unemployed. Failure to achieve these criteria led to a 4.65% reduction in unemployed people's benefit for the next three months.

4.   The first deviation from the job search obligation leads to a notification, which doesn't affect benefits. Repeated negligence leads to termination of the benefit for seven days, after which the benefit is suspended for 14 days. After this the job-seekers lose the right to the unemployment benefit until further notice. If the beneficiaries do not accept a job (without reasonable grounds), the benefit will be suspended for 45 days.

5.   The Katainen I cabinet had already launched local government pilots on employment, carried out between 2012 and 2015. The succeeding Sipilä government continued this experimentation with a trial between 2017 and 2018 (Act 505/2017). With the Marin cabinet, a third municipal trial was launched in 2020 (HE 87/2020), which was later extended until 31.12.2024 (HE 17/2022).

REFERENCES

Act 1353/1997. Laki työvoimapalvelulain muuttamisesta [Act on changing the public employment service]. Adopted in Helsinki on 30 December 1997. https://finlex.fi/fi/laki/alkup/1997/19971353

Act 1369/2014. Laki työllistymistä edistävästä monialaisesta yhteispalvelusta [Act on cross-sectoral joint service promoting employment]. Adopted in Helsinki on 30 December 2014. https://www.finlex.fi/fi/laki/alkup/2014/20141369

Act 505/2017. Laki julkisten tysvoima- ja yrityspalveluiden alueellista tarjoamista ja työelämäkokeilua koskevasta kokeilusta [Act on public employment and business services and local government pilots on employment]. Adopted in Helsinki on 10 July 2017. https://www.finlex.fi/fi/laki/alkup/2017/20170505

Andersen, J. G. (2012). Universalization and de-universalization of unemployment protection in Denmark and Sweden. In Anttonen, A., Häikiö, L., Stefánsson, K., & Sipilä, J. (eds.), *Welfare state, universalism and diversity*, Cheltenham, UK and Northampton, MA, USA: Edward Elgar Publishing, pp. 162–186.

Anttonen, A., Häikiö, L., Stefánsson, K., & Sipilä, J. (eds.) (2012). *Welfare state, universalism and diversity*. Cheltenham, UK and Northampton, MA, USA: Edward Elgar Publishing.

Bonoli, G. (2010). The political economy of active labour-market policy. *Politics & Society*, 38(4), pp. 435–457.

Bonoli, G. (2022). Research on active social policy. In Nelson, K., Nieuwenhuis, R., & Yerkes, M. (eds.), *Social policy in changing European societies*. Cheltenham, UK and Northampton, MA, USA: Edward Elgar Publishing, pp. 120–134.

Esping-Andersen, G. (1990). *The three worlds of welfare capitalism*. Princeton, NJ: Princeton University Press.

Gould, R., & Saurama, L. (2004). From early exit culture to the policy of active ageing: The case of Finland. In de Vroom, B., & Øverbye, E. (eds.), *Ageing and the transition to retirement*. Abingdon: Routledge, pp. 67–92.

Greve, B., Blomgvist, P., Hvinden B., & van Gerven, M. (2021). Nordic welfare states – still standing or changed by the COVID-19 crisis? *Social Policy and Administration* (special issue: *Social Policy in the Face of a Global Pandemic: Policy Responses to the COVID19 Crisis*), eds. Daniel Béland, Rod Hick, Amilcar Moreira, Peter Whiteford, & Bea Cantillon), 55(2), pp. 295–311. https://doi.org/10.1111/spol.12675

Greve, B., Harsløf, I., Van Gerven, M., Nieuwenhuis, R., & Strigén, J. (2023). How have the Nordic welfare states responded to the unexpected increase in inflation? *Social Policy and Society*, pp. 1–13. doi:10.1017/S1474746423000313.

Hämäläinen, K., Hämäläinen, U., & Tuomala, J. (2014). The labour market impacts of a youth guarantee: Lessons for Europe? VATT Working Papers 60. Available at: https://www.doria.fi/bitstream/handle/10024/148799/wp60.pdf?sequence=1&isAllowed=y.

HE 164/2005 vp (Parliament of Finland). Hallituksen esitys eduskunnalle laiksi julkisesta työvoimapalvelusta annetun lain muuttamisesta ja eräiksi siihen liittyviksi laeiksi [Bill to Change the Act on Public Employment Services and Certain Related Laws]. Helsinki: Parliament of Finland. https://www.eduskunta.fi/FI/Vaski/sivut/trip.aspx?triptype=ValtiopaivaAsiat&docid=he+167/2005.

HE 194/2009 vp (Parliament of Finland). Hallituksen esitys eduskunnalle laeiksi kuntouttavasta työtoiminnasta annetun lain 2 ja 10 §:n, työttömyysturvalain 8 luvun 6 §:n ja toimeentulotuesta annetun lain 10 ja 10 a §:n muuttamisesta [Bill on Rehabilitative Work Act and on Changing the Unemployment Security Act and the Social Assistance Act]. Helsinki: Parliament of Finland. https://www.eduskunta.fi/FI/Vaski/sivut/trip.aspx?triptype=ValtiopaivaAsiat&docid=he+194/2009

HE 124/2017 vp (Parliament of Finland). Hallituksen esitys eduskunnalle laeiksi työttömyysturvalain ja eräiden muiden lakien muuttamisesta [Bill on changing the Unemployment Security Act and Related Acts]. Helsinki: Parliament of Finland. https://www.eduskunta.fi/FI/vaski/KasittelytiedotValtiopaivaasia/Sivut/HE_124+2017.aspx

HE 87/2020 vp (Parliament of Finland). Hallituksen esitys eduskunnalle työllisyyden edistämisen kuntakokeilusta [Bill on Local Government Pilots on Employment]. Helsinki: Parliament of Finland. https://www.eduskunta.fi/FI/vaski/KasittelytiedotValtiopaivaasia/Sivut/HE_87+2020.aspx

HE 167/2021 vp (Parliament of Finland). Hallituksen esitys eduskunnalle työnhakijan palveluprosessin ja eräiden työttömyysetuuden saamisen edellytysten uudistamista koskevaksi lainsäädännöksi [Bill on Reforming Unemployed Job-seeker's Service Process and Certain Eligbility Criteria for Unemployment Benefits]: Parliament of Finland. https://www.eduskunta.fi/FI/vaski/KasittelytiedotValtiopaivaasia/Sivut/HE_167+2021.aspx

HE 17/2022 vp (Parliament of Finland). Hallituksen esitys eduskunnalle työllisyyden edistämisen kuntakokeilun voimassaolon jatkamista koskevaksi lainsäädännöksi [Bill to Continue Local Government Pilots on Employment]. Helsinki: Parliament of Finland. https://www.eduskunta.fi/FI/vaski/KasittelytiedotValtiopaivaasia/Sivut/HE_17+2022.aspx

HE 207/2022 vp (Parliament of Finland). Hallituksen esitys eduskunnalle julkisten työvoima- ja yrityspalveluiden uudelleen järjestämistä koskevaksi lainsäädännöksi [Bill on Reorganizing Public Employment and Business Services]. Helsinki:

Parliament of Finland. https:// www .eduskunta .fi/ FI/ vaski/ K asittelyti edotValtio paivaasia/Sivut/HE_207+2022.aspx

Jacques, O., & Noël, A. (2018). The case for welfare state universalism, or the lasting relevance of the paradox of redistribution. *Journal of European Social Policy*, 28(1), pp. 70–85.

Jans, W., Denters, B., Need, A., & Van Gerven, M. (2016). Mandatory innovation in a decentralised system: The adoption of an e-government innovation in Dutch municipalities. *Acta Politica*, 51, pp. 36–60.

Johansson, H., & Hvinden, B. (2007). Re-activating the Nordic welfare states: Do we find a distinct universalistic model? *International Journal of Sociology and Social Policy*, 27 (7/8), pp. 334–346.

Julkunen, R. (2001). *Suunnanmuutos: 1990-luvun sosiaalipoliittinen reformi Suomessa*. Vastapaino: Tampere.

Julkunen, R. (2013). Aktivointipolitiikka hyvinvointivaltion paradigman muutoksena. In Karjalainen, V., & Keskitalo, E. (eds.), *Kaikki työuralle! Työttömien aktiivipolitiikkaa Suomessa*. THL: Tampere, pp. 22–44.

Kalela, J., Kiander, J., Kivikuru, U., Loikkanen, H. A., & Simpura, J. (2001). Down from the heavens, up from the ashes. VATT 27:6. Helsinki.

Kangas, O. (2019). Finland: From the Deep Crisis of the 1990s to the Great Recession. In Ólaffson, S., Daly, M., Kangas, O., & Palme, J. (eds.), *Welfare and the Great Recession: A comparative study*. Oxford, 2019; online edition, Oxford Academic, 21 February 2019, https://doi.org/10.1093/oso/9780198830962.001.0001.

Kangas, O. (2021). The feasibility of universal basic income. In Kangas, O., Jauhiainen, S., Simanainen, M., & Ylikännö, M. (eds.), *Experimenting with Unconditional Basic Income*. Cheltenham, UK and Northampton, MA, USA: Edward Elgar Publishing, pp. 187–196.

Kangas, O., & Saloniemi, A. (2013). *Historical making, present and future challenges for the Nordic welfare state model in Finland*. Oslo: Fafo.

Kangas, O., Jauhiainen, S., Simanainen, M., & Ylikännö, M. (eds.) (2021). *Experimenting with Unconditional Basic Income lessons from the Finnish BI experiment 2017–2018*. Cheltenham, UK and Northampton, MA, USA: Edward Elgar Publishing.

Karjalainen, V. (2013). Aktiivipolitiikan ajankohtaisuus. In Karjalainen, V., & Keskitalo, E. (eds.), *Kaikki työuralle!: Työttömien aktiivipolitiikkaa Suomessa*. Tampere: THL.

Kautto, M. (2004). Sosiaaliturvalta työhön: suomalaisen hyvinvointivaltion reformi. *Yhteiskuntapolitiikka*, 69, pp. 11–30.

Kela (2023). Perusosan määrä 2023. www.Kela.fi.

Kildal, N., & Kuhnle, S. (eds.) (2005). *Normative foundations of the welfare state*. New York: Routledge.

Kuhnle, S. (2011). International modelling in the making of the Nordic social security system. In Kettunen, P., & Petersen, K. (eds.), *Beyond welfare state models: Transnational historical perspectives on social policy*. Cheltenham, UK and Northampton, MA, USA: Edward Elgar Publishing, pp. 65–81.

Kuivalainen, S., & Niemelä, M. (2010). From universalism to selectivism: The ideational turn of the anti-poverty policies in Finland. *Journal of European Social Policy*, 20(3), pp. 263–276.

Lähteenmaa, J. (2021). Nuorten työttömien orientaatiot aktivointitoimenpiteissä. *Nuorisotutkimus*, 39(1), pp. 37–57.

Lehtonen, H., Aho, S., Peltola, J., & Renvall, M. (2001). Did the crisis change the Welfare State in Finland? In Kalela, J., Kiander, J., Kivikuru, U., Loikkanen, H. A., & Simpura, J. (eds.), *Down from the heavens, up from the ashes.* VATT 27:6. Helsinki 2001, pp. 102–129.

Mähönen, E., Alatalo, J., & Ylikännö, M. (2022). Työ- ja elinkeinoministeriön lyhyen aikavälin työmarkkinaennuste, syksy 2022. *TEM analyyseja* 111/2022. https://julkaisut.valtioneuvosto.fi/bitstream/handle/10024/164434/TEM%20ty%C3%B6markkinaennuste%20syksy%202022%20FINAL.pdf.

Missoc (2022). Mutual Information System on Social Protection database. https://www.missoc.org/missoc-database/.

OECD (2020). Faces of joblessness in Finland: A people-centred perspective on employment barriers and policies. https://www.oecd.org/els/soc/OECD-2020-FoJ-Finland.pdf.

OECD (2023a). Labour market programmes: expenditure and participants, OECD Employment and Labour Market Statistics (database), https://doi.org/10.1787/data-00312-en.

OECD (2023b). Long-term unemployment rate (indicator), doi: 10.1787/76471ad5-en

OECD (2023c). Social expenditure: Aggregated data, OECD Social and Welfare Statistics (database), https://doi.org/10.1787/data-00166-en

OECD (2023d). Labour Force Statistics: Summary tables, OECD Employment and Labour Market Statistics (database), https://doi.org/10.1787/data-00286-en

OECD (2023e). Social Expenditure: Reference series (Edition 2023), OECD Social and Welfare Statistics (database), https://doi.org/10.1787/c4f50f0b-en

OECD (2024). Annual GDP and components - expenditure approach (database), https://stats.oecd.org/Index.aspx?DataSetCode=SNA_TABLE1

Pylkkänen, E. (2022). Työmarkkinat koronakriisissä. *Kansantaloudellinen aikakausikirja*, 2, pp. 142–150.

Rawls, J. (1971). *A theory of justice.* Cambridge, MA: Harvard University Press.

Saikkonen, P., & Ylikännö, M. (2020). Is there room for targeting within universalism? Finnish social assistance recipients as social citizens. *Social Inclusion*, 8(1), pp. 145–154.

Saikku, P. (2018a). Valtion ja kuntien vastuunjako pitkäaikaistyöttöminen aktivoinnissa: Sisällönanalyysi hallitusohjelmista ja hallituksen esityksistä vuosina 1995–2015. *Janus Sosiaalipolitiikan ja sosiaalityön tutkimuksen aikakauslehti*, 26(2), 104–122.

Saikku, P. (2018b). Hallinnan rajoilla: Monialainen koordinaatio vaikeasti työllistyvien työllistymisen edistämisessä. Valtiotieteellisen tiedekunnan julkaisuja. Helsinki University.

Simpura, J., Blomster, P., Heikkilä, M., Häkkinen, U., Kautto, M., Keskimäki, I., Lehto, J., Rastas, M., Rissanen., P., & Valtonen, H. (2001). The survival of the Finnish health care and social service system during the economic depression of the 1990s. In: Kalela, J., Kiander, J., Kivikuru, U., Loikkanen, H. A., & Simpura, J. (eds.), *Down from the heavens, up from the ashes.* VATT 27:6. Helsinki 2001, pp. 102–129.

Sosiaaliturvakomitea (2022). Palvelujen ja etuuksien yhteensovittaminen: Sosiaaliturvakomitean ongelmaraportti 4/2022. http://urn.fi/URN:ISBN:978-952-00-8448-6.

Statistics Finland (2023). Key indicators of the Labour Force Survey and their seasonal adjusted series and trends adjusted for random and seasonal variation by month and information, Labour force survey (database). https://www.stat.fi/en/statistics/tyti.

STM (2023). Sosiaaliturvauudistus. https://stm.fi/sosiaaliturvauudistus.

TEM (2022). Työllisyyskatsaus. Maaliskuu 2022. https://julkaisut.valtioneuvosto.fi/ bitstream/handle/10024/164034/TKAT_Maalis_2022.pdf.

TEM (2023).TE-palvelut 2024 uudistus. https://tem.fi/te-palvelut-2024-uudistus.

van Gerven, M. (2008). *The broad tracks of path dependent benefit reforms: A longitudinal study of social benefit reforms in three European countries, 1980–2006.* Vammala: KELA.

van Gerven, M. (2022). Nordic welfare states: Up to challenge? In Greve, B. (ed.), *De Gruyter handbook of contemporary welfare states*, pp. 47–65. https://doi.org/10 .1515/9783110721768-004

van Gerven, M., Mesiäislehto, M., Saikku, P., Ollongvist, J., Malava, T., & Tuominen, N. (2022). *Eri poluilla työllisyyteen. Suomen sosiaaliturvajärjestelmän erityispiirteet ja ongelmakohdat kansainvälisessä vertailussa. Valtioneuvoston selvitys- ja tutkimustoiminnan julkaisusarja,* 2022:51. http://urn.fi/URN:ISBN:978-952-383 -369-2

van Gerven, M., Malava, T., Saikku, P., & Mesiäislehto, M. (2023). Towards a new era in the governance of integrated activation: A systematic review of the literature on the governance of welfare benefits and employment-related services in Europe (2010–21). *Social Policy & Administration*, pp. 1–15. https://doi.org/10.1111/spol .12960

van Gerven, M. & Ruckenstein, M. (forthcoming). The unhappy marriage of standardization and discretion: the conflicting logic of digital welfare administration and activation in Finland. *Journal of European Social Policy.*

VN (2020). "Sosiaaliturvan uudistamisessa keskeistä on sosiaalinen oikeudenmukaisuus ja toimeentulon turvaaminen sosiaalisten riskien kohdatessa". https:// valtioneuvosto.fi/ marinin -hallitus/ hallitusohjelma/ sosiaaliturvan -uudistaminen (accessed on 13.2.2023).

VN (2023). Vahva ja välittävä Suomi Pääministeri Petteri Orpon hallituksen ohjelma 20.6.2023. https://julkaisut.valtioneuvosto.fi/handle/10024/165042.

Ylikännö, M. (2011). Vuoden 2006 työmarkkinauudistus – aktivointia Arkadianmäeltä. In Niemelä, M., & Saari, J. (eds.), *Politiikan polut ja hyvinvointivaltion muutos.* Tampere: Kela, pp. 206–231.

6. An activation U-turn? From pro-market employment orientation to investment in human capital

Werner Eichhorst and Michaela Schulze

INTRODUCTION

Labour market policy has a volatile history in Germany. At the end of the 1990s and entering the early 2000s, the labour market was characterized by medium employment rates and high unemployment. Both the public employment service and many instruments of active labour market policy were estimated as costly, inefficient and ineffective. In that regard Germany has often been described as providing "welfare without work" (Esping-Andersen, 1998) and labelled "kranker Mann Europas" ("the sick man of the Euro") (*The Economist*, 1999). The German system has been criticized in terms of generating a circle of high labour costs deriving from benefits that are based on payroll-tax financing and high unemployment. Due to several labour market policy reforms and a prospering economic environment, the German labour market changed fundamentally. This is often attributed to a successful employment and labour market policy, which is true to the extent that several reforms in the fields of active and passive labour market policies were adopted that modified the functioning of the labour market during the early to mid-2000s.

In common with many other countries, Germany has embarked upon an activation path (Bonoli, 2010). This was the main impact of the unprecedented structural changes implemented via the so-called Hartz reforms between 2003 and 2005. Stricter eligibility criteria, sanctions, a stronger emphasis on reciprocity and the willingness to take a job became central elements of active labour market policy. Moreover, qualification and training were reformed massively and geared towards faster labour market integration. During the early activation years, unemployed persons and recipients of social assistance were seen as the main focus group of activation. Several reforms that aimed at deregulation and decentralization of collective bargaining are clearly visible and potentially at least as important (Dustmann et al., 2014). However, since the end of the 2010s, a remarkable turn towards human capital investment is traceable for the employed and the unemployed.

In his often-cited article, Bonoli (2010) distinguishes between four types of active labour market policies (ALMPs). He differentiates them on the basis of two criteria: the pro-market employment orientation of policy and the emphasis on human capital investment. First, there is *incentive reinforcement*, which aims at strengthening incentives to work for those receiving benefits by cutting benefits' duration or amount. Benefits are made conditional, and sanctions are used systematically. Here pro-market employment orientations are quite strong, whereas investment in human capital has no priority (Bonoli, 2010: 440). The second is *employment assistance*, a type of ALMP that is oriented towards removing barriers to labour market integration and participation. Bonoli argues that counselling and job subsidies, job placement, and job search programs might contribute to discharge into the labour market. With regard to this type, pro-market employment orientation is strong too. Investment in human capital is weak here (Bonoli, 2010: 440f.). *Occupation*, the third type of ALMP, is generally more directed towards keeping unemployed persons engaged, to avoid a reduction of human capital. Job creation and work experience programs in the public or non-profit sector are common. As a consequence, both pro-market employment orientation and investment in human capital are weak (Bonoli, 2010: 441). Finally, *upskilling*, as the fourth type of ALMP, provides a job-related vocational training for unemployed persons. Here, both pro-market employment orientation and investment in human capital are strong (Bonoli, 2010: 441).

Even though Bonoli argues that the four types are ideal types, we can see elements of them in Germany. As mentioned above, Germany was long described as a welfare state without work. But the country has also managed to reduce unemployment enormously, and the perception has changed to a model that combines activation and a rather favourable economic development. Moreover, a noticeable increase of employment is visible. The aim of this chapter is to show what role activation policies have played over this period and to what extent activation policies were remodelled over time, mirroring also the perceived pressure emerging on the labour market. We will show the development of activation and argue that there was a strong activation path until the end of the 2010s, whereas newer reforms indicate a stronger orientation towards investment in human capital. We see this as an activation U-turn. We also evaluate the configuration of active labour market policies in relation to Bonoli's types of active labour market policy. And finally, we ask what future perspectives are discussed with regards to activation in Germany.

To address the main interests of the chapter, we proceed as follows. In the first section, we briefly introduce the institutional settings of activation, which can be characterized as fragmented governance. Next, the German path to activation is outlined. This is complemented in the section that follows, in which we analyse the developments of German activation from the early 2000s to the late 2010s in more detail. We then examine the change from activation to an approach more oriented towards investment in human capital. Subsequently we assess the German activation path, before taking a look at the Covid-19 pandemic and the implications for active labour market policies. Finally, implications and current discussions in Germany are considered, by way of conclusion.

INSTITUTIONAL SETTINGS OF ACTIVATION IN GERMANY: FRAGMENTED GOVERNANCE

The institutional settings of activation in Germany are rather complex and can best be described as fragmented governance (Dingeldey, 2011). It is essential to see that in the Bismarckian tradition, unemployment insurance is a crucial cornerstone for social protection of the core labour force, in particular those with long-lasting employment relationships. Traditionally, unemployment insurance provides a temporary income-related benefit that helps stabilize not only individual income after a job loss (for some time), but also occupation-specific human capital (Estevez-Abe et al., 2001). This is fundamentally different from the second tier of means-tested social assistance (or minimum income) that is mainly focused on poverty relief or avoidance. In that sense, the German model is dual to the extent that unemployment insurance is part of the protective institutions constituting standard employment relationships, while assistance is more relevant for those who are not (fully) integrated into the core of the German labour market. Over time, this dual setting has been recalibrated, but activation policies and governance reforms have mostly addressed the second tier, mirroring the strong politico-economic support to maintain a well-protected core that, however, has become more flexible internally, combining long-lasting employment with flexible wages and working time, while employment protection and unemployment insurance remained virtually unaffected (Eichhorst and Marx, 2011).

Before the activation turn, Germany had a three-tier benefit system for the unemployed and the poor. The unemployment insurance system covered all unemployed persons who were close to the labour market (Arbeitslosengeld) and was mainly financed by contributions of the employed and their employers. Furthermore, there were two tiers for the long-term unemployed. Unemployment assistance (Arbeitslosenhilfe) was a benefit that was paid in relation to the prior income in case unemployment insurance benefits expired. In contrast to the unemployment insurance, it was means tested and financed by taxes. Finally, social assistance (Sozialhilfe) aimed at preventing poverty. It was tax financed, administered by the municipalities and means tested. With regards to organizational responsibilities, in terms of benefit payments for all three tiers, the system could be characterized as one of multi-level governance (Dingeldey, 2011: 62). The activation reforms aimed at a "homogenization of the institutional structures, namely the improvement of inter-agency cooperation and coordination" (ibid.). However, instead of homogenization, more fragmented governance structures – in some respects – were the results of the activation reforms. The Hartz commission had suggested a one-stop shop for all jobseekers, but the reforms have created a three-tier system (public employment services, Arbeitsgemeinschaften (ARGEn) and Optionskommunen) (Konle-Seidl et al., 2007: 38).

Responsibilities for the insured unemployed are determined by the Third Book of the Social Code (SGB III). For this group, the Bundesagentur für Arbeit (Federal Employment Agency) is responsible for the administration of unemployment insurance benefits and for the implementation of related ALMP and activation policies. This first tier has proven to be relatively stable over time, despite tighter job search requirements and changes in benefit duration, in particular for older unemployed persons. As unemployment and social assistance schemes had been merged with the Hartz reforms, as laid down in the Second Book of the Social Code (SGB II), governance structures had to be reorganized. This has led to a dual model resulting from a political compromise. On the one hand, in most districts, joint agencies of the local branches of the Federal Employment Agency and (former) municipal social assistance administration were established (so-called "Arbeitsgemeinschaften"). In some districts, no joint agency of the Public Employment Service (PES) and municipal offices were created, but the municipalities took over the full responsibility of labour market integration and complementary social services for the long-term unemployed ("Optionskommunen"). Both joint agencies and municipal offices represented organizational bodies responsible for the long-term unemployed. However, this new mixed administration caused a more complex governance structure. With a decision of the Federal Constitutional Court (2007), mixed responsibilities were heavily criticized as a violation of the constitutionally guaranteed autonomy of the municipalities. As a result, the two types of models survived with new names: "gemeinsame Einrichtungen" (gE) as a joint organization of PES and the municipalities, and "zugelassene kommunale Träger" (zkT) as an autonomous organization independent from the PES. Even though complexity of governance has not been reduced, a clear separation of tasks and structures is visible now, and this has become much less contested and controversial.

THE PATH TO ACTIVATION: OVERCOMING THE PASSIVE CHARACTER

This section summarizes the historical development of German active labour market policy. We argue that activation was not an essential part of the early phases of active labour market policy. While certain instruments have existed for a long time, some principles of activation were only implemented more coherently later on.

The Passive Character of the German System

Going back in time, the main setting was defined in the late 1960s with a massive modernization and systematization of active labour market policies under the AFG ("Arbeitsförderungsgesetz", Act on the Promotion of Employment). The main aim was to ensure full employment and a systematic skill adjustment in a prosperous era. The AFG also brought about a modernization of the public employment service that was rebaptised to "Bundesanstalt für Arbeit" (Weishaupt, 2019: 673). From that period on, the three pillars of German labour market policy have been defined clearly: unemployment insurance, employment services and active labour market policy. This came along with the advancement of vocational training, training (Fortbildung) and retraining (Umschulung). The main aim was to foster occupational advancement and avoid poorly paid jobs (Dingeldey, 2020: 39). Vocational (re)training was the main field of activity of the Bundesagentur für Arbeit (Federal Employment Agency). However, instruments of the AFG should be used not only to reduce unemployment but also to avoid unemployment and a shortage of skilled labour, a topic that was deemed relevant in an era of virtually full employment. The main element was the right to vocational training for the unemployed and also for the employed (ibid.).

However, this model came under intense pressure after the mid-1970s, with increasing unemployment, mediocre employment and particular problems in creating jobs in the post-industrial setting, not least in the private service sector (Manow and Seils, 2000). In this context, ALMPs were rather used in a "passive" way to avoid open unemployment, in line with other policies to reduce labour supply such as early retirement. However, trying to contain registered unemployment was not sustainable in the long run. It tended to erode the fiscal base of the welfare state, as in the social insurance system of the German Bismarckian welfare state, resulting in massively rising social insurance contribution rates. After reunification in the 1990s, this became particularly visible on the basis of its heavy reliance on large-scale public job creation, short-time work or training programmes. Hence, one could argue that traditional ALMP, such as direct job creation and large-scale training, including transfer instruments and massive short-time work, had a rather "passive orientation" and was not able to stimulate (sustainable) job creation in phases of massive economic restructuring and high unemployment – quite in contrast to the original layout and objectives. Unemployment was a major friction. It is obvious from the data on expenditure on passive measures in Table 6.1, that unemployment (see also Figure 6.1) was a lasting problem in the German context. Furthermore, there was no systematic activation in unemployment insurance, unemployment assistance and social assistance at the time, leaving the impression that Germany was a laggard with regard to the activation turn in Europe, i.e. relative to countries such as Denmark, Finland, Sweden and the UK. This is also visible in Table 6.1 and is consistent with the results of previous research (Aust and Arriba, 2005; Caliendo and Steiner, 2005). Spending for passive measures of ALMP is always higher than spending for active measures.

Table 6.1   *Development of spending for active and passive measures of labour market policies 1985–2020 (as a percentage of GDP)*

	1985	1990	1995	2000	2005	2010	2015	2020
Active programmes	0.56	0.77	1.16	1.25	1.12	0.90	0.64	0.60
Active measures	0.39	0.59	0.96	1.02	0.81	0.52	0.28	0.28
Passive measures	1.24	0.97	2.25	1.81	1.93	1.29	0.88	1.30

Source: OECD (2023).

Table 6.1 differentiates between active programmes and active measures. Active programmes can be described as the subordinate category, as they combine spending for PES and administration, and programmes of activation (active measures). Overall spending for active programmes has been decreasing continuously since 2000. However, the spread between active programmes and measures is somehow in conflict with the activation turn. Spending for PES and administration has been rising since the turn of the century, whereas spending for active measures declined from 1.02 percent in 2000 to 0.28 percent in 2020. It is clear that Germany prioritized spending for administration instead of activation. Due to the fact that a massive reorganization of public employment service was accompanied by the activation path, this result is rather unsurprising. Spending for passive measures includes spending for unemployment benefits, unemployment insurance, unemployment assistance, partial unemployment benefits and early retirement. After reunification we see an immense increase of spending for passive measures. That goes along with our description of the activation path. Before the implementation of the Hartz reforms, spending declined and increased after the activation turn for a short time. Afterwards, over time, we see a continuous decline in spending, which is consistent with our argumentation according to the development of employment and unemployment. As the coronavirus broke out, in 2019, Germany spent 0.72 percent of GDP on passive measures.

The decline in spending may be discerned across all three categories. This development, on first sight, does not fit with our argumentation concerning the rising importance of the investment in human capital. Also, according to Bonoli, a stronger orientation towards upskilling is not obvious. However, spending data are often criticized as not convincing, as they are unable to show developments properly. It is obvious that spending for passive measures (e.g., unemployment benefits) has increased in the times after reunification. At this time, Germany was faced with high labour costs deriving from benefits that are based on payroll-tax financing and high unemployment. Moreover, the initial activation turn is also obvious from the spending for active measures and programmes. The Job-AQTIV-Gesetz, the following paradigmatic Hartz reforms and subsequent activation programmes find their expression in a temporary increase in spending. The fiscal costs of this strategy were hardly sustainable given that they drove up non-wage labour cost (which was perceived as a massive problem for job creation in service occupations and in the exposed sector) and public expenditure in a phase of increasing global economic integration – and neither service-sector job creation nor a reduction of persistent unemployment seemed within reach without structural changes. The main phase of labour market and welfare state reforms in Germany was the first half of the 2000s, with the "Agenda 2010" and the four "Hartz Acts". Besides, the development of employment and unemployment might also contribute to the decline in spending (see Figure 6.1).

The Activation Turn in Germany: The Hartz Reforms

To overcome the notorious weakness of the German economic and employment model – high non-wage labour costs, public deficits, and high unemployment – at the time, the Red Green Schröder government adopted a dual strategy of deregulating non-standard employment on the one hand (to stimulate job growth) and shifting towards the activation principle in labour market policies, inspired by countries such as Denmark, the UK or the Netherlands. This had particular consequences for, (a) the internal governance of the public employment, (b) the design of unemployment benefits (unemployment insurance and minimum income support), (c) the set-up of ALMP measures, and (d) activating links between benefit receipt and participation in ALMP or job search, combining so-called enabling and demanding elements (Clasen and Goerne, 2014; Eichhorst et al., 2010). The main aim of the reforms in the area of ALMP was to reduce unemployment (in terms of entries and duration), to encourage economic self-dependence and thus to reduce benefits dependency. Moreover, one central aim was to reduce the welfare costs of unemployment. Recipients should have been enabled to be integrated into the first labour market.

The above-mentioned reform efforts are seen as the most far-reaching labour market reforms after the introduction of the AFG in 1969 and went hand in hand with the parallel reorganization of German ALMP. First of all, the PES was modernized according to the principles of new public management, and this, the efficiency and effectivity of the administration, gained centre stage of the administration and of politicians (Sowa and Staples, 2014). Also, a new modus operandi in the governance of long-term unemployed was established. Benefit administration and activation activities for the long-term unemployed should be allowed by the newly established joint agencies (local branches of national PES and municipal social services) and – in some cases – municipal administration. Scientists assess this as a decentralization of counselling and job placement. In 2010, it was transformed into a more consistent model of coordination between the levels of government (Noe, 2017: 419). Furthermore, there were cuts in the unemployment benefits that have been heavily criticized (Bothfeld and Betzelt, 2013; Segbers, 2016). On the one hand, there were some cuts for older unemployed as regards the maximum duration of their benefits. On the other hand, unemployment assistance, a specific benefit for long-term unemployed people, which was located between unemployment benefits and social assistance and had provided a somewhat more generous benefit for the long-term unemployed, was abolished, effectively referring the long-term unemployed only to minimum income support.

The creation of Social Code II made the distinction between unemployment assistance (for long-term unemployment with some prior employment) and social assistance (for all other needy people in the working age) obsolete. This effectively resulted in the creation of an encompassing and more easily accessible minimum income support system for people in need in the working age. Most notably this system was now available both to unemployed persons (with no or insufficient UI entitlements) and those in work if their earnings were insufficient to pass the means test, effectively establishing a permanent in-work benefit. Furthermore, a stricter activation pattern was pursued (Eichhorst et al., 2010). This includes a stricter means-testing system, stricter availability criteria, the emphasis of job readiness and the willingness to accept nearly every reasonable job. Additionally, the Federal Employment Agency was restructured, implementing the ideas of new public management. The execution of tasks was divided between the jobcentres (Bürgergeld, responsible for recipients of unemployment benefit II, since 2023) and the employment agencies (Arbeitsagentur, responsible for the recipients of regular employment benefits). Several activation measures of job creation were also implemented. This included part-time employment (mini-jobs and midi-jobs) and self-employment (Ich-AG) for the unemployed. In particular, several special programmes and employment opportunities for young and elderly unemployed were established. The aims were a broader access to the labour market and a better integration into the labour market (emphasizing permanent instead of fast integration). The reforms were often criticized for dismantling the welfare state (Segbers, 2016; Fervers, 2019; Promberger, 2010). A huge scholarly debate ensued. One focus within the political scientist debate was the question of how far-reaching and pathbreaking the reforms have been (Ruddat, 2016).

In terms of Bonoli (2010), this activation period can clearly be ascribed to incentive reinforcement as benefits were reduced and restructured and made more conditional. In this interpretation, pro-market employment orientation is stronger than before. However, we can see more strategies of investment in human capital in the sense of employment assistance and upskilling.

REINFORCED ACTIVATION IN THE POST-HARTZ ERA: A CONTINUOUS ACTIVATION PATH UNTIL THE LATE 2010S

In the aftermath of the Hartz reforms, the public and scholarly debates about activation continued. At no time has the overall direction of activation been questioned by politicians. Against this background, it is not at all surprising that the aftermath of the Hartz reforms is characterized as a continuation. That is why one could interpret this as first-order change, because instruments are changed while maintaining the activation goals (Hall, 1993).

However, what can be said about the activation turn with reference to employment and unemployment? German active labour market policy has long been criticized for being too passive and for investing too little into human capital development (Jacobi and Kluve, 2006). High unemployment and comparatively low employment rates were two results. Especially from the 1990s to the early 2000s, Germany was faced with high unemployment. After reunification, we see rising unemployment in Germany (Figure 6.1). The market was characterized by medium employment rates and high unemployment. Both the public employment service and many instruments of active labour market policy were estimated as costly, inefficient and ineffective. The German system was considered and criticized as a circle of high labour costs deriving from benefits that are based on payroll-tax financing and high unemployment. The peak was reached in 2005, with 11 percent. But it is also obvious from the data that Germany has managed to reduce unemployment significantly in the years after the activation turn (Figure 6.1). This can be interpreted as the combined effects of the activation turn and the deregulation of the labour market as well as wage restraint, based on concession bargaining, and increased internal flexibility within firms (Eichhorst and Marx, 2011; Dustmann et al., 2014). The actual share of the activation turn in explaining the decline in unemployment has been a topic of intense political and scholarly debates, however. Compared with the OECD country average, it is noticeable that Germany is no longer the sick man of Europe. On the contrary, employment has also risen considerably above the OECD country average (Figure 6.2).

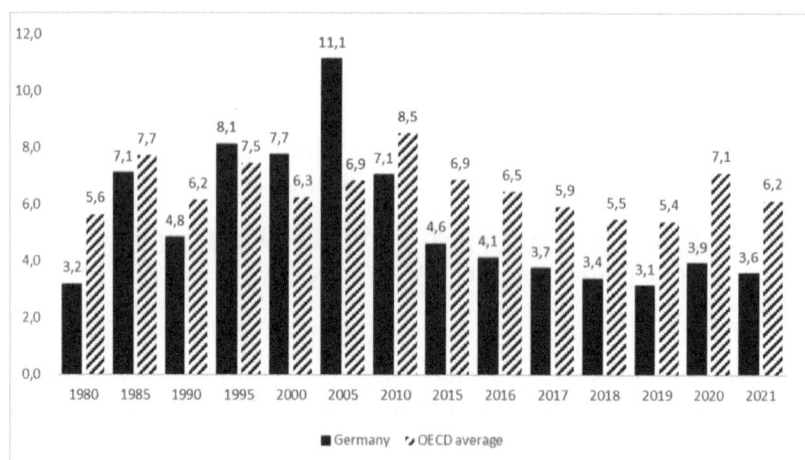

Source: OECD (2023).

Figure 6.1   German unemployment rate 1980–2021

By the end of 2001, the Federal Audit Office (Bundesrechnungshof) found out that officials of the public employment service had falsified their statistics. According to the investigations, only one third of all placements were adequate for the legal definitions of placement. Another one third have been manipulated or were not reasonable. The last third occupied a grey area, because the measure requiring clients' cooperation with regards to the filling of open positions ("Mitwirkung bei der Besetzung offener Stellen") was hard to control. This meant that the PES announced a higher activity level combined with the high deficit of the PES, which paved the way for a structural reform. The Hartz reforms contributed to a more careful monitoring of job placement.

We have argued above that this period can be characterized as a continuous activation path. Only minor changes were passed. In 2010, the German Federal

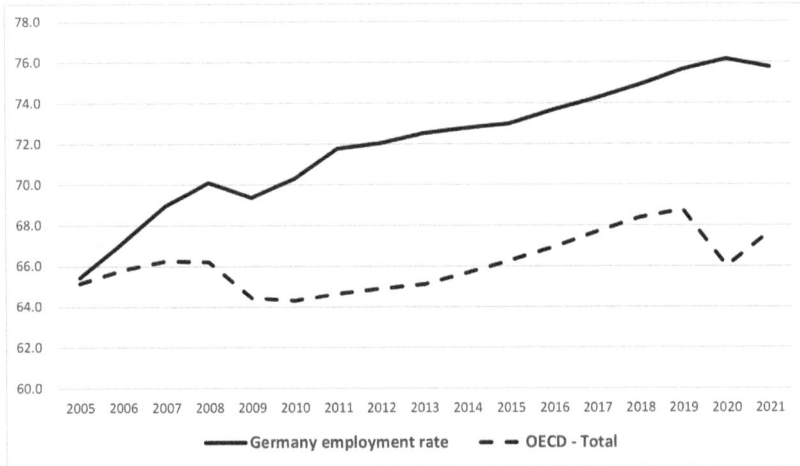

Source: OECD (2023).

Figure 6.2   German employment rate (2005–2021, person 15–64 years)

Constitutional Court decided that the minimum income support schemes had to be changed with regards to decent living conditions (Eichhorst and Hassel, 2018). Moreover, as long ago as 2007, the same court had decided that mixed constitutional competences are not consistent with the German constitution. The court had criticized that there were unclear structures with regards to staff, budget and responsibilities. Both decisions resulted in a slight improvement of the situation (higher benefits) and clarification of responsibilities.

In 2011, activation instruments have been adjusted (reform of instruments) with the aim of axing public expenditures. This has major implications for recipients of unemployment benefits and unemployment benefit II. The overall aim was a more efficient and effective employment service. Instead of profiling, an immediate potential analysis with a stronger obligation for the unemployed to cooperate was established. The employment agencies receive a placement budget at their own disposal, which aims at an individual, targeted and unbureaucratic support. Apart from the placement budget, the newly sorted instruments were subsumed as measures for activation and work related to integration (Maßnahmen zur Aktivierung und beruflichen Eingliederung). Basically, activation instruments are combined and unused instruments were removed (e.g., job rotation, aptitude assessment scheme) (Schulze and Brandl, 2023).

Moreover, a kind of pragmatism in the integration of long-term unemployed persons developed. Politicians had to admit that some barriers with regards to the integration of long-term unemployed persons are not easy to overcome and that integration into the labour market is also partly dependent on the cooperation of the clients (Noe, 2017). Unsurprisingly, the minimum income scheme became the most important pillar of benefits and activation policies. Long-term unemployment has once more proven to be sticky and hard to tackle. However, in this period, unemployment generally and continuously declined. This is especially valid for the short-term unemployed (Bundesagentur für Arbeit, 2022).

One result of the German activation path has been to reduce unemployment from more than 50 percent to one third of all unemployed. Over this time period, one could argue that the use of ALMPs in the country became more effective and more systematically evaluated. However, a kind of pragmatism emerged in terms of the need to consider that there are complex barriers for long-term unemployed. A successful and sustainable integration into the labour market will have to address these barriers. Recent statistics indicate that older workers, low-qualified people, and people who are affected by too few childcare places experience particular obstacles to labour market integration (Bundesagentur für Arbeit, 2022).

A NEW ACTIVATION TURN IN THE LATE 2010S? PRIORITIZING INVESTMENTS IN HUMAN CAPITAL

The late 2010s can be interpreted as a policy shift towards a new interpretation of activation. More investment in human capital can be seen now, while the activation path has not been relinquished. We can see new policy instruments manifested in several reforms that will be discussed in this section. We describe this period as second-order change (Hall, 1993).

Since the late 2010s, there has once more been an increased focus on human capital-oriented labour market. The "Arbeit von morgen-Gesetz" and the "Qualifizierungschancengesetz" 2019 (Qualification Opportunities Act) are good examples of policies that focus more on those who are at risk of losing their jobs due to structural changes (i.e., on employed rather than unemployed). Instruments that could in principle provide publicly subsidized training for broad groups of working-age people (including those in employment) were rolled out (Klaus et al., 2020). Also, PES has started to play an increasingly important role as a more general advisor for working-age people during their whole working life (lifelong vocational counselling, "lebensbegleitende Berufsberatung") (Nixdorf and Swiderski, 2022). The main reason behind this expansion of investment in human capital is the expected and perceived economic restructuring due to the digital transition and de-carbonization and the demographic change (Eichhorst and Marx, 2019), but one could also argue that the creation of the statutory minimum wage in 2015 created the need to raise productivity at the lower end of the occupational structure in Germany. According to our argumentation, we see a changed paradigm in German ALMPs. It comprises not only investing in unemployed or long-term unemployed (the traditional target groups of ALMP training); it includes human capital-oriented strategies for the employed. It tries to ensure employment and skills supply. The new strategy is to avoid unemployment and mismatch (instead of reducing unemployment).

Overall, activation policies in Germany have become oriented towards human capital investment most recently again (which does not yet show clearly in the time series data). While there were several adjustments in terms of a rearrangement of activation measures (e.g. in 2011), the years after 2010 can be characterized as a period with only small adjustments of the overall activation path. The Qualifizierungschancengesetz (Qualification Opportunities Act) and the Arbeit-von-morgen-Gesetz (Law on Work of Tomorrow) have both contributed to the investment in human capital strategy. Both laws provide further allowances for training for employed and unemployed people. The Qualifizierungschancengesetz (2019) establishes a strong advancement of further training especially for those workers who are affected by the technological structural transformation (Enoch and Stanik, 2022). The labour administration has a legal obligation to counsel employees and employers in the field of training. Funding is only possible if employers share the costs for further training (Bäcker et al., 2024: 43–44).

The Arbeit-von-morgen-Gesetz (2020) has specified the funding possibilities according to the company size. The more employees a company has, the lower will be the funding for training. As we have argued above, the focus of the government shifted overall from funding for unemployed persons to funding for all people. In addition, unemployed and employed people without professional qualification are legally entitled to support to gain this. However, a recent study has shown that disinformation is prevailing. Many companies assume that the funding is only for unemployed people (Biermeier et al., 2023). A clear shift towards investment in human capital (for all people) is noticeable. This has been confirmed, once more, with the most recent law on adult learning that has made publicly supported continuous vocational training even more generous and accessible (Gesetz zur Stärkung der Aus- und Weiterbildungsförderung, 2023; Bäcker et al., 2024: 21).

As is obvious from our argumentation, there is a strong shift towards training and investment in human capital for the employed and the unemployed. However, Germany is faced with a huge amount of long-term unemployed. This group should not be underestimated, as the share of long-term unemployed is comparatively high. In 2004, nearly 52 percent of all unemployed were long-term unemployed. Due to sound economic development and activation of unemployed persons, their numbers are decreasing. In 2019, 38 percent belonged to this group. In 2022, the figure was 33 percent. The German government realized that long-term unemployment is a specific point that needs to be addressed. In 2018, the Participation Opportunities Act established two new activation instruments with the aim of integrating unemployed persons who are very distant from the labour market into jobs (Ramos Labato et al., 2023; Schulze and Brandl, 2023). One could argue that it is a revival of supported employment, as wage costs are mainly financed by public subsidies. The first new instrument is determined in Social Security Code II §16i and is named participation in the labour market (Teilhabe am Arbeitsmarkt). It provides funding for an employment that is subject to social security contributions. It is only intended for people who are very distant to the labour market. That means, the unemployed person has to be more than 25 years old and to have drawn benefits (unemployment benefit II) for at least six years within the last seven years. Companies will receive wage subsidies at the level of the minimum wage for a maximum of five years. During the first two years, the pay is 100 percent. In every following year, the subsidy will be cut by 10 percent. This subsidy is not limited to the social labour market, which clearly indicates that the aim is to bring people back into the first labour market. Another element is the support for the employee by the job centres. The employers are obliged to enable the participant to take part in an accompanying support (beschäftigungsbegleitende Betreuung). The second new instrument is determined in Social Security Code II §16e as integration of long-term unemployed persons (Eingliederung von Langzeitarbeitslosen). Employers will receive wage subsidies for persons who are unemployed for more than two years, but they have to grant an employment of more than two years. The wage subsidy is lower: 75 percent in the first year and 50 percent in the second year can be attained. It is not that surprising that the subsidy is lower, as these unemployed are closer to the labour market.

We saw in Figure 6.1 that unemployment decreased until the beginning of the pandemic. In 2019, unemployment in Germany reached 3.1 percent. Compared with the OECD average, this is very low, as a result partly of the activation reforms and partly of sound economic development. This is also obvious from Figure 6.2. Employment rates had been continuously rising until the beginning of the pandemic.

OVERALL ASSESSMENT OF THE GERMAN ACTIVATION PATH

In this section, we discuss the developments of the activation path related to (long-term) unemployment, employment and the overall assessment of spending. We have worked out that there is a shift towards investment in human capital. As the changes in policy have been passed comparatively late, this is not obvious from the data yet.

In Figures 6.1 and 6.2, we showed the developments with regards to employment and unemployment. Compared with the OECD average, employment in Germany has developed satisfactorily. Employment has continuously increased, whereas unemployment decreased.

With regards to the basic measures of ALMPs for unemployed people in Germany, several developments (Table 6.2) are obvious. There is no clear indication that there was an immense expansion of spending for activation measures. Compared with the early 1990s, spending declined in the fields of training, employment incentives, supported employment and job creation. Compared with other countries, start-up incentives have not played a pivotal role in Germany. Moreover, the modernization of the labour administration caused an expansion of spending for public employment services and administration. These expenses doubled between 1990 and 2019 (see Table 6.2). During this time period, the labour administration had been reorganized substantially according to the principles of new public management and private efficiency (e.g. controlling and objective agreement). This included a shift from training job placement. These developments implied a change in the personnel structure of the federal employment agency and explain the decline of spending.

Table 6.2   *Public expenditure for active measures 1990–2020 (in % of GDP)*

Date	1990	1995	2000	2005	2010	2015	2020
10: PES and administration	0.18	0.20	0.22	0.31	0.38	0.36	0.33
20: Training	0.34	0.43	0.53	0.39	0.27	0.20	0.19
40: Employment incentives	0.05	0.07	0.09	0.06	0.10	0.03	0.02
50: Sheltered and supported employment and rehabilitation	0.12	0.12	0.12	0.13	0.03	0.02	0.02
60: Direct job creation	0.09	0.32	0.25	0.09	0.05	0.02	0.03
70: Start-up incentives	0.00	0.02	0.04	0.15	0.08	0.01	0.01

Source: OECD (2023).

We argued above that there is a more recent shift in the direction of activation towards more investment in human capital. This was obvious from the latest reforms in the late 2010s and early 2020s. However, spending data, especially with regards to training, do not show this development. On the contrary, spending for training since the activation turn has continuously declined, whereas spending in 2000 was 0.53 percent of GDP and in 2020 it was 0.19 percent. One possible explanation is the timing of the reforms. Reforms were passed comparatively late, so results in spending will become visible only somewhat later. From our perspective, it is far too early for an overall assessment. We see a clear change in the direction of policy towards more investment in human capital. If one considers the participants (Table 6.3), it is obvious that fewer people are taking part in training. The reasons are rather complex. Some people simply might not need training, while others probably find a job because of investment in human capital.

Table 6.3   *Participants stocks in German activation as a percentage of the labour force (2000–2021)*

Date	2000	2005	2010	2015	2016	2017	2018	2019	2020	2021
20: Training	1.99	1.75	2.45	2.40	1.31	1.29	1.27	1.25	1.29	1.23
40: Employment incentives	0.44	0.27	0.67	0.21	0.22	0.24	0.21	0.22	0.20	0.20
50: Sheltered and supported employment and rehabilitation	0.34	0.38	0.07	0.06	0.06	0.06	0.06	0.06	0.06	0.05
60: Direct job creation	0.81	0.69	0.63	0.23	0.22	0.24	0.22	0.23	0.24	0.22
70: Start-up incentives	0.11	0.79	0.38	0.08	0.07	0.07	0.06	0.06	0.05	0.05

Source: OECD (2023); here only categories 20–70.

As well as the spending on ALMP, it is important to have a look at the participants. It is clear from our argumentation that training plays a pivotal role in German ALMP, even though it is not obvious from the data discussed above. In Table 6.3 it is shown that most recipients take part in training and that all other measures are not that relevant anymore. With a closer look into training data, it becomes clear that external vocational training with specialized providers is the most important element of activation here, whereas workplace training and special support for apprenticeship are less relevant and integrated training is no longer of relevance (OECD, 2023). Overall, the number of participants has declined from the 2010s on. This is one indicator of sound economic development and an activation policy that takes full effect. Moreover, according to

Bonoli, we can see a clear tendency towards investment in human capital. The aim is to improve the chances of finding employment (Bonoli, 2010).

Even though there are good reasons to believe that German activation is a success story, we have to keep in mind that there is still a remarkable share of long-term unemployed persons who have remarkable difficulties finding and keeping a job. As overall unemployment has declined, the group of the hard to place has become relatively more visible, representing a larger share of the remaining unemployment. Senghaas has argued that the activation approach is not working fully for this group (Senghaas et al., 2019). In the middle of the 1980s, half of the German unemployed were long-term unemployed (1985: 47.8 percent). This amount increased until the beginning of the activation reforms (2005: 53 percent). In line with the activation path, Germany was able to reduce long-term unemployment to 32.8 percent in 2021) (OECD, 2023).

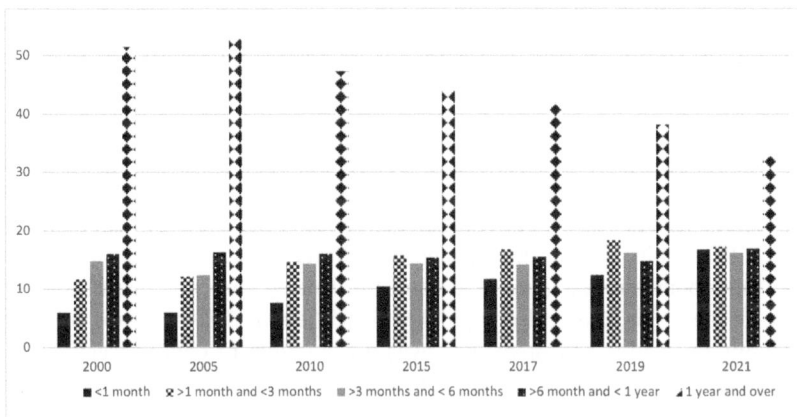

Source: OECD (2023).

Figure 6.3   *Development and duration of long-term unemployment in Germany (2000–2021)*

Figure 6.3 provides a clear picture of the detailed development and duration of German unemployed. First of all, most of them are still unemployed long term. Even though the percentage declined from more than 50 at the beginning of the activation period to 32.8 in 2021, people who are unemployed for more than one year are still the largest subgroup. Research has long discussed the long-term unemployed as the most vulnerable group (Clasen and Goerne, 2014; Dingeldey, 2020). Nevertheless, it is obvious that, meanwhile, the German activation policy reaches the long-term unemployed more. The newer reforms discussed above mainly address the unemployed and might contribute to a further reduction. In the other four groups, we can see a homogenization of the numbers. In 2021, all other unemployed were nearly at the same level.

With reference to the first two groups (unemployed for less than three months), a double reversal is clear from the date. First of all, the short-term unemployed need more time to find employment. Second, the share of short-time unemployed who are unemployed from one to three months has increased perceptibly from 6 (2000) to 16.8 percent in 2021. We can also see that this is not only an effect of the pandemic. Also, the second group (people who are unemployed for more than one month but less than three months) has increased from 11.7 (2000) to 17.3 percent in 2021. If one takes together the first two groups in 2021, 34.1 percent are unemployed for less than three months. Numbers for 2022 are more sweeping. In 2022, 37.5 percent are unemployed between one and three months. It seems that Germany has to focus not only on the most vulnerable groups. However, the better-qualified unemployed have it easier in finding a job.

THE COVID-19 EXPERIENCE: A GAME CHANGER FOR ACTIVATION?

The Covid-19 pandemic was a key challenge for German ALMPs. Due to the lockdown, employment agencies and job centres had to be closed quickly. Two developments had a direct influence on activation (Brandl et al., 2022; Schulze et al., 2022). First, due to the closing, all efforts with regards to integration into the labour market came to a standstill. Counselling was nearly impossible because the technical equipment of the German PES was not suitable for online consulting. Moreover, it was not possible to continue activation activities for the unemployed. As a consequence, sanctions for the unemployed were suspended. One can argue that the pandemic has weakened the activation idea, even in a wider sense. In order to soften the effects of the crisis, unemployment insurance (UI) benefits were extended and generous short-time allowances were implemented again. Following the idea that successful and sustainable activation and integration to the labour market needs a personal interaction between client and case manager, the pandemic virtually stopped this part of ALMPs. In addition, requirements regarding means testing and the appropriateness of housing were reduced regarding those receiving welfare (Social Code II). Moreover, there were no sanctions in practice. Second, the Federal Employment Agency had to react fast to reduce the effects of the pandemic (Schulze et al., 2022). A huge number of employees were delegated to process short-time allowance submissions and requests. People had to be trained in how to proceed. These developments have concentrated manpower and currently there are still employees who work on the short-time allowance submissions (especially final invoices "Abschlussrechnungen").

One might ask to, what extent might the pandemic have been a game changer for activation and ALMPs? We expect several developments, initiated by the pandemic and the resulting crisis. Short-time allowance is once more seen as a successful way to deal with the economic consequences of a massive shock (Ebbinghaus and Lehner, 2022). However, by now the financial resources of the Federal Employment Agency are exhausted, and there is a clear need for a new phase of economic prosperity to recharge the unemployment fund (which might take longer given current post-pandemic economic uncertainties). Moreover, there will be a stronger emphasis on the digital interaction between the PES and their clients. This also includes virtual consultations. We expect a digitalization of measures of ALMPs and administration. Consultation and job placement are becoming more and more digitalized. First projects on digital counselling show that there are promising ideas, but it is also clear that a direct and personal contact is key to a successful integration into the labour market (Bähr et al., 2022). Germany is, of course, a latecomer here, as it is with many aspects of digital government. At the same time, however, by now we can see that the benefit regime in unemployment insurance will remain largely unchanged. This is then also valid for the activation path. In fact, there has been a more structural change in the minimum income support system.

A first reform package moving beyond the system established in 2005 has been implemented in 2023 ("Bürgergeld", Citizen's Income) and is building upon ideas that were developed during the pandemic, namely the suspension of sanctions and less strict means testing (Bernhard et al., 2022). Despite its name, this is not a basic income, as it is bound to certain conditions that show the affinity to the German UB II. It continues to provide a means-tested minimum-income support benefit to those in need, i.e. after the expiry of unemployment insurance benefits or if entitlements to UI benefits are insufficient to pass the means test. The benefit rate was uprated significantly and will from now on be set in line with expected inflation (rather than past inflation). Politically, the Bürgergeld should arguably provide social participation and respect the dignity of all persons. That means a less strict means test. The costs of accommodation and heating are supported unconditionally during the first year of benefit receipt, while personal wealth is not considered as rigorously as in the past, as a higher threshold value is set for the first year, but also in later phases. However, sustainable integration into the labour market is another central aim restated with the new benefit. In the new model, an integration agreement between the client and the caseworker should be struck on equal terms and facilitate a more individualized provision of advice and support. In line with the general activation approach, it is also important to note that sanctions will not be abolished but implemented more selectively. In this context, the new arrangement does not require a quick take-up of available jobs anymore but allows for more extensive preparatory (re)training. Further, the built-in permanent earnings disregard clause is extended to strengthen work incentives. One important aim of the reform is a new model of counselling the unemployed. Street-level bureaucrats and clients should see each other at eye level. The focus will be more on the resources of the unemployed and thus a tendency towards more investment in human capital is clear (Bonoli, 2010). The focus will be on the benefits of active employment promotion (aktiven Arbeitsförderung) instead of a direct integration into the labour market by employment or training. A cultural turn is necessary to achieve both; however, this is not possible by only changing the laws (Bernhard et al., 2022).

The softening of activation as embodied in the new benefit system has been perceived with some ambiguity. It might lead to a more "friendly" and human capital oriented and sustainable type of activation. But it might also lead to a more divided labour market, less (rather than better) inclusion of those with multiple obstacles to labour market integration, and a more permissive approach towards benefit receipt, thereby weakening the links to the labour market for certain target groups. There has also been more emphasis on enabling policies to be delivered to this target group. Recently, however, at the end of 2023 and the beginning of 2024, there was a heated debate in German politics about the appropriate level of generosity of the Citizen's Income (Bürgergeld). It became obvious that vulnerable groups (e.g., the long-term unemployed) have suffered most from the various crises and are less reached by ALMP instruments. That is why the benefit was increased substantially in 2024. However, one third of all unemployed persons are still long-term unemployed in Germany. The country is faced with a significant amount of people who cannot be reached by ALMP instruments (see Figure 6.3). Furthermore, social and economic challenges have contributed to a renewed discussion about the generosity of the German welfare state and about the willingness of benefit recipients to work. The German government is currently discussing a reform that could result in stricter sanctions for Bürgergeld recipients who are unwilling to work for a determined period. In addition, the controversy on the appropriate distance between the level of minimum income benefits pay levels in the low-wage sector is reignited, focusing on the strength or weakness of work incentives. Within one or two years or so, a shift from a discussion on a more generous policy to a stricter policy that also allows cutting benefits for some time is obvious.

CONCLUSION

Germany has changed substantially since being described as the sick man of the Euro in the late 1990s and early 2000s, transforming itself into a country with a model employment-oriented active labour market and activating labour market policies, combined with a renewed set-up of governance in this policy area. With the implementation of the Hartz reforms in 2004, the German acti-vation path started in a comprehensive and effective manner. Until the 2010s, several reforms were passed that stressed integration into the labour market more than investment in human capital. Combined with a strong economy and a partly deregulated labour market, this has helped overcome mass unemployment and stimulate significant job growth, not least in the service economy. However, this was associated with rising inequality within the labour market and considerable political uneasiness regarding the downsides of labour market divides and demanding aspects of activation. More recently, we have seen an activation U-turn. Form the late 2010s on, Germany has embarked upon an activation path that is more oriented towards human-capital investment, responding indirectly to policies that raised effective wage floors, most notably through the introduction of the statutory minimum wage in 2015 and its subsequent upratings. Continuing a significant softening of activation during the Covid-19 phase, in 2023, the new Citizen's Income or "Bürgergeld" was introduced, renaming not only the minimum income support scheme created with the Hartz reforms, but also tuning down the demanding side of activation. For the foreseeable future, we can expect this path of recalibrating protective, enabling and demanding aspects of labour market policies to continue; however, austerity poses new challenges. While contributory unem-ployment insurance is remarkably stable in institutional terms, and while the employed are increasingly addressed by publicly supported training measures to cope with the economic transitions, we see a renewed discourse about the deservingness of those in minimum support. This concerns a controversial debate about the appropriate level of benefits, the strength of work (dis) incentives and the extent of sanctions in case of non-cooperative behaviour, bringing a pro-market orientation to the forefront once more, although until recently a softer and more human capital-oriented approach was favoured with regards to those out of jobs for a longer time. Hence, in an era of sluggish economic growth and potentially increasing benefit dependence, we might likely see another U-turn in order to cut costs in the minimum income support scheme while keeping the protective mechanism in unemployment insurance unchanged, while investing more into the human capital of those in employ-ment rather than on enabling policies for the long-term unemployed. But again, there is no unambiguous and coherent setting emerging, rather another phase of adjustment, responding to the perceived pressure.

REFERENCES

Aust, A., and Arriba, A. (2005) 'Towards Activation? Social Assistance Reforms and Discourses' in Taylor-Gooby, P. (ed.) *Ideas and Welfare State Reform in Western Europe*. London: Palgrave Macmillan, pp. 100–123.

Bäcker, G., Schmitz-Kießler, J., Sommer, P., Zink, L., and von der Weydt, L. (2024) *Dauerbaustelle Sozialsstaat 2023*. Duisburg: IAQ Forschung.

Bähr, H., Broder, H., Dietz, M., Förster, M., and Klier, M. (2022) *Neue Wege bei Beratung und Arbeitsvermittlung durch Digitalisierung: Online-Chat ermöglicht Informationsaustausch und gegenseitige Unterstützung*. Nürnberg: IAB Kurzbericht 09/2022.

Bernhard, S., Röhrer, S., and Senghaas, M. (2022) 'Auf dem Weg zum Bürgergeld: Die Sanktionspraxis nach dem Urteil des Bundesverfassungsgerichts und "in Zeiten von Corona"', *Sozialer Fortschritt*, 71(99), pp. 1–17. https://doi.org/10.3790/sfo.2022 .00.0000.Berhard_Roehrer_Senghaas.

Biermeier, S., Dony, E., Greger, S., Leber, U., Schreyer, F., and Strien, K. (2023) *Geförderte Weiterbildung von Beschäftigten: Hürden der Inanspruchnahme aus Sicht von Arbeitsagenturen und Betrieben*. Nürnberg: IAB-Forschungsbericht 13/2023.

Bonoli, G. (2010) 'The political economy of active labor-market policy', *Politics & Society*, 38(4), pp. 435–457. Doi: 10.1177/0032329210381235.

Bothfeld, S., and Betzelt, S. (2013) 'How do activation policies affect social citizenship? The issue of autonomy', *Social Policy Review*, 25, pp. 249–270. https://doi .org/10.51952/9781447312840.ch013.

Brandl, S., Matuschek, I., and Schulze, M. (2022) 'Die Bundesagentur für Arbeit als Krisenakteurin in der Pandemie', *Soziale Sicherheit*, 71(6), 232–235.

Bundesagentur für Arbeit. (2022) *Arbeitsmarktsituation von langzeitarbeitslosen Menschen. Blickpunkt Arbeitsmarkt März 2022*. Nürnberg: Bundesagentur für Arbeit.

Caliendo, M., and Steiner, V. (2005) *Aktive Arbeitsmarktpolitik in Deutschland: Bestandsaufnahme und Bewertung der mikroökonomischen Evaluationsergebnisse*. Berlin: DIW Discussion Papers No. 515.

Clasen, J., and Goerne, A. (2014) 'Germany: Ambivalent Activation' in Lødemel, I., and Moreira, A. (eds.) *Activation or Workfare? Governance and Neo-Liberal Convergence*. Oxford: Oxford University Press, pp. 172–202.

Dingeldey, I. (2011) 'Fragmented governance continued: The German case' in van Berkel, R., de Graaf, W., and Sirovatka, T. (eds.) *The Governance of Active Welfare States in Europe*. Basingstoke: Palgrave Macmillan, pp. 62–84.

Dingeldey, I. (2020) 'Mehr als 50 Jahre Arbeitsförderungsgesetz: Die Entwicklung der deutschen Arbeitsmarktpolitik als Fortschritt oder Rückschritt?', *Momentum Quarterly – Zeitschrift für Sozialen Fortschritt*, 9(1), pp. 35–49. https://doi.org/10 .15203/momentumquarterly.vol9.no1.p35–49.

Dustmann, C., Fitzenberger, B., Schönberg, U., and Spitz-Oener, A. (2014) 'From sick man of Europe to economic superstar: Germany's resurgent economy', *Journal of Economic Perspectives*, 28(1), pp. 167–188. https://doi.org/10.1257/jep.28.1.167.

Ebbinghaus, B., and Lehner, L. (2022) 'Cui bono – business or labour? Job retention policies during the COVID-19 pandemic in Europe', *Transfer: European Review of Labour and Research*, 28(1), pp. 47–64.

Eichhorst, W., Grienberger-Zingerle, M., and Konle-Seidl, R. (2010) 'Activating labor market and social policies in Germany: From status protection to basic income support', *German Policy Study*, 6(1), pp. 65–106.

Eichhorst, W., and Hassel, A. (2018) 'The German exception: Welfare protectionism instead of retrenchment' in Theodoropoulou, S. (ed.) *Labour Market Policies in the Era of Pervasive Austerity: A European Perspective*. Bristol: Policy Press, pp. 115–140.

Eichhorst, W., and Marx, P. (2011) 'Reforming German labour market institutions: A dual path to flexibility', *Journal of European Social Policy*, 21(1), pp. 73–87. https://doi.org/10.1177/0958928710385731.

Eichhorst, W. and Marx, P. (2019) 'Der Wandel der Arbeitswelt als Herausforderung für die Sozialpolitik' in Obinger, H. and Schmidt, M. G. (eds.) *Handbuch Sozialpolitik*. Wiesbaden: Springer VS, pp. 409–430.

Enoch, C., and Stanik, T. (2022) 'Rechtliche und konzeptionelle Grundlagen der Beratung der Bundesagentur für Arbeit', *Hessische Blätter für Volksbildung*, 72(1), pp. 54–64. DOI:10.3278/HBV2201W006.

Esping-Andersen, G. (1998) 'Welfare states without work: The impasse of labour shedding and familialism in continental European social policy' in Esping-Andersen, G. (ed.) *Welfare States in Transition: National Adaptations in Global Economies*. London: SAGE-Publications, pp. 66–87.

Estevez-Abe, M., Iversen, T., and Soskice, D. (2001) 'Social Protection and the Formation of Skills: A Reinterpretation of the Welfare State' in Hall, P., and Soskice, D. (eds.), *Varieties of Capitalism: The Institutional Foundations of Comparative Advantage*. Oxford: Oxford University Press, pp. 145–183.

Fervers, L. (2019) 'Economic miracle, political disaster? Political consequences of Hartz IV', *Journal of European Social Policy*, 29(3), pp. 411–427. https://doi.org/10.1177/0958928718774259.

Hall, P. A. (1993) 'Policy paradigms, social learning, and the state: The case of economic policymaking in Britain', *Comparative Politics*, 25(3), pp. 275–296.

Jacobi, L., and Kluve, J. (2006) *Before and After the Hartz Reforms: The Performance of Active Labour Market Policy in Germany*. Bonn: IZA Discussion Paper No. 2100.

Klaus, A., Kruppe, T., Lang, J., and Roesler, K. (2020) *Geförderte Weiterbildung Beschäftigter: Trotz erweiterter Möglichkeiten noch ausbaufähig*. Nürnberg: IAB-Kurzbericht 24/2020.

Konle-Seidl, R., Eichhorst, W., and Grienberger-Zingerle, M. (2007) *Activation Policies in Germany: From Status Protection to Basic Income Support*. Nürnberg: IAB-Discussion Paper 06/2007.

Manow, P., and Seils, E. (2000) 'Adjusting Badly: The German Welfare State, Structural Change, and the Open Economy' in Scharpf, F. W., and Schmidt, V. A. (eds.) *Welfare and Work in the Open Economy. Diverse Responses to Common Challenges*. Oxford: Oxford University Press, pp. 264–307.

Nixdorf, C. P., and Swiderski, J. (2022) 'Bildungsberatung in Arbeitsagentur und Jobcenter', *Blätter der Wohlfahrtspflege*, 169(4), pp. 146–148. https://doi.org/10.5771/0340-8574-2022-4-146.

Noe, T. (2017) 'Strategische Ausrichtung bei der Beratung und Vermittlung von Langzeitarbeitslosen in Optionskommunen' in Sowa, F., and Staples, R. (eds.) *Beratung und Vermittlung im Wohlfahrtsstaat*. Baden-Baden: Nomos, pp. 417–436.

OECD. (2023) OECD Statistics. https://stats.oecd.org/.

Promberger, M. (2010) 'Fünf Jahre SGB II: Kontinuitäten und Brüche in der Armutspolitik', *IAB-Forum*, 01/2010, pp. 86–93.

Ramos Lobato, P., Globisch, C., and Lange, J. (2023) 'Das Teilhabechancengesetz – Geschichte, Zielsetzung und Ausgestaltung der Förderinstrumente', *Sozialer Fortschritt*, 72(9–10), pp. 673–689. https://doi.org/10.3790/sfo.72.9–10.673.

Ruddat, C. (2016) 'Eine überraschende Reform? Politikwissenschaftliche Interpretationen und Erklärungsansätze zu Hartz IV', *Zeitschrift für Sozialreform*, 57(2), pp. 221–236. https://doi.org/10.1515/zsr-2011–0206.

Schulze, M., and Brandl, S. (2023) 'Zum Ausbleiben eines paradigmatischen Wandels: Die aktivierende Arbeitsmarktpolitik in der Ära Merkel', *Sozialer Fortschritt*, 72(7–8), pp. 597–614. https://doi.org/10.3790/sfo.72.7–8.597.

Schulze, M., Brandl, S., and Matuschek, I. (2022) 'Politische Steuerung in turbulenten Zeiten: Die deutsche Arbeitsverwaltung als Akteurin der Corona-Pandemie', *Zeitschrift für Sozialreform*, 68(3–4), pp. 267–297. https:// doi .org/ 10 .1515/ zsr -2022–0011.

Segbers, F. (2016) 'Das Menschenbild von Hartz IV. Die Pädagogisierung von Armut, die Zentralität von Erwerbsarbeit und autoritärer Sozialstaat' in Anhorn, R. and Balzereit, M. (eds.) *Handbuch Therapeutisierung und Soziale Arbeit*. Wiesbaden: Springer VS, pp. 687–708.

Senghaas, M., Freier, C., and Kupka, P. (2019) 'Practices of activation in frontline interactions: Coercion, persuasion, and the role of trust in activation policies in Germany', *Social Policy & Administration*, 53(5), pp. 613–626. https://doi.org/10 .1111/spol.12443.

Sowa, F., and Staples, R. (2014) 'Accounting in der Arbeitsverwaltung: Vermittlungsfachkräfte zwischen Steuerungsimperativen und autonomem Vermittlungshandeln', *Zeitschrift für Sozialreform*, 60(2), pp. 149–174. https:// doi .org/10.1515/zsr-2014–0204.

The Economist. (1999) 'The sick man of the Euro', June 3.

Weishaupt, J. T. (2019) 'Arbeitsmarktpolitik' in Obinger, H. and Schmidt, M. G. (eds.) *Handbuch Sozialpolitik*. Wiesbaden: Springer VS, pp. 669–696.

7. Activation policies in the Netherlands: the vicissitudes of general social policy and activating labour market policies since the 1990s

Romke van der Veen and Ferry Koster

INTRODUCTION

Since the 1990s, welfare systems have been transformed from passive benefits systems towards systems that activate benefit recipients and that in general promote social inclusion and participation. The turn towards activation includes various policy instruments – financial incentives, stricter obligations, sanctions, employment services – but the specific composition and order of the mix of policy changes varies from country to country.

This chapter presents the state of the art concerning activation policies in the Netherlands. To understand these policies, it is necessary to take the following into account. First, some attention needs to be paid to the broader set of policies and institutions related to these activation policies. And, second, since the specific nature of these policies is hard to grasp without knowing how they came about, some information about the changes in the system is required. Hence, before discussing the current characteristics of the activation policies in the Netherlands, we provide a short historical overview of the development of social security and labour market policies in the Netherlands. These policies are increasingly oriented at control of costs and at activation, and are implemented in all elements of the system of (social) policies that affect the supply and demand of labour, the take-up of benefits, and the re-integration of benefits recipients. This includes, for example, the system of tax benefits, as well as the governance and administration of the system of social security. The reorganization of governance and administration of the system of social security is an important element of these policies and highly determined by the path-dependent logic of the evolution of the Dutch welfare system (Pierson 1996).

The high level of unemployment, but especially of occupational disability in the 1980s, the so-called 'Dutch disease' (Visser and Hemerijck 1997), is a decisive factor in the process of restructuring of the system of social insurances and labour market policies that has taken place since the 1980s. The high level of occupational disability – the highest in Europe, at almost 20% of the working-age population in 1982 – was explained as the unintended and unwanted consequence of the role of the social partners in the governance and administration of the system of social insurances. The reorganization of governance and administration was therefore characterized by 'decorporatization' and 'privatization' and aimed at restructuring the incentives the system gave to all participants in the system, in such a way that participation and re-integration became the primary goal of employers, workers, organized interests and administrators.

Since the so-called 'Akkoord van (agreement of) Wassenaar', which the social partners reached in 1982, social policies in the Netherlands are primarily oriented at enhancing labour market participation of men and women. Next to part-time work, more flexible employment relations were promoted. In this agreement, increased labour market participation became an important element in promoting the social security of Dutch citizens, partially at the cost of the accessibility, level and duration of social security benefits (Visser 1999).

Following the sketch of the development of the Dutch policies oriented at increasing control and activation in *social and labour market policy* in general in the next section (1), we will review the developments that have taken place in more specific *active labour market policies* (section 2). Having described these developments, we will consequently sketch the situation on the labour market in the year 2023 (section 3) and ask the question, how might this affect the evolution of activation policies in the coming years? The Dutch labour market is characterized by a high level of participation, but it is also highly dualized: on the one hand, there are flex-workers and self-employed with little social security, while there is also a group of workers with a permanent contract and relatively high social security. This dualization has been amplified by the consequences of the Covid crisis and will, combined with the still-fragile labour market position of vulnerable groups, probably be the main driver of developments in social policy and labour market policy in the coming years.

1.   DEVELOPMENTS IN SOCIAL POLICIES SINCE THE 1990S: TOWARDS INCREASING CONTROL AND ACTIVATION

As noted, in the 1980s unemployment and occupational disability rocketed sky-high in the Netherlands. This set the stage for fundamental changes in social security and labour market policies.

Main Trends in the Transformation of Social Security and Labour Market Policy[1]

Decorporatization and privatization

The governance and administration of social security has been fundamentally reorganized since the 1990s. Social partners lost their role in the administration of social insurance, and their role in the governance of the system was severely limited. The administration of social insurance and employment services was first privatized, but, in the end, social security is now administered by the state (by the public social insurance administration, the UWV). Privatization also took place in risk protection and employment services.

Processes of decorporatization and privatization as well as administration by the state were all intended to lay the ground for an incentive structure in which all participants are confronted with the 'costs' of the choices they make to promote prevention of sickness and unemployment and re-integration of unemployed and disabled workers, and thus to promote labour market participation and cost control.

Restructuring incentives

Promotion of prevention and re-integration was organized by *privatizing* risks to the employer and by *decentralizing* social provisions to the municipality.

Employers are obliged to continue the payment of salary during the first two years of sickness. (They are free to re-insure this risk on the private insurance market; 75% of employers do so, and the level of reinsurance is lowest with the smaller companies, CPB 2015.) The incentive of this obligation serves to stimulate prevention of sickness and to promote a speedy re-integration once someone is sick.

A comparable reorganization of the incentive structure took place on the municipal level. Municipalities receive a lump-sum budget from which they must pay social assistance. Since 2006, if the municipality runs out of funding it is obliged to finance social assistance from other budgets. If any monies are left over, they may be invested in other municipal activities. This incentive intends to make the municipality a strict gatekeeper and financially interested in promoting re-integration.

In order to harmonize incentives in social provision policies, in 2015 all social provisions were integrated into one act, the Participation Act, which is implemented by the municipalities and – as the name already suggests – primarily focused on promoting participation. In a later section, we will go into more detail with regard to the working of the Participation Act as activation policy.

Finally, the incentives for workers and people dependent on social security, were also changed: the height and duration of benefits were shortened, and the obligation to look for and accept work was strengthened.

Flexibilization of labour relations

Labour market participation was also stimulated by organizing more flexibility on the labour market. Private employment agencies received more leeway and part-time employment was stimulated (the right to part-time employment was laid down by law). Different forms of flexible contracts ('on-call contracts' or so-called 'zero-hours contracts') were made possible. Participation was also stimulated by giving more leeway to self-employment, mainly by tax reliefs and by reduction (in case of health insurance) or by exemption (in case of disability insurance, as the self-employed are not insured) of social security premiums.

Dismantling employment services

Public employment offices have been terminated and employment services have been taken over by the public social insurance administration (the UWV). The UWV developed its employment services in a separate organization, the Workcompany, which is organized across 35 regions. Only in a few large cities are the region and municipality the same. Some of these services are conditional upon receiving insurances benefits. The range of employment services is limited, and the implementation of these services is mainly organized online.

On the sectoral level, the social partners stayed active with employment services, but these services are mainly oriented towards workers and aimed at preventing unemployment and sickness. These services are often delivered by private re-integration companies. Many employers have a contract with a re-integration company. Municipalities and the public social insurance administration make use of these re-integration companies.

The Development of Participation and Social Security Take-up since the 1990s

As far as labour market participation and social security take-up are concerned, the policy changes discussed above were successful. The take-up of disability insurance declined: official statistics in the Netherlands show a decline from almost 900,000 recipients of a disability benefit in the 1990s to 750,000 in 2020. Consequently, public spending related to incapacity declined. In relative figures, the decline is more impressive because labour market participation rose in the same period from less than 70% to more than 80% (2022, 85.4%). Unemployment has also declined. Between 2013 and 2022 it declined from almost 400,000 persons receiving unemployment benefits in 2014 to 150,000 in 2022. Unemployment is at a historically low level in 2022 of 3.5% (Figure 7.1).[2]

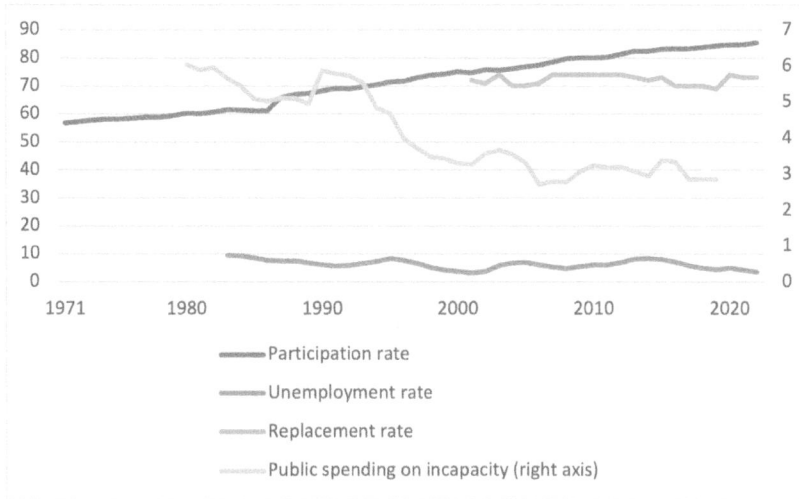

Figure 7.1   Participation and social security take-up

To what extent the changes in general social policies facilitate the more specific activation policies, is still to be seen. In line with the framework that regulates these policy changes, and based on the assumption that the general system of social security and labour market policies is made more activating and re-integrative, public employment services and administration are seen to be less necessary and therefore partially dismantled. Spending on public employment services and administration as a percentage of GDP more than halved between 1990 and 2022. In the next section, we will go into more detail concerning these specific activation policies.

2.   THE DEVELOPMENT OF ACTIVATION POLICIES

Next to general social security and labour market policies, we distinguish activation policies that are directly oriented at activation and re-integration of (mainly) people receiving social security benefits. In this section, we give a (necessarily brief) overview of the development of the most important instruments that are used in activation policies, and we conclude with a short sketch of the job agreement (2015) between the social partners and the government, and the introduction of the Participation Act (also in 2015). In this act the different re-integration instruments for people receiving social assistance are integrated. Both initiatives are intended to solve some of the problems that play a prominent role in the daily practice of implementing re-integration policies. Indicators of these developments are presented in Figure 7.2.

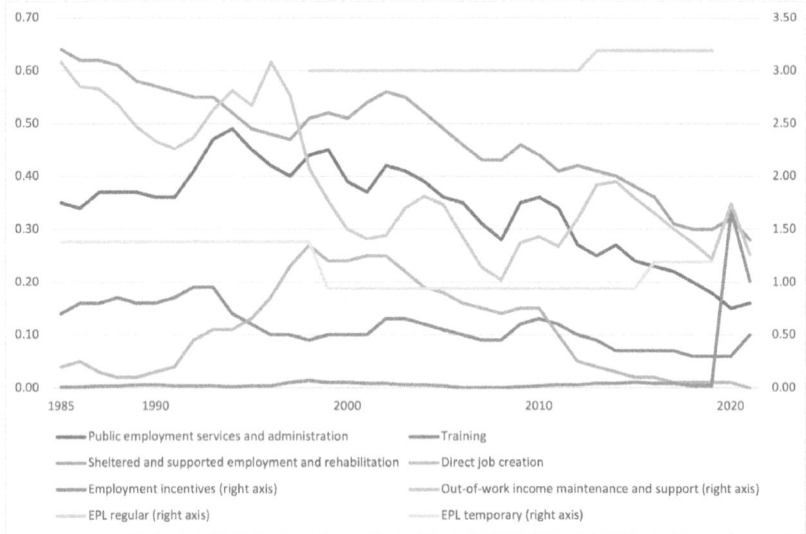

Figure 7.2   Developments in activation policies

Main Trends in Activation Policy

Employment services and training and schooling

The first instrument in activation policies concerns the services offered to people looking for a job. This involves information about and orientation on the labour market, and job vacancies and assistance during the job search. Next to these services, people can be offered training and schooling options to increase their chances on the labour market.

Until 2009, these services were delivered by a dedicated employment service organization (the CWI). Since 2009 the social security administration, the UWV, has delivered these services. Most of the services are directed at jobseekers with a low labour market value and are, as said, increasingly organized online. The Workcompany also delivers services to employers, helping employers to find personnel or helping employers to employ workers with a low labour market value. In so-called regionally organized 'employers service points', the Workcompany cooperates with municipalities. The UWV is confronted with diminishing budgets. As mentioned before, the implementation of some of these services therefore takes place mainly online, especially where job searching and orientation are concerned.

Municipalities deliver employment services for people who receive social assistance benefits. Until recently, municipalities received separate budgets for benefits and employment services. These budgets were merged in 2018. (This merger is partial, however; municipalities still receive a separate budget for support of people indicated for sheltered work.) Consequently, the budget used for employment services has diminished (SCP 2019).

The integration of employment services in social insurance administration is a result of the fact that the use and requirements of some of these services must be aligned with the benefit administration.

Training and schooling can be part of re-integration activities, yet at the same time can be at odds with stimulating labour market participation because people will be temporarily unavailable for the labour market due to training and schooling activities. This is the so-called 'lock-in effect' (Benda 2019). It is therefore necessary to target the people who qualify for training and schooling carefully (Kok 2011). In combination with the general development in social and labour market policies towards control of costs and take-up, this has resulted in a gradual decrease of the use of training and schooling facilities.

Obligations

In order to increase incentives to participate on the labour market, the level and duration of benefits has decreased. In line with this, work obligations have been gradually strengthened. Benefit recipients must look for work more intensively and have to accept employment quicker, meaning they have to accept work that is below their former level or under their level of schooling.

The enforcement of these obligations has also gradually been strengthened. Due to the dismantling of the employment services agency (the CWI), the public social insurance administration (UWV) and the municipalities became responsible for the administration and enforcement of these obligations. These obligations became, above all, a conditionality for receiving any benefits.

A far-reaching variety of an obligation is workfare, labour that one is required to do to receive a benefit. With the introduction of the Participation Act in 2015 – we will return to this act below – municipalities were given the opportunity to make use of the instrument of workfare. Some municipalities, though few, have done so. Finally, a so-called reciprocation is made possible by the Participation Act for those benefit recipients who are not active in sheltered work or in an activating labour market program. The reciprocation involves unpaid, socially useful activities (Fenger, Kip and van der Veen 2022).

Subsidized jobs and job subsidies
Activating labour market policies started in the 1990s with the so-called 'Melkert-jobs' (Mosselman and Muysken 2020). These were jobs in the public sector that were created for people who had little or no chance of finding a job on the regular labour market. The jobs created were not supposed to compete with jobs on the regular labour market. The history of these jobs is short. From the beginning, it was contested that these jobs did not compete with jobs on the regular labour market and that accepting such a job did not hinder people from finding a job on the regular labour market. The selection of people that qualified for these jobs was also contested, and selection of the more promising people – instead of people with the lowest labour market chances – was foreseen.

The 'Melkert-jobs' became 'inflow and throughflow' jobs, meant to help people find a job on the regular labour market. The selection of people for these jobs as well as the throughflow to the regular labour market, however, stayed contested, so in 2004 these jobs were abolished, and the instrument of job subsidies replaced them.

Job subsidies were (conditionally) available for employers on the regular labour market and were thus intended to solve the issue of competition and of a lack of throughflow towards the regular labour market. The conditionality and the targeting of these job subsidies, that still exist, among others in the Participation Act, has increased since they were introduced (SCP 2019).

Sheltered work
Until 2015, sheltered work, for people who are not fit for the regular labour market, was organized and financed separately from social security (in the WSW act) (Torre 2016). Organizations for sheltered work were (more or less) independent of social security administration and workers received a salary that was higher than the minimum wage. However, in 2015, all social provisions (including the WSW) were taken together in one act, the Participation Act, to be administered by the municipalities. Employment services, including sheltered work, were also integrated in the Participation Act.

People engaged in sheltered work now receive a salary at the minimum level. The arguments to incorporate sheltered work into the Participation Act and to lower the earnings to the social minimum level are the same we have seen before: issues of competition with the regular labour market, of selection of workers and of throughflow to the regular labour market. These issues were first taken up within the original act for sheltered employment (the WSW): organizations for sheltered employment had to second a percentage of their employees on the regular labour market, had to have a certain percentage of throughflow of employees and had to be, to some extent, profitable. These requirements were to some extent contradictory – profitability and throughflow – and led to selection of the most promising and to a low throughflow. The disappointing throughflow to the regular labour market was also seen as a consequence of the fact that it was possible for people in sheltered work to receive a salary above the minimum wage. So, in the end, the WSW was abolished and sheltered work was organized in the Participation Act.

Employment protection

Employers have limited means to dismiss workers, given the level of employment protection. This particularly holds for permanent workers, who enjoy higher levels of employment protection than temporary workers. The level of protection is quite stable and increased somewhat for permanent workers.

While higher levels of employment protection may be a disincentive for employers to hire employees, the benefits of it lie, for example, in a stronger incentive to invest in training employees to enhance their employability (e.g. Koster and Benda 2020). The shift from training via public policies to training that is paid by employers and employees indicates the increasing emphasis on activation.

The job-agreement (2015) and the Participation Act (2015)

Two recent developments in the field of activation policies are the so-called job-agreement and the Participation Act. Both were introduced in 2015 (SCP 2019).

The diminishing budgets for activation policies, mentioned before, are partially compensated for by the so-called 'job-agreement' that social partners and the state reached in 2015. This job-agreement intends to engage employers more directly in providing jobs for people with lower chances on the labour market and thus tries to solve some of the dilemmas concerning competition and throughflow prominent in activation policies. In the agreement, employers commit themselves to guaranteeing jobs for partially disabled workers and for workers who cannot earn a minimum wage because of a handicap or illness. The agreement was developed in relation to the introduction of the Participation Act and the abolishment of the law on sheltered work (WSW). Employers promised to create 125,000 jobs on the regular labour market for the agreement's target groups. If this target was not met in 2022, a quota (and a sanction) could be introduced. The target appears to have been met, albeit not by organizations in the public sector, which had to create 25,000 jobs. By 2021 they had created only 12,000 of the 25,000 jobs. However, a quota has not yet been considered.

The Participation Act integrates all provisions and services for people receiving social benefits. It integrates the former social assistance act (WWB), the act for sheltered employment (WSW) and the social assistance for disabled people without working experience (Wajong). The integration is meant to solve unwanted differences between beneficiaries that can hinder reintegration activities (for example, between people in sheltered employment who receive a salary above the minimum wage and people receiving social assistance on the social minimum). It also intends to bring all employment services for people receiving social benefits together in one administrative organization at the municipal level.

The first evaluations of this Participation Act show that, although general labour market participation rose, labour market participation of vulnerable groups has hardly increased and in some cases even decreased. The number of persons in sheltered employment, for example, has declined since the introduction of the Participation Act. However, this decline is compensated for by the job-agreement, mentioned before. In the Participation Act, the number of people in sheltered work is gradually increasing (SCP 2019: 215). The first evaluations also show a slow start followed by a gradual increase of the use of job subsidies (SCP 2019: 204–205). According to the researchers, a good match between employer and potential employee as well as adequate support of employers, are necessary for better use of the instruments the Participation Act provides.

Unwanted and Unintended Consequences Explain the Development of Activation Policies

The development of the different instruments of activation policies, as discussed, is comparable. Issues of selection of people who qualify for the different instruments, of competition between chances on the regular labour market and participation in activation programs and issues of limited through-flow, play a role with every instrument that is used in activation policies. We can witness a gradually increasing awareness of the unintended and unwanted consequences of activation policies. Benda (2019) summarizes these effects. First, targeting can lead to stigmatization, which can reduce instead of enhance the chances on the labour market of the targeted groups. Second, schooling and training can have 'lock-in effects', because the participants of these programs are not available for the labour market for the duration of training and schooling. This prolonged unemployment can reduce their labour market chances. And third, the administrative focus on the throughflow towards realization of the regular labour market activation policies, can lead to cream skimming – the selection of clients with the highest chances on the labour market.

Growing awareness of these unintended and unwanted consequences of activation policies, within the broader context of social policies increasingly oriented at control of costs and take-up, explains the developments sketched above and also the diminishing budgets for activation policies, which have been addressed before.

3. THE DUTCH LABOUR MARKET, DUTCH POLITICS AND THE FUTURE OF ACTIVATION POLICIES

Concerning the future of activation policies in the Netherlands, there are a number of issues that have to be mentioned. The first is the current situation on the labour market in the Netherlands. We have characterized this as a dualized labour market and we suggest that the dualization is to some extent produced by the policy developments we have sketched. Second, a re-orientation is taking place concerning the politics of retrenchment and control, that will affect the direction of and room for future social policies. Related to this, a re-orientation in perceptions of rights and duties, but also of what can be demanded of citizens, is taking place (WRR 2017). This, too, will affect the future of activation policies. We will discuss these issues and wrap up with a view on the foreseeable future of activation policies.

The Dutch labour market of today (Veen 2023) is characterized by one of the highest levels of participation in the EU (2022, 81.7%; the EU average is 73.1%) and by almost the lowest level of total hours worked per year (2021, 1400h/pw; the average is 1750h/pw).

This high level of participation results (among other things) from the strong increase of the participation of women (to 68% in 2022) and recently from the steep rise of the exit age (to 64 in 2022; the official retirement age is currently 66 years and 7 months). The participation of disabled people, however, is still lagging in comparison with other European nations (SCP 2016). The persistent low level of unemployment and the declining take-up of disability insurance also contributes to the high level of participation and illustrates the relative success of the Dutch social security and labour market policies.

The Dutch labour market is also characterized by a high number of people with part-time contracts (35% in 2022, the highest in the OECD), a high number of people with temporary employment (28%, the third highest in the OECD) and a high number of self-employed (16% in 2021, which means a slight drop from the 17% in 2020). In 2020, about 35% of the labour force was either a flex worker or self-employed. In 2021, this figure jumped to 42%. While sometimes attributed to the rise of the platform economy, it seems that this is not the major explanation for the increasing number of self-employed. Instead, it may be a matter of other conditions such as a weak position of labour unions (Koster 2023). The flexibility of the Dutch labour market results in a high level of participation but also in dualization. The social protection of flex workers and the self-employed, especially in cases of sickness and old age, is low. This has stimulated the European Commission in the European semester to ask the

Dutch government, for several years in a row, to increase the protection of flex workers and self-employed (European Commission 2022).

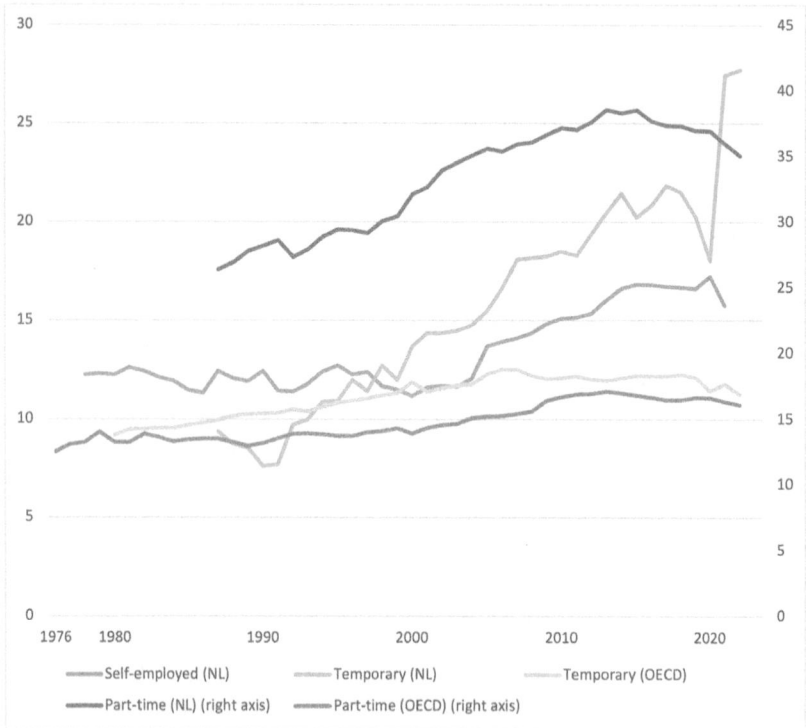

Figure 7.3   Developments in the Dutch labour market

Since the 1990s, activation and participation have been the main goals of social security in the Netherlands. The policies and instruments sketched before have intended effects, being stimulating activation and participation, but also unintended effects, such as the growth of flexible labour contracts and self-employed workers and a still-fragile position of vulnerable groups (e.g. disabled workers and the self-employed). The Dutch labour market thus has a Janus face. Social policies have also contributed to the growth of an increasingly dualized labour market and social protection of workers. Social policies in the Netherlands have developed towards selective policies, towards targeting, and towards strengthened obligations and responsibilities for citizens, as indicated before. This is not only visible in social security and labour market policies but is dominant in other policy fields too. In income policies, for example, it has led to the growth of a complicated system of allowances to target income support as much as possible. However, the selectivity of income policies (including social security) has not resulted in the intended outcomes. Many people are at risk of poverty or already have an income below the poverty line. A recent commission advising the government on the level of the social minimum explains this by pointing to the complexity of the system that often generates perverse effects, to the non-use of allowances because people lack the knowledge or the will to apply, and to the low level of the social minimum especially for single earner households (Commissie Sociaal Minimum 2023).

Selective policies are accompanied by a harsh enforcement. Selective policies ask for more enforcement than universal policies (because they are more complex), and this is amplified by a sceptical view of citizens and by incidents of fraud. Since the introduction of the Fraud Act of 2012, the Dutch Ombudsman has reported almost yearly about the harsh enforcement of social policies and about the devastating consequences of the fines and pay-back rules that are applied.

The combination of ineffective selective policies and a harsh enforcement, confirmed in recent parliamentary inquiries into the allowance system (2021), has resulted in a strong decline of trust in government and its administrative agencies (SCP 2023).

The dualization of the labour market and of social protection is increasingly experienced as a perverse effect of decades of activation policy. The social protection of workers with flexible labour relations and of the self-employed is low. But workers with permanent contracts experience the negative effects of the Dutch approach too. The minimum-income level has not risen for years and is experienced as too low. It is the flexibility of the labour market that probably limited the power of workers and their unions to negotiate a rise of income levels. Recently government has raised the legal minimum-income level for the first time in years, by more than 8%.

The experience of the perverse effects of the dualized labour market has been amplified by the Covid crisis. It was the workers with flexible labour contracts and the self-employed who experienced the economic consequences of the crisis most severely (see Cantillon, Seeleib-Kaiser and van der Veen 2021). Owing to the limited social protection of these groups, the government had to create new (temporary) provisions to prevent joblessness and poverty.

Next to the dualization of the labour market and of social security, the increasingly tight labour market will probably also be a driver of future changes in social policy and labour market policy. For the first time in many years, the number of open positions is larger than the number of unemployed. Given the aging working population, it is to be expected that the labour market will stay tight for years to come. This will probably lead to a gradual shift in the distribution of bargaining power, from employers to workers and unions.

It is to be expected that under the pressure of the negative effects of a dualized but increasingly tight labour market, social policy will change in the direction of more attention to security and less focus on flexibility. Recent developments support this hypothesis. Not only is the minimum-income level rising, but government also intends to decrease the flexibility of the labour market and to make self-employment less attractive. Administrative agencies are also stimulated to use their discretionary powers more often and to be more responsive.

The development in the direction of more attention for security is probably stimulated by the strongly felt unintended and perverse effects of selective policies and a harsh enforcement.

The focus on flexibilization at the cost of security in general social security and labour market policies, is accompanied by diminishing budgets and increasing targeting in activation policies, as we have shown. A policy change in the direction of more attention for security will probably stimulate a development in activation policies towards less targeting, an increase in budgets and more supportive implementation.

NOTES

1.   This section is based on a more comprehensive description in Romke van der Veen (2023).
2.   Data of Central Statistical Agency (CBS), the Netherlands. See also Vuuren et al. (2020).

REFERENCES

Benda, L. (2019) *Understanding Active Labour Market Policies*. Rotterdam: Erasmus University (dissertation).

Cantillon, B., M. Seeleib-Kaiser and R. van der Veen (2021) The Covid-19 crisis and policy responses by continental European welfare states, *Social Policy and Administration*, 55(2): 326–338

Central Planning Agency (CPB) (2015) *Kansrijk arbeidsmarktbeleid* (Promising Labour Market Policies). 's Gravenhage.

Commissie Sociaal Minimum (2023) *Een zeker bestaan. Naar een toekomstbestendig stelselk van het sociaal minimum* (A secure livelihood: Towards a future-proof system of the social minimum). 's Gravenhage

European Commission (2022) *Landverslag 2022 – Nederland, Aanbeveling voor een aanbeveling aan de Raad* (Country Report 2022, the Netherlands, recommendation for a recommdnation to the council). Brussels.

Fenger, M., T. Kip and R. van der Veen (2022) *Tien jaar beleid voor werk en inkomen in Rotterdam: een terugblik* (Ten years policy for work and income in Rotterdam: An overview). In: F. Dekker, M. Fenger and M. Van Kooij (eds.) *Waardevol aan het werk in Rotterdam*, Rotterdam, pp. 47–68.

Kok, L. (2011) *Onderzoek ontsloten. Lessen Reintegratie: wat werkt voor wie?* (Research into reintegration: What works for whom?). Nijmegen (SEO/ Gemeentelijke Rekenkamer Nijmengen).

Koster, F. (2023) Self-employment and technology: Different models of labour relations. In *Welfare States in a Turbulent Era* (pp. 28–47). Cheltenham, UK and Northampton, MA, USA: Edward Elgar Publishing.

Koster, F., and L. Benda (2020) Explaining employer-provided training. *Zeitschrift für Sozialreform*, 66(3), 237–260.

Mosselman, K., and J. Muysken (2020) *Lessen voor de baangarantie. Wat we kunnen leren van de Melkertbanen* (Lesson for the job-guarantee: What we can learn from the Melkertbanen). Den Haag (Wiardi Beckman Stichting).

Pierson, P. (1996) The new politics of the welfare state. *World Politics*, 4(2), 143–179.

Social and Cultural Planning agency (SCP) (2016) *Beperkt in functie* (Limited in function). 's Gravenhage.

SCP (2019) *Eindevaluatie van de Participatiewet* (End-evaluation of the Participation Act). 's Gravenhage.

SCP (2023) *Burgerperspectieven 2023* (Perspectives of citizens in 2023). 's Gravenhage.

Torre, L. van der (2016) *Sociale Werkvoorziening tussen overheid, markt en samenleving* (Sheltered employment between state, market and community). Rotterdam: Erasmus University (dissertation).

Veen, R. van der (2023) Sturing van arbeidsmarktbeleid en van arbeidsparticipatie. Een (deels) bestuurskundige agenda voor de toekomst (Labour market policies and labour market participation: A (partly) administrative agenda for the future). In: T. Overmans (ed.), *Maatschappelijke Bestuurskunde* (Social public administration). The Hague: Boom, pp. 169–190.

Visser, J. (1999) *De sociologie van het halve werk* (Sociology of part-time work). Amsterdam (inaugural lecture).

Visser, J., and A. Hemerijck (1997) *A Dutch Miracle: Job Growth, Welfare Reform and Corporatism in the Netherlands.* Amsterdam: Amsterdam University Press.

Vuuren, D. van, W. Zwinkels, A. Heijne, J. Kossen and D. Ooms (2020) *Beleidsdoorlichting artikel 1 (Arbeidsmarkt) 2012–2019* (Labour market policies 2012–2019). Amsterdam (de Argumentenfabriek)

Wetenschappelijke Raad voor het Regeringsbeleid (WRR) (2017) Weten is nog geen doen. Een realistisch perspectief op redzaamheid (Knowing is not the same as doing: A realistic perspective of self-reliance). 's Gravenhage.

8.   Norway: activation in the labouring society

Ivan Harsløf and Ivar Lødemel

INTRODUCTION

This chapter critically assesses the evolution of Norwegian policies targeted at workless people. Its historical outlook lays out the roots of present-day debates on the design of activation policies and their role in the welfare state. This analysis serves as a background for assessing future directions of these policies. Activation is a relatively new term, which has been increasingly used by policymakers and researchers since the late 1990s. It involves policies targeted at groups distant from the labour, and with the use of conditionality as a key policy instrument. Consistent with the other contributions to this volume, we use a broad understanding of the term, embracing both active labour market policies for the insured and later extensions to include groups further from the labour market. It is with these later extensions that conditionality has become more widely applied in Norwegian programmes targeted at workless people.

The chapter is organized as follows. Through a historical review of developments in employment and activation policies in Norway, we set out to identify key features of the policies, on a general level and with specific regard to the main tiers in the benefit hierarchy. This analysis is followed by a discussion of the important role played by the social partners in decisions on employment policies and their implementation. We then provide an account of the special employment measures that were adopted to tackle the challenges imposed by the COVID-19 pandemic from 2020 to 2022. In the final section, we offer a perspective on the likely direction of Norwegian activation policies in the years to come.

HISTORICAL DEVELOPMENT AND GENERAL TRAITS OF ACTIVATION IN NORWAY

Throughout the 20th century, full employment featured as a prominent goal in the Norwegian welfare state, to the extent that in 1954, the (symbolic) 'right to work' was enshrined in the constitution (Moe, 2000; Hanisch, 1977). Indeed, Norway encapsulates Hannah Arendt's notion of the 'labouring society', i.e. a society that glorifies labour (Arendt, 1958; Halvorsen and Stjernø, 2008). All the same, compared with Sweden, active labour market policies were for many years less prioritized. Instead, Norwegian policymakers preferred to stimulate employment through expansionist macroeconomic instruments (Dølvik and Oldervoll, 2019). Hence the state often intervened to promote employment, either directly through the expansion of state-owned enterprises or indirectly by offering advantageous loans through the state's Industrial Bank (established 1936) (Huber and Stephens, 1998; Hanisch, 1977).

In the 1920s and 1930s, most larger cities established local employment offices. Throughout the 1930s, many municipalities initiated 'emergency work' to alleviate the consequences of the deep recession and staggering unemployment. These efforts were supported by the state through special emergency work loans to the municipalities (Hanisch, 1977; Johansson, 1980). However, such efforts differed from later activation programmes by their lack of attachment to benefit entitlements, being solely demand side oriented and reserved for people who had recently lost their jobs (Lødemel and Dahl, 2000).

The Norwegian parliament reinvigorated the general work orientation in the early post-war years. The encompassing political programme initiated by a broad political coalition was headed 'Work for everyone' (Thorsvik, 2021). Following up on this programme, in 1947, the government adopted the Act respecting measures to promote employment (Norwegian Directorate for Labour, 1967). With a considerable number of men (particularly seafarers) being disabled during the war, rights to vocational rehabilitation and training were expanded and institutions were set up to cater to this group (Hvinden, 1994). The Labour Directorate was established, and local efforts to promote adequate supply and demand of labour were strengthened. National and local efforts concentrated on countering frictional and seasonal unemployment. To address seasonal unemployment, which is relatively large due to the country's geography and climate, short training measures were offered particularly to building and construction workers to allow them to broaden their employment possibilities (Hanisch, 1977).

In the 1950s to 1960s, a Norwegian type of 'spatial Keynesianism' (Brenner, 2004), a comprehensive regional policy to develop regions that were falling behind ('distriktspolitikk'), saw the light (Hersoug and Leonardsen, 1979). Among the many policy tools adopted under this banner in the following decades, the most important was the reduction in employers' contributions, introduced in 1975 to stimulate employment in outer districts (NOU, 2012). During the 1960s, Norway instituted encompassing and long-term vocational rehabilitation programmes that combined elements of treatment, work capacity assessment, education and job placement. The launching of rehabilitation programmes coincided with the introduction of more generous disability benefit programmes (Drøpping, Hvinden and Van Oorschot, 2000). Indeed, vocational rehabilitation programmes can be regarded as a 'gatekeeping' intervention to counter the inflow into costly, permanent disability benefits programmes (Lindqvist, 2000). In 1960, the state took over the responsibility for the local employment offices. This rescaling allowed for better coordination across the country. Hence, a stronger emphasis was put on encouraging workers in peripheral districts to seek work in new industrial projects in growth areas (Hanisch, 1977). By the end of the 1960s, well over 15 per cent of the matching between workers and jobs facilitated by the employment offices happened *across* district territories (Norwegian Ministry of Local Government and Labour, 1969).

For many decades, in any practical manner, Norway's goal of full employment only concerned male workers. Women's participation in the labour force was low by international standards, with only 18 per cent participating as of 1960 (Norwegian Directorate for Labour, 1967). However, during the 1960s, the state turned to promoting the employment of women. Between 1959 and 1968, the proportion of women participating in adult vocational training grew to 23 per cent from 8 per cent. Moreover, from 1963, state grants were paid to municipal day-care institutions to broaden the child-care services on offer (Norwegian Ministry of Local Government and Labour, 1969). Rather than a proactive policy to facilitate gender equality, the further expansion of day-care in the 1970s was primarily a reaction to women's large-scale entry into working life (Johnsen and Løken, 2013). Yet, the steady growth of social services not only relieved women from domestic care burdens, but simultaneously stimulated demand for women in the local labour markets (Kolberg and Esping-Andersen, 1991; Kjeldstad, Kautto and Hatland, 2001).

Activation of Recipients of Unemployment Benefits, Health-related Benefits and Minimum Income Schemes

We next consider the main developments in activation policies pertaining to different target groups. The governance structures prevailing in the field are best described as divided into two tiers. The first tier concerns the national programmes provided for groups of people out of employment who enjoy entitlements in the social insurance system. Here, our account separates between services for the unemployed and services for those on health-related benefits. The second, lower tier is provided at the local level and is attached to minimum income schemes – first and foremost, social assistance. This lower level integrates income maintenance and social services (Lødemel, 1997b). Groups covered by the first tier may also resort to the second tier for supplementary support; and as we shall see, during recent decades, governance reforms and new programming have resulted in a less clear-cut division between the two tiers.

Activation of the Unemployed in the First Tier

A government white paper entitled 'On Labour Market Policy' (Norwegian Ministry of Local Government and Labour, 1969), is often referred to as signalling a first expansion of active measures, from offering relocation support to redundant workers to creating new vocational training measures. A suggestion to establish quotas for older workers at enterprises was not adopted. Indeed, Norway has seen little of such overt regulations in favour of groups in vulnerable positions (Harsløf, Poulsen and Larsen, 2019). To implement the planned expansion of activation measures and public employment services, a preceding white paper called for deepened collaboration with the social partners, particularly at the local level (Norwegian Directorate for Labour, 1967: 14).

In the early 1990s, as Nordic countries experienced an economic crisis, active labour market policies were put high on the political agenda in Norway (Vartiainen, 2011). In 1989, an activation measure for people on unemployment benefits was introduced ('Arbeid for trygd'). It entailed offering unemployed persons temporary work practice in the public sector to do extraordinary work tasks. The measure only applied when possibilities for reintegration through regular employment services and training measures had been exhausted.

Furthermore, aligning with the policy orientation towards developing peripheral regions, in the three northernmost counties, special funds were set aside to try out the same measure in the private sector. Before this trial, the private sector had almost never been involved in such activities. This scheme was reserved for enterprises subject to collective agreements, and the work tasks involved had to be negotiated with representatives of the social partners. Placements were up to six months, with 80 per cent of the time allotted to work and 20 per cent for job searches. While certain pressure could be leveraged to encourage the target group to participate, in practical terms, it was unnecessary; most people were eager to join (Pedersen, 1990).

Generally, however, in this period, the authorities preferred educational measures over job-training measures. In modern-day terminology, this strategy is called 'train then place' (as opposed to the 'place then train' strategy) (Corrigan and McCracken, 2005). Hence, short vocational training courses were the measure most frequently used – and further expanded during the 1989–1995 recession (Moe, 2000). In the 1990s, Norway strengthened its emphasis on active measures. Research has found modest but positive effects of the (first-tier) activation measures applied in the 1990s. Work-oriented measures were found to have higher effects than educational measures. The effect was highest during recessions (Moe, 2000).

Figure 8.1 shows how the ratio of active to passive measures increased in that decade. The notable increase in 2006–2008 is likely related to the implementation of the Labour and Welfare Administration Reform and the ensuing extra spending to expand public employment services (to be discussed below). Over the whole 1990–2020 period, however, the ratio of active to passive measures has only grown marginally. The decline in 2014 can be attributed to a significant fall in oil prices that raised unemployment in oil-related industries, and, hence, expenditures on 'passive' unemployment benefits. For 2020, the last year we have data, the marked decline is clearly the effect of the pandemic.

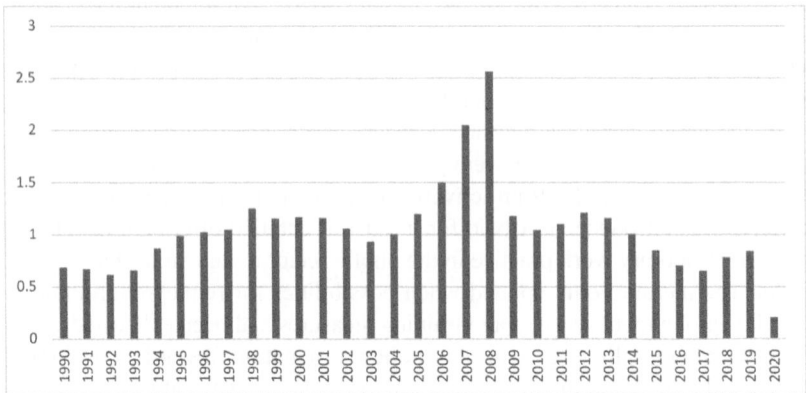

Figure 8.1   Ratio of active to passive measures 1990-2020

Activation within Health-related Benefit Programmes

Health-related benefits are also part of the first tier. Arguably, Norway's success in largely fulfilling the goal of full employment can partly be attributed to a social security system that allows a relatively large proportion of people of working age to live on a health-related benefit. Norway has the highest proportion of people on disability pension among OECD countries (MacDonald, Prinz and Immervoll, 2020). In 2007, Norway's expenditures on health-related benefits were 24 times higher than what was spent on unemployment benefits (Hatland and Øverbye, 2011).[1] For this reason, Norway's activation efforts – in addition to the policies concerning people on minimum-income schemes, to be discussed below – have mainly concerned people in receipt of sickness benefits and other health-related benefits.

When ill, Norwegian employees are guaranteed 100 per cent income replacement (up to a relatively high ceiling), with the state covering the costs from the 16th day of sickness leave. In response to concerns about the remarkedly high sickness absence rate in Norway, the sickness benefit programme has been subject to several changes throughout the years. In 2000, the Labour government proposed a cut in the sickness benefit level. However, this proposal was met with fierce protests from the labour unions. Instead, in 2001, the state entered into an agreement of intent with the social partners, setting up ambitious targets and measures. The agreement aimed to reduce the general sickness absence rate, retain vulnerable groups in current jobs, and bring new groups into paid employment. In 2004, several activity requirements were introduced for recipients of sickness benefits who received this allowance for more than eight weeks – unless there were special medical reasons. Furthermore, eligibility rules were adjusted to ensure better 'targeting towards employees with a stable labour market attachment' (Norwegian Government, 2003: 6).

Based upon disappointing results from the first agreement of intent, in 2006, the Labour government proposed that employers be required to co-finance part of the sickness absence period. Again, the labour unions strongly opposed the proposal, this time in an alliance with the Employers' Association. The proposal was subsequently shelved (Kjønstad, 2007). This incident exemplifies the strong power of the social partners in Norwegian welfare and employment politics, something that becomes particularly conspicuous when considering simultaneous welfare cuts that the government succeeded in carrying out, which affected less powerful groups (Bay and Hellevik, 2019).

A main policy development related to the group on health-related benefits, has been the 2010 restructuring of a number of vocational rehabilitation programmes into the Work Clarification Programme (AAP). Recipients of AAP are expected to undergo active treatment, participate in job-oriented measures, or receive other forms of support with the aim of either gaining or retaining employment. AAP recipients have an obligation to report to the Labour and Welfare Administration and are required to actively contribute to the process, cooperate in developing an activity plan, and follow through with the designated activities (Pedersen, Grødem and Wagner, 2019). Since its introduction, AAP has been subject to several tightening measures, both in duration (significantly limiting the possibility of staying on this programme for more than four years) and expansion of sanction possibilities (Kann and Lima, 2020).

Activation within the Lower-tier Minimum Income Programmes

There has traditionally been a sharp distinction between social insurance and social assistance programmes in Norway (Gubrium, Harsløf and Lødemel, 2014). In the Norwegian welfare model, social insurance programmes have been prioritized and social assistance has intentionally been given a marginal role (Halvorsen, Schøyen and Harsløf, forthcoming). Norway has a strong tradition of local autonomy in welfare provision, particularly in relief for the poor (Seip, 2007). Hence, throughout the 20th century, municipalities have had considerable autonomy in organizing and determining levels of social assistance for people in need.

Defined nationally in the Law on Social Services, social assistance programmes are administered and financed by the municipalities. Since 2001, national guidelines have been issued regularly regarding benefit rates, specified for different types of households, but the municipalities determine the exact level, allowing for adjustments to the local situation (particularly as local housing costs vary significantly across the country) and individual needs. To be eligible for social assistance, the person must have legal residence in Norway and must have exhausted all alternative economic resources, including those of other family members in the household (except for income generated through children's spare-time jobs).

Paralleling developments in most other Western welfare states, in 1991, municipalities were allowed to require that a person participate in training or work activities if they wished to receive full social-assistance benefits (Lødemel and Trickey, 2001). This change in policy was only passed by a small majority of centre-right parties against the will of the Labour Party government. Only four years later, however, in 1995, the Labour Party also decided to support such work requirements in the social assistance scheme (Vik-Mo and Nervik, 1999; Lødemel, 1997a). Looking back, the Norwegian activation policies for recipients on minimum-income schemes, as they were implemented in the 1990s, stood out as harsh and 'work first' oriented (Lødemel, 2001). Caseworkers were including broader groups of participants than what was observed in other European countries (Dahl and Pedersen, 2001).

During the 2000s, the use of mandatory activation varied between municipalities. The large municipalities were considerably more inclined to impose activation conditions than the small municipalities. The use of such conditions increased significantly during 2010–2015 (Proba, 2015). However, studies have found that sanctions for not complying with conditions were 'mild and client sensitive' (Sadeghi and Terum, 2020: 222). One study indicated that municipalities requiring work activities (sometimes supplemented with job-search activities) and attendance on all weekdays, with social assistance eliminated in case of unjustified absence, reduced the number of social-assistance claimants in the target group by 11–17 per cent (Dahl and Lima, 2016).

In the 2000s, consecutive governments of different political colours put the fight against poverty on the policy agenda. Minimum-income schemes became further stratified, which added new, more 'human-resource-development' -oriented and more generous activation programmes. Hence, in 2004, a new

Introduction Programme was launched, targeting newly arrived immigrants and refugees, groups who were strongly represented among those at risk of poverty. Under the programme, an individual plan consisting of full-time work and training activities, including language training, is arranged for up to two years. The monthly allowance paid to participants differs from social assistance by being considerably higher, taxable, and not means-tested (Fernandes, 2013). While the social assistance was intended for short-term support, the Introduction Programme and allowance, being fixed term and extending over a longer period, provided recipients with a more predictable income source.

We note that policymakers were cautious that the target group would develop a 'dependency' on public welfare. They wanted to prevent participants from coming in too close contact with the local social welfare offices and thus initially organized the programme in independent municipal units (Econ, 2008). Heralding a new, more centralized orientation in policies concerning marginal groups, the municipalities were obliged to implement the programme for everyone in the target group. Within three months after a person in the target group registers as a resident, the municipality is required to enrol this person in the programme (Djuve and Kavli, 2007).

Largely modelled on the Introduction Programme, the 2007 Qualification Programme introduced the first national activation programme for long-term social-assistance claimants. Intended as a 'close follow-up of individual clients', it entailed positive economic incentives with an allowance level that is higher than the means-tested social assistance. The Qualification Programme changed the balance between rights and obligations towards the former. Yet, the entrance criteria for the Qualification Programme are somewhat ambiguous. Presented as a statutory right, in practice it is left to the discretion of the municipalities to decide whether a person is eligible, balancing several concerns. Hence, the person's ability to work must be 'considerably reduced' while showing potential for improvement through participation in the programme. Whether these conditions are satisfied is to be determined through a systematic 'mapping' of the person's work ability.

The Qualification Programme is not an explicit obligation for potential participants. However, following the general provisions of the Social Services Act, not accepting an offer to participate in the programme can be regarded as contrary to the demand that one use all possible alternative means to provide for oneself before social assistance can be paid out. The Qualification Programme is a one-year full-time programme, with the possibility of extension. Participants in the programme receive a taxable allowance identical to the one provided to participants in the Introduction Programme. The payment of benefits can be brought to a halt if the participant is repeatedly absent for no legitimate reasons (Norwegian Government, 2007). From 2011, the national character of the programme weakened, as instead of earmarked grants to the municipalities, financing was shifted to national framework grants. As a result, it was left to the autonomy of the local authorities to decide how much funds to dedicate to the programme. Indeed, the following years saw a decline in the number of participants, despite a growth in the target group and the programme's considerable employment effects, as found by rigorous evaluations (Markussen and Røed, 2016).

From its inception in the early 1990s, conditional activation in social assistance was enacted as an instrument that the local authorities were *able* to use. In 2017, the conservative government changed this and made participation in activation a *mandatory* requirement for people under the age of 30 to receive social assistance. Only recipients with grave personal circumstances were exempt (Grødem, 2016). Members of the Norwegian Association of Local and Regional Authorities were sceptical of the new policy, which they saw as challenging the traditionally strong autonomy enjoyed at the local level. Evaluations of the new regulation of the municipalities' activation efforts found that it did not result in more young people getting into education or employment. The evaluator of the expanded programme argued that the lack of effect could be because municipalities, even before the regulation, were already taking measures to select participants whom they saw as most likely to benefit from it. Being forced by central government to expand activation beyond this group meant providing measures to young people whose problems made them unlikely to enter education or employment anyhow (Hernæs, 2021).

INSTITUTIONS AND COLLECTIVE ACTORS INVOLVED IN ACTIVATION

As already implied in the preceding section, collective actors have a strong say in the formulation of labour market policies in Norway. The most important channel of influence is through the participation in government-appointed committees (Engelstad, 2015). Social partners are involved on an ad-hoc basis in the organizational set-up of activation provision (Lauringson and Lüske, 2021). Concrete activation measures are supposed to be designed locally and adapted to local needs. Hence, local employers are meant to be consulted when vocational qualification offers are developed, to ensure that they match the skills needed in the labour market (Moe, 2000). Studies report satisfaction among collective actors and state agencies involved in negotiating, planning and implementing active labour market policies (Pedersen, 1992).

The Norwegian Confederation of Trade Unions has generally been supportive of activation measures. The Confederation's overall position is that activation programmes, considered a qualification strategy, are necessary to avoid the emergence of a low-wage labour market segment, which would undermine the Norwegian model of compressed wage structures. For example, the Confederation calls for an expansion of the Qualification Programme, targeting social-assistance claimants. Moreover, it encourages placing more emphasis on skills enhancement and greater involvement of the shop stewards – the person elected by workers to represent them in dealings with management – when activated persons are integrated into a workplace through the wage subsidy scheme. Confederation members have noted that shop stewards may be instrumental in ensuring that the scheme does not lead to substitution effects (Norwegian Confederation of Trade Unions, 2020).

Another central issue for trade unions is countering the outsourcing of activation to private actors (Norwegian Union of Municipal and General Employees, 2022). With the strengthened political emphasis on Norway's 'work approach' throughout the 1990s, more activation measures were contracted out. Initially, this was set up in the form of special enterprises (with municipalities or counties as main shareholders) being preapproved to deliver such services. Later, a larger part of outsourcing came in the form of public tenders, allowing for broader competition among commercial and non-profit actors. According to analyses commissioned by a public committee set up to assess the use of private actors, the increased engagement of private actors has improved the quality and efficiency of activation (Norwegian Committee for Welfare Services, 2020). Yet, there are concerns that some private actors form complex corporations that de facto extract profit, instead of reinvesting it into activation and vocational rehabilitation activities, as one is supposed to (National Audit Office, 2020). From 2014 to 2018, international companies' share of the total turnover among private actors increased to 24 per cent, from 13 per cent (Norwegian Committee for Welfare Services, 2020).

Since 2007, activation of unemployment benefit recipients, people on sickness benefits, and social assistance recipients has been handled by the Labour and Welfare Administration, which was created through an encompassing administrative reform, and which merged the Public Employment Services (Arbeidsmarkedsetaten), the National Insurance Administration (Trygdeetaten) and parts of the municipal social services. The reform was meant to align the different – and sometimes contrasting – institutional logic of the involved agencies and provide more coordinated and holistic support. The reform process deviated from the traditional corporatist tradition, having been designed and implemented mainly by policymakers and bureaucrats with less involvement from the social partners (Andreassen and Aars, 2015: 162). The Confederation of Norwegian Enterprises declared during the consultation that they wanted to keep separate a unit to handle pensions so that the new organization could concentrate on work-oriented measures (NHO, 2004).

COVID-19 EXPERIENCES, MEASURES AND INSTRUMENTS USED, EFFECTIVENESS, AND NEW NORMALIZATION

During the COVID-19 pandemic, the Norwegian economy experienced markedly lower fluctuations than other EU countries, but saw a relatively higher increase in unemployment (Statistics Norway, 2022).[2] Young people, low-income groups, the low educated and immigrants were most affected (Bratsberg et al., 2020). At the outbreak of the pandemic, and the imposing of lockdowns, the Norwegian government responded with a number of measures aimed at preventing bankruptcies among private businesses and alleviating financial hardship among individuals affected by the sudden loss of work income (Greve et al., 2021). The unemployment insurance benefit for low-income groups was temporarily increased so that people with a previous annual income under NOK 320,000 would – during the pandemic – be compensated 80 per cent of previous pay, while compensation for earnings of NOK 320,000–638,000 remained the same as before, at 62.4 per cent (*FriFagbevegelse*, 2021). Moreover, the three-day waiting period for persons (temporarily) laid off before being entitled to benefits was suspended (Norwegian Government, 2020). A temporary measure was introduced for the self-employed and freelancers losing their income due to the pandemic, covering 80 per cent (later reduced to 60 per cent) of lost income (up to a certain ceiling) (Norwegian Labour and Welfare Directorate, 2022). Providing social benefits for these groups is a novelty and can be regarded as an expansion of the welfare state (Greve et al., 2021).

Norway's temporary lay-off scheme was gradually expanded in several ways. These changes were decided in close cooperation with the social partners. The period in which companies were allowed to furlough employees was doubled to 52 weeks, from 26. Additionally, the rule that ordinarily prevents temporarily laid-off workers from participating in training programmes while receiving unemployment benefits was suspended (Svalund, 2021). In December 2021, a temporary wage-subsidy scheme was adopted to allow companies to retain employees instead of laying them off or furloughing them (Norwegian Government, 2021). During the lockdown, participants in activation programmes were, as the rest of society, not allowed to meet in person. Instead, providers of activation measures were to arrange for online activities. Private suppliers of activation measures were compensated for the decline in turnover through the general support scheme for enterprises, as well as a special scheme where they could receive compensation for documented losses (Norwegian Committee for Welfare Services, 2020).

The pandemic required many industries to adopt rapid changes. Most importantly, it enforced a digital transformation, affecting both customer relations and internal work processes. According to a 2019 government-appointed employment committee (The Employment Committee, 2021), the pandemic increased the need for restructuring. In the report, committee members referred to the intensified pressure on industries that were already being affected by megatrends such as globalization and automatization. The committee called for training and skills development in working life, to respond to the needs of workers in industries that are likely to face closures and high unemployment in the future. On this basis, the committee recommended a strengthened focus on active labour market policies. In particular, they called for more qualification and job-training measures with wage subsidies. They proposed a tripartite industry programme, where the state and the social partners develop a relevant offer of training and further education measures (The Employment Committee, 2021).

In summary, the pandemic broadened the scope of the welfare state to accommodate new segments of individuals. But in terms of activation policies, the fundamental understanding of the problem's nature remains: activation measures in Norway focus mainly on groups with low skills and whose members are likely to be increasingly marginalized in the post-industrial labour market.

CONSIDERATIONS FOR THE FUTURE OF ACTIVATION IN NORWAY

Proponents of activation have faced criticism from two opposite ideological quarters: from groups advocating the decommodification of labour on the one hand, most notably the basic income movement (e.g. Standing, 2020), and from actors in support of free market forces (commodification), on the other. This latter perspective was most clearly expressed by British conservatives in the early 1990s who argued that activation represents market interference (Grover and Stewart, 1999).

Activation in the larger welfare state regime – and the social contract it is predicated upon – is often discussed in terms of whether the target group is receiving 'less' or 'more'. Activation policies regarded as implying 'less' entail strong sanctions, few rights and little funding, and prioritize work activities that do not stimulate skills development. This approach is often referred to as the 'work first' strategy. In contrast, policies that potentially provide 'more' to the participant, have a greater emphasis on rights and skills development and are backed by sufficient national funding. There policies are associated with the 'human resource development' strategy (Lødemel and Trickey, 2001).

Following Room (2000), policies promoting human resource development may be considered as furthering decommodification.

Norwegian activation for the unemployed with entitlements in the social insurance system is arguably closest to the human resource development strategy. Although, on paper, Norway has strict availability requirements and criteria for what is considered a suitable job (Immervoll and Knotz, 2018), such rules have often not been implemented or followed up very enthusiastically by the national authorities' representatives at the local level (e.g. Scharle, Váradi and Samu, 2015; Hansen and Rusten, 2005). Unemployed persons are met with few de facto work-first obligations. For those on minimum-income programmes, policies and programmes have over the last fifteen years departed from Norway's relatively coercive work-first strategy as it was practised in the 1990s (Gubrium, Harsløf and Lødemel, 2014). Hence, current programming is, more than before, based on a social-rights discourse and offers higher benefits, a more stable income, and a focus on skills development. Drawing on Titmuss's (1963) classic argument that universalism improves services, arguably the governance reform that merged the agencies catering to groups with or without entitlements in the social insurance system added 'more' to the people served in the lowest tier. With the reform, they were now referred to the same one-stop shop as first-tier users, hence more likely to benefit from the wider group's abilities to exert demands on service quality.

The development away from work-first approaches in the lower tier was, however, set back by the 2011 devolution of the economic responsibility for the Qualification Programme. The change replaced earmarked state funding for the programme with block grants, which resulted in municipalities giving lower priority to this type of activation. And the 2017 policy development mandating municipalities to activate all young social-assistance claimants can also be interpreted as a step in the work-first direction. However, considering the evaluations of this policy, as we have discussed, it may be more of a symbolic invocation of the Norwegian labouring ethos than a real policy change. Yet also the current Social Democratic-led government is contributing to this discourse. Hence, in the presentation of the 2024 national budget, its representatives resorted to statements that may signal a harsher future for those most distant from work. This included statements such as the group needing to 'get out of bed in the morning' and that 'presenting people with demands is to care' (*Nordlys*, 2023).

In the Norwegian case, the most difficult issue to assess concerns the activation of people on health-related benefits. Certainly, the Norwegian 'work approach' as first rolled out in the early 1990s has taken a relatively coercive approach towards this group with more mandatory meetings and activities. That said, there has also been considerable investment in skills enhancement and other measures oriented to human resource development (Håvold,

Harsløf and Andreassen, 2018). Recipients of health-related benefits face a dilemma with measures meant to promote work. The measures may help the recipient find employment, but that may barely increase the recipient's net earnings. Meanwhile, the recipient may lose their eligibility for health-related benefits, including the prospect of a permanent disability pension. If work integration should fail at a later stage, the recipient risks being relegated to the means-tested social assistance programme.

To assess future developments, one can consider several trends. First, globalization and service-sector expansion are carving out a new segment in the labour market that is characterized by low wages and precarious employment. We see this is reflected in the steady growth in in-work poverty, which has risen 15 per cent during 2011–2019 (Eurostat, 2023), alongside a moderate drop in union membership (Nergaard, Barth and Dale-Olsen, 2015). Second, and related to this, the target group for activation (in particular in the lower tier) is increasingly made up of people from ethnic-minority backgrounds (Statistics Norway, 2021). Combined, these developments may cause a drift in activation policies (cf. Hacker, 2004). This implies that even if the government may devote the same level of resources, the face of activation policies may change. As the labour market into which one is supposed to become integrated deteriorates, the pressure on unemployed people seeking work will, in effect, become harsher. Likewise, as the target group faces greater challenges in getting a stable foothold in the labour market – due to language barriers, ethnic discrimination, lack of relevant education, or other reasons – more resources will be needed to achieve the same effects in building people's qualifications and chances of employment.

NOTES

1. To compare, on average OECD countries were only spending three times more on health-related benefits (Hatland and Øverbye, 2011).
2. The relatively high rise in unemployment may be due to the initial Norwegian choice of policy response. In some countries, e.g. Denmark, the government chose from the outset to offer wage substitution to employers, hereby preventing (temporary) layoffs (Fløtten and Trygstad, 2020).

REFERENCES

Andreassen, T. A. and Aars, J. (2015) *Den store reformen: da NAV ble til (The great reform: When the Labour and Welfare Administration was created)*. Oslo: Universitetsforlaget.
Arendt, H. (1958) *The Human Condition*. Chicago: University of Chicago Press.

Bay, A.-H. and Hellevik, T. (2019) 'Politisk styring' (Political governance), in Bay, A.-H., Hatland, A., Hellevik, T. and Terum, L. I. (eds.) *Trygd i aktiveringens tid* (Social security during the activation period). Oslo: Gyldendal, pp. 128–144.

Bratsberg, B., Raaum, O., Alstadsæter, A., Eielsen, G., Markussen, S., Røed, K. and Kopczuk, W. (2020) *The First Weeks of the Coronavirus Crisis: Who Got Hit, When and Why? Evidence from Norway*. Cambridge: National Bureau of Economic Research.

Brenner, N. (2004) *New State Spaces: Urban Governance and the Rescaling of Statehood*. Oxford: Oxford University Press.

Corrigan, P. W. and McCracken, S. G. (2005) 'Place first, then train: an alternative to the medical model of psychiatric rehabilitation', *Social Work*, 50(1), pp. 31–39.

Dahl, E. and Pedersen, L. (2001) 'Workfare in Europe: does it work?', *Workfare in Six European Nations Findings from evaluations and recommendations for future development*. Oslo: Fafo Institute for Applied Social Science.

Dahl, E. S. and Lima, I. A. Å. (2016) 'Krav til å stå opp om morran – virker det? (Do requirements of getting up in the morning work?)', *Arbeid og velferd*, 3, pp. 115–130.

Djuve, A. B. and Kavli, H. C. (2007) 'Integreringspolitikk i endring' (Integration policy in change), in Dølvik, J. E., Fløtten, T., Hernes, G. and Hippe, J. M. (eds.) *Hamskifte: Den norske modellen i endring* (Hamskifte: The changing Norwegian model). Oslo: Gyldendal Akademisk, pp. 196–218.

Dølvik, J. E. and Oldervoll, J. (2019) 'Norway: Averting crisis through coordination and Keynesian welfare policies', in Ólafsson, S., Daly, M., Kangas, O. and Palme, J. (eds.) *Welfare and the Great Recession*. Oxford: Oxford University Press, pp. 210–227.

Drøpping, J. A., Hvinden, B. and Van Oorschot, W. (2000) 'Reconstruction and reorientation: changing disability policies in the Netherlands and Norway', *European Journal of Social Security*, 35(2), pp. 35–68.

Econ (2008) *'Opp om mårran': Forslag til innhold i og organisering av kvalifiseringsprogrammet* (A proposal to the content of and the organisation of the Qualification programme): Econ18.

Engelstad, F. (2015) *Cooperation and Conflict the Nordic Way: Work, Welfare, and Institutional Change in Scandinavia*. Warsaw, Poland; Berlin, Germany: De Gruyter Open.

Eurostat (2023) *In-work at-risk-of-poverty rate*. Available at: https:// ec .europa .eu/ eurostat/databrowser/view/tespm070/default/table?lang=en (accessed: 2023-20-01).

Fernandes, A. G. (2013) 'Ethnification of New Social Risks: Programmes for Preparing Newly Arrived Immigrants for (Working) Life in Sweden, Denmark and Norway', in Harsløf, I. and Ulmestig, R. (eds.) *Changing Social Risks and Social Policy Responses in the Nordic Welfare States*. Basingstoke: Palgrave Macmillan, pp. 189–219.

Fløtten, T. and Trygstad, S. (2020) *Post korona – en ny fase for den nordiske modellen?* (Post Corona – A new phase for the Nordic model?). Oslo: Fafo.

FriFagbevegelse (2021) 'Her er korona-ordningene som gjelder for arbeidsløse og permitterte fram til 28. februar 2022' (Here are the COVID-19 measures applying to unemployed and furloughed until 28 February 2022), 15 December. Available at: https:// frifagbevegelse .no/ nyheter/ her -er -koronaordningene -som -gjelder -for -arbeidslose -og -permitterte -fram -til -28 -februar -2022 -6 .158 .839674 .8dbfbe5a9e (accessed: 2024-24-08).

Greve, B., Blomquist, P., Hvinden, B. and van Gerven, M. (2021) 'Nordic welfare states—still standing or changed by the COVID-19 crisis?', *Social Policy and Administration*, 55(2), pp. 295–311.

Grødem, A. S. (2016) 'Mandatory activation for recipients of social assistance in Norway', *Social Europe*, 6. Available at: https:// ec .europa .eu/ social/ BlobServlet ?docId=15052&langId=en (accessed: 2024-24-08).

Grover, C. and Stewart, J. (1999) '"Market workfare": Social security and competitiveness in the 1990s', *Journal of Social Policy*, 28(1), pp. 73–96.

Gubrium, E., Harsløf, I. and Lødemel, I. (2014) 'Norwegian activation reform on a wave of wider welfare state change', in Lødemel, I. and Moreira, A. (eds.) *Activation or Workfare? Governance and Neo-Liberal Convergence*. New York: Oxford University Press, pp. 19–46.

Hacker, J. S. (2004) 'Privatizing risk without privatizing the welfare state: The hidden politics of social policy retrenchment in the United States', *American Political Science Review*, 98(2), pp. 243–260.

Halvorsen, K. and Stjernø, S. (2008) *Work, Oil and Welfare*. Oslo: Universitetsforlaget.

Halvorsen, R., Schøyen, M. A. and Harsløf, I. (forthcoming) 'Minimum income in Norway', in Jessoula, M. (ed.) *Minimum Income Schemes in Europe*. Cheltenham, UK and Northampton, MA, USA: Edward Elgar Publishing.

Hanisch, T. (1977) *Hele folket i arbeid: et essay om sysselsettingspolitikken i Norge. Pax-bok* (All the people at work: An essay on employment policy). Oslo: Pax.

Hansen, H.-T. and Rusten, G. (2005). 'Arbeidskontorenes kontakt med næringslivet' (The Work offices' contact with business life), *Tidsskrift for Velferdsforskning*, 8(1), pp. 34–46.

Harsløf, I., Poulsen, I. and Larsen, K. (2019) 'Northern European rehabilitation services in the context of changing healthcare, welfare, and labour market institutions: a theoretical framework', in *New Dynamics of Disability and Rehabilitation: Interdisciplinary Perspectives*. Singapore: Palgrave Macmillan, pp. 23–42.

Hatland, A. and Øverbye, E. (2011) 'Syk eller arbeidsledig?' (Sick or unemployed). Bergen: Fagbokforl., pp. 71–89.

Håvold, O. K., Harsløf, I. and Andreassen, T. A. (2018) 'Externalizing an "asset model" of activation: creative institutional work by frontline workers in the Norwegian Labour and Welfare Service', *Social Policy and Administration*, DOI: 10.1111/spol.12305.

Hernæs, Ø. M. (2021) 'Liten virkning av vilkår om aktivitet til unge sosialhjelpsmottakere' (Little effect of conditions on activity for young social assistance recipients), *Stat & styring* (State & Governance), 31(2), pp. 28–30.

Hersoug, B. and Leonardsen, D. (1979) *Bygger de landet? Distriktspolitikk og sosialdemokrati 1945–1975* (Are they building the country? Regional policies and social democracy 1945–1975). *Pax-bøkene*. Oslo: Pax.

Huber, E. and Stephens, J. D. (1998) 'Internationalization and the social democratic model: crisis and future prospects', *Comparative Political Studies*, 31(3), pp. 353–397.

Hvinden, B. (1994) 'Den norske velferdsstaten 100 år – men hva så? Arbeidslinjen i ny og gammel drakt' (The Norwegian welfare state 100 year – but so what? The work line in new and old guise), *Sosial trygd* (Social Security), 7/8(8), pp. 26–30.

Immervoll, H. and Knotz, C. (2018) 'How demanding are activation requirements for jobseekers?' *OECD Social, Employment, and Migration Working Papers*, 2018-07(215), pp. 1–52.

Johansson, T. (1980) *Fra sosialpolitikk til krisepolitikk? Arbeiderpartiets syn på krisepolitikk, nødsarbeid og bureising under arbeidsløshetskrisa 1920–1939* (From social policy to crisis policy? The Labour Party's view on crisis policy, emergency work and housing during the employment crisis 1920–1939). Oslo: T. Johansson.

Johnsen, J. V. and Løken, K. V. (2013) 'Ved veis ende: Har familiepolitikken spilt fallitt som likestillingsverktøy?' (At the end of the road: Has family policy failed as an equality tool?), *Nytt norsk tidsskrift* (*New Norwegian Journal*), 30(1), pp. 79–89.

Kann, I. C. and Lima, I. (2020) 'Ny lavterskelsanksjonen på arbeidsavklaringspenger er lite brukt, og effekten på mottakernes aktivitet er usikker' (The new low-threshold sanction on work assessment allowance is seldom used, and its effect on recipients' activity is uncertain), *Arbeid og velferd* (*Work and Welfare*), 2, pp. 81–100.

Kjeldstad, R., Kautto, M. and Hatland, A. (2001) *Nordic Welfare States in the European Context*. London: Routledge.

Kjønstad, A. (2007) *Folketrygdeloven med kommentarer* (The National Insurance Act with comments). Oslo: Gyldendal norsk forlag.

Kolberg, J.-E. and Esping-Andersen, G. (1991) 'Welfare states and employment regimes', in Kolberg, J.-E. (ed.) *The Welfare State as Employer*. New York: M. E. Sharpe, Inc, pp. 3–35.

Lauringson, A. and Lüske, M. (2021) *Institutional set-up of active labour market policy provision in OECD and EU countries: Organisational set-up, regulation and capacity*. Organisation for Economic Co-operation and Development.

Lindqvist, R. (2000) *Att sätta gränser: Organisationer och reformer i arbetsrehabilitering*. Umeå: Boréa.

Lødemel, I. (1997a) *Pisken i arbeidslinja* (The whip in the work line). Oslo: Forskningsstiftelsen Fafo.

Lødemel, I. (1997b) *The Welfare Paradox: Income Maintenance and Personal Social Services in Norway and Britain 1946–1966*. Oslo: Scandinavian University Press.

Lødemel, I. (2001) 'National objectives and local implementation of workfare in Norway', in Lødemel, I. and Trickey, H. (eds.) *'An Offer You Can't Refuse': Workfare in International Perspective*. Bristol: Policy Press, pp. 133–158.

Lødemel, I. and Dahl, E. (2000) Public Works Programmes in Korea: A comparison to Active Labour Market Policies and Workfare in Europe and the US. Preliminary Report prepared for the World Bank. Oslo: Fafo Institute for Applied Social Science.

Lødemel, I. and Trickey, H. (2001) 'A new contract for social assistance', in idem. (eds.) *'An Offer You Can't Refuse': Workfare in International Perspective*. Bristol: Policy Press, pp. 1–49.

MacDonald, D., Prinz, C. and Immervoll, H. (2020) *Can Disability Benefits Promote Re)employment)? Considerations for Effective Disability Benefit Design*. Paris: OECD Publishing.

Markussen, S. and Røed, K. (2016) 'Leaving poverty behind? The effects of generous income support paired with activation', *American Economic Journal: Economic Policy*, 8(1), pp. 180–211.

Moe, A. (2000) 'Aktiv arbeidsmarkedspolitikk i Norge 1989–95: effekter av kvalifisering og arbeidstrening' (Active labour market policy in Norway 1989–95: effects of qualification and work training), *Tidsskrift for samfunnsforskning* (*Journal for Social Research*), 41(1), pp. 3–37.

Nergaard, K., Barth, E. and Dale-Olsen, H. (2015) 'Lavere organisasjonsgrad, et spørsmål om nykommere?' (Declining unionization, a question about newcomers?), *Søkelys på arbeidslivet* (*Spotlight on Working Life*), 32(1–2), pp. 91–110.

NHO (2004) *Horing av NOU 2004:13: En ny arbeids – og velferdsforvaltning – Om samordning av Aetats, trygdeetatens og sosialtjenestens oppgaver* (Response to consultation on the New labour and welfare administration). Oslo: Confederation of Norwegian Enterprise. Available at: https://www .regjeringen .no/ globalassets/ upload/kilde/sos/hdk/2004/0008/ddd/pdfv/225649-nho.pdf (accessed: 2022-08-16).

Nordlys (2023) 'Full fress i "Debatten"' (Fierce debate in 'Debatten'), 12 October.

Norwegian Committee for Welfare Services (2020) *Private aktører i velferdsstaten: velferdstjenesteutvalgets delutredning I og II om offentlig finansierte velferdstjenester: utredning fra et utvalg oppnevnt ved kongelig resolusjon 28. september 2018. Avgitt til Nærings- og fiskeridepartementet 1. desember 2020* (Private actors in the welfare state: The welfare committee's sub-investigation I and II on publicly funded welfare services: report from a committee appointed by royal decree on 28 September 2018. Submitted to the Ministry of Trade and Fisheries on 1 December 2020). *Norges offentlige utredninger* (Norway's public investigations). Oslo: Departementenes sikkerhets- og serviceorganisasjon, Teknisk redaksjon.

Norwegian Confederation of Trade Unions (2020) *LO-notat om Sysselsettingsutvalgets rapport* (LO memo on the Employment Committee's report). Oslo: LO, Samfunnspolitisk avdeling.

Norwegian Directorate for Labour (1967) *Aktiv arbeidsmarkedspolitikk: Melding fra Arbeidsdirektoratets styre* (Active Labour Market Policies: Memorandum from the board of the Directorate for Labour). Oslo: Styret.

Norwegian Government (2003) *Om lov om endringer i folketrygdloven* (On the law on changes in the Act of Social Security). Ministry of Labour and Social Inclusion.

Norwegian Government (2007) *Law proposal No. 70. Om lov om endringer i sosialtjenesteloven og i enkelte andre lover (On changes in the Act on social services).* Ministry of Labour and Social Affairs.

Norwegian Government (2020) *Slik blir endringene i permitterings- og dagpengeregelverket* (These are the changes in the rules for temporary lay-offs and unemployment insurance). Available at: https://www.regjeringen.no/no/dokumentarkiv/ regjeringen -solberg/ aktuelt -regjeringen -solberg/ asd/ pressemeldinger/ 2020/ slik -blir -endringene -i -permitterings - -og - dagpengeregelverket/ id2694346/ (accessed: 2022-08-02).

Norwegian Government (2021) *Ny lønnsstøtteordning – oppdatert informasjon (A new wage subsidy scheme).* Available at: https://www.regjeringen.no/no/tema/ okonomi-og-budsjett/norsk_okonomi/ny-lonnsstotteordning-oppdatert-informasjon/ id2893529/ (accessed: 2022-08-04).

Norwegian Labour and Welfare Directorate (2022) *Midlertidig ordning for selvstendig næringsdrivende og frilansere som mister inntekt på grunn av koronautbruddet* (Temporary measure for self-employed and freelancers having lost their income due to Corona). Available at: https://www.nav.no/no/person/innhold-til-person-forside/ nyheter/ midlertidig -ordning -for -selvstendig -naeringsdrivende -og -frilansere -som -mister-inntekt-pa-grunn-av-koronautbruddet#chapter-1 (accessed: 2022-08-04).

Norwegian Ministry of Local Government and Labour (1969) *Om arbeidsmarkedspolitikken. St.meld* (About labour market policy. St-report). Oslo: Departementet.

Norwegian national audit office (2020) *Arbeids- og velferdsetatens forvaltning av tilskudd til arbeidsmarkedstiltak* (The Labour and Welfare Agency's management of grants to labour market measures). Oslo.

Norwegian Union of Municipal and General Employees (2022) *Nytt utvalg skal finne ut hvordan kommersielle aktører i velferdstjenestene kan utfases* (New committee set up to find out how private actors in the delivery of welfare services can be eliminated). Available at: www.fagforbundet.no/a/365765/nyheter/nytt-regjeringsutvalg -skal -finne -ut -hvordan -kommersielle -aktorer -i -velferdstjenestene -kan -utfases/ (accessed: 2022-08-22).

NOU (2012) *Utenfor og innenfor: Norges avtaler med EU*. Oslo: Norwegian Ministry of Foreign Affairs). Available at: www.regjeringen.no/contentassets/5d3982d042a24 72eb1b2063 9cd8b2341/ no/ pdfs/ nou20 1220120002 000dddpdfs .pdf (accessed: 2022-08-22).

Pedersen, A. W., Grødem, A. S. and Wagner, I. (2019) *Trygdepolitikk og trygdemottak i åtte nordeuropeiske land* (Social security policies in eight countries in Northern Europe). Oslo: Institute of Social Research.

Pedersen, P. (1990) *Arbeid for trygd i private bedrifter. Report (FORUT : trykt utg.)* (Work for social security in private companies. Report). Tromsø: FORUT.

Pedersen, P. (1992) *Hvordan fungerte 'arbeid for trygd'? Report (FORUT : trykt utg)* (How did 'work for social security' function?). Tromsø: FORUT.

Proba (2015) *Aktivitetsplikt for sosialhjelpsmottakere – Virkninger for kommunene* (Activity condition for recipients of social assistance – implications for the municipalities). Report no. 12. Available at: https://proba.no/wp-content/uploads/rapport -2015-12-aktivitetsplikt-for-sosialhjelpsmottakere.pdf (accessed: 2024-08-24).

Room, G. (2000) 'Commodification and decommodification: A developmental critique', *Policy & Politics*, 28(3), pp. 331–351.

Sadeghi, T. and Terum, L. I. (2020) 'Frontline managers' perceptions and justifications of behavioural conditionality', *Social Policy and Administration*, 54(2), pp. 219–235.

Scharle, Á., Váradi, B. and Samu, F. (2015) Policy convergence across welfare regimes: the case of disability policies, WWWforEurope Working Paper, No. 76, Vienna.

Seip, Å. A. (2007) 'Poor relief and welfare legislation in Norway, 1814–1920', in King, S. and Stewart, J. (eds.) *Welfare Peripheries: The Development of Welfare States in Nineteenth and Twentieth Century Europe*. Bern: Peter Lang, pp. 97–124.

Standing, G. (2020) *Battling Eight Giants: Basic Income Now*. London: I.B. Tauris.

Statistics Norway (2021) *Over halvparten av sosialhjelpsutbetalingene går til innvandrere* (More than half of social assistance payments to immigrants). Available at: https://www.ssb.no/ sosiale -forhold -og -kriminalitet/ artikler -og -publikasjoner/ over -halvparten -av -sosia lhjelpsutb etalingene -gar -til -innvandrere (accessed: 2023-01-20).

Statistics Norway (2022) *Hvordan gikk det? Korona i Norge og EU* (How did it go? Corona in Norway and EU). Available at: www.ssb.no/helse/faktaside/konsekvenser -av-korona (accessed: 2022-08-01).

Svalund, J. (2021) *Job Retention Schemes in Europe: Norway*. Brussels: European Trade Union Institution.

The Employment Committee (2021) *Kompetanse, aktivitet og inntektssikring: tiltak for økt sysselsetting* (Skills, activity and social security: Measures to increase employment). Norges offentlige utredninger. Oslo: Departementenes sikkerhets- og serviceorganisasjon, Teknisk redaksjon.

Thorsvik, J. (2021) *Hvordan vårt politiske system fungerer.* 1st edition. Bergen: Fagbokforlaget.

Titmuss, R. M. (1963) *Essays on the Welfare State*. 2nd edition. London: George Allen & Unwin.

Vartiainen, J. (2011) 'Nordic collective agreements – A continuous institution in a changing economic environment', in Mjøset, L. (ed.) *The Nordic Varieties of Capitalism Comparative Social Research*. Bingley: Emerald Group, pp. 331–363.

Vik-Mo, B. and Nervik, J. A. (1999) *Arbeidsplikten i arbeidslinjen: Kommunenes iverksetting av vilkåret om arbeid for sosialhjelp* (The obligation to work in the Work Approach: The municipalities' implementation of the condition of work for social assistance). ISS rapport (trykt utg.) Trondheim: Institutt for sosiologi og statsvitenskap, Norges teknisk-naturvitenskapelige universitet.

9. Institutional fragmentation and low effectiveness in the Spanish activation turn

Laureano Martinez and Begoña Cueto

INTRODUCTION

This chapter addresses the main characteristics of activation in Spain in terms of institutional setting and governance, instruments and outcomes. The Spanish case is characterized by a labour market with high unemployment rates and a non-negligible coverage of its unemployment protection mechanisms, which implies that activation measures and services should respond to a significantly high volume of population. This is a distinctive feature compared with other countries that address problems of a quantitatively and qualitatively different nature when it comes to measures aimed at the return of unemployed people to the labour market.

Activation involves various degrees of engagement for benefits claimants to participate in programmes aimed at labour market entry (Clasen and Mascaro, 2022). This participation is subject to the capacity of public services to carry out actions such as training, job search activities and subsidized employment, generally encompassed under the term active labour market policy (ALMP). Previous studies have shown that the main problems of the Spanish ALMP have been their relatively low and misallocated expenditure and the limited effectiveness of the measures due to their low capacity to implement social programmes from an underfunded and poorly coordinated administrative system (AIReF, 2019; Arranz et al., 2013; Malo and Cueto, 2015). The aim of this chapter is to show that despite the tightening of obligations for benefit recipients since the beginning of the activation turn in the 1990s, the implications have been limited, due to the limited ability of the system to provide skills upgrading or access to employment. The crisis related to the Covid-19 pandemic has drawn additional attention to the shortcomings of activation policies and triggered policy reforms. In contrast to previous reforms, many of which have lacked effectiveness, the boost from European funds might lead to a higher impact of these measures.

To meet the proposed objective, this chapter is organized into four main sections. First, it presents the institutional setting of employment policies since the democratic transition (1975–1980) and highlights the current configuration, inherited from the decentralization process at the beginning of the twenty-first century. Second, it analyses the evolution of benefits for the unemployed and the emergence and development of the principles of activation. Third, it deals with the results in terms of ALMP expenditure, showing its evolution and most salient aspects. The final section analyses the changes produced in the context of the crisis caused by the Covid-19 pandemic and reflects on the future challenges of activation in Spain.

INSTITUTIONAL SETTING OF EMPLOYMENT POLICIES

Like other southern European countries, the period of dictatorship in Spain left behind an inefficient public administration with an underdeveloped social protection system (Guillén, 2010). The main axes of contemporary social and employment policies in Spain began to develop out of this scenario in the 1980s. The key aspect to highlight in the institutional configuration of employment policies in Spain involves the shift from a centralized model that arose during the period of democratic transition, which for the first time brought together in a single body unemployment protection policies and the incipient activation measures, and then moved towards a process of decentralization that began in the early 1990s and culminated in 2003. This process has been characterized as a "hierarchical model of regionalisation" (López-Santana and Moyer, 2012) due to the preponderant role of the central government in the management of unemployment benefits and in the design of activation measures. Problems of coordination between the central government and the seventeen regional governments (Autonomous Communities, which are in charge of implementing active policies) have been constant in the assessment of the obstacles facing active policies. Fragmentation has thus been a hallmark of Spanish employment policies, in terms of both the unemployment protection system (Mato-Díaz, 2011) and activation policies (Serrano Pascual, 2007).

The 2008 crisis severely tested the capacities of ALMPs in Spain. After reaching a relatively low 8.2 per cent in 2007, the unemployment rate rose to 26.1 per cent in 2013, with some six million people unemployed. The response in terms of active policies was largely shaped by the orientation of the revised Lisbon Strategy and primarily by the Europe 2020 Strategy, as well as the successive recommendations of the European Council (Moreno and Serrano Pascual, 2011). Many of the reforms adopted in this period aimed to improve the provision of services, including the promotion of individualized activation plans and more personalized employment guidance, as well as to improve the coordination of the different actors involved in labour activation.

In this context, a set of strategies emerged to coordinate the National Employment System – namely, the Spanish Employment Strategy (2012–2014), then the Employment Activation Strategies (2014–2016 and 2017–2020) and finally the Spanish Active Employment Support Strategy (2021–2024). Since 2012, these strategies have materialized in the Annual Employment Policy Plans, which are the instruments for coordinating all active policy measures. With these measures, Spain has introduced a management-by-objectives approach for Public Employment Services (PES), on a yearly basis, in which distribution of funds between the state and regional governments is based on the results of the annual plans.

With the aim of making the system more coherent, in the context of a new reform in 2015 the main instruments of the ALMPs were organized in the Common Portfolio of Services of the National Employment System, which has since been made up of four main services: vocational guidance service; placement and advice service for companies; training and qualification service for employment; and advice service for self-employment and entrepreneurship. These services are financed by the State and the European Social Fund and are implemented by the regional PES throughout the national territory. Regional governments can complement this common portfolio with their own programmes and actions, although most of them limit themselves to offering common services (AIReF, 2019).

Activating Out-of-Work Benefit Recipients

Activation applies to several types of income benefits recipients, with different instruments and objectives. The Spanish unemployment protection system originally included an insurance benefit, dependent on the person's employment records, and a second tier, with a set of flat-rate, means-tested benefits. In addition to the second tier, a series of extraordinary benefits that combine in a single instrument a financial benefit and active measures have been implemented,[1] partly in response to repeated calls from European institutions for the better coordination of passive and active policies (Mato-Díaz, 2011). These decisions have only increased the complexity of the system, which has been repeatedly pointed out as a constraint on its effectiveness (Aguilar and Arriba, 2019). A contributory benefit for the self-employed was added to this initial scheme in 2010. Finally, minimum income schemes provide the last social safety net for people in need.

Since 1980, there has been a succession of reforms in the field of unemployment protection. Although the most notable milestones that currently characterize the Spanish system occurred in 1992 and in 2002, the pattern of reform has been described as a "drip-feed" process, with numerous small regulatory changes between major transformations (del Pino and Ramos, 2009). As in other countries in the European context, the reforms have affected what Clasen and Clegg (2007) call conditions of category (i.e. changes in the definition of the category of the "unemployed" with access to unemployment benefits), conditions of circumstance (i.e. the eligibility and entitlement criteria) and conditions of conduct (i.e. actions that the person must carry out to continue receiving a benefit).

The beginning of the activation turn
If we take the Employment Act 1980 as a point of reference, the orientation of subsequent reforms was, with some exceptions, towards a tightening of eligibility and unemployment benefits entitlement criteria. Throughout the 1980s, in the field of contributory unemployment, these reforms established a close relationship between the requirement of previous employment and the period for the receipt of the benefit, while extending the duration of unemployment insurance from eighteen to twenty-four months, which has remained unchanged ever since. The tightening of the conditions of access to contributory benefits was accompanied by the consolidation of a set of non-contributory means-tested benefits, with less generous amounts, which led to a loss in the quality of the guarantee of entitlement against the risk of unemployment (Mato-Díaz, 2011).

At the beginning of the 1990s, re-commodification measures were taken under the imperatives of recalibration, deficit reduction and European convergence (Moreno and Serrano Pascual, 2011). The reform to unemployment benefits in 1992 took the form of a tightening of the eligibility conditions through the extension of the employment/contribution requirement to twelve months in the previous six years, where it has remained ever since. In this framework, as in other countries in the region, cuts in unemployment protection were justified on budgetary grounds and on the basis that a high level of protection discouraged jobseeking (Palier and Martin, 2008). However, evidence denies or nuances this idea (Toharia Cortés et al., 2010).

It is noteworthy that the reform points to "a new conception of the role that active policies are called upon to play in the new EU context" (BOE, 1992, p. 27113). This conception was aimed at correcting imbalances in the labour market and highlighted the need to reallocate public expenditure to strengthen active employment policies (mainly training and employment incentives) as opposed to passive ones. As far as the balance between rights and obligations is concerned, a clear activating turn took place in the introduction of the obligation to "actively seek" employment as a condition of conduct to prove the involuntariness of the unemployment situation (del Pino and Ramos, 2009). At the same time, sanctions were toughened. Young people, workers over the age of 45 and women were the main target groups of these measures.

The strengthening of activation and the aftermath of the 2008 crisis

Since the implementation of the European Employment Strategy (1997), especially in the framework established at the Lisbon (2000) and Nice (2000) summits, activating policies in Spain have been strongly influenced by European guidelines (Guillén and Álvarez, 2004; Aragón et al., 2007; Moreno and Serrano Pascual, 2011). It is of interest to note that the reforms deepening the activation turn taken at the beginning of this period were carried out in a context of economic growth, with a relatively low unemployment rate, unlike the previous reforms of the early 1990s. Viewed in this way, the reforms did not respond to a context of crisis and the consequent pressure on the unemployment protection system (del Pino and Ramos, 2009).

In 2000, the activating trend was reinforced by regulating the system of sanctions, at both the contributory and assistance levels, in the event of non-compliance with the conditions of conduct. The activating trend in the contributory segment was strengthened with the reform introduced by Law 45/2002, which was presented as a law "to improve employability", and Law 56/2003 on Employment. This renewed regulatory framework deepened the activation turn in Spain with the introduction of new conditions of conduct, including the signing of the so-called "activity agreement". The obligation to subscribe to an active job search plan thus became a formal condition for benefit eligibility. At the same time, the concept of a "suitable job" that a person registered as a jobseeker must accept on the part of the PES was made more flexible for the long-term unemployed (Torrents, 2006).

The Great Recession put immense pressure on the unemployment benefit system and led to a reinforcement of negative incentives. Although no substantial reforms were made to the eligibility criteria, from 2011 onwards the permanence criteria were tightened with the aim of encouraging active job search (Casa Quesada et al., 2011a). The obligations of unemployment benefit recipients were tightened, which compelled them to remain registered as jobseekers throughout the entire period of receipt of unemployment benefits in order to continue to be eligible for them. The activation logic of the benefit was also strengthened with the signing of a "Personal Employment Agreement", which reinforced the logic of individualization and contractualization of situations protected by social rights (Fernández Rodríguez and Serrano Pascual, 2014).

In 2012, with the end of the government led by the Socialist Party and the rise of the Popular Party, the replacement rate of the benefit from the seventh month was reduced from 60 per cent to 50 per cent. Sanctions were also toughened, as in cases of non-appearance in response to calls from employment agencies, and pressure was increased regarding job search accreditation.

Despite this, although the total number of sanctions increased in absolute terms, it did not increase in relative terms, due to the large increase in the number of unemployed people (see Appendix 9.1).

Strictness of activation requirements

While the introduction of activation requirements has been common to all European countries, the level of strictness varies considerably between countries (Immervoll and Knotz, 2018). On the basis of data provided by the OECD (2023), it is possible to compare the strictness of activation requirements. The indicator has three components: availability requirements, job-search requirements and sanctions. Spain shows an overall score of 2.67 out of 5 in the first-tier unemployment benefit programme, which is comparatively low. Only two European countries, Greece and Hungary, have a lower score. The Czech Republic shows an equal score, with the exception of 2014, when it was somewhat lower. Ireland, Finland and Belgium have a similar score, generally somewhat higher than Spain and always below 3 points. As far as the second tier (unemployment assistance) is concerned, Spain has the same score as for the first tier, as it has the same levels of conditionality. In comparative terms, this score represents a somewhat higher level of strictness. Countries such as the Slovak Republic, Belgium, Lithuania, Iceland, Norway and Hungary have a somewhat lower score, while Denmark, Finland, the Czech Republic and Ireland have a slightly higher score.

Within the set of items assessed, the one in which Spain has among the highest overall scores is that referring to sanctions, which is mainly driven by voluntary resignation from employment (entitlement criteria) and by repeated refusal of a job offer and repeated refusal of participation in ALMP, which is specifically linked to activation criteria.

Despite this greater strictness in sanctions from a formal point of view, their effective implementation does not seem to have been high. The data provided by the Spanish Ministry of Labour on sanctions for refusal of job offer and refusal of participation in ALMP are aggregated with the data on sanctions for fraud (see Appendix 9.1), so it is not possible to determine their weight specifically. However, we can see that even between the two causes their share has been low over the last two decades, with a minimum of 2.4 per cent in 2001 and a maximum of 4.2 per cent in 2015, with no significant variations in the period of the Great Recession. From 2016 onwards, levels fall, particularly during the Covid-19 pandemic crisis, when some obligations were suspended. Although a more detailed analysis would be necessary to reach more robust conclusions, it appears from the above that the level of strictness of the Spanish system is relatively low compared with the systems in other European countries. Moreover, in the area where its level of strictness is highest – that is, sanctions – its level of enforcement appears to be low, judging by the available data.

The network of last resort: minimum income schemes

The set of income support schemes is completed by means-tested minimum income programmes aimed at the population of working age and in need. Between 1989 and 1995, seventeen programmes were created, which, unlike unemployment benefits that depend on the state level, are the responsibility of the regional governments. This latter safety net is territorially heterogeneous both from the point of view of coverage and generosity and in terms of the introduction of conditionality criteria in the search for employment and training, which makes it difficult to identify a common activation model (Aguilar and Arriba, 2019). However, it is possible to point out that, from the outset, many of these schemes have been oriented towards the insertion of their beneficiaries through an integration plan involving training or work activities on the basis of different levels of conditionality (Pérez Eransus, 2005), in a vein similar to other countries in the European context (Lødemel and Moreira, 2014).

In most cases, beneficiaries of working age had to be registered as jobseekers, which makes them "activable" subjects, in a way similar to those receiving unemployment benefits; however, their conditionality was linked to "social insertion" plans, a term that was later replaced by "social inclusion" plans. These plans are generally designed and implemented by Social Services, of shared regional and local responsibility. Hence, fragmentation and lack of coordination between social and employment services have been identified as two of the problems with activating people within minimum-income programmes in the labour market (Pérez Eransus and Martínez Virto, 2020), as in other European countries (Heidenrich and Rice, 2016). This last safety net has led to some relaxation in conditionality levels since 2015 and has undergone a fundamental change with the approval, in 2020, of a state-level benefit (*Ingreso Mínimo Vital*, IMV), which has entailed a reordering of the subnational programmes in terms of both cash benefits and activation measures.

Outcome in Terms of ALMP Spending

As mentioned earlier, activation implies participation in labour market programmes for benefits claimants (Clasen and Mascaro, 2022). The outcome in terms of ALMP spending makes it possible to assess the capacity of public services to carry out activation measures and thus to obtain an overall picture of active policies in the Spanish case.

Active versus passive spending

The spending on active and passive policies and the unemployment rate in Spain are shown in Figure 9.1. In the pre-recession period, when Spain had an unemployment rate close to the European average, the ratio between active and passive measures was stable, with spending on passive policies at around 1.4 per cent of GDP and around 0.8 per cent on active policies. These values are above the OECD average of around 0.7 per cent and 0.5 per cent, respectively. From 2008 onwards, the behaviour of spending begins to show a pattern that differentiates the Spanish case in the period of the Great Recession. Spending on income maintenance policies soared, reaching around 3 per cent of GDP between 2009 and 2013, a period in which the unemployment rate rose from 18 per cent to 26 per cent. If we look at total spending on employment policies, it is notable that the proportion of these allocated to income maintenance policies is among the highest in Europe, while the proportion of those allocated to active policies, at around 25 per cent, is well below the EU average of 40 per cent.

Although spending on active programmes initially increased, it soon declined due to a reduction in public expenditure, reaching a minimum of 0.5 per cent in 2013. Considering that the volume of unemployed persons increased from less than two million in 2007 to six million in 2013, the relative maintenance of spending shows the insufficient response of active policies in terms of spending per unemployed person. Indeed, this is reflected in the stock of participants in all activation services and programmes (see Figure 9.3, later), which fell from 16 per cent in 2007 to 6.6 per cent in 2013. With the economic recovery, spending has grown, and it is now above the OECD average. In 2020, the spending on active programmes peaked at 1.18 per cent, as a result of the increase in spending linked to the measures put in place during the pandemic – in particular, short-time work schemes.

Employment incentives: much ado about nothing

ALMP spending in Spain is illustrated in Figure 9.2. The main active programme has been employment incentives, mostly during the pre-crisis period and at the beginning of the crisis, which occupied almost a third of the resources allocated to active policies in 2014, while in the European Union average, they did not reach 20 per cent. It should be noted that this policy includes the hiring of unemployed people belonging to specific target groups, and also the transition from temporary to permanent contracts, driven by the high level of temporary employment in the Spanish labour market.

With specific reference to incentives for hiring the unemployed, over the years the target groups, the amount of aid and the forms of payment (a fixed amount or a reduction in the company's social security contributions) have been modified (Molina, 2016). Evaluations of hiring subsidies have shown that

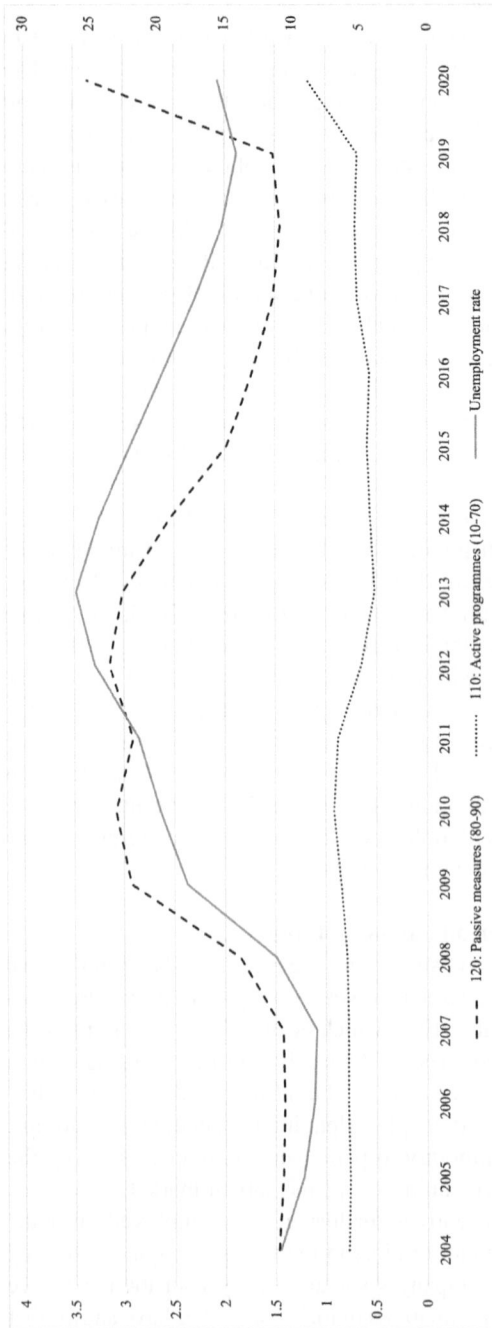

Source: OECD Public expenditure and participant stocks on LMP.

Figure 9.1   *Spending on active and passive policies (left) and unemployment rate (right) in Spain*

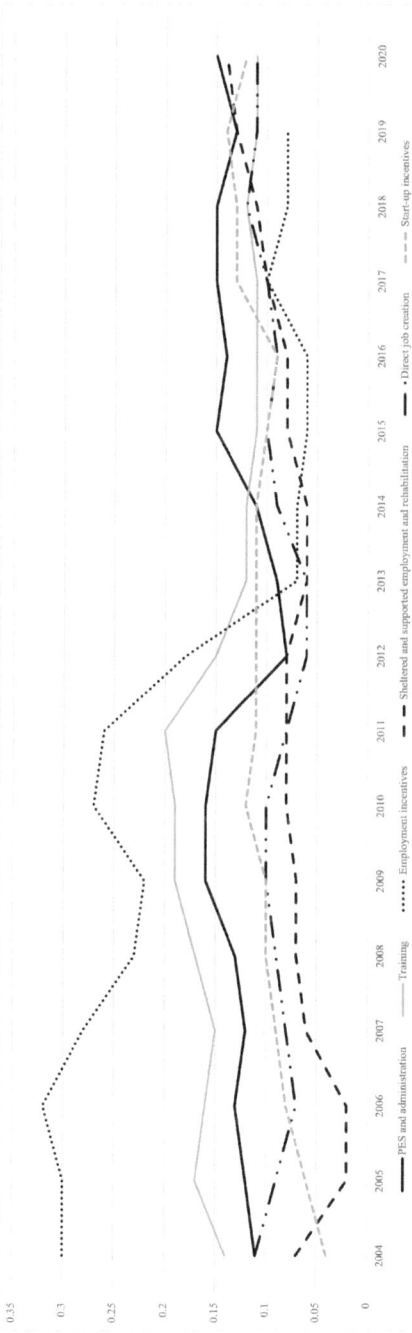

Note: Employment incentives data for Spain include an employer subsidy for the conversion of temporary contracts into permanent contracts.
Source: OECD Public expenditure and participant stocks on LMP.

Figure 9.2   Public expenditure on ALMP in Spain as a percentage of GDP by type of programme

this type of programme has large deadweight and displacement effects (AIReF, 2020; Malo and Cueto, 2015), and that their positive effects are clearly limited. Moreover, these incentives are also considered largely ineffective in terms of quality employment creation, fostering non-standard or fixed-term types of employment contracts (Corti and Ruiz de la Ossa, 2023).

During the period 2004–2007, these types of active programmes accounted for around 0.25 per cent of GDP and 35–30 per cent of total expenditure. Participant stocks as a percentage of the labour force remained below 4 per cent (Figure 9.3). Molina (2016) points out that the evolution of hiring incentive policies during the period of economic crisis that began in 2007 has followed different stages. In the first stage, from 2007 to 2010, changes were made to focus the policy on vulnerable groups. These changes occurred cumulatively and without a clear design for the incentive policies. In the period 2010 to 2011, a twofold change is observed. On the one hand, the concentration of incentives on particularly vulnerable groups increased, while at the same time there was a shift in instruments from bonuses to reductions, for budgetary reasons. Since 2012, the trend towards rationalization of the incentive system has been consolidated, both in terms of the subjective scope (beneficiary groups) and time (duration of the incentives over time). Since 2015, there has been an increase in spending, but without returning to previous levels.

During the Great Recession, spending shifted from employment incentives to start-up incentives, promoting entrepreneurship – a buzzword for promoting self-employment – as a way out of unemployment. Aid for entrepreneurship in Spain has had the highest relative weight in the entire European Union. Once again, however, evaluations of such measures that are not very focused on specific groups have revealed little or no effect (Cueto, Mayor and Suárez, 2017; AIReF, 2020).

Apart from the economic variations and attempts to rationalize the system, the prioritization of this type of instrument has been a constant feature of ALMPs in Spain since the early 1990s. Palacio (1991) already pointed out early on that this feature of employment policy showed the primacy of the direct lowering of labour costs as an objective, a complementary criterion to the flexibilization of hiring that has characterized employment policies in recent decades (Fernández Rodríguez and Serrano Pascual, 2014).

PES and administration: too small not to fail
It is at this point that the weakness of the Spanish activation model in its objective of improving skills and the return to employment can be more clearly observed. To put it briefly, employment services do not show sufficient capacity to respond to the size and complexity of the benefit claimant population. This results in a low capacity to implement the formal obligations that activation entails.

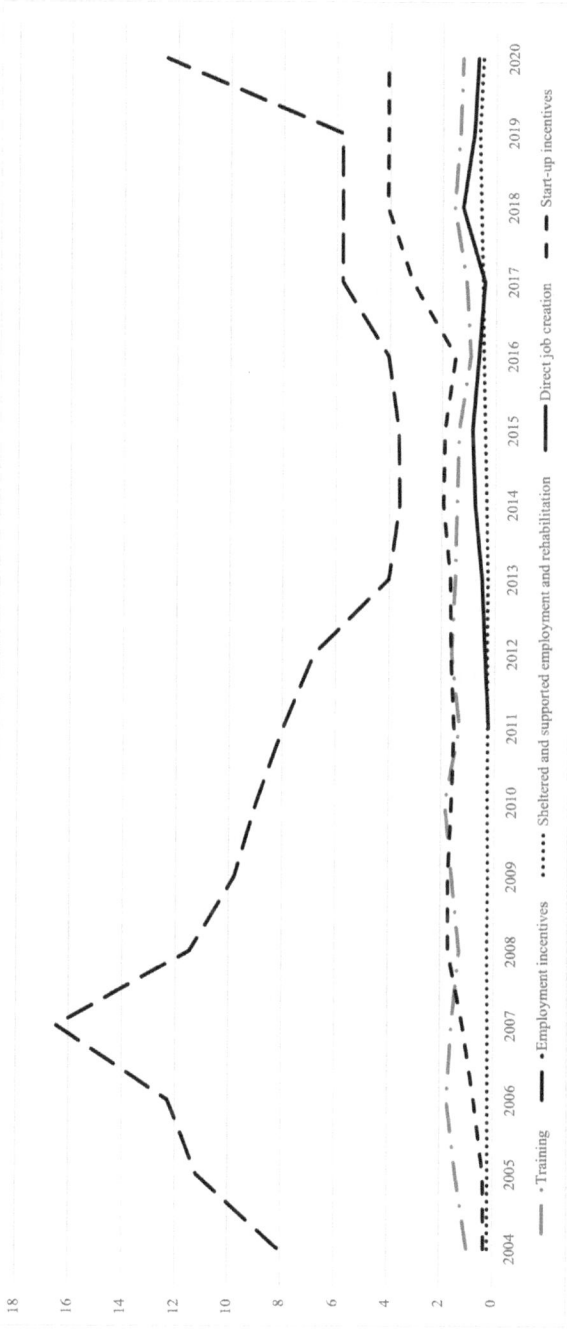

Source: OECD Public expenditure and participant stocks on LMP.

Figure 9.3 *Participant stocks as a percentage of the labour force*

Spending on PES and administration – and particularly placement and related services – has been comparatively low, even in periods of lower unemployment. The initial response to the 2008 crisis saw a slight increase, largely for staff recruitment, but then declined in 2012, and only in 2015 did it return to pre-crisis levels. The call for improvements in personalized service delivery came early on (Alujas Ruiz, 2003) and was reinforced in the context of the Great Recession. Since 2011, particular emphasis has been placed on the development of a personalized support for the unemployed through an individualized itinerary, the strengthening of public employment services, the establishment of a catalogue of basic services for citizens, and a greater boost to the relationship between active policies and the social protection system. However, the objectives of the different laws have clashed with the reality of the lack of PES resources, where there is an insufficient number of staff to deal with the high number of unemployed people in the Spanish labour market. The continued focus on regulation, with a repeated lack of impact on implementation, has been described as an "eternal modernisation deferred" (Casa Quesada et al., 2011b, p. 162).

One of the problems when analysing the performance of PES in Spain is the difficulty of accessing harmonized and quality data. Nevertheless, there is some evidence that provides a general picture of the situation. According to Escudero and Khatiwada (2011), in 2010, with an unemployment rate of 20 per cent and a total of 4.5 million people unemployed, the client-to-staff ratio was nearly 450, which was about fifteen times higher than the ratio in Germany and the United Kingdom. According to data from Casa Quesada et al. (2011b), in 2010, the number of staff per thousand unemployed in Spain was 4.4 compared with a European average of 17.4, with Spain's ratio being the lowest in Europe. The AIReF report (2019), with data from 2016, pointed out that each civil servant attended to 188 jobseekers, which is a much higher number than in all of the countries analysed in the report (Germany, Finland, Australia, Belgium and France). Although figures may differ depending on the source, they clearly indicate a very low ratio for meeting the objectives of personalized and individualized support. The relative weight that the private, mostly non-profit, actors carrying out guidance activities may have – for which no reliable data have been found – would not change the scenario described either, given that the PES are the main gateway to activation services.

This is not characteristic of the PES in Spain only during crises, but also during expansionary phases. For 2017, with a declining unemployment rate, the European Commission (2018) in its Country Report for Spain states that the lack of resources and weak coordination have had a negative effect on the effectiveness of the PES. According to the European Commission (2018) data, in 2017, PES staff numbers were 3 per cent lower than in 2015, while expenditure was 33 per cent lower than in 2012. This low capacity within the employment services is reflected in the low level of outreach of services for unemployed people. García Pérez (2017) analysed a sample of the main employment guidance programmes and showed that in the period 2011–2015, around 90 per cent of unemployed people did not receive any services from public employment offices. The study analysed individual tutoring (which only 3 per cent of the registered unemployed receive); career guidance (from which only 1 per cent benefit); personalized itineraries (0.57 per cent); and search techniques (which only 0.15 per cent of job seekers receive).

The lack of the necessary resources in terms of staffing and funding to properly carry out their activities may also clarify the low share of total vacancies managed by the PES in Spain. According to Eurostat data, in 2007, 36.1 per cent of unemployed persons used public employment offices as a search method. Since then, this proportion has been falling steadily. In 2016, it stood at 24.6 per cent, which placed Spain as the country with the lowest use of public employment services in the EU; and in 2019, it showed similar data, with only Italy below it. This may be due to the flexibilization, between 2010 and 2012, of labour intermediation, with the introduction of private for-profit actors. Since then, temporary employment agencies can be constituted as private for-profit employment agencies. Even so, the figures still clearly show the very poor performance of public services.

In addition to the low proportion of staff and the reduced scope of its services, other aspects that have been pointed out are the lack of advanced statistical profiling methods for jobseekers, as well as deficiencies in its IT systems (mainly oriented towards the administrative treatment of data) and the lack of evaluations of major programmes (AIReF, 2019). The lack of coordination between employment and social services in the activation of recipients of the last safety net, apart from some isolated reforms at regional level, has also been pointed out (Laparra and Martínez, 2021).

Training policy: a weak contribution to the human capital approach
Training is a key element in human capital investment (Bonoli, 2010). Training policies have been promoted according to the different governments when talking about active labour market reforms. However, they do not seem to have found their rightful place as a priority in Spain. Their effectiveness depends both on sufficient resource allocation and on adequate design and implementation. In the Spanish case, problems can be observed related to both aspects.

The share of training expenditure ranged from 0.14 to 0.17 per cent of GDP in the period 2004–2008. At the onset of the crisis, it increased slightly, reaching 0.2 per cent in 2011. Thereafter it declined and stabilized at 0.11 per cent. Within the training expenditure as a whole, this corresponds to institutional training, which has been around 0.10 per cent of GDP in the period

2004–2011. In 2012, it showed a significant decline to 0.5 per cent since 2015. In terms of total expenditure, institutional training has ranged from a high of 58 per cent in 2007 to a low of 41 per cent in 2015. This trajectory in terms of expenditure is also observed in terms of participants. Participants in institutional training peaked at 1 per cent of the labour force in 2010 and then fell to 0.4 per cent in 2013. In terms of spending intensity, measured as a share of GDP over the unemployment rate, a significant drop can be seen as a consequence of the 2008 crisis.

According to data from the Ministry of Labour of Spain (Figure 9.4), in terms of participants, on-the-job training has been given greater weight than training for the unemployed. In the former case, the number was six times larger than that of the latter before the recession. Since then, training for employed persons has declined, in correspondence with the employed population, to equalize in 2012, it fell in the period 2014–2018 and, in 2019, again outnumbered training for unemployed persons. The volume of the latter has been relatively stable over the period, which points to the low responsiveness of the training system during a crisis period and speaks to a structural weakness, when taking into account the volume of long-term unemployed, which reached 13 per cent in 2013.

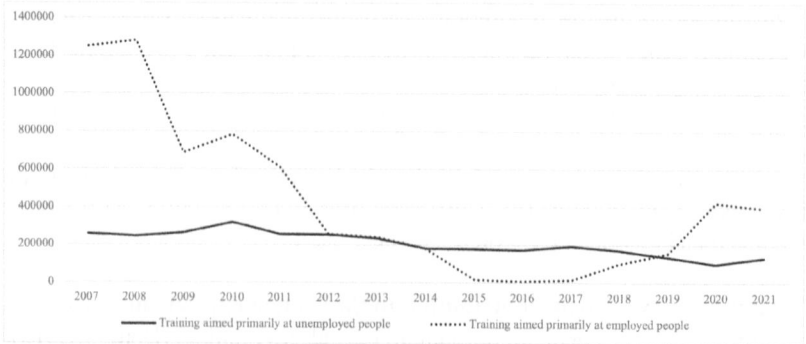

Source: Ministry of Labour and Social Economy of Spain, Yearbook of Labour Statistics.

Figure 9.4   *Evolution of training according to people's situation in the labour market: number of people trained 2007–2020*

Integrated training remained stable between 2004 and 2020, oscillating between barely 0.1 per cent and 0.2 per cent of the active population, which speaks of the poor reach of this instrument. Training contracts are a way for young people to improve their human capital and thus their employability. Throughout the decades studied, the training and apprenticeship contract has undergone constant comings and goings, in which the training component and the logic of labour market insertion have gained or lost ground, depending on the labour market situation at any given time. None of the reforms has managed to substantially improve the success of this contractual formula, which continues to have a derisory percentage use.

The lack of effectiveness of training is linked not only to its clear lack of budgetary resources, but also to the institutional design. The vocational training system for employment has undergone several reforms, but none of them has achieved a substantial change in its efficiency or effectiveness in improving the labour market integration of unemployed people (Malo and Cueto, 2015). Despite the reforms introduced in 2011 and 2015, the current system is more focused on "how" or "who trains" (service oriented) than on "who is trained" (personalized approach). Institutional inertia and provider criteria often take precedence over the needs of the unemployed or the labour market. This service orientation instead of person orientation is a limit in the model of service provision to the implementation of individualized pathways repeatedly mentioned in the regulations (Cueto and Menéndez, 2022).

The logic of the training system, in which trade unions and employers' organizations participate, has been to offer a wide menu of training courses; however, decisions on courses are not taken on the basis of solid evidence of their effectiveness but, at best, on the basis of "soft" evidence, such as the gross insertion rates of beneficiaries, satisfaction evaluations and costs per trainee. This has favoured the tendency to maintain the same courses over time even when they are known to be ineffective. In other words, there is no planning between the professional skills offered, the requirements of the labour market and the profiles of the unemployed. Nor does the top-down model of the training programme design contribute to improving this aspect. Although efforts have been made since 2015 to give greater weight to local entities, their role continues to be marginal, which makes it difficult to comply with the principle of proximity and adaptation to the needs of the territories (Cueto and Suárez Cano, 2011). However, although there is evidence that courses of longer duration and more specialized training are more effective, it is precisely those of short duration and general content that are more numerous (Cueto, 2010). The courses are focused on certain typologies that do not quickly find a place in the labour market or for which there is an oversupply of labour.

In summary, it has been pointed out from the outset that this is a field in which there is a lack of coherence in many actions and in which many of the policies developed, especially internship and training contracts, have constituted a mechanism for cheapening the labour force rather than a coherent attempt to promote training (Recio, 1998).

Changes under Covid-19 and the future of activation in Spain

The pandemic has posed a major challenge for Spanish employment policies. On the one hand, the social distancing measures and the lockdowns in most countries have meant an unprecedented scenario in which it was necessary to respond to the increase in unemployment and the need for attention to unemployed people in the management of benefits, in the search for employment and in re-qualification. On the other hand, beyond conjunctural measures, and as usually happens in periods of crisis, Covid-19 has highlighted the problems and limitations of the system, while at the same time accelerating transformations that were previously on the agenda but, for different reasons, had not been launched. If these reforms achieve their objectives, the future of activation policies in Spain will show the continuity of the guiding principles of recent decades, with an adjustment in the weight of their instruments, to the benefit of those instruments which, following the classification of Bonoli (2010), are oriented towards facilitating (re-)entry into the labour market (placement services, counselling and job search programmes) and improving human capital (vocational training).

Immediate responses: is it different this time?

The Spanish labour market has been characterized by a high level of job destruction during periods of crisis. The measures aimed at maintaining jobs in the context of the crisis unleashed by Covid-19 are thus worth mentioning. Short-time work schemes (STWSs), largely EU funded, affected more than three million workers during the first two months of the pandemic – equivalent to around one in five wage earners. These mechanisms helped to preserve workers' wages and prevented firms from using dismissals to adjust to the drastic fall in production, as was the case in the Great Recession. These STWSs were modified throughout 2020 and in 2021 to continue their use when necessary. Both telecommuting and STWSs clearly helped to reduce the negative effects of the pandemic and the economic downturn measures on the labour market (García Serrano, 2022).

An aspect to highlight regarding labour activation mechanisms has been the need to adapt the services offered by the PES to lockdowns and social distancing. The PES were thus confronted with the need to offer remote access to the range of activities undertaken. The obligation to renew registration as a jobseeker was also temporarily suspended. A study carried out by the OECD (2021) shows that a group of countries such as Belgium (Flanders), Estonia and Sweden, with good remote access prior to the pandemic, had to make relatively few changes to service delivery. On the other hand, Spain was confronted with the need to make changes to the range of services offered. In the same vein, to adapt to the pandemic's new work reality, the Spanish government invested in digitalization to facilitate teleworking and online training.

As can be seen in Figure 9.2 above, expenditure on training and PES services remained unchanged from the previous trend during the pandemic. Conversely, spending on employment incentives and start-ups did increase. The aforementioned study showed that while some countries such as Norway and Sweden introduced temporary reductions in social security contributions applying to all employers, Spain, along with other countries such as the Czech Republic, Estonia and Portugal, targeted the reductions to particular employers such as SMEs and companies or sectors hit by the pandemic. It also increased spending on start-up support.

Subsequent reforms: the same philosophy, with the support of EU funds
Beyond the need to respond to an unprecedented scenario, the crisis served as a backdrop to trigger reforms that had been on the agenda but for several reasons had not been launched. In this matter, what has undoubtedly marked the post-pandemic scenario has been the role of the European Recovery Instrument ("Next Generation EU"), of which Spain has been one of the main beneficiaries. These funds are conditional on the implementation of far-reaching reforms, embodied in the Recovery, Transformation and Resilience Plan (RTRP). Due to several problems in the Spanish labour market, an entire component of the RTRP has been allocated to labour market reforms and modernization, with a total planned budget of EUR 69.5 billion, equivalent to 4.8 per cent of Spanish GDP in 2021.

At the end of 2021, as part of the RTRP – but also as a previous agreement of the coalition government – a new labour reform was approved, focusing on the fight against temporary employment. Early evidence seems to show that it has been successful in reducing the high level of temporary employment in the private sector (Felgueroso et al., 2023), but more time will be needed to assess the real impact of the reform.

Reform 5 of the Plan is dedicated to the "Modernisation of active employment policies", and this has been reflected in the Employment Act 3/2023, where activation is presented as a guaranteed right for all unemployed people. The reform aims to make improvements in all areas of ALMP: the modernization and reinforcement of training policy, particularly aimed at young and older people, and the improvement of the efficiency of the PES, the digitalization of services, the improvement of data collection and the exchange of information. The reform of hiring incentives is seen as a prerequisite for improving the effectiveness of investments and producing a lasting impact in response to the compelling evidence of their lack of effectiveness (AIReF, 2020). The plan points to the need to simplify incentives and requirements for beneficiary companies and to focus them on specific groups.

Moreover, the reform insists once again, as in previous reforms, on improving the configuration of personalized employment guidance trajectories. At this point, it is worth highlighting the creation of a network of twenty Centres for Guidance, Entrepreneurship, Accompaniment and Innovation for Employment. The aim of these centres is to design and evaluate innovative actions and develop experimental projects in the fields of guidance, prospecting, intermediation and job training.

From the point of view of governance, the need to improve multilevel coordination between central and regional governments is emphasized, and the need to give a greater role to local authorities is highlighted. Improved coordination between social and employment services, in particular for people benefiting from minimum income schemes, has also been a focus, along with the strengthening of social dialogue, with an important emphasis on the role of enterprises in active policies.

Also as part of the RTRP, in December 2023 the government launched a reform of the unemployment subsidy with three main changes: an increase in the amount during the first year, an increase in coverage (through the inclusion of the unemployed under 45 years of age without family responsibilities, and workers in the agricultural sector) and the extension of the situations in which it is possible to remain in the programme with income-generating work, which is permitted for a period of six months. In this case, the benefit becomes an "employment support complement" to facilitate a transition into work.

Finally, reforms after Covid-19 also aim to address one of the structural problems of Spanish of public policies in general, and of activation in particular – the lack of evaluation. In 2022, the Law for the Institutionalization of Public Policy Evaluation was approved, which constitutes one of the milestones of the RTRP, linked to the "Modernisation of Public Administrations", and aims at the consolidation of evidence-based policymaking. Two aspects that appear to be cross-cutting should be pointed out: the gender perspective to address the significant gender gap in the labour market, and digitalization as a fundamental aspect both in the contents of training policies and in the improvement of PES digital tools.

Beyond the relevance of the mentioned reforms, the area that has most specifically affected activation has been that concerning the last safety net, with the approval of a state-level benefit, the IMV. Although its implementation in the first years after its approval encountered various obstacles and was less far-reaching than expected (Ayala Cañón et al., 2022), the policy for activating IMV recipients seems to lead towards a human capital investment approach and was launched with a relatively soft level of conditionality of conduct, continuing a trend observed since 2015 in some regional programmes (Arriba and Aguilar-Hendrickson, 2021). Recipients were required to register as jobseekers within the first six months after the benefit was granted, unless they were already working, under 28 years old and in education, were caring for a dependent person, or had a severe disability. Those without the afore-mentioned impediments were required to participate in the inclusion itineraries promoted by the Ministry of Social Inclusion. As a novelty, under the princi-ples of "making work pay" and with the aim of avoiding the so-called "poverty trap", in-work support mechanisms have been introduced by disregarding a proportion of earned income from the standard means test, which had only previously been present in a few regional programmes.

To design social inclusion pathways, more than thirty pilot projects have been launched based on the principles of active inclusion and supported by the EU's Recovery and Resilience Funds. These projects aim to implement reforms of different types and scopes, ranging from the implementation of social inclusion pathways that address the multidimensionality of social exclu-sion (region of Castilla La Mancha); the improvement of digital skills (region of Asturias); to changes in the service delivery model through the integration of social and employment services (region of Navarra). These pilot projects aim to generate evidence based on experimental designs, mainly randomized controlled trials (RCTs).

CONCLUSIONS

This chapter has analysed the introduction and development of activation in Spain. Since the 1990s, Spain has implemented an increasing number of work-oriented obligations for unemployment benefit recipients, while at the same time tightening eligibility criteria, particularly in the first tier. The incre-mental introduction between 1992 and 2002 of active job search obligations has accompanied the unemployment benefit system ever since. In line with comment on most mature welfare states in Europe, it can be stated that the contractualization of the unemployed, reconverted into an active – legally and contractually committed – "jobseeker" subject, has been consolidated as a fundamental piece of this model of activation, in a clear tendency towards commodification. This has increased over time the distance of unemployment benefits from the logic of the social right, which was supposed to keep the individual apart from his or her position in the market, in favour of a con-tractual logic by which the beneficiary entitled to the right must formally undertake to repay a part of the public solidarity he or she receives through the formalized and enforceable commitment to get involved in the process of improving employability and access to employment (Casa Quesada et al., 2011a). However, this growth in benefit recipients' obligations has not been sufficiently supported by actions to ensure the objective of skills upgrading or return to work. In this sense, following the idea of Lødemel and Trickey

(2001), it can be said that activation in Spain means certainly, "An offer you can't refuse", but it should be added, "in the unlikely event that you receive it."

Indeed, when analysing the outcomes in terms of expenditure in activation programmes over the last two decades, the Spanish case presents three elements that set it apart from other European countries in terms of the structure of spending on active policies: the high weight of employment incentives for job creation, the low expenditure on public employment services and a low spending on training for the unemployed. The negative evolution for all programmes except employment incentives and, especially, start-up incentives, suggests that Spain's strategy has been to reduce unemployment rates through a limited spending effort, with greater dominance given to work-first approaches to the detriment of measures aimed at promoting human capital.

From the above, it follows that when formal obligations are compared with the institutional capacity to enforce those obligations, what can be seen is an implementation gap that is characteristic of the Spanish case, similar to what has been pointed out about other countries such as Italy or the Czech Republic (Barberis and Baumann, 2010). For this reason, the pressure on the unemployed does not correspond to the capacity of public services to make effective the commitment to offer individualized pathways to employment, through personalized itineraries, nor to have an effective impact through instruments linked to the promotion of human capital, such as training, or to re-entry into the labour market, such as placement services, counselling or job search programmes.

The reforms launched in a context marked by the post-Covid-19 pandemic seem to have favoured progress towards some "stagnant" changes, such as improvement in the digitalization of the PES, the reorganization of employment incentives or the reform of the vocational training system. In this sense, it can be noted that the reforms underway are aimed at strengthening what has been called enabling instruments and positive incentives (Bonoli, 2010, 2013; Taylor-Gooby, 2004), with the support of recovery funds being fundamental in this respect, which makes it possible to solve the historical problem of the lack of adequate funding for human capital investment and employment assistance. However, it is too early to assess whether these measures will indeed mean a modernization of employment services and programmes or whether they will be yet another chapter in the "eternal deferred modernization" that has characterized the Spanish model for decades.

All the above-mentioned changes do not imply, however, a change in active policy principles and goals, but rather a reinforcement of the measures adopted in previous decades. It should be stressed that the ongoing reforms do not affect the balance between rights and obligations of unemployment benefit recipients. In any case, the reform aims to strengthen the capacity of public services to provide content to the actions related to the obligations of beneficiaries. In addition, apart from some minor adjustments aimed at improving the governance of the system, there is no evidence of a type of reform aimed at solving the problems of coordination between the different bodies involved in the return-to-work policy, such as reducing the number of entry points to the system or integrating benefits. In this sense, the institutional fragmentation and the weaknesses in the implementation of measures, noted early on (Serrano Pascual, 2007), have shown no signs of significant change.

It is perhaps in the state-level minimum income scheme that activation has shown a change in orientation towards an approach closer to human capital investment, reinforcing a trend that began in 2015. The level of conditionality of the IMV assumes a rights-guaranteeing model, with a flexible "active inclusion" approach. However, this orientation could be connected to the political cycle, with centre-left governments pushing the measures, so it would be premature to conclude that we are witnessing a model of soft obligations that will remain in place over time. It will be necessary for these reforms to mature to be able to assess whether they have brought about a change in activation strategies or whether they will continue the path of recent decades.

NOTE

1.   The main one is the *Renta Activa de Inserción*, in force since 2006. It has been followed by a series of programmes that have been successively implemented to fill the gaps in unemployment protection. These are: *Programa Temporal de Protección por Desempleo e Inserción* (PRODI), between 2009 and 2011; *Programa de Cualificación Profesional* (PREPARA) between 2011 and 2018; *Plan de Activación para el Empleo* (PAE), between 2015 and 2018; and *Subsidio Extraordinario por Desempleo* (SED), which has been in force since 2018.

REFERENCES

Aguilar, M. and Arriba, A. (2019) 'Crisis económica y transformaciones de la política de garantía de ingresos mínimos para la población activa', *Panorama social*, 29, pp. 91–103.

AIReF (2019) *Programas políticas activas*. Madrid: Autoridad Independiente de Responsabilidad Fiscal (AIReF).

AIReF (2020) *Incentivos a la contratación y al trabajo autónomo*. Madrid: Autoridad Independiente de Responsabilidad Fiscal (AIReF).

Alujas Ruiz, J. (2003) *Políticas activas de mercado de trabajo en España*. Madrid: Consejo Económico y Socia de España.

Aragón, J., Rocha, F., Santana, A. and Torrents, J. (2007) 'The commitment to be actively available for work and employment Policy in Spain', in Serrano, A. and Magnusson, L. (eds) *Reshaping Welfare States and Activation Regimes in Europe*. Brussels: Peter Lang, pp. 173–205.

Arranz, J. M., García Serrano, C. and Hernanz, V. (2013) 'Active labour market policies in Spain: a macroeconomic evaluation', *International Labour Review*, 152(2), pp. 327–348. Doi: 10.1111/j.1564–913X.2013.00184.x.

Arriba, A. and Aguilar-Hendrickson, M. (2021) 'Between recalibration and continuity: the context of the birth of the MVI', *Revista Espanola de Sociologia*, pp. 1–12. Doi: 10.22325/fes/res.2021.46.

Ayala Cañón, L., Jurado Málaga, A. and Pérez Mayo, A. J. (2022) 'El ingreso mínimo vital: adecuación y cobertura', *Papeles de economía española*, 172, pp. 155–169.

Barberis, E. and Baumann, B. (2010) 'A comparative perspective on labour market changes', in *Rescaling Social Policies: Towards Multilevel Governance in Europe*. New York: Routledge, pp. 106–142.

BOE (1992) Boletín Oficial del Estado no. 186. Ley 22/1992, de 30 de julio, de medidas urgentes sobre fomento del empleo y protección por desempleo, pp. 27112–27116.

Bonoli, G. (2010) 'The political economy of active labor-market policy', *Politics & Society*, 38(4), pp. 435–457. Doi: 10.1177/0032329210381235.

Bonoli, G. (2013) *The Origins of Active Social Policy: Labour Market and Childcare Policies in a Comparative Perspective*. Oxford: Oxford University Press.

Casa Quesada, S. de la, Vallecillo Gámez, M. R. and Molina Navarrete, C. (eds) (2011a) *Empleo, mercado de trabajo y sistema productivo: el reto de la innovación en políticas de empleo*. Albacete: Bomarzo.

Casa Quesada, S. de la, Vallecillo Gámez, M. R. and Molina Navarrete, C. (2011b) 'Empleo a tiempo parcial y temporal, "reciclaje" profesional e "itinerarios personalizados de empleo": ¿modernizarse haciendo siempre lo mismo?', *Revista de Trabajo y Seguridad Social, CEF*, 336, pp. 123–176.

Clasen, J. and Clegg, D. (2007) 'Levels and levers of conditionality: measuring change within welfare states', in Clasen, J. and Siegel, N. (eds) *Investigating Welfare State Change: The 'Dependent Variable Problem' in Comparative Analysis*. Cheltenham, UK and Northampton, MA, USA: Edward Elgar Publishing, pp. 166–197.

Clasen, J. and Mascaro, C. (2022) 'Activation: a thematic and conceptual review', *Journal of European Social Policy*, 32(4), pp. 484–494. Doi: 10.1177/09589287221089477.

Corti, F. and Ruiz de la Ossa, T. (2023) *The RRF's role in strengthening active labour market policies and public employment services: Italy, Spain and Croatia*. Brussels: European Parliament. Economic Governance and EMU Scrutiny Unit.

Cueto, B. (2010) 'Los efectos de la formación ocupacional: ¿Importa la duración de las acciones?', *Hacienda Pública Española / Review of Public Economics*, 195, pp. 9–36.

Cueto, B. and Menéndez, P. (2022) 'El sistema de formación de trabajadores y parados en el proceso de recualificación', in *Informe España 2022*. Madrid: Universidad Pontificia de Comillas, pp. 135–182.

Cueto, B. and Suárez Cano, P. (2011) 'Formación para el empleo en España. ¿Quién se forma?', *Moneda y crédito*, 233, pp. 73–105.

Cueto, B., Mayor, M. and Suárez, P. (2017) 'Evaluation of the Spanish flat rate for young self-employed workers', *Small Business Economics*, 49(4), pp. 937–951. Doi: 10.1007/s11187–017–9853-y.

Del Pino, E. and Ramos, J. A. (2009) 'Proceso político y reformas de la protección por desempleo en España', in *Reformas de las políticas del bienestar en España*. 1st edn. Siglo XXI de España, pp. 137–170.

Escudero, V. and Khatiwada, S. (2011) *Spain: Quality jobs for a new economy*. International Labour Office, Research Department.

European Commission (2018) *Assessment report on PES capacity*. Brussels.

Felgueroso, F., Doménech, R., Arellano, A., De la Fuente, A., García, J. R., Jansen, M., Viola, A. (2023) Observatorio trimestral del Mercado de Trabajo. [Quarterly labour market observatory.] *Fedea Apuntes: Bulletin no. 4.* https://fedea.net/observatorio-trimestral-del-mercado-de-trabajo/

Fernández Rodríguez, C. J. and Serrano Pascual, A. (2014) *El paradigma de la flexiguridad en las políticas de empleo españolas: un análisis cualitativo.* Madrid: Centro de Investigaciones Sociológicas.

García-Pérez, J. I. (2017) 'Una primera evaluación del impacto sobre la salida del desempleo de las políticas activas ofrecidas por los servicios públicos de empleo en España', *Fedea Policy Papers 2017/07.*

García Serrano, C. (2022) '¿Dos años que estremecieron el mundo? Los efectos de la pandemia del covid-19 sobre el mercado de trabajo', *Papeles de Economía Española*, 173, pp. 16–40.

Guillén, A. M. (2010) 'Defrosting the Spanish welfare state: the weight of conservative components', in Palier, B. (ed.) *A Long Goodbye to Bismarck? The Politics of Welfare Reforms in Continental Europe.* Amsterdam: Amsterdam University Press, pp. 183–206.

Guillén, A. M. and Álvarez, S. (2004) 'The EU's impact on the Spanish welfare state: the role of cognitive Europeanization', *Journal of European Social Policy*, 14(3), pp. 285–299.

Heidenrich, M. and Rice, D. (eds) (2016) *Integrating Social and Employment Policies in Europe: Active Inclusion and Challenges for Local Welfare Governance.* Cheltenham, UK and Northampton, MA, USA: Edward Elgar Publishing.

Immervoll, H. and Knotz, C. (2018) 'How demanding are activation requirements for jobseekers?', *IZA Discussion Papers 11704, Institute of Labor Economics (IZA).* Doi: 10.1787/2bdfecca-en.

Laparra, M. and Martínez, L. (2021) 'La integración de servicios sociales y de empleo en el debate entre protección y activación', *Papers*, 106(3), pp. 467–494. Doi: 10.5565/rev/papers.2839.

Lødemel, I. and Moreira, A. (2014) *Activation or Workfare? Governance and the Neo-liberal Convergence.* New York: Oxford University Press.

Lødemel, I., and Trickey, H. (eds.) (2001) *An Offer You Can't Refuse: Workfare in International Perspective.* Bristol: Policy Press.

López-Santana, M. and Moyer, R. (2012) 'Decentralising the active welfare state: the relevance of intergovernmental structures in Italy and Spain', *Journal of Social Policy*, 41(4), pp. 769–788. Doi: 10.1017/S0047279412000335.

Malo, M. Á. and Cueto, B. (2015) 'El impacto de las políticas activas de mercado de trabajo en España', *Documentación Social*, 178, pp. 105–120.

Mato-Díaz, F. (2011) 'Spain: fragmented unemployment protection in a segmented labour market', in Clasen, J. and Clegg, D. (eds.) *Regulating the Risk of Unemployment: National Adaptations to Post-industrial Labour Markets in Europe.* Oxford: Oxford University Press, pp. 164–186.

Molina, O. (2016) 'De racionalización a extensión: los incentivos al empleo en la crisis económica en España', *Anuario IET de trabajo y relaciones laborales*, 3, pp. 74–93.

Moreno, L. and Serrano Pascual, A. (2011) 'Europeanization and Spanish welfare: the case of employment policy', in Guillén, A. M. and León, M. (ed.) *The Spanish Welfare State in European Context.* Farnham: Ashgate, pp. 39–58.

OECD (2021) 'Active labour market policies and COVID-19: (Re-)connecting people with jobs', in OECD (ed.), *OECD Employment Outlook 2021: Navigating the*

COVID-19 Crisis and Recovery. Paris: OECD Publishing. https://doi.org/https://doi .org/10.1787/5a700c4b-en.

OECD (2023) 'Strictness of activation requirements', Organisation for Economic Co-operation and Development. Available at: https:// stats .oecd .org/ Index .aspx ?DataSetCode=SBE.

Palacio, J. I. (1991) 'La política de empleo', in Miguélez, F. and Prieto, C. (eds) *Las relaciones laborales en España*. Madrid: Siglo XXI de España, pp. 307–329.

Palier, B. and Martin, C. (2008) *Reforming the Bismarckian Welfare System*. Oxford: Blackwell.

Pérez Eransus, B. (2005) *Políticas de activación y rentas mínimas*. Madrid: Fundación Foessa: Cáritas.

Pérez Eransus, B. and Martínez Virto, L. (eds) (2020) *Políticas de inclusión en España: viejos debates, nuevos derechos. Un estudio de los modelos de inclusión en Andalucía, Castilla y León, La Rioja, Navarra y Murcia*. Madrid: Centro de Investigaciones Sociológicas.

Recio, A. (1998) 'La política laboral: acuerdo y conflicto en un contexto de reforma continua', in Gomà, R. and Subirats, J. (eds) *Políticas públicas en España. Contenidos, redes de actores y niveles de gobierno*. Madrid: Ariel, pp. 113–132.

Serrano Pascual, A. (2007) 'Activation regimes in Europe: a clustering exercise', in Serrano Pascual, A. and Magnusson, L. (eds) *Reshaping Welfare States and Activation Regimes in Europe*. Brussels: Peter Lang, pp. 275–316.

Taylor-Gooby, P. (2004) *New Risks, New Welfare: The Transformation of the European Welfare State*. Oxford: Oxford University Press.

Toharia Cortés, L., Arranz, J. M., García-Serrano, C. and Hernanz, V. (2010) 'El sistema de protección por desempleo y la salida del paro', *Papeles de economía española*, 124, pp. 230–246.

Torrents, J. (2006) 'El marco jurídico de la activación de los demandantes de desempleo', *Cuadernos de relaciones laborales*, 24(2), pp. 21–36.

APPENDIX

Table 9A.1   *Percentage of sanctions as a percentage of total unemployment benefit withdrawals*

2001	2002	2003	2004	2005	2006	2007	2008	2009	2010	2011	2012	2013	2014	2015	2016	2017	2018	2019	2020	2021
3.3	3.1	3.1	3	2.7	3.2	4.2	4.2	2.8	3	3.2	2.9	2.4	2.9	3	0.9	1.2	1.2	1	0.2	0.3

Source: Ministry of Labour and Social Economy of Spain, Yearbook of Labour Statistics.

10. Switzerland: activation in a fragmented welfare state

Giuliano Bonoli

INTRODUCTION

Like other European countries, over the last three decades, Switzerland's welfare state has undergone a transformation that can be seen as an activation turn. Before the mid-1990s, in spite of the fact that social security legislation did stress the important role of the state in supporting labour market (re-)entry, the system was de facto rather passive. Following a sharp increase in case-loads, the main social security schemes were reformed repeatedly starting in the mid-1990s, and now Switzerland has a social security system in which acti-vation and, more generally, active labour market policy feature prominently.

While the activation turn is clearly observable as a broad trend, upon closer scrutiny one finds significant differences across programmes and across cantons. Switzerland is a fragmented and highly decentralised federal state, which means that the rolling out of the activation strategy is not uniform. This is especially the case regarding social assistance, a scheme that is entirely governed by the cantons and the municipalities. As a result, an important dif-ference exists in the country. To an extent, these differences can be considered problematic, given that the right to a decent minimum standard of living is upheld by the federal constitution (Conseil fédéral 2015).

Institutional fragmentation generates a second type of policy problem that has to do with the lack of coordination among social security schemes that belong to different government departments and different levels of the federal state. This high level of institutional fragmentation has resulted in the devel-opment of cost-shifting practices that have proved difficult to eradicate and that have prevented the development of effective interagency collaboration. In addition, access to different services, especially training and activation for individuals with health problems, is not available to all non-working people, but only to those entitled to a specific benefit. Finally, fragmentation is also a source of tension among the different levels of the federal state: disability and unemployment insurance are under the responsibility of the federal government, while social assistance is a cantonal and municipal task (Bonoli and Champion 2014; Bonoli and Trein 2016).

Today, activation remains a key theme in social policymaking in Switzerland. However, the topic seems to be less central to policy debates and developments than a decade ago. This may have to do with the fact that over the last few years, and especially after the COVID pandemic, the main labour market problem is labour shortage and not so much rising caseloads, the problem that motivated the activation turn in the 1990s. Skill shortage arguably may require a different type of active labour market policy, linked to the provision of skills and possibly better employment conditions. However, at the time of writing, there is little sign of a broad reorientation of the Swiss system of active labour market policy in a way that reflects the changing economy context and employers' needs.

The chapter is organised in the following way. First, I briefly sketch the development of activation across the various schemes that make up the Swiss social security system. Second, the focus moves on to the practice of activation in today's welfare state. Given the fragmented structure of the Swiss welfare state, the three main social security schemes, i.e. unemployment insurance, disability insurance and social assistance, are discussed separately. The next section focuses on what seems to be the main unresolved problem in relation to activation and also the efficiency of the whole social security system: how to coordinate a highly fragmented system. The final section concludes and considers a number of current trends that might shape future developments in activation policy in Switzerland.

THE DEVELOPMENT OF ACTIVATION IN SWITZERLAND

Switzerland can be considered a late developer in relation to social policies, as the construction of the welfare state was not completed until the mid-1980s (Armingeon 2001; Bonoli 2001).[1] There were delays at every stage during the construction of the welfare state, which can be largely explained with reference to the country's political institutions: direct democracy, federalism, and the interaction between the two (Armingeon 2001; Bonoli 2001; Obinger 1998).

Unemployment insurance is no exception. For most of the postwar years, unemployment insurance was provided on a voluntary basis by the unions. The state's involvement was limited to the provision of benefits. The first compulsory state-run unemployment insurance scheme was introduced in 1976 on the basis of temporary legislation and made permanent in 1984 (Armingeon 2001).

Disability insurance and social assistance existed before, but their connection to the labour market was relatively weak. Disability insurance was introduced in 1960 and has a two-pillar structure: a universal state-run first pillar and an occupational top-up that is compulsory for employees earning above a certain threshold. Social assistance, finally, is provided by the cantons. The Federal Constitution obliges the cantons to guarantee a last-resort safety net, but federal law is very open in terms of the form this assistance should take. The result is a fragmented welfare system with significant differences from canton to canton.

Like other European welfare states, Switzerland underwent an "activation turn" that started in the mid-1990s. The activation turn was visible in legislation but perhaps even more strongly in the implementation of the various social programmes. The legislation that was in place until then did put emphasis on return to work, but the reality of implementation had somehow lost sight of this objective. This was very clear in disability insurance, where disability pensions were often attributed for labour market reasons and reintegration was not attempted. The same was true for social assistance, which did once cater for highly marginalised people and did not have a strong reintegration dimension, even though the laws expected clients to make efforts to leave social assistance. Change was spurred by a rapid increase in the caseloads of each of the three main social security schemes for working-age people: unemployment insurance, disability insurance and social assistance.

As can be seen in Figure 10.1, the immediate result of the crisis of the early 1990s was a sharp increase in the number of unemployment insurance clients. This was rapidly followed by clear increases in caseloads for both disability insurance and social assistance. As a result of these trends, we saw a rapid succession of reforms in all social security schemes. These reforms included various elements, but in general they introduced and/or strengthened the activation dimension of the programme.

The first scheme to be reformed in the direction of activation was unemployment insurance. In a reform adopted in 1995, two key changes were introduced. On the one hand, a time limit on recipiency of 18 months for most unemployment people was adopted. At the same time, however, the new legislation also made provision for developing and expanding the active labour market policy system. The reform established a network of regional placement offices and vastly increased the amounts available to finance labour market programmes (Giriens and Stauffer 1999; Bonoli and Mach 2000). A few years later, it was the turn of disability insurance. The fifth revision of disability insurance, adopted in 2007, essentially pursued the same objective: to strengthen the active dimension of occupational integration and to make it possible to access a disability pension only if reintegration measures have failed or cannot reasonably be applied (Champion 2011: 130; OECD 2006).

For cantonal social assistance, the reorientation process was more mixed. Indeed, some cantons and cities moved faster than others have and have been

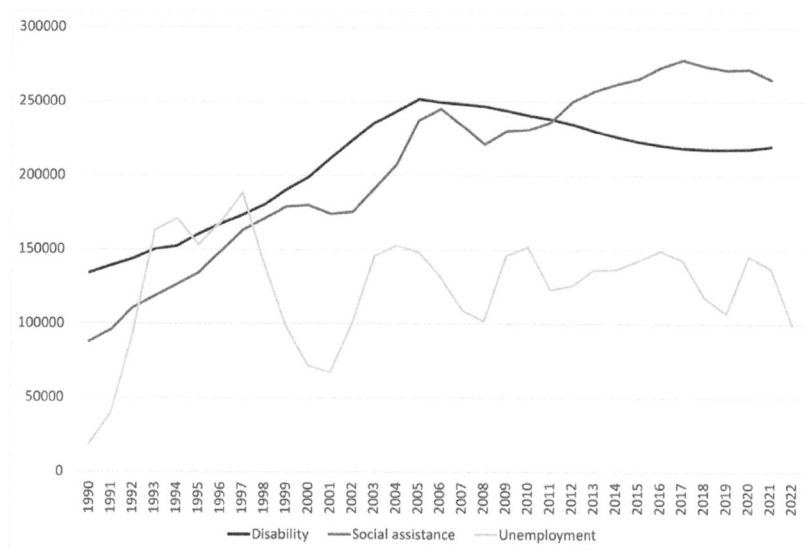

Sources: For disability insurance, BSV (https://www.bsv.admin.ch/bsv/fr/home/
assurances-sociales/iv/statistik.html); for social assistance, BSF (https://www.bfs.admin.
ch/bfs/fr/home/statistiques/securite-sociale/aide-sociale.html); and for unemployment
insurance, SECO (https://www.seco.admin.ch/seco/fr/home/wirtschaftslage--
-wirtschaftspolitik/Wirtschaftslage/Arbeitslosenzahlen.html

Figure 10.1   Social security caseloads, 1990–2021/2022

trying to reorient themselves in different ways. In French-speaking Switzerland
(especially Vaud, Fribourg and Geneva), social assistance services are encouraged to work with employment services and regional employment offices and
provide labour market integration services. However, in the German-speaking
part of Switzerland, the combination of social assistance and employment
services is concentrated more in the large cities, where social services have
acquired competence in labour market integration and are thus increasingly
able to make it available to target groups (Bonoli and Champion 2013).

ACTIVATION IN SWITZERLAND TODAY

Forms of activation exist in each of the three main social security schemes for
working-age people. However, the principles they follow and the way they
are shaped are somewhat different. Unemployment insurance pursues above
all an objective of quick labour market re-entry. The law on unemployment
insurance states that the objective of the policy is to promote fast and sustainable labour market reintegration.[2] However, the benchmarking system used

by the federal government to evaluate the performance of the cantonal Public Employment Service (PES) is mostly based on how fast jobseekers are put back into jobs. This creates a context in which "fast" integration takes priority over "sustainable".

In order to promote rapid labour market integration, the system relies on a mix of support and negative incentives. The PES can provide labour market services but is also entrusted with monitoring the efforts made by the jobseekers and requested to impose sanctions on those who are deemed non-cooperative. Sanctions are widely used, but with some notable differences across cantons. Differences have been observed in the processes that are followed in order to decide to sanction a jobseeker, but also in the frequency. In general, German-speaking cantons tend to use more sanctions than French/ Italian-speaking cantons (Conseil fédéral 2016).

Things are rather different in disability insurance, where the logic is much more one of status protection. As a result, the type of support a client can expect to receive depends crucially on the level of insured earnings. Disability insurance can provide long-term and high-quality training if this is what is needed to reconstitute the previous earning capacity. The notion of activation in a strict sense is less relevant in the context of disability insurance. The right to benefits and services is strictly regulated, and non-cooperative clients risk losing access.

Finally, in social assistance, the situation is patchier, and the kind of support and activation services available to clients varies across cantons, and even across municipalities. In general, however, one can say that support is rather limited. Sometimes cantons offer "social insertion" programmes that do not really have an explicit objective in terms of labour market participation but are more meant to provide an alternative to market employment for individuals who experience severe difficulties in accessing jobs (Pfister 2009; Bonoli and Champion 2013). Sanctions are also possible but limited because of the existence of a constitutional right to an absolute minimum income.

The fact that the three main social security schemes for working-age people follow different logics, makes the coordination of activation difficult. For instance, clients of different schemes have access to different types of support and are subjected to different levels of pressure. Another important factor that makes collaboration difficult is the fact the two federal insurance programmes, unemployment and disability insurance, can control access to their benefits. Uncooperative claimants can simply be excluded. This can be done in unemployment insurance by declaring a claimant unfit for work; and in disability insurance by calculating the benefit on the basis of a "reasonable" income that the client could obtain in a balanced labour market. In contrast, social assistance, by definition the last resort safety net, has no control over inflow.

THE CONTENT OF ACTIVATION POLICY

Activation takes place in the three main social security schemes for working age people: unemployment insurance, disability insurance and social assistance.[3] It is important to point out that these schemes have different governance structures. Unemployment and disability insurance are both governed by the federal level but belong to two different ministries. Their implementation, however, is delegated to the cantons. Social assistance instead is entirely run by the cantons, and in some case in conjunction with the municipalities. Fragmentation is both a source of tensions between the different actors and an obstacle to effective collaboration among the various agencies.

Unemployment Insurance

Unemployed people who are eligible for unemployment insurance are registered with the PES and are eligible for all the activation services and measures available within unemployment insurance. The range of services is very broad, and includes the standard package of active labour market policies that one finds in the most-developed European welfare states.

First, unemployment insurance can provide training. There are language courses for immigrants who need to improve the local language, but also English or other language courses for locals. Computing courses are also widespread, as are other technical courses related to specific professions. These are generally of short duration, from a few week up to a few months. The PESs also provide training and support with job searching. Finally, for unemployed people who do not have a professional or academic degree, and who are over 30, unemployment insurance can pay a full vocational training, lasting generally 3 years.

Second, there are job subsidies paid to employers who hire a long-term-unemployed or a difficult-to-place jobseeker. These consist of a sliding subsidy covering 40% of the salary over a period of 6 months. To receive the subsidy, the employer must prove that some training or practice is necessary before the new employee becomes fully productive. It must provide some form of training or induction. The subsidy can last up to 1 year for unemployed people who are over 55. The employer must offer an open-ended contract or a contract of at least twice the duration of the subsidy.

Third, unemployment insurance provides job creation programmes in the public or non-profit sector. These must fulfil the condition of non-competition with market employment. So, theoretically, the activities that are developed in order to provide work experience to unemployed people should be different from those that exist in the economy. In reality, this principle is applied with moderation. Many of the job creation programmes, for instance, provide recycling services, simple activities that are contracted out by private commercial companies, etc.

Job search conditions are strictly enforced. A certain number of applications per month is decided with the relevant case worker, and failure to comply (in terms of quantity or quality) results in sanctions. Sanctions take the shape of suspensions in the payment of the benefit for a number of days. They can last for up to 30 days. If an unemployed person is repeatedly sanctioned for failure to comply with the job search requirement, he or she can be declared "unfit for work", and as a result loses the entitlement to the insurance benefit.

Recent and current trends in activation within unemployment insurance go in the direction of a more agile and modern activation policy. For example, jobseekers are activated earlier, but with shorter programmes. Also, the traditional subsidised temporary job, while it has not disappeared, plays an increasingly smaller role (interview, SECO, 22.02.2023).[4]

Social Assistance

The situation is more complex for unemployed people who rely on social assistance, because of the great degree of diversity we see across the country. In a few cantons, social assistance clients deemed fit for work are systematically required to register with the public employment service. In others, the request is sometimes made, but not systematically; and in others still, social assistance provides integration/employment services on its own. What emerged through attempts to map services for social assistance clients is that these tend to have a strong social orientation, and are often not so much geared towards labour market re-entry. Some large cities have started enacting more ambitious programmes. Overall, however, Swiss social assistance has not undergone a generalised "activation turn" as in other EU countries (Bonoli and Champion 2013; 2014).

For social assistance clients, pressure to actively look for a job is in general arguably lower than for unemployed people receiving insurance benefits, even though cantonal legislations have been gradually adapted to the new context throughout the 1990s, by including some form of activation such as incentives for those who agree to follow labour market programmes. However, in many cases (especially in French-speaking cantons), the objective of these activation programmes was not labour market participation, but "social reinsertion". An important development was the adoption, in 2005, of a set of guidelines by the influential SKOS-CSIAS (Swiss conference of social assistance organisation).[5] The guidelines explicitly encouraged cantons to introduce activation measures in their social assistance legislation. These guidelines are not legally binding and their adoption has proved rather controversial, with the strongest resistance coming from the French-speaking cantons. The guidelines are none-theless being adopted in a growing number of cantons, but the extent to which social assistance is genuinely reoriented towards activation and employment promotion is probably limited and varies by canton.

For example, there is evidence that for many years at least some cantons continued to use cantonal (or municipal) employment programmes not to help people back into jobs, but in order to reopen an entitlement period to federal unemployment insurance. In addition, activation measures for social assistance beneficiaries are often unrelated to labour market participation, aiming more at providing them with some sort of occupation than enhancing their employment chances (Wyss 1997; Pfister 2009; Bonoli and Champion 2013).

In the second half of the 2010s, continuing rising numbers of social assistance beneficiaries, including in a period of good economic performance, have pushed cantonal and municipal authorities to promote a bolder activation and social investment agenda. Some cantons have been innovating too. In the canton of Vaud, for example, a programme that aims to provide full vocational training to young social assistance clients was significantly expanded.[6] Various cantons are experimenting with activation projects based on the collaboration between social assistance offices and unemployment insurance (Bonoli and Champion 2014).

One such example is the canton of Vaud, where a joint unit of the social affairs office and the public employment service has been in operation in the city of Lausanne since 2015. An evaluation study has shown that relative to standard practice, this approach can produce employment gains of around 9 percentage points, with a non-negligible favourable impact on the social assistance budget (Bonoli et al. 2017). The cantonal government has decided to extend the collaboration beyond the city of Lausanne to the whole canton.

Disability Insurance

Disability insurance offers a range of different programmes and is less concerned with activation than the other two social programmes. Unlike in unemployment insurance and social assistance, training plays an important role in disability insurance. The basic principle is status maintenance. As a result, if a person cannot work in the job they learned because of a long-term illness, disability insurance will pay what it takes for them to learn another job that provides a roughly equivalent wage. In addition, beyond training, various typical active labour market policy tools are also available. These include supported employment programmes, job subsidises, internships, sheltered employment programmes. These programmes are very specific for people with disabilities and are more about supporting them than about strengthening work incentives. Due to strict access conditions, which require an earning loss due to a long-term medical problem, disability insurance can easily control inflow. Activation in the strict sense, i.e. as a mix of positive and negative incentives aiming to put jobless people rapidly into jobs, is less relevant in this context.

CURRENT DEBATES AND DIRECTIONS IN ACTIVATION POLICY

The debate on activation is less central than it was when it started in the late 1990s/early 2000s. Recent policy developments have been limited and, perhaps more importantly, caseloads have stopped rising since the late 2010s. This has arguably reduced pressures on policymakers to expand or reform activation. Recent and current debates have focused on other aspects. First, a constant preoccupation of policymakers has been coordination. As argued above, the Swiss welfare state is characterised by a high degree of fragmentation, both vertically (i.e. federalism) and horizontally (i.e. divisions between ministries at each level of government). Fragmentation constitutes a problem for the coordination of the various social security schemes. Second, like other European countries, Switzerland is facing a serious problem of labour and skill shortage in a large number of sectors. While this development has not prompted a reorientation of the Swiss ALMP system, it has changed the context in which activation takes place. This development is bound to have consequences.

The COVID pandemic had a large short-term effect on social and labour market policy. As in other countries, a big effort was made to maintain individuals in their jobs, by providing a replacement income. For employees, this was done via unemployment insurance, which included provision for short-time work. For the self-employed, a similar mechanism had to be developed virtually overnight. This was done within the old age pension system (which already collected contributions for the self-employed). In addition, some loans were made available to the self-employed to help them cover their fixed costs (Bonoli et al. 2022). These various programmes have now been phased out, and in the end the COVID pandemic did not have a lasting effect on ALMPs in Switzerland.

The Coordination Problem

The problem of coordinating social policies targeting people of working age emerged in the early 1990s.[7] This was due to the economic crisis that hit Switzerland in those years. More or less simultaneously, all social security schemes came under pressure due to a strong increase in the number of beneficiaries and thus of expenditures. This development makes the previous, mainly informal, collaboration more difficult. It makes institutions more 'selfish' in the sense that, under pressure, they prioritise the protection of their budget rather than the general interest when the latter implies devoting resources to beneficiaries covered by other social schemes. In practice, the lack of coordination gives rise to three different problems.

The first problem identified is the so-called carousel effect, i.e., when beneficiaries apply to one institution, they are referred to another, sometimes several times, and end up excluded from the social protection system. A typical example is a person who is unemployed and has health problems. The unemployment insurance may, because of the health problems, not recognise the person as fit for work and therefore exclude him or her from its benefits. Since the decisions of the unemployment insurance are not coordinated with those of the disability insurance, the same person may be considered capable of work by the latter and thus also be excluded from its benefits (Champion 2008).

Secondly, following the reorientation of all social schemes towards reintegration into the labour market, the managers of the various institutions are finding that they lack certain capabilities. For example, the social services do not have capabilities in terms of labour market placement and vocational reintegration, which is not the case with unemployment insurance. However, the latter are not at all specialised in caring for unemployed people with health problems, a competence that is found within the disability insurance offices. As a result, it soon became clear that the pooling of all these competences is essential to successfully meet the challenge of labour market integration (Champion 2008; Egger et al. 2010).

Finally, all actors develop strategies for cost shifting. Faced with the difficulty of containing the increase in the number of beneficiaries and reintegrating them into the labour market, all actors involved try to transfer them to other social schemes. This practice, known in the literature as "cost shifting" (Overbye et al. 2010; Bonoli and Trein 2016), is achieved in different ways. For example, for federal unemployment insurance, reforms have made it more difficult to access benefits by extending the period during which contributions must be paid.

These restrictions on access to unemployment insurance have probably led to a cost shift to cantonal and municipal social assistance, although this burden shift is difficult to quantify. An attempt was made in a study in relation to the latest of these reforms (4th revision of unemployment insurance in 2011). It concluded that in 15 cities the 2011 reform was responsible for an increase in the number of social assistance caseloads of between 5 and 15 percent (Salzgeber 2012: 64).

During the same period, cantons and municipalities also practised a cost-shifting strategy aimed at shifting part of the burden of social assistance to federal social insurance. For example, until 2009, the canton of Geneva had a job guarantee system for unemployed people who could not return to the labour market during the 18-month unemployment insurance compensation period. The job offered allowed unemployed people to regain entitlement to a new 18-month compensation period financed by federal unemployment insurance (de Coulon et al. 2002). Other cantons have implemented similar, but generally less generous and less visible programmes. Neuchâtel, for example, rather than guaranteeing a 12-month period of employment, has developed a system of job guarantees limited to 6 months, but renewable once (Bonoli et al. 2011).

Although there is no systematic overview of the extent of these practices, it is certain that many other cantons and municipalities have used the strategy of cost shifting to avoid the financial responsibility of the long-term unemployed. It is difficult to estimate the impact of these practices on the overall system. In 2008, the Federal Council estimated their cost to the unemployment insurance system at CHF 90 million per year, or 2.2 per cent of the expenditure on cash unemployment benefits (Conseil fédéral 2008: 7046). This possibility has been ruled out in a reform of unemployment insurance adopted in 2011.

LABOUR AND SKILL SHORTAGE

Labour shortages are observed and expected in several mid- to high-skilled occupations such as various technical professions, management, and health care professionals. In 2016, a government report identified the following professions as the most likely to be concerned by labour shortage: engineers, managers, technicians, legal professionals, health care professionals, computer specialists, advertising and tourism professionals, education professionals, technical professionals, scientists, sport and entertainment professionals, and social workers (SECO 2016).[8] The report has not been updated, but a recent enquiry by the main peak employer association published in 2022 confirms that labour shortages are experienced in most sectors, in particular in the ICT branch (UPS 2022). After the pandemic, labour shortage also affect low-skill sectors, such as the hospitality industry.

Various actors have been developing strategies to deal with labour and skill shortages. The federal government launched a high-profile initiative in the mid-2010s, targeting untapped potential among residents.[9] The key target groups are older working-age people, and parents of young kids. In an earlier version of the strategy, refugees were also considered a target, but this group has been dropped from more recent iterations. With regard to activation specifically, there are a few examples of schemes that try to profit from the context of a labour shortage. For example, in the German-speaking canton of Solothurn a programme aims to train jobless people so that they can work as bus drivers. In the French-speaking canton of Vaud, jobless people can follow a 10-month work experience and training programme that prepare them for jobs in the field of social care. However, the changed economic and labour market context has not resulted in a general reorientation of active labour market policy towards upskilling. According to a manager of unemployment insurance, this is probably because, legally, the objective of unemployment insurance is quick labour market integration (interview, SECO, 22.02.2023).

CONCLUSION

Activation, while still a key component of the Swiss welfare state, is less central than a decade ago in policy debates. This probably reflects the fact that caseloads have stabilised or are even declining in some contexts. In addition, the current labour market policy debate is focused mostly on the problem of labour shortage, in relation to the consequences of the pandemic and also to the process of aging of the workforce. Activation, understood in strict terms as an effort to put pressure on jobseekers so that they enter the labour market, seems less appropriate in the current context. Upskilling and, more generally, preparing jobseekers so that they can access employment in sectors characterised by labour shortage would seem a more appropriate approach. However, as mentioned above, with the exception of a few local schemes, there is, at the time of writing, little evidence of a broad reorientation of the active labour market policy system.

The issue of job quality also deserves some attention. In fact, what is an apparent skill mismatch could in reality, at least in part, be a problem of job quality in some low-skills segment of the labour market. Employers are having difficulties recruiting for low-skill jobs in sectors such as hospitality and catering. Since these are low-skill jobs, i.e. jobs that do not require more than some basic training (on the job), the fact that employers fail to recruit in sufficient numbers may be more an indication of insufficient attractiveness of employment than of a skill mismatch. If this is the case, the solution to labour shortage will come not from ALMPs, but from improvements in working conditions.

NOTES

1. This section draws on material published in Bonoli and Fossati (2024).
2. Law on unemployment insurance, art. 1.
3. This section draws on material published in Bonoli and Trein (2018).
4. In order to gain insights into the most recent developments, an interview was conducted with a person responsible for overseeing ALMPs at the federal level.
5. SKOS/CSIAS is an association of cantonal and municipal social services and NGOs involved in the fight against poverty (such as Caritas). This association, which is not a state nor a state-recognised body, issues guidelines

periodically with regard to how the cantons should run their social assistance schemes. These guidelines are not binding but tend to be followed by cantons. For more information, see www.skos.ch.

6.   The programme is known as FORJAD (Formation pour Jeunes Adultes en Difficulté).
7.   This section draws on material published in Bonoli and Fossati 2024.
8.   These professions are also the ones in which the vacancy rate is highest. Just before the pandemic (Q4 2019), the vacancy rate (i.e. number of vacancies/total employment) stood at 1.6% for the overall labour market, but was highest for computer specialists (4.2%), information and communication specialists (3.2%), finance and insurance (2.2%), machine industry (2.2%), real estate (2.1%), transport (2.1%), electronics and watch making (2.1%); source https://www.bfs.admin.ch/bfs/fr/home/statistiques/industrie -services/entreprises-emplois/statistique-emploi/places-vacantes.assetdetail .22604360.html, visited 11.08.2022
9.   See https://www.seco.admin.ch/seco/de/home/Arbeit/Fachkraefteinitiative .html, visited 04.03.2023.

REFERENCES

Armingeon, K. (2001). Institutionalising the Swiss Welfare State. *West European Politics*, *24*(2), 145–168.

Bonoli, G. (2001). Political Institutions, Veto Points, and the Process of Welfare State Adaptation. In P. Pierson (Ed.), *The New Politics of the Welfare State* (pp. 238–264). Oxford: Oxford University Press.

Bonoli, G., & Champion, C. (2013). *La réinsertion professionnelle des bénéficiares de l'aide sociale en Suisse et en Allemagne*. Lausanne: IDHEAP, Cahier de l'IDHEAP.

Bonoli, G., & Champion, C. (2014). Federalism and Welfare to Work in Switzerland: The Development of Active Social Policies in a Fragmented Welfare State. *Publius; The Journal of Federalism*, *45*(1), 77–98.

Bonoli, G., & Fossati, F. (2024). Social Policy. In P. Emmenegger, F. Fossati, S. Häusermann, I. Papadopoulos, P. Sciarini, & A. Vatter (Eds.), *Handbook of Swiss Politics* (pp. 695–713). Oxford: Oxford University Press.

Bonoli, G., & Mach, A. (2000). Switzerland: Adjustment Politics within Institutional Constraints. In F. W. Scharpf & V. Schmid (Eds.), *Welfare and Work in the Open Economy* (Vol. 2, pp. 131–174). Oxford: Oxford University Press.

Bonoli, G., & Trein, P. (2016). Cost-Shifting in Multitiered Welfare States: Responding to Rising Welfare Caseloads in Germany and Switzerland. *Publius: The Journal of Federalism*, *4*(46), 596–622.

Bonoli, G., & Trein, P. (2018). *ESPN Country Profile: Switzerland*. Brussels: European Commission.

Bonoli, G., Champion, C., & Schlanser, R. (2011). *Evaluation des mesures de résinerion professionnelles dans le Canton de Neuchâtel*. Lausanne: IDHEAP.

Bonoli, G., Fossati, F., Gandenberger, M., & Knotz, C. M. (2022). Sometimes Needs Change Minds: Interests and Values as Determinants of Attitudes towards State Support for the Self-employed during the COVID-19 Crisis. *Journal of European Social Policy*, *32*(4), 407–421.

Bonoli, G., Lalive, R., Oesch, D., Bigotta, M., Cottier, L., & Fossati, F. (2017). *Evaluation de l'unité commune ORP-CSR en Ville de Lausanne.* Canton Vaud, Dép. de l'Economie et du sport, Dép. de la santé et de l'action sociale.

Champion, C. (2008). *Bilan intermédiaire de la mise en oeuvre de CII_MAMAC.* Lausanne: unpublished MA thesis.

Champion, C. (2011). Switzerland: A Latecomer Catching Up? In J. Clasen & D. Clegg (eds.), *Regulating the Risk of Unemployment: National Adaptation to Post-Industrial Labour Markets in Europe* (pp. 121–141). Oxford: Oxford University Press.

Conseil fédéral. (2008). *Message relatif à la modification de la loi sur l'assurance-chômage du 3 septembre 2008.* Berne.

Conseil fédéral. (2015). *Aménagement de l'aide sociale et des prestations cantonales sous condition de ressources. Besoins et possibilités d'intervention.* Berne.

Conseil fédéral. (2016). *Efficacité et efficience du service public de l'emploi. Rapport en réponse au postulat 13.3361 de la Commission de l'économie et des redevances CN du 22 avril 2013.* Berne.

de Coulon, A., Flückiger, Y., & Vassiliev, A. (2002). *Les raisons de la différence entre les taux de chômage genevois et suisse.* Geneva: Université de Genève, Cahier du LEA no. 24.

Egger, M., Merckx, V., & Wütrich, A. (2010). *Evaluation du projet national CII-MAMAC.* Berne: OFAS, Rapport de recherche 9/10.

Giriens, P.-Y., & Stauffer, J. (1999). Deuxième révision de l'assurance chômage: genèse d'un compromis. In A. Mach (Ed.), *Globalisation, néo-libéralisme et politiques publiques dans la Suisse des années 1990* (pp. 105–144). Zurich: Seismo.

Obinger, H. (1998). Federalism, Direct Democracy, and Welfare State Development in Switzerland. *Journal of Public Policy, 18*(3), 241–263.

OECD. (2006). *Sickness, Disability and Work: Breaking the Barriers, Norway, Poland and Switzerland.* Paris: OECD.

Overbye, E., Strohmeier Navarro Smith, R., Karjalainen, V., & Stremlow, J. (2010). The Coordination Challenge. In Y. Kazepov (Ed.), *Rescaling Social Policies towards Multilevel Governance* (pp. 389–428). Farnham: Ashgate.

Pfister, N. (2009). *Integrationsauftrag der Sozialhilfe in der Praxis.* Bern: SKOS/CSIAS.

Salzgeber, R. (2012). Auswirkungen Der 4. AVIG Revision Auf Die Sozialhilfe. *Volkswirtschaftmagazin Fur Die Wirtschaftspolitik, 85*(9), 62–66.

SECO (2016). *Pénurie de main-d'œuvre qualifiée en Suisse. Système d'indicateurs pour évaluer la demande en personnel qualifié.* Bern: SECO.

UPS (Union Patronale Suisse) (2022). *Baromètre de l'emploi. Le redressement économique aggrave la pénurie de personnel.* Zurich: UPS.

Wyss, K. (1997). *Massnahmen zur sozialen und beruflichen Integration von Langzeitarbeitslosen bzw. SozialhilfeempfängerInnen.* Bern: CSIAS.

11. Between extension and emasculation: the UK activation regime in the 21st century

Daniel Clegg

INTRODUCTION

At the turn of the century, the United Kingdom (UK) was frequently held up as a model in the area of activation, which was central to the then recently elected New Labour government's so-called 'third way' in social and economic policy. The policy instruments that formed the UK's distinctive activation regime were not new, but under the first Blair administration they were refreshed, reinforced and extended. Although its causes were more complex, the steady decline in UK unemployment after the late 1990s lent credibility to New Labour's claim to have found a virtuous labour market policy formula, especially when governments in France and Germany were struggling with high joblessness.

This chapter takes stock of the fortunes of the UK activation regime in the two decades since the high point of its celebrity. Punctuated by the global economic shocks of the financial crisis and the Covid-19 pandemic, this has also been a period of major political upheaval in the UK. In 2010 the Conservative Party returned to government for the first time since 1997, and at the time of writing have been in power, alone or in coalition, for an uninterrupted 13 years. Moreover, in a 2016 referendum the UK narrowly voted to leave the European Union (EU), empowering a nationalist faction within the Conservatives who pushed for a 'hard Brexit' based on withdrawal from the single market and customs union while at the same time espousing a new rhetoric of economic interventionism intended to appeal to lower- and middle-income voters who had voted Leave. Brexit is arguably now generating a third big economic shock, albeit one that is UK specific and slower burning. While there is ongoing controversy over its impact, the government Office for Budget Responsibility estimates that separation from the EU will have cost the UK 4% of GDP by 2030.

How has the UK activation regime evolved in this turbulent period? Has it been further institutionalized or undermined? Do we observe mainly continuity or more substantial policy change? As this chapter shows, providing unequivocal answers to these questions is not straightforward. Over the period as a whole, the development of activation in the UK is characterized by two developments that appear partly contradictory. On the one hand, activation has been progressively *extended* to encompass ever more groups of working-age benefit recipients, including non-working lone parents, those who are economically inactive due to sickness or disability and latterly sections of the underemployed. On the other hand, however, many of the more enabling features of activation have been *emasculated* by sharp reductions in expenditure. The result is an activation regime that is today both broader and thinner, the limits of which have become increasingly evident as the UK struggles badly with post-Covid labour market recovery.

To reconstruct policy developments over the past two decades, this chapter draws on secondary academic literature complemented with policy documents, parliamentary papers and publications by authoritative think tanks. National and international statistical sources illustrate some key policy trends, though since 2012 the UK has no longer provided detailed data to the OECD–European Commission labour market policy database, limiting the scope for expressing labour market policy expenditure and participation trends in the accepted comparative categories. The focus of the chapter's analysis is on UK-wide policy developments. Although the Scotland Act 2016 devolved powers over employment programmes for some groups to the Scottish government, there has not been significant divergence between Scotland and the rest of the UK in this area subsequently,[1] and the other instruments that make up the UK activation regime remain the reserved prerogative of the UK government.

The chapter is organized in four main sections. The first section briefly sketches the pre-history of activation in the UK. The next section outlines a number of core features that differentiate the UK's activation regime most markedly from those found in other advanced democracies, especially elsewhere in Europe. This is followed by a reconstruction of the evolution of the regime in the two decades between the turn of the new millennium and the onset of the Covid-19 pandemic, distinguishing the markedly different phases of policy development under Labour- and Conservative-led governments. The final section assesses the prospects for the future of activation in the UK in the light of debates around policies to respond to the aftershocks of the pandemic and the UK's current political and economic direction of travel.

THE PRE-HISTORY OF ACTIVATION IN THE UK

Throughout the early post-World War II period, the UK had an essentially 'passive' labour market policy. In his 1942 report, William Beveridge unsuccessfully proposed making unemployment benefit entitlement unlimited in duration but conditional on attendance at a 'work or training centre' after a certain period of unemployment. The post-war Labour government preferred time-limiting unemployment benefits and vesting responsibility for professional training in the Department of Labour, without any link to administration of social security (Brown, 1990: 28–30). Buoyant labour demand ensured most jobseekers could find new employment quickly in any event, and encouraging labour reallocation was a more pressing policy problem than combating unemployment. UK governments' wider efforts to plan for manpower needs were meanwhile hampered by low esteem for vocational education and an industrial relations tradition that made businesses and trade unions alike wary of state intervention in employment questions (Whiteside, 1995).

The creation of the tripartite Manpower Services Commission (MSC) in the early 1970s attempted to address these issues by building quasi-corporatist economic governance institutions mimicking those found under more coordinated models of capitalism (Rhodes, 2000). Among other things, the MSC was handed the remit of modernizing the system of labour exchanges, which were rebranded as Job Centres and located in more prominent commercial locations. As the economic situation worsened in the mid-1970s, though, the MSC was redirected from its originally broader aims to the delivery of a succession of targeted job creation and training schemes, though these did little to stem a rising tide of unemployment. Indeed, with the election in 1979 of a Conservative government committed to a decisive shift in economic policy, the tide soon turned into a tidal wave. A combination of strict monetarist policies to control inflation and a badly overvalued currency saw the UK experience a particularly massive and abrupt loss of industrial employment in the first half of the 1980s, under the first Thatcher administrations (Tomlinson, 2021). Unemployment sky-rocketed, peaking at just under 12% of the labour force in 1984.

Massive employment or training programmes for the unemployed, many involving direct job creation in the public sector, were a key part of the UK policy response at a time when government still felt the electoral need to be seen to be helping the causalities of its economic policies. In the mid-1980s, expenditure on ALMP (Active Labour Market Policy) was around 0.5% of GDP, comparable to France and Germany though far less than Sweden, and in a context of much higher unemployment. The political need to be seen to be helping the jobless also partly protected unemployment benefits from feeling the full force of the government's attempts to bear down on public expenditure in the early 1980s, though an earnings-related element that had been introduced in the 1960s was abolished in 1982 (Clasen, 1999). As the economy began to improve in the second half of the decade, though, a series of measures was taken to restrict unemployment benefit eligibility and entitlement (Atkinson and Micklewright, 1991; Clasen, 1994, chapter 7). Alongside public expenditure objectives, unemployment benefit retrenchment was part of a wider supply-side agenda for promoting growth through labour market 'deregulation'. Restrictions on collective and individual employment rights, including the abolition in the early 1990s of the UK's system of sectoral minimum wages, were other key elements of this policy approach (Deakin and Reed, 2000).

When the country entered a deep recession in the early 1990s, the response revealed the UK government's growing faith in a straightforwardly neo-liberal approach to the management of the labour market. While new employment programmes were introduced, they were on nothing like the scale of those deployed in the early 1980s, and much more oriented towards subsidized employment in the private sector, which the weakened unions could no longer resist. While there was much talk in this period of US-style 'workfare', the Conservatives baulked at the cost of government taking on the role of employer of last resort (Grover and Stewart, 1999). The creation of Jobseekers Allowance (JSA) in the mid-1990s better reflected their preferred policy logic. This reform reduced the maximum duration of non-means-tested unemployment benefits from 12 to 6 months, cut benefit rates for under-25s, and increased conditionality for recipients of means-tested and non-means-tested benefits alike (Clasen, 2011).

Retaining JSA after 1997 was one of the more visible manifestations of New Labour's resolve to preserve aspects of the Thatcherite social and economic policy inheritance. Famously, the new government also committed to remain within its predecessor's public spending objectives during its first term. Policy continuity was not absolute, however. New Labour signed the European Social Charter, from which an opt-out had been secured at Maastricht in 1992, and modestly enhanced some trade union rights (Crouch, 2001). It also introduced the UK's first national minimum wage in 1999, though fixed at an initially rather modest level (Metcalf, 2008). The so-called New Deal programmes directed at various groups of the unemployed marked a return to grace of targeted employment measures, and occupied an important place in the new government's social policy rhetoric. It was, however, the less-heralded transformation of the in-work social security benefit Family Credit into a new Working Families Tax Credit (WFTC) that would ultimately prove to be a more decisive contribution to establishing a distinctive new activation regime in the UK.

THE ESSENTIAL FEATURES OF THE UK'S ACTIVATION REGIME

The singularity of the UK's contemporary activation regime can be described through four essential features: modest benefits for the unemployed; limited public expenditure on ALMP, and an emphasis on ALMP services (job-search monitoring and assistance) over measures (targeted programmes of training or subsidized work experience); a very important role for permanent in-work social transfers, with the dual objective of enhancing incentives to work and combatting poverty among households with working adults; and a highly centralized governance system giving neither sub-national tiers of government nor the social partners much involvement in policy design or delivery. While there have been significant reforms affecting all these aspects of policy since the turn of the millennium, they have operated within the parameters set by these fundamental characteristics of the regime, and in many cases further accentuated them.

Modest Benefits for the Unemployed and Strong Targeting

Poverty alleviation rather than income replacement has always been the key objective of the social security system in the UK (Clasen, 2011; Kelly and Pearce, 2023). For this reason, all non-means-tested benefits, such as contributory unemployment insurance, are generally paid at a flat rate. While in countries where unemployment benefits have a stronger insurance function replacement rates are often substantially higher for the short-term than the long-term unemployed, in the UK they don't vary across an unemployment spell. Replacement rates are also very low in comparative perspective, especially for the short-term unemployed. While the value of benefits has been further eroded by recent reforms (see the section below), at the turn of the millennium they replaced only 20% of a low earner's previous wages after 2 months of unemployment compared with well over 60% in countries with the most generous benefit systems (see Figure 11.1). Owing to the flat rate structure, benefits for average earners replaced an even lower share of their lost wages, a mere 14% compared with an OECD average of 52% in 2001 (OECD, 2023a).

One consequence of modest social insurance benefits is the lack of any meaningful distinction between unemployment insurance and social assistance (Clasen, 2011). Low unemployment insurance benefits mean many unemployed people have always needed to claim social assistance, especially when they have non-working dependents and/or high housing costs. With the inclusion of social assistance and housing benefits, the gap in replacement rates for

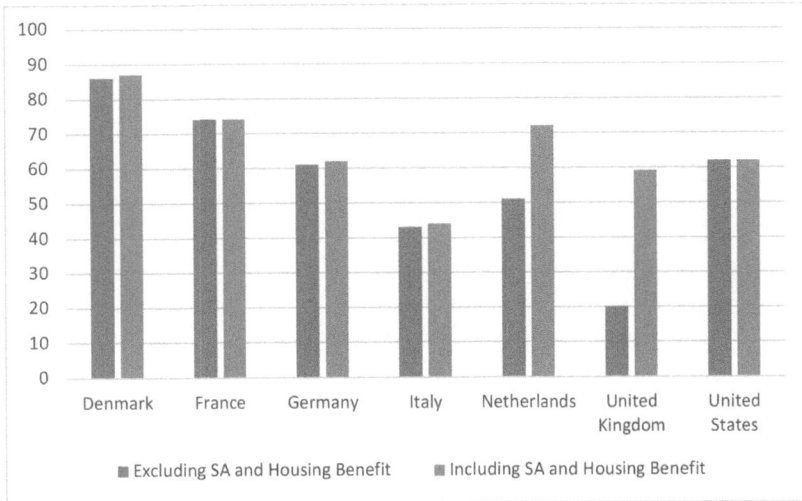

Note: Data for 2 months of unemployment and prior wage at 67% average.
Source: OECD (2023a).

Figure 11.1   *Net replacement rates in unemployment, select countries, 2001*

low earners in unemployment between the UK and other advanced economies narrows very considerably (see Figure 11.1). While in many other welfare states the debate about activation has been partially distinct for the insured unemployed and for recipients of social assistance, this has not been the case in the UK, where insurance and assistance are far more closely imbricated and the benefit system as a whole is heavily targeted on the poor.

Limited Public Expenditure on ALMP and an Emphasis on Placement

A second feature of the UK's activation policy regime is comparatively low expenditure on formal ALMPs. ALMP expenditure dipped below the OECD average in the early 1990s, and has remained consistently lower ever since (see Figure 11.2). Most European countries devote a far higher share of GDP to ALMP. In some cases – France, for example – this is in part explained by higher unemployment. But the UK has also markedly underspent countries that have comparable or even lower rates of unemployment, such as Denmark and, since 2010, Germany. As discussed below, ALMP expenditure was cut back considerably as part of the austerity drive of the 2010s, but this occurred from an already low base.

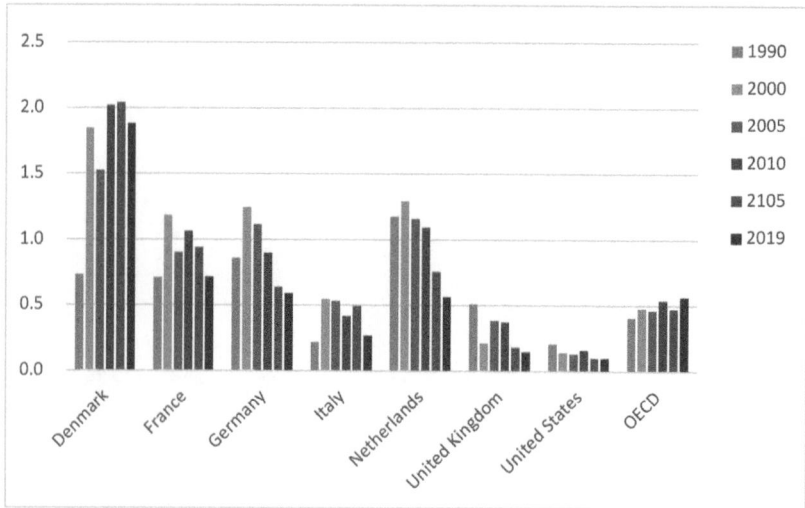

Source: OECD (2023b).

Figure 11.2   ALMP expenditure (% GDP), select countries, 1990–2019

Much of the difference in ALMP expenditure with other advanced economies is accounted for by the very limited role in the UK of training programmes and recruitment incentives targeted at the unemployed. Despite the rhetoric surrounding the New Deal programmes in its first term, in all the New Labour years, combined spending on these types of support for the unemployed never surpassed 0.1% of GDP. Of the conventional instruments in the ALMP toolkit, it is placement and related services provided by the public employment service that is most prominent in the UK activation policy regime. When the network of Job Centres was overhauled in the early 2000s and re-branded as Job Centre Plus (JCP), there was substantial investment in job-search support for the unemployed. In the early to mid-2000s, the UK was in absolute terms spending three to four times as much as the OECD average on placement services, and more than any of the other countries in Figures 11.1 and 11.2. While JCP has also fallen victim to austerity recently, placement expenditure in the UK is much more in step with the norm for advanced economies than overall expenditure on ALMPs.

The Role of In-work Transfers

Particularly since the turn of the millennium, dedicated social transfers targeted at low-income working households have become a third crucial feature of the UK activation regime. The UK was the first developed country to introduce such benefits in the early 1970s (Abbas and Robertson, 2023). Their main rationale was initially tackling child poverty at lower cost than universal child benefits and without harming incentives to work. As their names indicate, the first UK in-work benefits (Family Income Supplement and its more generous 1986 replacement Family Credit) were understood primarily as family policies rather than as labour market policies. Over time, however, the role they could play in reducing both the opposition to and the negative consequences of labour market flexibility, by subsidizing wages and boosting incentives to enter even part-time or low-paying work, were increasingly stressed (Grover, 2016; Sloman, 2019, chapter 6).

Under New Labour, this rationale moved front and centre, and in-work benefits came to be presented, along with the new minimum wage, as part of an agenda to 'make work pay'. Beguiled by the centrality of Earned Income Tax Credit to Clinton's active welfare reforms and the associated 'jobs miracle' in the USA, the first Blair administration expanded and rebranded Family Credit as WFTC, though in practice this continued to operate more like a social security benefit than a tax rebate (Walker, 1999; Clegg, 2015).[2] By the early 2000s there were 1.3 million UK households in receipt of in-work benefits, compared with 0.7 million in the mid-1990s (Millar, 2009). As described below, this number would increase yet further in the years to come, eventually ushering in greater contestation around this pillar of the UK activation regime.

A Highly Centralized System of Governance

Compared with other advanced economies, the UK has a highly centralized system of labour market policy governance. One aspect of this is a very limited role for trade unions and employer representatives in policy making in this area (Clasen, 2009). Except during the brief corporatist experiment brought to an end with the abolition of the MSC in the 1980s, representative organizations of labour and business have never had a formal consultative or executive role in UK labour market policy.[3] In part due to its residual nature, they also lack any institutional role in the governance of social security that the 'social partners' enjoy in many European countries (Crouch, 1999).

While for essentially political reasons there has been some decentralization of responsibility for ALMP to the Scottish government in recent years, overall the picture is also one of very limited involvement of sub-national political authorities in UK labour market policy. In the European context, the UK is unusual in having introduced a fully national system of social assistance already in the 1940s, removing the responsibilities that municipalities continue to have for this tier of income protection elsewhere (Clegg, 2016). While local authorities do commission and/or provide some employment support, prior to

Brexit this was funded largely through the European Social Fund, and seen as complementary to but not part of UK labour market policy, in line with additionally principles. National labour market policies are directed and funded by UK central government, and either delivered through JCP, now a part of the Department for Work and Pensions (DWP), or centrally commissioned to voluntary and private-sector providers (Wilson et al., 2022). Increasingly, this commissioning has occurred through a competitive process of tendering for contracts to deliver publicly funded employment support, on quasi-market principles (Wiggan, 2015).

THE RECENT EVOLUTION OF THE UK'S ACTIVATION REGIME

The evolution of activation policies in the UK between the start of the millennium and the onset of the Covid-19 pandemic can be divided into two main phases, divided by the 2010 general election. In the first period, the most important developments were the gradual extension of active welfare principles to an ever-larger population of working-age benefit claimants and a substantial expansion of in-work benefits. In the second, structural reform of the benefit system built on some of these developments, but at the same time sharp cuts to expenditure on both benefits and services time further weakened the modest enabling features of the UK activation regime.

The Extension of Activation under New Labour, 2000–2010

From early in its time in office, New Labour emphasized helping into work not only the unemployed but also a range of economically inactive groups in receipt of social benefits. Alongside the mandatory New Deal programmes for the unemployed, backed by the threat of benefit sanctions for non-engagement, voluntary New Deals for lone parents (July 1997), for people with disabilities and for the partners of the unemployed (both April 1999) were introduced. Over the following years this support became increasingly compulsory, however, in what Griggs et al. (2014: 82) call "a shift from ensuring equal access to enforcing participation through mandate". Changes made the principle of work-related conditionality increasingly a feature of all working-age benefits for those out of work, albeit with continuing differences of intensity.

In 2001, joint couple claims for JSA were introduced, subjecting non-working partners of the unemployed in childless couples to the same conditions as the main claimant. In 2004, mandatory Work Focused Interviews (WFIs) were brought in for non-working partners of the unemployed with children, requiring some level of engagement with JCP. Compulsory WFIs had already been introduced in 2001 for lone parents in receipt of previously unconditional

Income Support, and in 2005 the requirement was extended to the agreement of an action plan. In 2008, eligibility for Income Support – previously open to lone parents with children aged up to 16 – was restricted to lone parents with children under 12, and a year later this age threshold was further reduced to 10. Lone parents without work who were no longer able to claim Income Support were forced to turn instead to JSA, and came under its stricter conditionality regime.

The centrepiece of the 2007 Welfare Reform Act, which aimed to increase the employment rate to 80% and reduce claimants of disability benefits by 1 million, was the introduction of a new benefit system for people with work-limiting disabilities. Symbolically called Employment Support Allowance (ESA), and in the government's words "built on a clear framework of rights and responsibilities" (Department for Work and Pensions, 2006: 6), the new benefit included a stricter work test called the Work Capability Assessment. Claimants assigned to a 'work-related activity group' following this test were required to attend mandatory WFIs and to engage in 'work-related activities'. The same welfare reform also extended the full JSA conditionality regime to unemployed workers aged over 50, who had previously been exempted.

The other key development in this period was a major expansion of in-work benefits (Clegg, 2015; Sloman, 2019, chapter 7). The 2002 Tax Credits Act removed family support elements from WFTC and rolled them together with some family components of out-of-work benefits to create a new Child Tax Credit (CTC), payable to households below a certain income irrespective of work status. A new Working Tax Credit (WTC) was also created to replace WFTC. More targeted than CTC but more generous than WFTC, it also extended in-work support on somewhat more restrictive conditions to childless working households for the first time. These reforms were expansionary, increasing expenditure on the tax credit system from £10.1 billion in 2002/03 to £19.9 billion the following year (at 2022/23 prices) (DWP, 2023). Subsequently, Chancellor Gordon Brown used almost every annual budget to invest further resources in the improvement of tax credits (Sloman, 2019: 180). By the time New Labour left office in 2010, annual expenditure had ballooned to over £35 billion (DWP, 2023), making tax credits the largest area of social spending in the UK after the state pension, representing some 1.7% of GDP.

Not all of this expenditure strictly targeted low-income working households. Of the 6.2 million households receiving tax credits in 2009/10, 1.43 million were out of work, while a further 1.67 million were in receipt only of the 'family element' (or less) of CTC, and thus in middle- and not low-income households. Tackling child poverty once again became an important rationale for tax credits in the later years of New Labour,[4] meaning out-of-work households with children had to be better supported. Brown also viewed it as important for the system to reach quite far up the income distribution to secure middle-class support for it, an approach he termed 'progressive universalism' (Sloman, 2019: 195). Still, nearly 3.1 million low-income working households received wage supplements through tax credits in 2009/10. Moreover, as tax credits were designed above all to make work pay, the lion's share of the expenditure was targeted on these households, who received the most generous awards. In 2009/10, while low-income working households accounted for half of tax credit recipients, they received 70% of the spending (all figures from Her Majesty's Revenue and Customs, 2012).

New Labour's policy theory was that the combination of conditional out-of-work benefits and expanded in-work support would generate the combination of negative and positive incentives required to draw most of the workless into market employment. They nonetheless continued fine-tuning more intensive support through the New Deal ALMPs for those facing particular difficulties in returning to work, albeit at low levels of overall expenditure (see Figure 11.2 above). A key aspect of this was experimentation with new delivery systems intended to drive provider performance. Towards the end of Labour's final term in office, all pre-existing New Deal programmes were replaced by the so-called Flexible New Deal (FND), which was less prescriptive than its predecessors and partly based on a payment-by-results model. This was intended to incentivize providers operating under contract to develop more innovative, personalized solutions to the barriers to work facing those referred to them (DWP, 2007).

Measured from its arrival in office to the middle of the 2000s, New Labour's activation policy looks like a success story. By 2004, both the unemployment rate (4.75%) and the long-term unemployment share (20.5%) had fallen to their lowest levels in a quarter-century and were well below the OECD average. These declines had been underway before New Labour's arrival in office, however, and furthermore went into partial reverse after the middle of the decade, even before the onset of the global financial crisis. While the employment rate grew slightly from 71% in 1997 to 73% in 2004, the gains were much stronger for women, with many men leaving unemployment for economic inactivity (McKnight, 2005). Moreover, as Blundell et al. (2016) show, much of the employment growth precipitated by changes to the tax and benefit system was part time and at low earnings, with limited prospects for human capital development and progression in employment (see also Hoynes et al., 2023).

The 2007/08 global financial crisis and its aftermath wiped out much of what progress on labour market outcomes had been made under New Labour; unemployment was higher and employment lower when it left office in 2010 than when it had entered it 13 years earlier. Although in the wake of the crisis there was none of the improvements to unemployment benefits in the

UK seen in many other countries (Clegg, 2010), there was initially a partial departure from the established path of UK activation policy with the introduction in 2009 of the Future Jobs Fund (FJF). This £1 billion job subsidy programme, intended to create an initial 170,000 jobs for young people who had been in receipt of JSA for at least 10 months, was hailed by the UK Trade Union Confederation as "the most progressive jobs programme for more than a quarter of a century" (TUC, 2009). With youth unemployment still at a 25-year high of over 20%, FJF was, however, closed to new entrants for reasons of cost when a Conservative-led coalition came into office after the May 2010 election (Harari, 2011). This was a portent of the logic that would strongly shape UK activation policy in the years ahead.

The emasculation of activation under the Conservatives, 2010–2020

The two most significant changes in the UK activation regime since 2010 have been a far-reaching overhaul of the working-age benefit system and a strategy of extreme cost containment. While expenditure cuts were promised by the 2010 Conservative election manifesto, proposed changes to the working-age benefit system came out of the blue. The plans were drawn up by a think tank headed by the future Work and Pensions Minister, who was not even part of the Conservative Party leadership team (Timmins, 2016: 24). For that reason, benefit reforms were not originally connected to – and to some extent even conflicted with – the new government's plans for deficit reduction. The two agendas would, however, become increasingly intertwined over time.

The centrepiece of the 2012 Welfare Reform Act was Universal Credit (UC), an integrated new means-tested benefit that is gradually replacing all means-tested schemes for different claimant groups, including benefits for those out of work (e.g. JSA, ESA) and ones for those in work (WTC). New working-age claimants are now all directed to UC, and existing claimants of the pre-existing ('legacy') benefits are transferred when their circumstances change. Having been repeatedly delayed by information technology problems and associated costs, the transition is expected to be complete by 2024, fully 12 years after the legislation was adopted.

UC's main objective is simplification, primarily to avoid perverse interactions between the different existing benefits and particularly with a view to improving work incentives. UC builds, in certain respects, on New Labour's reforms, which as described had already partly eroded the distinction between different out-of-work benefits by incrementally extending work-related conditionality to them. UC means people in various situations now all receive the same type of benefit, though they are placed in one of four different 'conditionality groups' depending on their family situation and capacity to work. While the distinctions between these groups largely mirror the varying ways conditionality was previously applied to different legacy benefits, there have also been some further extensions of conditionality due to the introduction of UC's new 'claimant commitment', intended to intensify job-searching activities. And the 2012 Welfare Reform Act also sharply increased sanctions, both for UC and, in the interim, for the benefits such as JSA and ESA it would eventually replace. For JSA, the maximum period of benefit sanction was increased from 6 months to 3 years.

An even more significant change is that UC brings in-work support back under the administrative control of DWP, ending the clear-cut institutional as well as symbolic distinction between 'welfare' and in-work benefits that had been a major reason behind the development of the tax credit brand (Clegg, 2015). The main justification for this change is that remaining on the same benefit when moving into work represents a considerable simplification for jobseekers, lowering a possible barrier to entering work. Another important difference from tax credits is that UC does not have eligibility thresholds for working claimants based on minimum weekly hours of work. This is meant to improve financial incentives for people to enter jobs offering only a few hours of work, what might elsewhere be called 'mini jobs', a move that under the legacy benefit system generated some of the very highest marginal effective tax rates.

Although UC has in this respect expanded the scope of application of in-work support, it has also changed its logic. Working UC claimants with incomes below a specified level have become subject to conditionality (so-called 'in-work conditionality'), and are now required to make efforts to increase their wages or hours of work (Abbas and Chrisp, 2023; Wright and Dwyer, 2022). Violation of the welfare/in-work benefit frontier notwithstanding, this builds on earlier reforms by yet further extending conditionality, in this case to the underemployed. The underpinning argument is that 'dependency' on in-work support and out-of-work support is equally problematic, and activation should therefore no longer be just about supporting people into work but also about reducing financial reliance on the state (Millar and Bennett, 2017).

When the UC impact assessment was published by DWP in 2011, the legacy benefit system had already been subject to a first series of spending cuts. Albeit against this lower baseline, the analysis suggested that in its original form UC would have been an expansionary change overall. Somewhat crudely stated, on original design assumptions UC would be neutral for workless households, reduce benefits for working households with higher earnings (with particular implications for second-earner work incentives) and increase benefits for working households with lower earnings, especially due to part-time employment (Brewer et al, 2012). The gains for lower earners would have been higher still, and the losses for higher earners lower, if the Treasury had accepted the initially proposed standardized UC withdrawal rate (or 'taper') of 55% instead of ultimately insisting on a rate of 65% for reasons of cost.

As soon as they entered office in 2010, the Conservatives had also embarked on a programme of extensive public spending cuts, argued necessary to reduce the UK's budget deficit. Social security was earmarked for a third of the savings (HM Treasury, 2010), and with pensions protected this meant very substantial cuts to working-age benefits. Just as New Labour had repeatedly increased tax credit spending in the previous decade, so every fiscal event in the first half of the 2010s brought new cuts to working-age benefits. This culminated in the 2015 summer budget, shortly after a general election in which the Conservatives won an unexpected majority, which contained a massive package of cuts that were expected to generate savings of £13 billion per year by 2020/21 (Keep, 2015). Some of the most striking changes across the period as a whole included the uprating of working-age benefits being limited to 1% for three years in 2012, and then frozen entirely for four years in 2016; the introduction of a fixed maximum ceiling on benefit claims (a 'benefit cap'), particularly affecting large families; and the restriction of entitlement to child additions to tax credits and UC to two children within a household (the 'two child limit') (Hobson, 2020).

The sheer relentlessness of the cuts aside, their most striking feature was that the axe fell just as hard on in-work benefits as it did on benefits for those out of work. For the government this was the most politically delicate aspect of their retrenchment drive, prompting substantial opposition among even Conservative MPs. Planned cuts to tax credits announced in 2015 were actually cancelled some months later following a major Parliamentary rebellion. But the equivalent restrictions to the work allowances in UC – which at the time was being claimed by far fewer people, and thus less salient – were not reversed, and consequently the transition to UC became much more visibly a retrenchment of in-work support than it had previously been (Timmins, 2016: 55). This led to the 2016 resignation of the Work and Pensions Minister, who complained that successive rounds of welfare reforms had fatally undermined UC's original activation logic and made it simply a tool for delivering benefit cuts (O'Grady, 2022: 66).

Over this period as a whole, ALMPs were also sharply scaled back. To respect a pledge in the Conservative manifesto for the 2010 election – fought as unemployment spiked after the financial crisis – a large new employment programme was introduced in 2011. The Work Programme (WP) was fully outsourced to private providers through competitive contracting, using a 'black box' approach giving providers complete freedom over the design of support measures and a largely outcome-based payment model (Rees et al., 2014). It was thus noteworthy for intensifying the market-based delivery principles that New Labour had introduced to employment support in its last years in office. But more striking still is how quickly WP was scaled back. Its initial £2.5 billion annual budget was halved one year after its introduction, and by 2016/17 had fallen to little over £500 million (Wilson et al., 2022: 30). In what was reported in the media as "a massive shakeout of the government funded welfare to work sector that will see it shrink by 75%" (Butler, 2017), it was then replaced by the Work and Health Programme, which is much more narrowly targeted on people with work-limiting disabilities and the very long-term (+2 years) unemployed. In 2018/19 it was reported that the DWP spent less than £50 million on WHP (Powell, 2020a: 7).

JCP also saw substantial cuts. Once an executive agency, it was recentralized within DWP with the aim of reducing running costs by 40%. Between 2011–12 and 2015–16, the number of front-line employment advisors ('Work Coaches') was reduced by nearly half (Work and Pensions Select Committee, 2016, para 77). A programme to reduce the size of the DWP estate then closed over 100 JCP offices – about 15% of the total – between 2017 and 2018 (Finn, 2018). In parallel, the number of people required to have regular contact with JCP increased sharply due to the rollout of UC, mainly as a result of the extension of conditionality to new groups (Powell, 2020b). JCP thus faced increased demands on its services but diminishing resources to meet them. It squared this circle by making more use of call centres and automated online services (Fletcher and Wright, 2018: 331), while also cutting back on outreach work with local businesses (Ingold et al., 2017).

All types of public spending on the labour market – working-age benefits, employment programmes and the public employment service – were thus significantly retrenched between 2010 and 2020. In the second half of this period, however, these cuts were accompanied by significant increases in the value of the UK's statutory minimum wage. From 2016, a more generous National Living Wage was introduced for workers aged 25 and over, and by 2020 the UK's wage floor had climbed to 58% of median wages, putting it among the highest in the world (Cominetti et al., 2023: 39). Although minimum wages are less well targeted than means-tested transfers, the government presented this development as counterbalancing its spending cuts, in particular retrenchment of in-work benefits; indeed, creating a plausible narrative to justify benefit restrictions was a key motivation for the rate rise (Mabbett, 2023). Somewhat ironically, the rhetorical opposition between work and welfare that had been used as a key argument for the construction of the UK activation model under New Labour was now being used to justify its emasculation.

The government also justified its defunding of the UK activation regime with reference to the ostensible good health of the labour market. UK unemployment fell steadily from the end of 2011, and on the eve of the Covid-19 pandemic stood at only 3.8%, lower than at any time in the New Labour years (Figure 11.3). This good health was only temporary, however. The UK

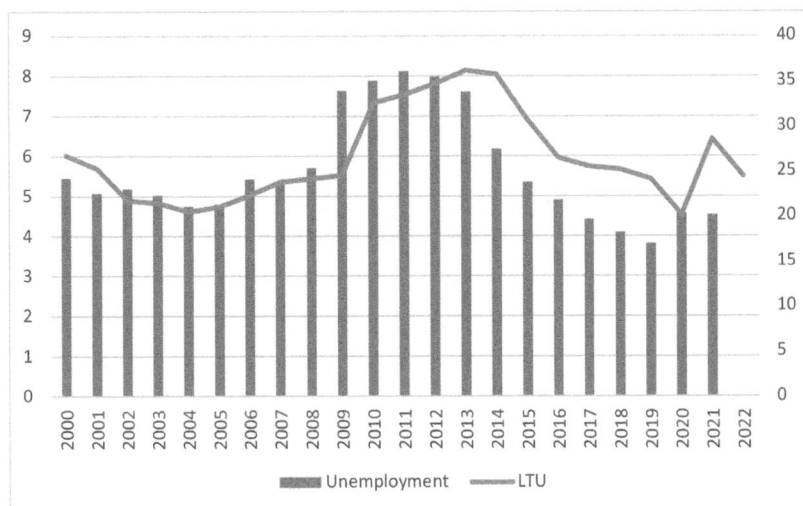

Source: OECD.

Figure 11.3   UK unemployment rate (left axis) and long-term
            unemployment rate (right axis), 2000–2022

economy has stagnated since the financial crisis, with zero real wage growth in the 2010s (Resolution Foundation, 2022). The puzzling boom in employment in this context was driven not by buoyant demand but instead by a labour supply shift provoked by stagnating wages and cuts to out-of-work benefits (Bell and Gardiner, 2019). Fully a third of the expansion of employment between 2012 and the end of 2016 was due to increasing self-employment (Office for National Statistics, 2018), while 'zero-hours contracts', where employees receive no advance notification of their regular working hours, grew rapidly after 2012 to around 3% of all employment – and as high as 12.2% in elementary occupations – by the end of the decade, having tradition-ally been relatively stable at between 0.1 and 1% of all UK employment (ONS, 2023). In reality it is the weakness, not the strength, of the UK labour market that explains cuts in spending on labour market policies under Conservative governments, who sought to deflect blame for stalling living standards by vilifying working-age beneficiaries of the welfare state (Lavery, 2017).

THE POST-COVID FUTURE OF THE UK ACTIVATION REGIME

The response to the Covid-19 pandemic saw some significant departures from the extant logic of UK labour market policy. First, basic rates of UC (and WTC) were sharply increased – by £20 per week, equivalent to an increase of between 24 and 30% for single people, depending on age – as soon as the first lockdowns were announced in March 2020. Coming after four years during which the value of these benefits had been totally frozen, this was a striking change of emphasis in policy. Secondly, a large short-time work scheme called Coronavirus Job Retention Scheme (CJRS) was rapidly devised and implemented. Through CJRS the state covered 80% of the wages of employees unable to work due to Covid-related restrictions, up to a ceiling of £2500 per month. Very much out of step with recent UK labour market policy norms, CJRS privileged simplicity and accessibility over efficient targeting (Clegg et al., 2023). Unlike in other countries, firms did not need to demonstrate adverse economic impacts for their employees to benefit from CJRS, and to simplify reporting requirements furloughed employees could not initially be placed on reduced hours but had to cease working entirely (National Audit Office, 2020). For this reason CJRS was exceptionally expensive; Drahokoupil and Müller (2021: 19) assess 2020 expenditure at 2% of GDP, double the cost of the French STW work scheme, which had a higher take-up rate. A final innovation was the announcement in 2020 of Kickstart, a subsidized employment measure targeting the young unemployed – the first such scheme in the UK since the 2009 FJF.

Despite speculation that this activist response to the pandemic might be a turning point in UK labour market policy, it looks today more like an interlude. While in some other liberal welfare states, such as Ireland and New Zealand, the success of pandemic income support schemes led governments to propose measures to bolster the earnings-replacement function of the regular benefit system (Kelly and Pearce, 2023: 14), such ideas have gained no traction in the UK political debate, despite interest from left-leaning think tanks (Harrop et al., 2023). Meanwhile, though extended until October 2021, the uplift to the value of Universal Credit was ultimately withdrawn despite intense campaigning for it to be made permanent. For working households, the government offset this removal by increasing the UC work allowance (i.e. earned income disregard) by £500 per year and reducing the taper rate from 63% to 55%, at a cost of £3 billion per year. However, analysis showed that nearly three-quarters of UC claimants would be worse off overall (Brewer et al., 2021). And while there were calls from the House of Lords Youth

Unemployment Committee for Kickstart to be expanded and made permanent, it was closed to applications in December 2021 (Powell, 2022).

While policy quickly reverted to type, the UK post-Covid labour market has seen some significant changes. As in many countries, the pandemic prompted widespread labour reallocation and the emergence of acute labour shortages in some sectors, especially care, hospitality and retail. In the UK, these have been exacerbated by a sharp rise in economic inactivity, which has not been seen in other countries. An increase of 1.5% (or 650,000 people) at its peak in mid-2022, at the time of writing there are still 350,000 more economically inactive people than before the pandemic. Most of this is due to a rise in health-related inactivity, with analysis showing that this is particularly concentrated among people who are older, have low skills, report mental health issues, and previously worked in customer-facing services and industries such as care, hospitality, sales and elementary occupations (Office for Budget Responsibility, 2023).

The share of the working-age population receiving sickness and disability benefits, which had fallen slowly since the early 2000s, had actually begun rising again before the pandemic. This trend has been greatly accelerated by the post-pandemic surge in health-related inactivity, and by late 2022 7.8% of the working-age population was in receipt of a health-related benefit, an all-time high. Trends in population health (then exacerbated by Covid-19) and an ageing workforce account for part of this tendency, but part of it may also be explained by the evolution of the UK activation regime. Though due to changes described above, actual benefit rates are now only higher for those assessed as having more severe levels of incapacity; unlike in many European countries, there is no positive financial incentive to register as unemployed on job loss rather than to leave the labour market altogether (Clegg, 2022). Moreover, as the risks of being subject to a benefit sanction are far higher for the unemployed than for people receiving benefits for reasons of ill-health, there is still more security to be had from being assessed as having even a mild incapacity for work, and this may be particularly important when households are under acute financial strain (OBR, 2023: 47).

Far from prompting a policy reassessment, the UK's post-Covid labour market problems seem to have encouraged the government to double-down on the extant approach. In the face of labour shortages, it was announced in January 2022 that job search conditions for the unemployed would be further tightened. The March 2023 budget then extended the scope of in-work conditionality by increasing the earnings threshold below which intensive conditionality applies, and introduced a trial programme in which unemployed people have to sign-on every day at JCP. The rate of unemployed benefit claimants receiving a benefit sanction has also spiked since the end of the pandemic, and was nearly three times higher in the middle of 2022 than in the middle of 2019

(OBR, 2023: 45). While there has been an increase in spending on ALMPs compared with the immediate pre-pandemic years – mainly devoted to a new 3-year contracted-out employment programme called Restart, targeted on those unemployed for at least 12 months – expenditure remains well below £1 billion annually in current prices (Wilson et al., 2022: 30). This compares to spending that was consistently above £1.5 billion annually in the early 2000s, when the unemployment rate was only slightly higher.

At the time of writing, the prospects for substantial change in the basic logic of the UK's activation policy regime therefore seem rather dim. However, though the opposition Labour Party has little to say about labour market policy as such, one high-profile policy commission has recommended the devolution of JCP to local/city or regional authorities (Labour Party, 2022). This could allow national policy to better connect with local-level initiatives that have developed in recent years, in part due to the emasculation of national policies, and involve far higher levels of employer engagement than national labour market programmes (Orton and Green, 2019). With systematic employer engagement, in-work conditionality might in turn mutate into a more effective emphasis on in-work progression, especially if the recent consensus around boosting the wage floor could be broadened into an agenda of promoting good work. This could begin to tackle a major weakness of the UK activation regime, which has tended to encourage the creation of jobs with low/uncertain hours and limited prospects (In-Work Progression Commission, 2021).

The major constraint on this agenda will be fiscal. The UK's poor recent economic performance, unfavourable trading situation after Brexit and the massive increase in borrowing during the pandemic coupled with higher interest rates have left the public finances extremely strained. The Labour Party's recent pledge not to reverse even extremely unpopular changes to the benefit system, such as the two-child limit, may be a tactic to reassure voters and the markets that it can be trusted to manage the economy, but is also an acknowledgement that any new government will face very hard decisions on spending priorities after the election. The dilemma is that while the UK economy would certainly benefit from at the very least reversing the damage inflicted on its activation regime since the financial crisis, the current state of and future prospects for the UK economy will make financing such a reversal of course very difficult.

CONCLUSION

Reforms since the turn of the century have made the UK activation regime broader. Initially focused mainly on the problem of unemployment, an activation logic has gradually been extended to a wider population of benefit claimants, including the economically inactive and underemployed workers.

Particularly since 2010, however, the activation regime has also become thinner. Spending cuts have lowered the value of out-of-work and in-work benefits, and reduced the resources committed to ALMPs and the public employment service. To the extent that the enabling aspects of activation make the demanding aspects morally acceptable, this double movement of extension and emasculation has arguably made the UK activation regime increasingly unjust. Despite low open unemployment, there are mounting signs that it is also ineffective.

Political partisanship has been a crucial factor in the recent evolution of the UK activation regime. While activation was extended by New Labour and Conservative governments alike, the policy of emasculation has been pursued only under the right. Whether political partisanship will once again change the course of policy development in this area seems more uncertain, however. The next UK government will not enjoy the relatively benign economic conditions of the New Labour years, but instead inherit an economy with low growth prospects, tax- and debt-to-GDP ratios both at historic highs and severe crises in many of its public services. It would be optimistic to think that the activation regime will be a priority area for major investment, however acutely it is now needed.

NOTES

1. Fraser of Allander Institute analysis (2021) shows that in 2019 and 2020 combined, UK, sub-national and local government expenditure on employment support was slightly above the UK per-capita average in Scotland, but below per-capita spend in Northern Ireland and all regions of Northern England.
2. As the UK has an individualized taxation system, integration of a payment targeted by household income in the tax system was technically impossible. The administration of WFTC was, however, transferred to the Inland Revenue (now Her Majesty's Revenue and Customs (HMRC), the executive agency of the Treasury).
3. A minor exception is the representation of employers and trade unions on the Low Pay Commission, an independent body that advises government on the National Minimum Wage (see Mabbett, 2023).
4. In 1999, Tony Blair had made a high-profile commitment to eradicate child poverty entirely by 2020.

REFERENCES

Abbas, J. and Chrisp, J. (2023) Working hard or hardly working? Examining the politics of in-work conditionality in the UK, *Social Policy and Society*, 22(1), 31–52.

Abbas, J. and Robertson, E. (2023) The rise of in-work benefits: Policy, politics and evaluation, in Clegg, D. and Durazzi, N. (eds.) *Handbook of Labour Market Policy in Advanced Democracies*, Cheltenham, UK and Northampton, MA, USA: Edward Elgar Publishing, pp. 280–94.

Atkinson, A. and Micklewright, J. (1991) Turning the screw: Benefits for the unemployed, 1979–1988, in Dilnot, A. and Walker, I. (eds.) *The Economics of Social Security*, Oxford: Oxford University Press, pp. 17–51.

Bell, T. and Gardiner, L. (2019) *Feel Poor, Work More: Explaining the UK's Record Employment*, London: Resolution Foundation.

Blundell, R., Costas Dias, M., Meghir, C. and Shaw, J. (2016) Female labour supply, human capital and welfare reform, *Econometrica*, 84(5), 1705–53.

Brewer, M., Browne, J. and Jin, W. (2012) Universal Credit: A preliminary analysis of its impact on incomes and work incentives, *Fiscal Studies*, 33(1), 39–71.

Brewer, M., Handscomb, K. and Try, L. (2021) *Taper Cut: Analysis of the Autumn Budget Changes to Universal Credit*, London: The Resolution Foundation.

Brown, J. (1990) *Victims or villains? Social Security Benefits in Unemployment*, York: Joseph Rowntree Foundation.

Butler, P. (2017) Thousands of jobs to go in government shakeout of welfare to work sector, *The Guardian*, 13 January.

Clasen, J. (1994) *Paying the Jobless: A Comparison of Unemployment Benefit Policies in Great Britain and Germany*, Aldershot: Ashgate.

Clasen, J. (1999) Beyond social security: The economic value of giving money to unemployed people, *European Journal of Social Security*, 1(2), 151–80.

Clasen, J. (2009) The United Kingdom, in de Beer, P. and Schills, T. (eds.) *The Labour Market Triangle: Employment Protection, Unemployment Compensation and Activation in Europe*, Cheltenham, UK and Northampton, MA, USA: Edward Elgar Publishing, pp. 70–95.

Clasen, J. (2011) The United Kingdom: Towards a single working-age benefit system, in Clasen, J. and Clegg, D. (eds.) *Regulating the Risk of Unemployment: National Adaptations to Post-Industrial Labour Markets in Europe*, Oxford: Oxford University Press, pp. 15–33.

Clegg, D. (2010) Labour market policy in the crisis: The UK in comparative perspective, *Journal of Poverty and Social Justice*, 18(1), 5–17.

Clegg, D. (2015) The demise of tax credits, *The Political Quarterly*, 86(4), 493–499.

Clegg, D. (2016) Institutional arrangements and policy coordination in national anti-poverty regimes, in Halvorsen, R. and Hvinden, B. (eds.) *Combating Poverty in Europe: Active Inclusion in a Multi-Level and Multi-Actor Context*, Cheltenham, UK and Northampton, MA, USA: Edward Elgar Publishing, pp. 85–108.

Clegg, D. (2022) *Post-Covid labour shortages, bad jobs and social security: Reflections on the British and French debates*, Social Policy Association Blog, October 18.

Clegg, D., Durazzi, N., Heins, E. and Robertson, E. (2023) Policy, power and pandemic: Varieties of job and income protection response to Covid-19 in Western Europe, *Journal of European Public Policy*, DOI: 10.1080/13501763.2023.2242907

Cominetti, N., McCurdy, C., Thwaites, G. and Viera-Marques, R. (2023) *Low Pay Britain 2023: Improving Low-Paid Work through Higher Minimum Standards*, London: The Resolution Foundation.

Crouch, C. (1999) Employment, industrial relations and social policy: New life in an old connection, *Social Policy & Administration*, 33(4), 437–57.

Crouch, C. (2001) A third way in industrial relations? in White, S. (ed.) *New Labour: The Progressive Future?* Basingstoke: Palgrave Macmillan, pp. 93–109.

Deakin, S. and Reed, H. (2000) River crossing or cold bath? Deregulation and employment in Britain in the 1980s and 1990s, in Esping-Andersen, G. and Regini, M. (eds.) *Why Deregulate Labour Markets?* Oxford: Oxford University Press, pp. 115–147.

Department for Work and Pensions (2006) *A New Deal for Welfare: Empowering People to Work (Cm 6730)*, London: HMSO.

Department for Work and Pensions (2007) *Ready to Work: Full Employment in Our Generation (Cm 7290)*, London: HMSO.

Department for Work and Pensions (2023) *Benefit Expenditure and Caseload Tables 2023*, London: DWP.

Drahokoupil, J. and Müller, T. (2021) *Job Retention Schemes in Europe: A Lifeline during the Pandemic*, Brussels: ETUI.

Finn, D. (2018) Why are Britain's Jobcentres disappearing? *The Conversation*, May 10.

Fletcher, D. and Wright, S. (2018) A hand up or a slap down? Criminalising benefit claimants in Britain via strategies of surveillance, sanctions and deterrence, *Critical Social Policy*, 38(2), 323–44.

Fraser of Allandar Institute (2021) *Election 2021 Issue Brief: The Employability Landscape in Scotland*, Glasgow: Fraser of Allander Institute.

Griggs, J., Hammond, A. and Walker, R. (2014) Activation for all: Welfare reform in the United Kingdom, 1995–2009, in Lødemel, I. and Moreira, A. (eds.) *Activation or Workfare? Governance and the Neo-Liberal Convergence*, New York: Oxford University Press, pp. 73–100.

Grover, C. (2016) *Social Security and Wage Poverty: Historical and Policy Aspects of Supplementing Wages in Britain and Beyond*, Basingstoke: Palgrave Macmillan.

Grover, C. and Stewart, J. (1999) 'Market workfare': Social security, social regulation and competitiveness in the 1990s, *Journal of Social Policy*, 28(1), 73–96.

Harari, D. (2011) *Future Jobs Fund, House of Commons Library standard note SN05352*, London: House of Commons.

Harrop, A., Reed, H. and Sacares, E. (2023) *In Time of Need: Building Employment Insurance for All*, London: The Fabian Society.

Her Majesty's Revenue and Customs (2012) *Child and Working Tax Credit Statistics, Finalised Annual Awards*, Newport: UK Statistics Authority.

Her Majesty's Treasury (2010) *Budget 2010: Securing the Recovery (HC 451)*, London: HM Treasury.

Hobson, F. (2020) The Aims of Ten Years of Welfare Reforms (2010–2020), House of Commons Library Briefing Paper no. 9090, London: House of Commons.

Hoynes, H., Joyce, R. and Waters, T. (2023) *Benefits and Tax Credits (Inequality: The IFS Deaton Review)*, London: Institute for Fiscal Studies.

In-Work Progression Commission (2021) *Supporting Progression out of Low Pay: A Call to Action*, London: DWP.

Ingold, J., Sarkar, M., Valizade, D., Garcia, R. and Scholz, F. (2017) *Employer Engagement in Active Labour Market Programmes in the UK and Denmark*, CERIC Policy Report no. 8, Leeds: CERIC.

Keep, M. (2015) *Summer Budget 2015: A Summary (Updated), House of Commons Library Briefing Paper no. 07521*, London: House of Commons.

Kelly, G. and Pearce, N. (2023) Beveridge at eighty: Learning the right lessons, *The Political Quarterly*, 94(1), 8–15.

Labour Party (2022) *A New Britain: Renewing Our Democracy and Rebuilding our Economy, Report of the Commission on the UK's Future*, London: The Labour Party.

Lavery, S. (2017) The legitimation of post-crisis capitalism in the United Kingdom: Real-wage decline, finance-led growth and the state, *New Political Economy*, 23(1), 27–45.

Mabbett, D. (2023) In the shadow of hierarchy: Minimum wage commissions in the UK and Germany, *Socio-Economic Review*, 21(4), 2117–35.

McKnight, A. (2005) Employment: tackling poverty through 'work for those who can', in Hills, J. and Stewart, K. (eds.) *A More Equal Society? New Labour, Poverty, Inequality and Exclusion*, Bristol: The Policy Press, pp. 23–46.

Metcalf, D. (2008) Why has the British minimum wage had little or no impact on employment? *Journal of Industrial Relations*, 50(3), 489–512.

Millar, J. (2009) Tax credits, in Millar, J. and Sainsbury, R. (eds.) *Understanding Social Security* (2nd edition), Bristol: The Policy Press, pp. 242–64.

Millar, J. and Bennett, F. (2017) Universal Credit: Assumptions, contradictions and virtual reality, *Social Policy and Society*, 16(2), 169–82.

National Audit Office (2020) *Implementing Employment Support Schemes in Response to the Covid-19 Pandemic (HC 862), Report by the Comptroller and Auditor General*, London: National Audit Office.

O'Grady, T. (2022) *The Transformation of British Welfare Policy: Politics, Discourse and Public Opinion*, Oxford: Oxford University Press.

OECD (2023a) *Net Replacement Rates in Unemployment, OECD Statistics*, Paris: OECD.

OECD (2023b) *Social Expenditure – Aggregated Data, OECD Statistics*, Paris: OECD.

Office for Budget Responsibility (2023) *Fiscal Risks and Sustainability (CP 870)*, London: OBR.

Office for National Statistics (2018) *Trends in Self-Employment in the UK*, London: ONS.

Office for National Statistics (2023) *EMP 17: People in Employment on Zero-Hours Contracts*, London: ONS.

Orton, M. and Green, A. (2019) Active labour market policy in the UK: At a (local) crossroads? *Local Economy*, 34(1), 3–9.

Powell, A. (2020a) *The Work and Health Programme, House of Commons Library Briefing Paper no. 7845*, London: House of Commons.

Powell, A. (2020b) *Universal Credit and the Claimant Count, House of Commons Library Briefing Paper no. 7927*, London: House of Commons.

Powell, A. (2022) *Coronavirus: Getting People Back into Work, House of Commons Library Briefing Paper no. 8965*, London: House of Commons.

Rees, J., Whitworth, A. and Carter, E. (2014) Support for all in the UK Work Programme? Differential payments, same old problem, *Social Policy & Administration*, 48(2), 221–39.

Resolution Foundation (2022) *Stagnation Nation: Navigating a Route to a Fairer and More Prosperous Britain*, London: Resolution Foundation.

Rhodes, M. (2000) Desperately seeking a solution: Social democracy, Thatcherism and the 'third way' in British welfare, *West European Politics*, 23(2), 161–86.

Sloman, P. (2019) *The Transfer State: The Idea of a Guaranteed Income and the Politics of Redistribution in Modern Britain*, Oxford: Oxford University Press.

Timmins, N. (2016) *Universal Credit: From Disaster to Recovery?* London: Institute for Government.

Tomlinson, J. (2021) Deindustrialisation and 'Thatcherism': Moral economy and unintended consequences, *Contemporary British History*, 35(4), 620–42.

TUC (2009) *The Future Jobs Fund*, London: TUC. https://www.tuc.org.uk/research-analysis/reports/future-jobs-fund

Walker, R. (1999) The Americanization of British welfare: A case study of policy transfer, *International Journal of Health Services*, 29(4), 679–97.

Whiteside, N. (1995) Employment policy: a chronicle of decline? in Gladstone, D. (ed.) *British Social Welfare: Past, Present and Future*, London: UCL Press, pp. 52–70.

Wiggan, J. (2015) Varieties of marketisation in the UK: Examining divergence in activation markets between Great Britain and Northern Ireland 2008–2014, *Policy Studies*, 36(2), 1–18.

Wilson, T., Patel, R., Edwards, M., Mason, B. and Muir, D. (2022) *Working for the Future: Launch Report for the Commission on the Future of Employment Support*, Brighton: Institute for Employment Studies.

Work and Pensions Select Committee (2016) *The Future of Jobcentre Plus (HC 57), Second report of session 2016–17*, London: House of Commons.

Wright, S. and Dwyer, P. (2022) In-work Universal Credit: Claimant experiences of conditionality mismatches and counterproductive benefit sanctions, *Journal of Social Policy*, 51(1), 20–38.

12. Activation in the United States: low effort, fragmented administration, and poor performance

Ian Greer

INTRODUCTION

European labour market experts once spoke of the United States as a liberal model to be emulated, unencumbered by generous welfare benefits and strict employment protection, and therefore effective at producing high employment levels and low levels of unemployment. Americans, according to one prominent authority, should be considered a model for Europeans facing down the erosion of their social model by virtue of their everyday capacity for "self-help and personal initiative, which are essential for prosperity and success", made possible by "optimistic willingness to take risks and compete. The faster we learn how to deal with more open markets, the better" (Streeck 2004, p. 9). In those years, the US was also often a reference point in critical discussions of "workfarism", in which such virtues were part of a discourse justifying punitive labour market institutions, privatization of employment services, and the rise of precarious work (Peck 2001).

In the US itself, activation has been a marginal topic in academia, and the term never gained much currency in policy debates. It is true that the policy principles behind the main programmes that support working-age people favour "activation", if we define it as "efforts to promote employability and labour market participation for both uninsured and insured unemployed people." A complex landscape of employment services exists to do this task, normally referred to as workforce development, which is organized as networks of service providers that assist disadvantaged jobseekers and employers through advice, training, and job-placement assistance. However, overall spending on workforce development is relatively low, and policymakers have not responded to the problems of the US labour market by expanding workforce development services.

One of the best-known examples of activation worldwide was embedded in the reform of the means-tested benefit for lone parents, known as Aid to Families with Dependent Children (AFDC), and then, after the 1996 Personal Responsibility and Work Opportunity Reconciliation Act (PRWORA), Temporary Assistance for Needy Families (TANF). The language of "workfare" was pioneered by Republican politicians and pundits starting in the 1970s, often working at the state level, as part of a broader political strategy to win over white voters while getting tough on racialized deviants (Kohler-Hausmann 2017). The reforms of the mid-1990s sought to generalize workfare by creating incentives for states to reduce spending on the benefits, introducing time limits, eliminating any entitlement to the benefit, and strengthening work requirements. This reform was effective in reducing caseloads. In 2022, the average monthly caseload included 1.9 million individuals, down from more than 12 million in 1996. Whether this policy improved employability and labour market participation is doubtful for reasons discussed below, but activation was among its stated objectives.

The promotion of work for recipients of benefits has a longer history than that of workfare. The acts that created unemployment insurance (UI), Wagner–Peyser (1933) and the Social Security Act (1935), used employment services to reduce the "moral hazard" of claimants not looking for work and to improve the labour supply to employers. These laws funded employment services at the state level and required them to work with unemployment insurance. This funding stream, however, has stagnated in nominal terms and declined in real terms since the mid-1980s, curtailing job-search assistance, assessments of clients, and the coordination of relevant agencies (Balducchi and O'Leary 2018).

TANF and UI are just one part of a sprawling landscape of policies, programmes, and projects in the US that serve as functional equivalents to activation, and it is quite unusual that the empirical literatures about them are synthesized (but see Quade et al. 2008; Anderson et al. 2014). Projects funded by states and the federal government to move jobless people into work continue to be evaluated (Card et al. 2018). Disparate literatures examine changes in the various policy fields that in a European country might be considered part of "labour market policy" and handled by a single ministry or public employment service. Beyond TANF, these include unemployment insurance (UI), disability benefits, Medicaid, Supplemental Nutrition Assistance Program (SNAP), housing supports such as Section 8 vouchers, and the Earned Income Tax Credit (EITC). Other state-level programmes compensating for federal inaction could be included in this list, such as childcare subsidies, means-tested social assistance for low-income people ineligible for TANF, or unemployment benefits for undocumented migrants. Further Federal programmes target Native Americans, veterans, the self-employed, and more. These benefits all have different rules to encourage job searching and different funding streams for services to support the job search. The task of interpreting and enacting these rules falls to overworked street-level bureaucrats in the vast and varied landscape of agencies that administer benefits (Brodkin 2011, Barnes et al. 2023). Reflecting the fragmented character of activation in the US, the relevant literature is diverse, and it is beyond the scope of this chapter to provide a thorough synthesis.

My aim in this chapter is to provide a starting point to make sense of how activation works in the US, and I will make three arguments. First, the US is an outlier in its lack of effort in activation, in the sense that spending on services is very low; in terms of spending per capita, it is the second lowest, with marginally more spending than Mexico (OECD databank). Austerity may seem consistent with the idea of the US as a liberal economic order, and is indeed consistent with much of the rhetoric and biases of conservative and centre-left policymakers. However, it prevents the expansion of activation, in its human capital investment or work-first variants. Second, even if activation efforts were adequately funded, they would not be coordinated. If activation is viewed as a system, it is characterized by severe horizontal fragmentation between programmes and vertical fragmentation between levels of government. Third, this lack of effort and fragmented administration is related to poor labour market performance. Unlike most other wealthy countries, in the US labour force participation has been dropping since around 2000, due not only to the weaknesses of activation policies, but also to a range of other political, institutional, and societal factors that create barriers to work. These barriers disproportionately affect people of colour, and are often gendered. Countering these barriers is a task for the under-funded workforce development system.

This chapter discusses these three points in turn and concludes with a critique of the widespread perception of the US labour market as embedded in a liberal, market-driven regime.

1.   LOW EFFORT

Despite its well-known innovations in work-first activation schemes, the US is a laggard in activation. Even if we consider the work-first variant, "workfare", policymakers have failed to heed the advice of advocates of activation. When Lawrence Mead bluntly advised "telling the poor what to do", he argued that only government had the democratic legitimacy to do this, and that this involved not only exercising authority but also allocating funding (1998). The principles of most welfare programmes do promote work, and in many instances can back up these principles with financial penalties; what is missing is adequate funding to support claimants in fulfilling work-search requirements. They are better at cutting claimants off of supports than finding them jobs. To refer to Peck and Tickell's (2002) pregnant image of neoliberalism: activation in the US has been far more *roll-back* than *roll-out*.

This can be seen in the Covid era, when the overall unemployment rate reached the highest level since the Great Depression, 14.7%. The number of Americans receiving unemployment benefits also reached unprecedented levels for the "regular" UI administered by states; on top of this were new Federal pandemic unemployment programmes. These included Pandemic Unemployment Compensation, which added a flat-rate $600 weekly payment for all claimants early in the pandemic and $300 later; Pandemic Unemployment Assistance, which provided 26 weeks of benefits for self-employed, "gig workers", low earners, new labour-market entrants, and other unemployed workers excluded from UI; and Pandemic Extended Unemployment Compensation, which added an extra 13 weeks for people who exhausted their 26 weeks of benefits. In the early months of the pandemic, the replacement rate of benefits was over 100% for about 74% of claimants (Ganong et al. 2020) and the new benefits significantly mitigated the increase in poverty (Traub 2021). These measures, however, were temporary.

As the pandemic progressed, the unemployment rate dropped, and employers reported difficulty recruiting and retaining staff. Starting in the summer of 2021, 26 Republican-led states cancelled their pandemic benefits programmes, and in September the Democrats who controlled both houses of Congress at the federal level, allowed the benefits to expire. Motivated by employer concerns about work incentives and the labour shortage, policymakers allowed nearly 10 million claimants to lose their benefits in the space of a few weeks. In his announcement that pandemic unemployment benefits would not be extended, Biden's secretary of Labor, Martin Walsh, called on Congress to make permanent fixes to the UI system. (Republicans and business interests responded by criticizing UI fraud and the tax burden on small business, a framing that in early 2023 dominates the national debate on UI.) This took place during one of the peaks of Covid cases, with around 2000 deaths per day.

At first sight, this would seem to be a case where arguments for activation won out over other considerations. The CARES Act had allowed states to suspend job search requirements and increased benefit levels specifically to slow the spread of the virus. Now, this policy was reversed with the explicit aim of intensifying the pressure on unemployed workers to find a job. Initial studies showed that the decision to end benefits led to only small increases in the labour supply (Greig et al. 2021; Holzer et al. 2021).

Aside from the question of ending pandemic-era unemployment benefits, activation was mostly absent from policy and academic discussions of how to address employer concerns about the labour supply. The focus of business lobbyists and Republicans was on benefits and work incentives; for progressive Democrats and labour, it was on labour-market disparities, poor job quality, and structural racism. Lobbyists for the workforce development system continued to make the argument for expanding funding, and there have been some new opportunities. Biden-era green energy infrastructure spending, for example, could drastically increase funding for apprenticeships in the unionized construction industry. However, the workforce development system did not receive extra funding to assist employers in recruiting and retaining workers, or assisting workers seeking to re-enter paid work. Indeed, Trade Adjustment Assistance, which provided benefits and services for workers laid off due to trade, was allowed to lapse in 2022.

This neglect of workforce development is nothing new for the United States. Consider the OECD public labour market spending numbers (Figure 12.1). Spending on active measures is relatively low, and as a share of GDP has slowly declined over time. Overall spending has fluctuated with the business cycle, but increases were until the pandemic entirely driven by spending on unemployment insurance benefits. During the pandemic this changed, as spending on "employment incentives" increased to more than 3% of GDP; this reflects the introduction of the Paycheck Protection Program (PPP), loans to cover two weeks of employees' pay, forgivable if employers did not lay workers off. PPP loans were aimed at containing the economic damage of the pandemic, along with the pandemic unemployment benefits and three stimulus checks in 2020–21 received by most workers. But this increase in spending is for stabilizing the economy, and not for activation. During this and previous recessions, spending on training, make-work schemes, and job-search supports for disadvantaged jobseekers has hardly changed.

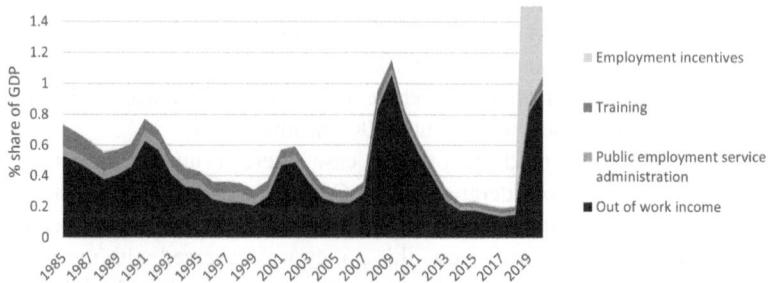

Source: OECD database, 2024. Public expenditure and participant stocks on LMP.

Figure 12.1   Public labor market spending in the US, main components

Medicaid is the largest means-tested programme in the United States, with 84.5 million recipients in July 2023. Enrolment expanded during the Obama administration and the pandemic as eligibility was expanded, accounting for

17% of health spending nationally. During the Trump administration, 13 states obtained permission to introduce work requirements; only Arkansas implemented the policy. Between June 2018 and March 2019, when the programme was thrown out by a court, 18,000 people were disenrolled. Court challenges, the pandemic, and opposition from the Biden administration ended the trend toward Medicaid work requirements (Guth and Musumeci 2022).

SNAP has, since the mid-1990s, imposed a general work requirement for "Able Bodied Adults without Dependents". These adults, however, comprise only 5% of claimants, 2.1 million out of 39.9 million. Claimants can satisfy this requirement by working or participating in employment services for 80 hours per month or more. This does not apply to claimants younger than 18 or older than 52, the disabled and homeless, veterans, and people with dependants. There is strong evidence that work requirements reduce caseloads among this group, by as much as 50%, but quite mixed evidence on the effects on income and employment (Bauer and East 2023).

The landscape is similar for other benefits. Even in the ever-shrinking caseloads of TANF a minority have engaged in work activity, and only about 5% at any given time were in a "workfare" programme (Anderson et al. 2014). Unemployment insurance has, since its inception, been attached to job search requirements. It also incentivizes work in most states by paying benefits for workers who take part-time jobs, but the attached employment services have been starved of funding. The two main disability benefits, means-tested SSI and social-insurance SSDI, have been reformed over the years to strengthen work incentives and improve access to employment services. Claimants are allowed to keep part of their earnings and under the "Ticket to Work" can opt into employment services (Bruyère 2019), but these lack the compulsory character of TANF and workfare.

In the United States, austerity trumps activation. The principles behind many of the most important benefits encourage work, and the intention behind excluding workers from benefits is to impose the discipline of the labour market on workers (Greer and Umney 2022). However, relatively low spending on out-of-work benefits is matched by low spending on training and other employment services. The next section discusses further the services and benefits that do exist and the challenge of coordination.

2.   FRAGMENTED ADMINISTRATION

Coordination is a persistent problem in activation worldwide. Benefits systems, the needs of workers and employers, and the public services relevant to matching supply and demand on the labour market are all varied and complex. The US, however, has never created a modern national agency like Britain's Jobcentre Plus or Germany's Bundesagentur für Arbeit to combine various public functions and enact a semblance of a coherent labour-market policy. TANF, the benefit attached to "workfare", is only one of many cash benefits, some means tested, some based on social insurance, managed by an alphabet soup of federal and state agencies. Meanwhile, employment services are provided by a separate and diverse landscape of public, for-profit and non-profit agencies.

In some ways, little has changed in the 25 years since Michael Wiseman wrote about the experience of a hypothetical single mother who seeks assistance:

> [She] goes to the local office of the state social services agency. She is required to provide information about her income, assets and if she is not receiving child support from the father of her children the particulars necessary for establishing a court order for such payments. Based on this information and the size of her family she receives a monthly cash payment from the income support program, TANF, and food stamps. She also receives a card (from the Medicaid) program that authorizes health care providers to bill the state for common medical services she and her children might require. If she is working, the food stamps and TANF benefits are reduced according to the amount of earnings she has. This reduction is offset in part by a refundable tax credit (EITC) that is most often collected when she files her income tax return at the beginning of the year following earnings. If she is not working ... workfare obligations are applied .... If she or one of her children is disabled, she may also receive Supplemental Security Income, a national program. (Wiseman 2000: 218)

It is true that welfare offices provide access to multiple benefits and services, and it is striking how the names of the programmes have nearly all remained the same. However, the experience was never as seamless as this seems to imply. If this woman receives unemployment benefits, she has to go to a separate employment office. If she receives SSI, she has to visit the social security administration. And for many of these benefits she faces confusing application forms, likely rejection, long appeals, cumbersome electronic systems, and other administrative burdens (Herd et al. 2023). Moreover, accessing employment services is not always just a matter of being mandated onto a workfare programme; in many cases there are also voluntary workforce development programmes that she can access if she can navigate the network of service providers and front-line workers who staff them.

Activation in the US is fragmented along two dimensions. First is horizontal fragmentation between different federal programmes and the bureaucracies that regulate and fund services. Federal departments with different functions fund and regulate activation services separately – a Department of Labor that governs unemployment insurance, a Department of Health and Human Services that governs Medicaid and TANF, a Social Security Administration that administers SSI and its social insurance counterpart SSDI, and a Department of Agriculture that administers SNAP. Second is vertical fragmentation, in which policies are implemented and programmes carried out by different levels of government. Political and cultural differences are particularly important here, especially the politics of race (Soss et al. 2011). Coordinating across these two dimensions is a hugely challenging task in the US.

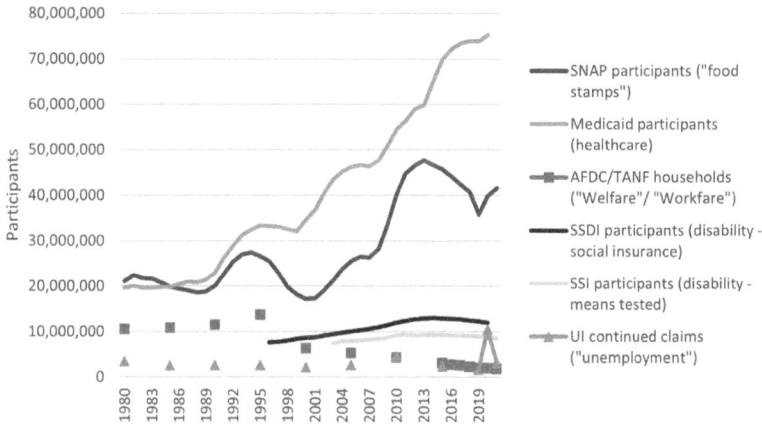

Sources: This is caseload data from the various agencies: SNAP, US Department of Agriculture, 2024, SNAP Data Tables, https://www.fns.usda.gov/pd/supplemental-nutritio n-assistance-program-snap; Medicaid, Center for Medicaid and CHIP Services (2024), Monthly Medicaid & CHIP Application, Eligibility Determination, and Enrollment Reports & Data, https://www.medicaid.gov/about-us/messages/index.html; AFDC/TANF, Office of Family Assistance, 2024, TANF Caseload Data, https://www.acf.hhs.gov/ofa/programs/ tanf/data-reports; SSI and SSDI, Social Security Administration, 2024, SSA State Agency Monthly Workload Data, https://www.ssa.gov/disability/data/ssa-sa-mowl.htm; UI, US Department of Labor, 2024, Unemployment Insurance Weekly Claims Data, https://oui. doleta.gov/unemploy/claims.asp.

Figure 12.2   Major social safety net and social insurance programs, average yearly caseloads

To understand horizontal fragmentation, consider the various benefits systems for working-age people who might be subject to activation (Figure 12.2). Unemployment insurance is managed by the federal Department of Labor and administered by 53 states (including the District of Columbia, Puerto Rico, and the Virgin Islands). Other means-tested programmes are also administered by states, but are run by different departments at the federal level – SNAP by the US Department of Agriculture, and TANF and Medicaid by the US

Department of Health and Human Services. Housing support is governed by the US Department for Housing and Urban Development and administered by local housing authorities. The two main disability benefits – means-tested SSI and social insurance SSDI – are managed by the federal Social Security Administration, which administers them through a national network of offices.

Most of these programmes have funding streams attached to support claimants' job search efforts. The US DOL provides funding to states for employment services, with programmes for young people, dislocated workers, Native Americans, migrant farmworkers, and other adults. One major funding stream comes directly from employer unemployment insurance contributions (Balducchi and O'Leary 2018). Attached to SNAP is funding for workforce training administered by USDA, and HUD funds a small workforce programme for residents in public housing. Although disability benefits are not subject to strict work requirements, there is considerable funding from the SSA and USDOL to support SSDI and SSI claimants. Work supports for TANF are funded by states out of their federal block grants.

Beyond the cash benefits and associated funding streams are the actual providers of services to promote activation. These services are coordinated by 53 state workforce boards and 591 local Workforce Development Boards. Under the Workforce Innovation and Opportunity Act (WIOA), states are required to draw up plans for spending the funds they are administered, and the local workforce development boards apply for and distribute these and other funds. The funding streams managed by these boards pay for services from for-profit training companies, community colleges, community-based non-profits, economic development agencies, private consultants, research organizations, and "American Job Centers", sometimes called one-stops, where client-facing services funded by some of these programmes and provided by more than one agency are located. "One-stop" is a misnomer, however, because (as mentioned above) cities and towns normally have separate additional offices for social services agencies delivering means-tested benefits, the Social Security Administration, and training providers. Unsurprisingly, states and locales vary widely in their success in coordinating these services (Myers and Kellogg 2022).

Providers of employment services face the difficult task of keeping in mind the differing work requirements attached to different benefits. Some benefits are characterized by strict conditionality enforced by federal law, most notably TANF, which requires most adult claimants to look for and take work. SNAP too has clearly defined federal job search requirements, but these only apply to "Able-Bodied Adults Without Dependents", and they were waived during both the Great Recession and the Covid pandemic. The opposite case is Medicaid with its brief Trump-era state-level experiments with work requirements. Similarly, the two largest disability benefits offer support services and income disregards to claimants looking for work, but job search is not mandatory. (See Congressional Budget Office (CBO) 2022 for an overview of these developments.) It must be kept in mind that these requirements are particularly challenging where funding is "braided" and programmes are devised that include recipients of different or multiple benefits.

UI is an interesting case of how activation principles work in US benefits systems. According to federal law, UI claimants have to be available and actively seeking work, and they may not turn down "appropriate" job offers. There are wide variations between states, however, in how an "appropriate" job offer is defined, which "job-search activities" are required, and how these requirements are enforced (United States Department of Labor (2023) provides a useful comparison of state laws and is updated annually). In some states, for example, a victim of domestic violence forced to quit her job because she may be targeted by her former spouse will receive UI benefits; in other states this is not a "good cause" to quit, and she will be denied benefits. During the pandemic, the Federal government permitted states to waive work search requirements; some did so, while others did not. Amid pandemic-era accusations that UI claimants were turning down suitable job offers and fraudulently collecting benefits, some states publicized "tattle-tale" lines, phone numbers for employers to report workers who do not accept job offers, allowing the state UI agency to reject applications for benefits. The 53 states also vary in the services they provide to UI recipients to help them re-enter work, although they have in common severe under-funding (Balducchi and O'Leary 2018).

Given this fragmentation, it is difficult to generalize about the character of workforce development services. To refer to Bonoli's (2010) typology, policies that seek to activate jobless people without investing in their human capital are easy to find – time limits, benefits conditionality, tax credits, and ending or reducing benefits when economic crises are passed are all thought to incentivize work. Programmes with little or no human capital investment are also common: about half of the TANF budget is spent on work-first services with an emphasis on job placement (CBO 2022). Also, in evidence, however, are "human capital investment" approaches, such as sector-specific programmes that use apprenticeships or college degrees to prepare workers for living-wage jobs with clear prospects for future career advancement (Osterman 2020). Due to the variation in the services, it is challenging to use either of these labels to categorize the system as a whole. More than the character of these services, their striking feature in international comparison is their scarcity: their overall low funding and participant numbers.

It is also difficult to generalize about the quasi-markets used to govern these services. Marketization and privatization were important features in the formative phase of workfare; promoting participation in the labour market took place at the same time as marketization of services in line with new public management doctrines (Brodkin 2011). However, there are several structural features of the market that may stunt competition. First, due to the fragmented institutional structure, there is no national market for employment services in the US, the way there has been in Great Britain, or even a clear national market structure as in Germany and Denmark (Greer et al. 2017). Privatization and contracting have been a contested terrain in workfare (Reese 2011) and also in unemployment insurance. In the latter, a longstanding demand by conservatives has been to end "merit-based staffing", first mandated by the 1933 Wagner–Peyser Act, which sought to root out corruption in the earliest make-work schemes (Shierholz et al. 2019). This prevents the privatization of core tasks of decision-making in UI, but it has not prevented the privatization of call centre work during the pandemic (when merit-based staffing rules were temporarily suspended) or the reliance of private IT systems on "modernization" (which is not subject to these rules but has a major effect on decision-making by state agencies). Austerity is also a problem for the expansion of these markets; a private market for activation services does not necessarily expand to compensate for inadequate public provision (Van Slyke 2003; Krachler and Greer 2015). Declining spending and a fragmented funding landscape lead to low-value contracts; and competition is restricted by a weak incentive to enter the market. To the extent that providers do compete, it is for increasingly scarce resources. Many of these markets are characterized by "network accountability" (Jantz et al. 2018): competition is on the basis of reputation rather than price, performance and outcomes are difficult to measure, and non-profits and the public sector dominate.

The neglect of benefits and services for jobless people is not only reflected in low spending figures; it is also reflected in poor coordination. Some states are more effective than others in coordinating their workforce development systems, but even studies on success stories contain important insights into the macro-level challenges (Giloth 2004; Myers and Kellogg 2022). The next section grapples with the question of how these problems are related to broader problems with the US labour market.

3.   POOR PERFORMANCE

The failure of the US to spend on services and coordinate administration is not caused by widespread satisfaction in the state of the labour market. Aside from headline unemployment rates during the Great Recession and Covid pandemic that were high both in international comparison and in historical perspective, longer-term trends are even more damning. For example, labour force participation among prime working-age adults has been dropping since around 2000, at a time when most other wealthy countries were experiencing increases. Since the 1950s there has been a continuous decline in participation by men;

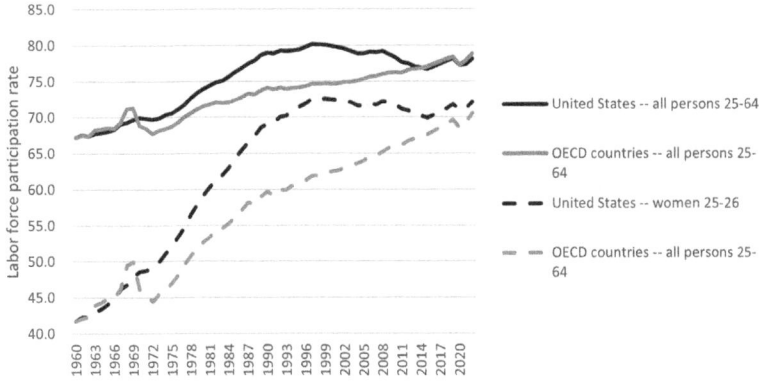

Source: OECD, 2024, Labour force participation rate. https://data.oecd.org/emp/labour-force-participation-rate.htm

Figure 12.3   Participation in the labor force: US vs. OECD countries

the opposite was true of women until about 2000, when the increase in labour force participation abruptly ended. This has come at a time when nearly every other country has experienced increases in labour force participation, driven by particularly rapid increases for women. At 78.1%, the US is now just below the OECD average for prime working-age labour force participation (Figure 12.3).

Over this period, spells of unemployment have been getting longer. During the Great Recession, average weeks of unemployment reached 40, and in the Covid pandemic 32. In the very tight labour markets of 2018, 2019, and late 2022, the average spell of unemployment ranged between 19 and 22 weeks, which is similar to the *peak* figures reached at the heights of mass unemployment during the three recessions prior to the Great Recession.

Declining labour force participation has been shaped not only by broader demographic shifts (for overviews, see Abraham and Kearney 2020, Krueger 2017, and Forsythe et al. 2022) but also by longstanding disparities by race. The population is aging, leading to more retirements, and younger people are increasingly either in full-time education or neither in education nor in the labour force. During the Covid pandemic, the participation rate dropped for all groups and, as of early 2023, remains below its 2019 level for all groups except black men. Figure 12.4 shows these figures for black and white workers, broken down by gender. (The figures for black people somewhat overstate the rate for prime working-age individuals because their life expectancy is shorter than white people; these figures include all individuals over the age of 20.)

Economists sometimes point to benefits systems as a possible cause of this decline. For example, in the wake of the Great Recession, a debate took place

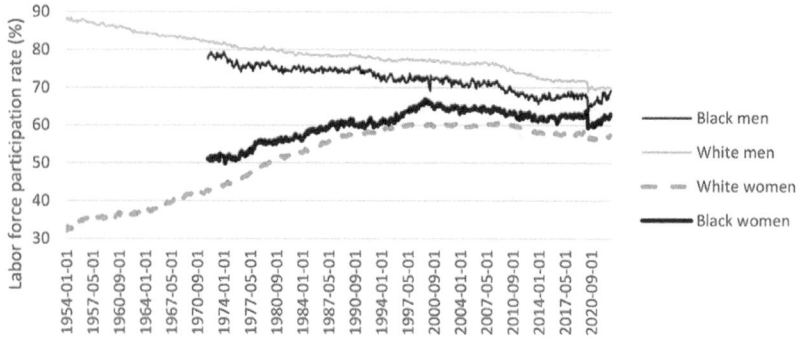

Source: OECD, 2024, Labour force participation rate. https://data.oecd.org/emp/labour-force-participation-rate.htm

Figure 12.4   *Disparities by race and gender in labor force participation, age 20+*

over expansion of disability benefit caseloads, which became many times those of unemployment insurance or TANF. Autor and Duggan (2006) argued that what had originally been provided for people too disabled to work had turned into social insurance for people who, for a wider variety of reasons, were unemployable. Similar arguments have been made about SNAP, TANF, Medicaid, unemployment insurance, and other benefits, the implication being that strictly enforced restrictions such as work requirements should lead claimants to re-enter the labour force (Abraham and Kearney 2020).

The claim that out-of-work benefits cause declining labour-force participation in the US is unconvincing. From the perspective of an international-comparative study, the most obvious problem is that the wage replacement and take-up rates are both relatively low in the US (OECD database). This has been the case for decades, as performance of the US labour market has deteriorated. Moreover, the domestic US literature shows that declining caseloads do not necessarily lead to low-income people getting jobs, a point often made in reviews of the evidence (e.g. CBO 2022). As caseloads for benefits with work requirements shrink, there are fewer clients who could be supported into work. This is indeed one of the purposes of UI: to support jobseekers, not only so that they will make transitions into work, but also so that they will *not* make the transition out of the labour force. When economists speculate about the decline in the unemployment rate that could be brought about by the abolition of UI, they forget to ask how much of this decline would be due to more employment and how much of it would be due to workers ending their job search and leaving the labour force (Quade et al. 2008).

What, then, explains the labour force exits of prime working-age adults? Here is a partial list of factors examined in the empirical literature.

1. *Mass incarceration and policing.* Since the 1970s and 1980s, the "war on drugs", "broken windows policing", and other anti-crime measures have swollen prison and jail populations, temporarily taking millions of people out of the labour market. Meanwhile, an even larger number of Americans have obtained criminal records. This can prevent people from entering certain kinds of work, leads to employer discrimination, and creates a variety of other barriers to work that disproportionately affect people of colour (Western et al. 2001).

2. *Lack of childcare and family-friendly policies.* During the 1990s and 2010s the United States fell behind most other OECD countries, including mandatory paid parental leave and working-time flexibility and publicly funded childcare. Blau and Kahn (2013) find that this substantially depressed women's labour force participation in the US relative to other countries.

3. *Deindustrialization and skills mismatches.* Like most European countries, the US has shed millions of manufacturing jobs since the 1970s due to automation and relocation of work to lower-cost countries. As regional economies dependent on manufacturing were slow to adapt, workers experienced long spells of unemployment, especially in trade-exposed regions (Autor et al. 2016).

4. *Health problems and opioids.* Alan Krueger (2017) finds that about half of prime-age men (25–54 years) outside of the labour force have a serious health condition that prevents them from working, and a similar percentage take pain medication daily, mostly opioid based; moreover, there is a strong correlation between regional opioid prescription rates and labour force participation. Opioids, therefore, have led not only to large numbers of overdose deaths, but are also related to the declining labour-force participation rates of prime working-age men.

Low spending on activation is another possible explanation for declining labour-force participation, but it is not commonly considered in these debates. Arguably, this is an important blind spot in the literature. Increasing labour force participation is one of the aims of activation policies, and all four of these issues are regularly tackled by the workforce development system. Formerly incarcerated people have become frequent users of employment services, and seeking relief for people with criminal records an important task in serving this clientele (Prescott and Starr 2020). Many of the same agencies that administer benefits with work requirements also issue childcare subsidies, which in New York State are narrowly targeted at low-income working parents. The retraining of displaced workers is a classic task of workforce development, especially for industrial unions, which have been active in seeking Trade Adjustment Assistance funds for unemployed workers affected by international trade (Decker and Corson 1995). Finally, workers with severe health problems who receive disability benefits can access targeted and specialized employment services, such as Ticket to Work (O'Leary and Roessel 2023). Workforce development providers also encounter a range of other barriers to work, depending on the provider's locale and clientele, and tackle them depending on the available funding.

One reason why inadequate spending on activation is so rarely mentioned may be the mixed evaluation results that schemes have received. Reviews of the evaluation evidence typically look at employment and wages as key outcomes, and consider the programme design features that lead to success or failure. These reviews are therefore unable to assess the macro-level impacts of these policies (Card et al. 2018). The track record of these schemes is not overwhelmingly positive, and one problem normally ignored in evaluation studies is privatization and marketization (but see Hipp and Warner 2008). It may be, however, that the problem load facing the workforce development system, the barriers to work in American society, are so severe that front-line workers face a Sisyphean task, as Robert Castel (2017) argued for the case of France.

4.   CONCLUSION

In this chapter, I have sketched the landscape of activation in the US. This is challenging, because the issue is so marginal in policy and academic debates; but it is possible, because the principles and practice of activation are present. My approach has been to piece together research findings from disparate literatures on the various benefits systems, workforce development, and labour market outcomes, along with some international sources as theoretical reference points. I hope this sketch gives some idea of the current state of play.

Comparative social science traditionally categorizes the US as a liberal, i.e. market-driven, regime, because it lacks the strong social services, welfare benefits, statutory rights in the workplace, left-of-centre political parties, and trade unions that exist throughout Western Europe. What comparative social science misses, however, is that the alternative to conservative or social democratic welfare states is not necessarily the free, open, or competitive market. The US labour market is no longer the engine of job creation that it once was, and an increasing number of potential workers are excluded from it. If the low effort and poor coordination of activation contribute to declining labour-force participation, then the modernization and expansion of the US welfare state could actually help revive the labour market.

PRWORA was not a law that aimed to empower individuals on the labour market. Its policy motivation was paternalistic and not laissez faire (Mead 1998), its political motivation was aimed at mobilizing whites to vote Republican (Kohler-Hausman 2017), its discourse was full of racist and sexist tropes (Nadasen et al. 2013), and its administration was far harsher in jurisdictions with large numbers of Black claimants (Soss et al. 2011). Workfare came about around the same time, and for many of the same reasons, that mass incarceration was removing large numbers of workers from the labour market, and the criminal justice system saddled many more with criminal records that created additional disadvantage on the labour market (Alexander 2020). During that time, the 1990s, the US also began to fall behind the rest of the OECD in "family-friendly" policies that would have continued the trend towards greater female labour force participation (Blau and Kahn 2013). Shortly thereafter, the labour force participation rate for prime working-age adults, including women, began to decline.

The outlook for activation in the US is unclear. During the Covid pandemic, the labour supply and benefits system have been salient political topics. For the political right, however, the main relevant social policy object has been to reduce caseloads and spending. For the political left it has been nearly the opposite: addressing the disparities in the US labour market by making benefits more inclusive, equitable, and generous, which means pushing back against work requirements and arguing that they don't improve the labour supply. Meanwhile, state and county agencies responsible for welfare and workforce development, community colleges, community-based organizations, and private companies that make activation happen at the street level have been gradually starved of resources. Their state-level and federal professional organizations publicize funding opportunities and lobby to extend programmes, but there is no sign of political will at the federal level to change this anytime soon. To the contrary, the Trade Adjustment Assistance (TAA) programme was allowed to expire, and expanding workforce development funding was not policymakers' preferred method for addressing labour supply problems.

The chapter is not the first to point out the difference between the reality of the US political economy and the stylized facts of comparative typologies. Consider the subtitles of such academic best-sellers as James Galbraith's (2008) *The Predator State: Why Conservatives Abandoned the Free Market and Why Liberals Should Do the same* and Thomas Philippon's (2019) *The Great Reversal: How America Gave up on Free Markets*. It is time for comparativists to appreciate how illiberal the US labour market is.

REFERENCES

Abraham, K. G., & Kearney, M. S. (2020). Explaining the decline in the US employment-to-population ratio: A review of the evidence. *Journal of Economic Literature, 58*(3), 585–643.

Alexander, M. (2020). *The new Jim Crow: Mass incarceration in the age of colorblindness*. The New Press.

Anderson, T., Kairys, K., & Wiseman, M. (2014). Activation and reform in the United States: What time has told. In Lodemel, I., & Moreira, A. (eds), *Activation or workfare? Governance and the neo-liberal convergence*. New York: Oxford University Press, 101–142.

Autor, D. H., & Duggan, M. G. (2006). The growth in the social security disability rolls: A fiscal crisis unfolding. *Journal of Economic Perspectives, 20*(3), 71–96.

Autor, D. H., Dorn, D., & Hanson, G. H. (2016). The China shock: Learning from labor-market adjustment to large changes in trade. *Annual Review of Economics, 8*, 205–240.

Balducchi, D. E., & O'Leary, C. J. (2018). The employment service–unemployment insurance partnership. In Wandner, D. (ed.), *Unemployment insurance reform: Fixing a broken system*. Kalamazoo, MI: WE Upjohn Institute for Employment Research, 65–100.

Barnes, C., Michener, J., & Rains, E. (2023). "It's like night and day": How bureaucratic encounters vary across WIC, SNAP, and Medicaid. *Social Service Review, 97*(1), 3–42.

Bauer, L., & East, C. (2023). *A Primer on SNAP Work Requirements*. Report, The Hamilton Project.

Blau, F. D., & Kahn, L. M. (2013). Female labor supply: Why is the United States falling behind? *American Economic Review, 103*(3), 251–256.

Bonoli, G. (2010). The political economy of active labor-market policy. *Politics & Society, 38*(4), 435–457.

Brodkin, E. Z. (2011). Policy work: Street-level organizations under new managerialism. *Journal of Public Administration Research and Theory, 21*(suppl_2), i253–i277.

Bruyère, S. M. (ed.) (2019). *Employment and disability: Issues, innovations, and opportunities*. Ithaca, NJ: Cornell University Press.

Card, D., Kluve, J., & Weber, A. (2018). What works? A meta analysis of recent active labor market program evaluations. *Journal of the European Economic Association, 16*(3), 894–931.

Castel, R. (2017). *From manual workers to wage laborers: Transformation of the social question*. Abingdon: Routledge.

Congressional Budget Office (2022). *Work requirements and work supports for recipients of means-tested benefits*. Washington DC: CBO.

Decker, P. T., & Corson, W. (1995). International trade and worker displacement: Evaluation of the trade adjustment assistance program. *ILR Review, 48*(4), 758–774.

Forsythe, E., Kahn, L. B., Lange, F., & Wiczer, D. (2022). Where have all the workers gone? Recalls, retirements, and reallocation in the COVID recovery. *Labour Economics, 78*, 102251.

Galbraith, J. K. (2008). *The predator state: How conservatives abandoned the free market and why liberals should too*. New York, NY: Simon & Schuster.

Ganong, P., Noel, P., & Vavra, J. (2020). US unemployment insurance replacement rates during the pandemic. *Journal of Public Economics, 191*, 104273.

Giloth, R. (Ed.). (2004). *Workforce intermediaries: For the 21st century*. Philadelphia, PA: Temple University Press.

Greer, I., & Umney, C. (2022). *Marketization: How capitalist exchange disciplines workers and subverts democracy*. London: Bloomsbury Publishing.

Greer, I., Breidahl, K. N., Knuth, M., & Larsen, F. (2017). *The marketization of employment services: The dilemmas of Europe's work-first welfare states*. Oxford: Oxford University Press.

Greig, F., Sullivan, D. M., Ganong, P., Noel, P., & Vavra, J. (2021). When unemployment insurance benefits are rolled back: Impacts on job finding and the recipients of the pandemic unemployment assistance program. https://papers.ssrn.com/sol3/papers.cfm?abstract_id=3896667

Guth, M., & Musumeci, M. (2022). *An overview of Medicaid work requirements: What happened under the Trump and Biden administrations?* Report, Kaiser Family Foundation.

Herd, P., Hoynes, H., Michener, J., & Moynihan, D. (2023). Introduction: Administrative burden as a mechanism of inequality in policy implementation. *RSF: The Russell Sage Foundation Journal of the Social Sciences, 9*(4), 1–30.

Hipp, L., & Warner, M. E. (2008). Market forces for the unemployed? Training vouchers in Germany and the USA. *Social Policy & Administration, 42*(1), 77–101.

Holzer, H. J., Hubbard, R. G., & Strain, M. R. (2021). *Did pandemic unemployment benefits reduce employment? Evidence from early state-level expirations in June 2021* (No. w29575). National Bureau of Economic Research.

Jantz, B., Klenk, T., Larsen, F., & Wiggan, J. (2018). Marketization and varieties of accountability relationships in employment services: Comparing Denmark, Germany, and Great Britain. *Administration & Society, 50*(3), 321–345.

Kohler-Hausmann, J. (2017). Getting tough. In *Getting tough: Welfare and imprisonment in 1970s America*. Princeton, NY: Princeton University Press.

Krachler, N., & Greer, I. (2015). When does marketisation lead to privatisation? Profit-making in English health services after the 2012 Health and Social Care Act. *Social Science & Medicine, 124*, 215–223.

Krueger, A. B. (2017). Where have all the workers gone? An inquiry into the decline of the US labor force participation rate. *Brookings Papers on Economic Activity, 2017*(2), 1.

Mead, L. M. (1998). Telling the poor what to do. *Public Interest*, (132), 97–112.

Medicaid, Center for Medicaid and CHIP Services (2024). Monthly Medicaid & CHIP Application, Eligibility Determination, and Enrollment Reports & Data. https://www.medicaid.gov/about-us/messages/index.html

Myers, J. E., & Kellogg, K. C. (2022). State actor orchestration for achieving workforce development at scale: Evidence from four US states. *ILR Review, 75*(1), 28–55.

Nadasen, P., Mittelstadt, J., & Chappell, M. (Eds.). (2013). *Welfare in the United States: A history with documents, 1935–1996*. Abingdon: Routledge.

O'Leary, P., & Roessel, E. (2023). Effects of the ticket to work program: Return on investment and overall assessment of outcomes versus design. *Social Security Bulletin, 83*(1), 1–39.

Osterman, P. (ed.) (2020). *Creating good jobs: An industry-based strategy*. Cambridge, MA: MIT Press.

Peck, J. (2001). *Workfare states*. New York, NY: Guilford Press.

Peck, J., & Tickell, A. (2002). Neoliberalizing space. *Antipode, 34*(3), 380–404.

Philippon, T. (2019). *The great reversal*. Boston, MA: Harvard University Press.

Prescott, J. J., & Starr, S. B. (2020). Expungement of criminal convictions: An empirical study. *Harvard Law Review*, *133*(8), 2460–2555.

Quade, B., O'Leary, C. J., & Dupper, O. (2008). Activation from Income Support in the US. In Eichhorst, W., Kaufmann, O., & Koule-Seidl, R. (eds.), *Bringing the Jobless into Work? Experiences with Activation Schemes in Europe and the US*, pp. 345–414. Berlin: Springer.

Reese, E. (2011). *They say cutback, we say fight back! Welfare activism in an era of retrenchment*. New York, NY: Russell Sage Foundation.

Shierholz, H., McNicholas, C., & Poydock, M. (2019). *Proposed rule to privatize the federal Employment Service would likely reduce services for unemployed workers*. Washington DC: Economic Policy Institute.

Soss, J., Fording, R. C., & Schram, S. F. (2011). *Disciplining the poor: Neoliberal paternalism and the persistent power of race*. Chicago: University of Chicago Press.

Streeck, W. (2004). Hire and Fire: ist der amerikanische Arbeitsmarkt ein Vorbild für Deutschland? *Berliner Republik*, 3, pp. 1–9.

Traub, A. (2021). *7 things we learned about Unemployment Insurance during the pandemic*. Washington DC: National Employment Law Project.

United States Department of Labor (2023). *Comparison of State Unemployment Laws 2022*. Washington DC: USDOL.

Van Slyke, D. M. (2003). The mythology of privatization in contracting for social services. *Public Administration Review*, *63*(3), 296–315.

Western, B., Kling, J. R., & Weiman, D. F. (2001). The labor market consequences of incarceration. *Crime & Delinquency*, *47*(3), 410–427.

Wiseman, M. (2000). Making work for welfare in the United States. In Lødemel, I., & Trickey, H. (Eds.), *'An offer you can't refuse': workfare in international perspective*. Bristol: Policy Press, 215–248.

13. Concluding remarks to a changing activation world

Henning Jørgensen and Michaela Schulze

UNEMPLOYMENT AND ACTIVATION IN TANDEM

Unemployment is harmful, a disease, for individuals and families involved and for society at large. It must be conquered on a collective level. All Western countries try to combat unemployment by the help of interventions, services, and different forms of measures. Selective interventions in the labour market are conceptualized as active labour market policy (ALMP) or employment policies. Such kinds of policies are here to stay, and so is activation, but not necessarily for producing full employment in all approaches, as was the case in the post-war period in the 1960s and 1970s. More crises, mass unemployment experiences, and political developments have given rise to different principal doctrines and employment policies (Eichhorst and Zimmermann 2011, Clegg and Durazzi 2023). But some kind of political action as to unemployment has constantly been taken. Governments have not retreated from interventions in labour markets. This is important. It is also essential to see activation in its historical and national contexts. The system of social protection provides income replacement for those out of work. The first systems of unemployment insurance were introduced in a first phase of LMP more than 100 years ago, as noted in Chapter 1. Four other phases have followed. Unemployment benefits reduce income disparities and partly "de-commodify" labour. ALMP was introduced in the Nordic countries, and the OECD had already promoted this concept as well, during the 1960s. Activation from the 1990s and intensifying during the 2000s has generally been promoted to compensate for the disincentives caused by "generous" unemployment benefits. A rhetoric – paying homage to methods and assumptions of neo-classical economics – of "passive" and "active" benefits, "structural unemployment", and "making work pay" has paved the way for policies to prevent welfare dependency. Workless people should be "activated", as should the whole social system. A triple activation was developed: unemployed people, street-level organizations, and the whole system of social protection should go from "passive" to "active". But implementation processes had a life of their own. It was discovered that the street-level bureaucrats shape, transform, and produce policy while developing services and decisions in encounters. It was thought that these should be "modernized" as well, and new public management (NPM) was implemented. Here, neo-liberalizations also had their reform impacts. Incentives for "good" behaviour and penalties for non-compliance were used. New menus of incentives and regulations also included private providers as part of the actor system. Narratives of unemployed people were changed, too. Functional and policy changes are mediated through discursive changes. And in some public employment systems (PESs), there is no longer talk of unemployed people but of jobseekers only.

The partial de-commodification of labour in universal welfare state developments (Esping-Andersen 1990) has been re-purposed as re-commodifying workers without work. Activation tries to push or help unemployed people back into paid work, at a rapid pace in workfare and "work-first" editions. Conditionality, restricted benefit periods, and the use of sanctions have been new ways of putting pressure on workless people. Entry into any kind of employment should improve employability and well-being. Employment sustainability is, however, not considered very much in workfare and work-first activation. Workfare has even been seen as a departure from welfare. However, other activation approaches try to combine more goals and measures in welfare policies. A combination of enabling and demanding elements is to be seen in most policies. Activation, ALMP, and social policy all bear a defining ambiguity in them, in having support and punishment embedded in stronger logics of politics. But ways of conducting activation are in no way one-dimensional, and encounters cannot be totally steered from a centre. Administrative programming and street-level behaviour result in a variety of national and sub-national activation arrangements, the latter based on adjustments to local peculiarities. And policies and implementation processes are recalibrated in more rounds of renewals. This is also a reason why dichotomous classifications are oversimplifications and not very useful. The content of activation measures has been changed again during recent years, presumably paving the way for more social investments and a renewed ethos of universal welfare alongside active inclusion.

DEVELOPMENTS OF ACTIVATION

Up-to-date information as to activation has been provided in this book. The contributions have shown us how strongly activation systems are dependent on national traditions, actor systems, and path dependency in central reform processes. The importance of politics is obvious. Policies reveal different doctrines and employment policies implemented in Northern and Southern Europe, in the US, and in the UK, compared with Continental European countries and within national systems over time. Finally, polity shows its importance in the administrative structures and governance reforms of the public sector. Federal systems give special conditions as to autonomy of decentralized authorities, as seen in the US, Germany, and Switzerland. It is the interplay between politics, policies, and polity that can bring us closer to explanations supplementary to contextual factors.

The activation turn came with a promise of strong employment results with the help of active programmes placing incentives and sanctions in pivotal positions. Individualized and incentivized activation has been the way of combatting unemployment by "motivation effects". As to the functioning of activation systems, it has proven difficult to have people in vulnerable positions react to incentives and the threat of sanctions. At the time of writing, more building both on trust through productive talks with workless people and on "qualification effects" is necessary. This is a lesson learned from the analysis. Over-steering of PES systems must be conquered at the same time. After a reform has been decided upon at the central level and implementation starts, wishing to know what happens and "what works" leads central authorities to place requests for decentralized agents and institutions to supply a lot of data for documentation, evaluation, and system development. Conflicting demands as to operations come from multiple institutional logics (Røhnebæk and Breit 2022). At the local level, a lot of time, energy, and double communication seems to be used for purposes other than helping unemployed people. Bureaucratic overload can lead to poor implementation.

The chapters have highlighted changes in activation over time and especially after the COVID-19 period. COVID-19 showed us that viruses are part of the "natural environment" – that is part of ourselves – and that it is our common efforts to cope with problems that bring innovation to social, economic, and political life. Lessons have been learned – also as to activation. Now, less coercive activation and more investments in upskilling and reskilling are taking place in more countries. The EU and the OECD are also supporting such changes in policies. This could look like support for those who consider "human capital" the most important way of conducting activation. But, in Chapter 2, we tried to avoid being trapped by a classical economic theory foundation and proposed a new understanding of investments in capabilities. Training, skill formation, and competence development are among the topics involved. Again, differences as to developments in Anglo-Saxon countries, Nordic countries, and Continental and Southern European ones must be stressed. There is and will be no strong convergence even if we are entering a fifth period of activation. More transformation of policies is to be expected. The state seems to be bouncing back from austerity and coercive activation in most European countries. COVID-19 had the economy and social relations partially "frozen" for some time. This was bridged by a bonanza of fiscal stimuli, regulations, and new ways of working, including conducting new activation practices. Meanwhile, restrictions and abolishment of "hardcore" activation were mushrooming. High-income countries were the first to recover from the crisis (Greve 2023). Unemployment in Europe was down to 6.2 per cent in 2022. A strong expansion of state interventions has taken place. The social contract between citizens and the state has been strengthened, too. The economy has gone from crisis to partial lack of manpower. But the deepened skill-biased job polarization has not been effectively met by existing activation measures or ALMP initiatives. New initiatives will have to be created and implemented. It is a question of putting activation and ALMP on a more suitable and forward-looking footing, with the productive capacities of the welfare state contributing to sustainable employment, well-being, and productivity.

CONCEPTS AND THE LACK OF A COMPREHENSIVE THEORY

However, conceptual confusion as to activation exists. We are still without a firm and well-elaborated theory of activation – partly because of the fact that no consensus exists as to the definition and clarification of concepts. Analytical distinctions are most important. But activation has no self-evident meaning. This must be constructed intellectually.

Unemployment has been an object of study for perhaps the greatest variety of social scientists, and a lot of empirical documentation, statements, evaluations, analytical generalizations, in addition to many policy recommendations, have been seen. Unemployment is regarded as the eternal opposite of "work", a familiar feature of modern life in a capitalist society, even though more understandings and theories are developed, and even if some are still competing. The same analytical reflexivity cannot be seen in the study of activation. Political, economic, and social conditions for policies have had the attention of many scholars during the last three decades, but we are still lacking comprehensive theories and a common analytical framework. Disagreement exists as to concept formation, analytical statements, methodologies, and the basis of assessments. The "constructedness" of unemployment is better elaborated than the one of activation, the policy side. Politics, policy, and polity are to be seen in relation to each other if we are to explain the way in which activation is governed, elaborated, implemented, and outcomes and impacts are produced. This is to be investigated as part of burgeoning interdisciplinary efforts.

Our definition of activation has been formulated with the aim to bring unemployed people quickly back into the open labour market by restoring a balance between rights and duties. The latter have been strengthened, and now all workless people should be ready to participate in some kind of activation and actively be seeking jobs. A blend of services and sanctions are recorded to intensify the job search. Definitions of activation have been focusing on instruments, programmes, and policy goals, and in shifting combinations. Chapters 1 and 2 have been devoted to discussions regarding understanding and analysing activation. We have many concepts but few theories – if any.

Theory building is also about theorizing change, which is not only about variety in the form of paradigmatic shifts of activation policies, but also about varietals in the form of policy recalibrations and reform processes. Explaining change as a complex interplay of collective actors and institutional forces is an urgent but also difficult task. To develop explanatory accounts, you need more than understandings of national variation and styles of activation. You also need to analyse blind spots.

Among these blind spots are interrelationships between the micro, meso, and macro levels. Economic effect analysis and evaluations typically concentrate on the micro level, with data on individuals as the basis for assessing measures (spotting moves from public support to self-employment). We also know a lot about different target groups and their perception of treatment. Process-oriented studies have enriched our understanding of experiences and views of participants in programmes. Studies of the encounter between the state and the street (Zacka 2017) tell us of the importance of mutual trust and local organizational places for positive motivation of people. In more and more multicultural societies, programmes work differently for some people, such as immigrants and refugees.

Political scientists, especially, often analyse activation changes as the results of partisan politics at the macro level and the coalition dynamics that lie behind policy choices. Some studies also relate this to perceptions of deservingness among voters. Other scholars concentrate on the budgeting and programming of implementation. Included in these kinds of analysis are governance reforms taking place in systems, most often in the name of NPM recalibrations.

However, we know comparatively less about the meso level – about the rules, regulations, institutions, and norms governing organizational behaviour. These meso factors can affect both microeconomic behaviour and macroeconomic outcomes and impacts. We also know too little about the long-term impacts of programmes. Often, results first materialize some time after leaving a programme or a measure. And configuration of policies and programmes ought to be investigated much more, in addition to side effects and indirect outcomes with regard to inequality, poverty, productivity, and labour market performance.

These questions also address the future of welfare state developments. The welfare state is not having an "ethical neutrality", as Max Weber told us. There is a moral foundation of welfare programmes that give the welfare state its values and responsibilities. Universalism in social policy and equality have been two of these basic principles for Nordic welfare states. Other European and Anglo-Saxon systems have given priority to other conservative and liberal values. The welfare state changes too, as challenges, economic conditions, and collective actors put pressure on established policies and polity arrangements. This is also the story of activation in Europe and the US. But public interventions as to unemployment developments are constitutive for arrangements and activities.

After having all the empirical and historical materials collected, we know a lot more about activation in individual countries and developments over time. Progress has been more than marginal. More than "what works" questions have been addressed. However, international comparative and integrative investigations are still to be made. Analytically, a difference between activation strategies and activation programmes has been argued here, and we have stated possible policy legacies. This is also a step away from "dichotomization" within early activation literature. Programmes have been in a pivotal position as to typologies (as documented by Giuliano Bonoli), and they inspire and direct many empirical investigations. The relation between policies/strategies and implementation of programmes is to be scrutinized much more intensely. We will try to contribute further to this discussion below.

TYPOLOGY OF ACTIVATION STRATEGIES

Typologies are a way to follow towards theorization. We will propose a new activation strategy typology, trying to overcome some of the shortcomings of more existing ones. It is about trying to develop a new two-dimensional activation typology of strategies – not on instruments – and building on two axes: one regarding investments in skills and competences and programmes as to capacitation (or the lack of these skill-oriented initiatives); and the other based on profiles of implementation approaches – citizen-oriented encounters (trying to enable integration), versus disciplinary approaches (using incentives and sanctions).

The two axes proposed are a continuation of our discussion on activation policies formulated on the central level and activation encounters at the local level (Chapter 2). Policies and programmes are connected in the typology. And as the two axes are not dependent on each other in a direct way, a typology is made possible. Put together, they can be illustrated as in Figure 13.1.

The first quadrant, cell I in Figure 13.1, illustrates a paternalistic strategy, building on strong central initiatives to have people – and first, youngsters – go into education and to have unemployed people with some qualifications take up jobs offered, supported by some upskilling. Capacitation is first and foremost for those who are considered strong as to employability. In reality, the strategy distinguishes between the deserving and the less deserving workless people. Inequality is produced by creaming and parking; but this is no problem

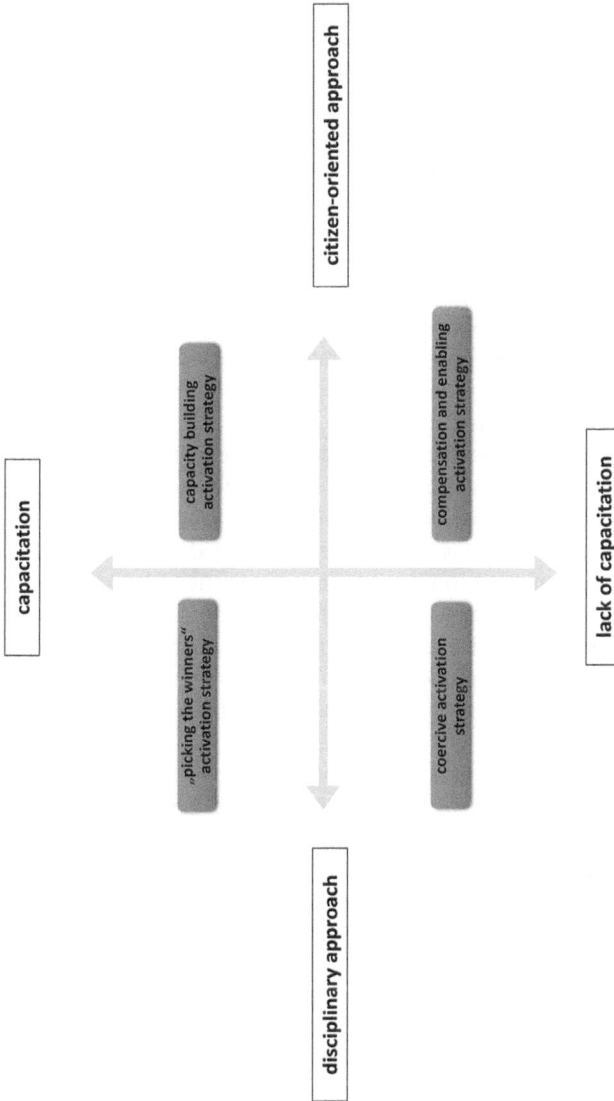

Source: Own compilation.

Figure 13.1 *Two-dimensional typology of activation strategies*

as to the policymakers. Still, a disciplinary-based encounter is typical for the strategy from the side of the PES systems, and for private providers this is a preferred strategy, too. The authorities and private providers are mostly interested in stocks of workless people with some qualifications. These have higher chances of using their skills. This can be called a disciplinary selection and a "picking the winners" activation strategy.

Quadrant II shows a social investment strategy in both vocational training and education, in order to foster skill formation, skill preservation, and skill mobilization, built on a premise of a linear relationship between investments, motivation, and productivity/economic growth. Supplementary to these investments, job creation measures could also be supplied. Citizens are treated on an enabling basis, trying to give the workless people involved influence in encounters and paving the way for co-production and co-creation in activation. But clear potentials for competence development must be present on the individual level. Here the interest is concentrated on stocks, flows, and buffers of manpower, and qualifications among people of working age. This can be called a capacity-building activation strategy.

Quadrant III corresponds to the traditional coercive form of activation in which incentives and sanctions should push people back into work (disregarding pay and working conditions). No investment in skills is made. "Workfare" is one of the trademarks. The interest is closely connected to flows within the labour market as part of the neo-liberalization of societies. Workfarist practices have been central together with "work-first" practices (close to Bonoli's incentive reinforcement). Critics talk of Matthew effects and poverty as possible negative consequences, proponents of the positive results of incentives and sanctions. This disciplinary approach, we will call a coercive activation strategy.

Quadrant IV, finally, presents a strategy of enabling encounters and social compensation in continuation of well-known welfare legacies. One could also talk of more forms of muddling through the activation turn. Employment performance is a primary goal for the economy, and workless people are to experience both pressure and protection, "fordern und fördern", but in "soft" editions of employment assistance and job search measures only. It is a pro-market strategy. However, capacitation is rare or non-existing. This can be called a compensation and enabling activation strategy.

These four types of activation strategies can serve as ideal types for classification and can amplify existing classifications, using the types of national configurations and developments depicted on the basis of a two-dimensional approach. But there is more to it than placing nations in a "box". It could seem rather easy to place the UK and the US in quadrant III, Spain, perhaps, in IV, and Norway and Germany in quadrant II when it comes to present-day activation strategies. However, it is even more interesting (and demanding) to use the typology heuristic to follow changes in strategies over time. Denmark, for example, was clearly to be placed in quadrant II, with a strong capacity-building activation strategy in the form of "learnfare" of the 1990s, but the strategy then changed and moved towards quadrants I and III during the 2000s. Germany, from the Hartz reforms of the early 2000s, has moved the other way, towards a rising capacity-building activation strategy – an activation U-turn. Exercises as to the strategic direction finding and changes in Finland, Holland, Austria, and Switzerland can be made from reading the relevant chapters in this book.

Social investments are said to raise employment, consolidating the state's revenues, and improving the changes for people in the labour market to find "good" jobs (Hemerijck and Metsaganis 2024) and improving productivity afterwards. This would be a strong argument for capacity and capability-building strategies (Sen 1998, 2009). Critics point to the fact that most activation can trigger detrimental Matthew effects to the disadvantage of vulnerable people and low-income families (Bonoli, Cantillon, and Van Lancker 2017). In the future, capacitation will have to install conversion factors that can be reused, preventing social Matthew effects, if the social investment strategy is to succeed. You cannot deny problems in combatting inequality in existing policies. This has been witnessed in many of the contributions in this book, from Spain in the South to Denmark, Norway, and Finland in the North, and from the Netherlands, Austria, Germany, and Switzerland to the UK and the US.

The interest in skills must also be explained. Reference must be given to unevenly distributed opportunities for workers and to structural mismatches between skills demands and capacities and resources of the working population. The demand for skills is unevenly distributed in labour markets. But a general trend is the reliance on higher skills in more sectors. Dynamic services call for this, now including basic IT skills. Occupational changes are also visible: "routine" jobs will have diminished demand as repetitive tasks and personal services will see low-skill demand, while cognitive-based jobs call for stronger skills development (Garritzmann and Palier 2023). We could see "polarised upgrading" in the new activation phase – both as a trend and as a threat (Carlo and Durazzi 2023). As to low-skilled jobs, activated people might have different chances for getting a job. The ambition of the PES is to have upskilling and reskilling combined with a view to higher-skilled and more sustainable jobs. Capabilities and lifelong learning can be even higher ambitions than ongoing training (Evans et al. 2023). But then the capacity-building strategy should be for all working people. Competences need to be seen as broader than narrow goal-oriented skills, abilities, and attitudes.

Activation does not affect the total number of hirings and firings in the labour market. Employment protection is weak in this respect. And employers are not met by much legislation with claims of taking responsibility for hiring workless people (Ingold and McGurg 2023). Employers can shift most of the social costs of unemployment to the public sector. Left to the market, there will be no strong investment in skills either. Public institutions to secure adequate provision of skills are essential, especially for workless people. Skills are a collective good and are social production factors, but the individual firms will act according to their rational profit choice model. They might also fear losing investments to competitors. Thus, the necessary investments will, probably, not be taken. That is why we will have an almost chronic undersupply of skilled labour in the case where no public responsibility is developed. But the collective skills needed may also fail to be produced by the public sector. Training in schools is, for example, not equal to training in firms. But skill-enhancing initiatives are strongly in demand in many places now.

There is, however, more to activation than improving the motivation and the qualifications of unemployed people. Socializing with the help of measures such as guidance and employment projects, and work-related network formation in the form of traineeships and wage subsidies are also part of the activation package. Structural and long-time unemployment are some of the most difficult challenges as there will be institutional barriers and employer strategies – including discrimination practices – to be influenced. This calls for more and stronger interventionist programmes.

Help from more kinds of actors is necessary in order to implement activation and capability approaches. Private and public employers are in a pivotal position as to the success of activation policies. But the social partners and other organizations (including private actors) need to be involved as well. This could also be another way of conquering the general coordination and cooperation deficit in employment systems uncovered in the chapters in this book. Fragmented, multi-level governance has been recorded almost everywhere. Different institutional logics and understandings have shaped the form and operation of interaction between agencies and actors. For workless people – and especially those with multiple barriers to employment – inter-agency collaboration between local organizations and actors is strongly required.

A fifth phase of activation has been started with some new orientations and ambitions, but there is no uniform trend. Difference and normality are not mutually exclusive. Big differences between North and South, West and East in Europe are recorded. The US again forms a special case, as documented here. High-skill formation has been much more common in Northern and Anglo-Saxon countries than in Southern and Eastern European countries. Welfare state regimes are challenged differently. Political priorities differ, too.

AGAIN: THE FUTURE OF ACTIVATION

The most important question of the future of activation cannot be answered without knowing how the welfare states will develop in the future and be able to secure socially cohesive societies. Activation and welfare states are bound up with capacities for fostering a well-functioning labour market and strong social security at the same time. ALMP and activation are political responses to socio-economic tensions, conflicts, and imbalances brought along by the dynamic development of capitalist labour markets. Provision of social security on the one hand and services and public help on the other have been two sides of policy developments. In the past, countries have proved only partially able to cope with unemployment and the increasing number of people on social assistance and other beneficiaries. However, it was not the ineffectiveness of the market, but the malfunctioning public sector itself that was blamed for unemployment from the 1980s first in Anglo-Saxon and then Continental European countries. Neo-liberal approaches of retrenchment and austerity were mushrooming – but not everywhere. And now new policy developments have been started with the state in a stronger and more interventionist position. Lessons have been learned, also during and after the COVID-19 period.

But clashes of interests are obvious. Group and class conflicts as to strategies are to be expected, and tensions within the state systems will persist, too. Wicked problems – such as demographic challenges, migration, and climate change – do put strong pressure on advanced democracies. More policy changes are to be expected. But technological developments also put stronger demand on activation and ALMP in the future to have a better balance between supply and demand, and to enhance qualifications at all levels. Capacitation is already given priority in more systems. But all systems seem to be challenged. New ways of working – platforms, independent contract work, unregulated jobs, self-employment – have become widespread and will also pose new challenges. The risk of more insecure and precarious employment relationships is big. Transformed gender relations and inequalities are obvious. And decarbonization will strongly affect the labour market, calling for just transition policies resonating with green jobs and skills approaches (Ding and Hirvilammi 2024). Socio-economic developments – including unemployment – and political developments are interconnected. We also know that there are strong differences as to the wishes, expectations, claims of citizens, and legitimacy towards the welfare state. How these develop will also have repercussions as to the future of activation.

Economic growth needs to be greener, having environmental challenges tackled too. And unemployment must be conquered at all levels by many collective actors. Lower economic growth will imply a reduced room for manoeuvre for welfare states services and benefits. This again will threaten redistributions. Next, the support for a more interventionist economic policy and policy mixes must not be depressed in case activation is going to have the chance to combat unemployment successfully. If unemployment should be kept low, domestic demand must be supported by the state. Countries with a big public debt are less able to cope with new crises in this respect. The way economic policies are organized together with activation strategies will define some of the opportunities of national policies. Priorities will, however, still be different. These will also be influenced by new technologies and knowledge demands. The relevance of artificial intelligence also has implications for PES and activation. Political, normative, and ethical issues will still be given various priorities, as before. We will see varieties of activation and even varietals – variations within variety. However, activation will be redirected in a number of ways and coloured by capacitation in more systems in the future. Complementarities of policies will have to be scrutinized much more, as policy mixes seem to be necessary if Western societies will be able to cope with the many shifting, complex, and fluctuating problems facing us.

Activation has survived under the conditions of permanent crises. It is here to stay. It has entered a fifth period with less coercive activation and more capability-oriented renewals. This is our assessment based on the national contributions in this book and on the existing, comprehensive literature on activation. Capacity-building initiatives together with other policy arrangements are, presumably, also a better way to cope with inequality within the labour market and to invest in opportunities for both workless people and people in work. However, it is important not to end up with the result of a "picking-the-winners" strategy only, leaving many less qualified people behind. "The security of wings" should be for all. More kinds of arrangements for workless people are relevant, improving capabilities, and it should also be secured that these people will have an influence on processes and ways ahead. The potential for public value creation is to be used more effectively. However, value creation is also an "outside-in" perspective. Framing and reframing processes will be needed to have public values embedded in interactions and in organizational changes and mindsets. These improvements can still happen within a universal welfare state approach, supplemented by new policy mixes for sustainable developments.

New discussions as to alternatives to "traditional" work are spreading, including proposals for Universal Basic Income with a lack of targeting and for in-work benefits. Experiments have started – and pose a real challenge to activation, as these experiments could decouple the work and welfare nexus that has dominated activation and activation research until now. We need to end up with a solid answer. To this end, much more research in activation, ALMP, and other related policies is urgently required.

REFERENCES

Bonoli, G., Cantillon, B. and Van Lancker (2017) 'Social investment and the Matthew effect: Limits to a strategy', in Hemerijck, A. (ed.), *The Uses of Social Investment*. Oxford: Oxford University Press, pp. 66–76.

Carlo, D.D. and Durazzi, N. (2023) 'Skill formation: part of and complement to labour market policy?' in Clegg, D. and Durazzi, N. (eds.), *Handbook of Labor Market Policy in Advanced Democracies*. Cheltenham, UK and Northampton, MA, USA: Edward Elgar Publishing, pp. 327–341.

Clegg, D. and Durazzi, N. (eds.) (2023) *Handbook of Labor Market Policy in Advanced Democracies*. Cheltenham, UK and Northampton, MA, USA: Edward Elgar Publishing.

Ding, J. and Hirvilammi, T. (2024) 'Three pillars of just transition labour market policies', *Contemporary Social Science*, 19(1), pp. 1–18. doi.org/10.1080/21582041.2024.2316656.

Eichhorst, W. and Zimmermann, K.F. (2011) *Combatting Unemployment*. New York: Oxford University Press.

Esping-Andersen, G. (1990) *The Three Worlds of Welfare Capitalism*. Princeton, NJ: Princeton University Press.

Evans, K., Lee, W.O., Markowitsch, J., Zukas, M. (eds.) (2023) *Third International Handbook of Lifelong Learning*. Cham: Springer.

Garritzmann, J.L. and Palier, B. (2023) 'Welfare states, growth regimes, and the emergence of the knowledge economy: Social policy in turbulent times', in Greve, B. (ed.), *Welfare States in a Turbulent Era*. Cheltenham, UK and Northampton, MA, USA: Edward Elgar Publishing, pp. 127–141.

Greve, B. (ed.) (2023) *Welfare States in a Turbulent Era*. Cheltenham, UK and Northampton, MA, USA: Edward Elgar Publishing.

Hemerijck, A. and Matsaganis, M. (2024) *Who's Afraid of the Welfare State Now?* Oxford: Oxford University Press.

Ingold, J. and McGurg, P. (eds.) (2023) *Employer Engagement: Making Active Market Policies Work*. Bristol: Bristol University Press.

Røhnebæk, M.T. and Breit, E. (2022) 'Dammed if you do and dammed if you don't: A framework for examining double binds in public service organizations', *Public Management Review*, 24(7), pp. 1001–1023.

Sen, A.K. (2009) *The Idea of Justice*. London: Penguin.

Sen, A.K. (1998) *Development of Freedom*. New York: Knopf Press.

Zacka, B. (2017) *When the State Meets the Street: Public Service and Moral Agency*. Cambridge: The Belknap Press of Harvard University Press.

Index